INSURANCE IN PRIVATE INTERNATIONAL LAW

This book provides a much-needed analysis of this very important subject for international business lawyers, including discussion of the jurisdictional and choice of laws issues arising from cross-border contracts of insurance and reinsurance concluded by electronic means.

This book is the first published in England to devote itself to a detailed analysis of the choice of laws rules in the EC Insurance Directives. It is aimed at academics and practitioners, at private international lawyers and at insurance lawyers. The private international law rules of the EC Insurance Directives deal with the applicable law to insurance contracts covering risks situated within the EU. They do not deal with the applicable law to reinsurance contracts and insurance contracts covering risks situated outside the EU. This should be ascertained by reference to the choice of laws provisions in the 1980 Rome Convention on the law applicable to contractual obligations. Detailed discussion of these rules is also provided, and proposals for reform suggested.

Insurance in Private International Law

A European Perspective

FRANCESCO SEATZU

·HART·
PUBLISHING

OXFORD – PORTLAND OREGON
2003

Published in North America (US and Canada) by
Hart Publishing c/o
International Specialized Book Services
5804 NE Hassalo Street
Portland, Oregon
97213-3644
USA

Hart Publishing is a specialist legal publisher based in Oxford, England. To order further copies of this book or to request a list of other publications lease write to:

Hart Publishing, Salter's Boatyard, Folly Bridge,
Abingdon Road, Oxford OX1 4LB
Telephone: +44 (0)1865 245533 or Fax: +44 (0)1865 794882
e-mail: mail@hartpub.co.uk
WEBSITE: http//www.hartpub.co.uk

British Library Cataloguing in Publication Data
Data Available
ISBN 1–84113–335–3 (hardback)

Typeset by Hope Services (Abingdon) Ltd.
Printed and bound in Great Britain on acid-free paper by
Biddles Ltd, *www.biddles.co.uk*

To my parents and my sister Carla
for their unfailing support and
encouragement throughout the years

Preface

The entire problem of the conflict of laws with regard to insurance is much in need of monographic treatment

Otto Kahn Freund[1]

Insurance is a fascinating area of private international law. It brings into focus the very basis of private international law including the reasons for displacing the law of the forum and the methods of selecting the governing law. Moreover, it raises some unique issues in private international law, as by its own character, it combines contract principles with those of tort.[2] For instance, a claimant to recover in a personal injury action from an insurer for the conduct of the insured must prove, first, that the insured is liable for his injuries and, secondly, that the insurance grants coverage for that liability. Choice of law questions usually arises in such cases as the place of the contract and the place of the accident often are not the same.

The curious dearth of subject-specific literature in the United Kingdom tends to give a peculiarly pioneering tinge to any effort to collate and analyse what rightly can be described as earlier attempts to focus on aspects of a subject which has been recognised by some writers as incapable of being reduced to simple coherent rules.[3] Yet increasing travel and multistate commercial activity have created factual situations which were and are bound, at some stage, to involve the law of insurance and the conflict of laws. The introduction of a foreign element in an insurance or reinsurance contract inevitably raises potential problems of private international law. These range from establishing which court has jurisdiction and which is the applicable law to securing recognition and enforcement of foreign judgments. Not surprisingly, in recent years something of a revolution has occurred in the United Kingdom and the other Member States of the European Union where new approaches to choice of law in insurance contracts have been adopted as a result of the implementation of the European Insurance Directives.

It is well known that the Second and Third 'Generation' of Insurance Directives provide very detailed choice of law rules which apply to insurance contracts covering risks situated within the EC.[4] Moreover the EEC Convention

[1] [1959] *Modern Law Review* 198.

[2] Mengis (1987) *Louisiana Law Review*.

[3] See Ubertazzi, (1962) *Diritto internazionale*, 353; Carnaham, *Conflict of Laws and Life Insurance Contracts* (Buffalo, Dennis, 1958); Rabel, *The conflict of laws: a comparative study* (Ann Arbor, The University of Michigan, 1958) 359–352.

[4] See Art 7 of the Second Council Directive on Non-Life Insurance, 88/357EEC (OJ 1998 L172/1), and Art 4 of the Second Council Directive on Life Assurance, 90/619, (OJ 1990 l330/50), Arts 27 and

on the law applicable to contractual obligations of 1980 (the Rome Convention) contains contract choice of law rules which apply to insurance contracts covering risks situated outside the EC.[5] Unlike the Insurance Directives, this Convention contains no provision to deal specifically with insurance contracts. When it comes to jurisdiction, the Council Regulation on jurisdiction and the recognition and enforcement of judgments in civil and commercial matters of 2000 (the Brussels I Regulation) and the EC/EFTA Convention (the Lugano Convention) provide specific rules of jurisdiction for insurance contracts regardless of whether these contracts cover risks situated within or outside the EC/EFTA.[6]

The time is ripe for a thorough examination of the regime of private international law for insurance and reinsurance contracts in Europe, and the possible options for reform of the European rules on jurisdiction and the law applicable to insurance and reinsurance contracts. But this has to be carried out against the substantive law background in Europe. Part I will therefore look at the substantive law background and its significance for the private international lawyer. Part II will provide a critical analysis of the rules on jurisdiction for insurance and reinsurance contracts and possible options for reform. Parts III and IV will provide a critical analysis of the choice of law provisions and possible options for reforms. Finally, Part V will look at jurisdiction and applicable law problems that arise in Europe in relation to insurance and reinsurance

28 of the Third Council Directive on Non-Life Insurance, 92/49/EEC (OJ 1992 L228/1) and Articles 27 and 28 of the Third Council Directive on Life Assurance, 92/96 (1992) OJ L360/1. These choice of law rules are discussed in: Dicey and Morris, *The Conflict of Laws* by L Collins *et al*, 13th edn (London, Sweet & Maxwell, 1999) 1350–76; Kaye, *The New Private International Law of Contract of the European Community* (Aldershot, Ashgate Publishing, 1993) 13–40; Plender, *The European Contracts Convention* (London, Sweet & Maxwell, 1992) para 4.49–4.53; MacNeil (1995) 44 *International and Comparative Law Quarterly* 19; Smulders and Glazener (1992) 29 *Common Market Law Review* 775; Reich (1992) 29 *Common Market Law Review* 861 at 870 *et seq*; Forlati Picchio in Bellando (ed), *Le Assicurazioni in Europa* (Torino, Utet, 1984) 155; Blanco Morales Limones, *El seguro español en el Derecho internacional privado* (Madrid, Caser, 1989); Frigessi di Rattalma, *Il contratto internazionale di assicurazione* (Padova, Cedam, 1990); Claret, *Contrats d'Assurance et Conflits de Loi en Droit Communautaire* (Doctoral thesis, University of Lille, 1994); Dubuisson, *Le droit applicable au contrat d'assurance dans un espace communitaire integré* (Doctoral thesis, Université Catholic de Louvain; Reichert and d'Oliveira (eds) *International Insurance Contract Law* (The Hague, Kluwer Law International, 1994); Fuentes Camacho, *Los contratos de seguro y el Derecho Internacional Privado en la Unión Europea* (Madrid, Civitas, 1999); Celle, *I contratti di assicurazione grandi rischi nel diritto internazionale privato* (Padova, Cedam, 2000).

[5] Art 1, para 3 of the Rome Convention, (1980) OJ L 266 of 9 October.

[6] Arts 8 to 14 of the Brussels Regulation deal with matters relating to insurance. The text of the Brussels Regulation is to be found in OJ 2001 L 12/1. The Brussels Regulation replaces the 1968 Brussels Convention. The original text of the Brussels Convention is to be found in OJ 1978, L 304/77. The text of the United Kingdom, Danish and Irish Accession Convention of 1978 is set out in OJ 1978, L 304/1. For the text of the Greek Accession Convention of 1982 see OJ 1982 L 388/1. For the text of the Spanish and Portuguese Accession Convention of 1989 see OJ 1989 L 285/1. The text of the Austrian, Finnish and Swedish Accession Convention of 1996 is found in OJ 1997 C 15/1. A consolidated version of the 1968 Convention and 1971 Protocol, as amended by the four Accession Conventions in set out in 1998 OJ C 27/1.

contracts concluded by electronic means, and the possible solutions to these problems.

The perspective will be unashamedly European. For it is in Europe that the fundamental and unique developments in relation to the private international law for insurance and reinsurance contracts have taken place. At the same time, when thinking of solutions for reform, much can be learnt from an examination of developments in non-European States, in particular the Latin American countries and the United States.

Acknowledgements

I would like to thank Professor James Fawcett for his time and patience in reading successive drafts and for his helpful and constructive comments and encouragement. Many thanks must also go to Professors Jonathan Harris and Robin Morse. Their comments and views were of particular assistance in converting my thesis into a book.

Gratitude should be expressed to the Departamento de Derecho Internacional Publico y Privado, Universitad Complutense de Madrid, Spain for the assistance and facilities afforded to me during the course of my research.

I would like to take this opportunity to thank Professors Isabella Castangia, Paolo Fois, Marco Frigessi di Rattalma and Riccardo Pisillo Mazzeschi who have helped me at various stages during my career.

Within the School of Law, University of Nottingham, my appreciation for Simone Degeling, Paolo Galizzi, Stephen Girvin and Martin Trybus who were a source of support as well as enjoyable companions.

Finally, I would like to express my appreciation to my family and friends: to my parents, grand-mother, sister and brother in law for their unfailing support and encouragement; to my friends Edward Bates, Roxana Belecheanu, Peter Braun, Peppe Conte, Chiara Eberle, Carole Fayad, Catherine Georgiou Kyrieri, Aris Georgopoulos, Andreas Kouzupis, Monica Lagazio, Teresa Marat Mendes, Chitra Massey, Lilin Meng, Enrico Milano, Marco Odello, Despina Pachnou, Slawomir Sujecki and Samantha Velluti for their friendship and understanding; to the Warden, tutors and students of Lincoln Hall who made my time in Nottingham as enjoyable as it was productive.

Nottingham, August 2002

Contents

Table of Cases

Abbreviations

AA	Ars Aequi
AC	Appeal Cases, English Law Reports
Act Dr	Actualités du Droit
AG	Advocate General
All ER	All England Reports
An Der Civ	Anuario de Derecho Civil
Ann Dr Lv	Annales de Droit de Louvain
Ann Fr Dr Int	Annuaire français de droit international
Arb Int	Arbitration International
Arch civ	Archivio civile
Arch giur	Archivio giuridico "Filippo Serafini"
ASDI	Annuaire suisse de droit international
Assicurazioni	Rivista di diritto, economia e finanza delle assicurazioni priv.
AIDA	Association Internationale du Droit des Assurances
AIRAC	All-Industry Research Advisory Council
AYIL	Australian Yearbook of International Law
BBTC	Banca, Borsa e Titoli di Credito
Benelux Jur	Jurisprudentie van het Benelux Gerechtshof
BGB	Bürgerliches Gesetzbuch (Germany)
BGH	Bundesgerichtshof
BJ	Belgique judiciaire
Bus Law	The Business Lawyer
Clunet (see JDI)	
Contratti	I Contratti
Corr giur	Il Corriere giuridico
CS	Comunicazioni e studi dell'Istituto di diritto internazionale privato e straniero dell'Università degli studi di Milano
Dalloz	Revue Dalloz
Danno e resp	Danno e Responsabilità
DCI	Diritto del commercio internazionale
Dir com e scambi int	Diritto comunitario e degli scambi internazionali
Dir econ ass	Diritto e pratica dell'assicurazione
Dir giur	Diritto e Giurisprudenza
Dir int	Diritto internazionale
Dir maritt	Diritto marittimo
Dir publ comp eur	Diritto pubblico comparato ed europeo

Riv trim dir e proc civ	Rivista trimestrale di diritto e procedura civile
Dir UE	Il Diritto dell'Unione europea
ECC	European Commercial Cases
ECR	European Community Law Reports
EdD	Enciclopedia del Diritto
EFTA	European Free Trade Association
Etudes Lalive	Etudes de droit international en l'honneur de Pierre Lalive, Bâle-Frankfurt am Main, 1993
Europa e diritto	Europa e diritto
Europa e diritto privato	Europa e diritto privato
Foro it	Foro italiano
Foro pad	Foro padano
Gaz Pal	Gazette du Palais
Giur it	Giurisprudenza italiana
Giur comm	Giurisprudenza commerciale
Giust civ	Giustizia Civile
Hague Recueil	Recueil des Cours de l'Acaemie de Droit International de La Hague
IAIS	International Association of Insurance Supervisors
INA	Istituto Nazionale delle Assicurazioni
IJIL	International Journal of Insurance Law
IPrax	Praxis des Internationalen Privat und Verfahrens-rechts
IYIL	Italian Yearbook of International Law
Liber Amicorum K Siehr	Private Law in the International Arena, The Hague, 2000
JDI	Journal de Droit International
JMLC	Journal of Maritime Law and Commerce
JT	Journal des Tribunaux
Jur Rev	Juridical Review
Jus	JUS-Rivista di Scienze Giuridiche
Liber Droz	E pluribus unum. Liber amicorum Georges AL Droz. On the Progressive Unification of Private International Law, The Hague, Boston, London, 1996
Lloyd's Rep	Lloyd's Reports
Mélanges Loussouarn	L'internationalisation du droit. Mélanges en l'honneur de Yvon Loussouarn, Paris, 1994
NGCC	La Nuova Giurisprudenza Civile Commentata
NLCC	Le Nuove Leggi Civili Commentate
RabelsZ	Rabels Zeitschrift für ausländisches und internationals Privatrecht
RBDI	Revue belge de droit international
RDCiv	Rivista di diritto civile

RDE	Rivista di diritto europeo
REDE	Revista Española de Derecho Europeo
REDI	Revista Española de Derecho Internacional
Resp civ prev	Responsabilità civile e previdenza
Rev Esp Seg	Revista Española de Seguros
Rev giur ass terr	Revue giuridique de l'assurance terrestre
Rev dir eur	Revue trimestrelle de droit européen
Rev Marché Commun	Revue de Marché Commun
Riv not	Rivista del Notariato
Studi Broggini	Collisio legum. Studi di diritto internazionale privato per Gerardo Broggini, Milano, 1997
Studi Capotorti	Divenire sociale e adeguamento del diritto. Studi in onore di Francesco Capotorti, Milano, 1999
Studi Giuliano	L'unificazione del diritto internazionale privato e processuale. Studi in memoria di Mario Giuliano, Padova, 1989
Trav Com fr de dip	Travaux du Comité français de droit international privé

PART I

The Substantive Law Background in Europe and its Significance for Private International Law

1

The Substantive Law in Europe

1. INTRODUCTION

EU INSURANCE law is undeniably complex, resulting, as it does, from different types of Directives.

First, there are Directives which attempt to harmonise Member States' laws. Examples of this category are the Motor Insurance Directives, which harmonise much of the substantive law of motor vehicle insurance in the European Union States which have implemented the Directives.[1]

Secondly, there are three 'Generations' of Insurance Directives, which are designed to realise a single insurance market in Europe.[2] Alongside the Non Life and Life Insurance Directives there is the Reinsurance Directive which abolishes all restrictions on the establishment and provision of services relating to reinsurance in the Single Market.[3]

Thirdly, there are other Directives not directly concerned with insurance but which may have an impact on the insurers' activities. An example is the Directive on unfair terms in consumer contracts.[4] This Directive applies to the terms of all contracts or supplies made between a seller or a supplier and a consumer who is a natural person.

After a brief discussion of the Single Insurance Market and an exposition of the Treaty of Rome provisions on freedom of establishment and services, the rest of this chapter will consider the European Directives concerned with insurance and reinsurance.

2. THE EU INSURANCE MARKET

The Single Insurance Market in Europe has been achieved through three 'generations' of insurance directives: the 1973 and 1978 'First Generation' Insurance Directives which aim to abolish obstacles to the freedom of establishment in direct non-life and direct life business; the 1988 and 1990 'Second Generation'

[1] Council Directive 72/166 EEC; *OJ* 1972 L 103 02. 05. 1972 pp 1 *et seq*; Council Directive 84/5; *OJ* 1984 L 008 11. 01. 1984 p 17; Council Directive 90/232 EEC; *OJ* 1990 L 129 19.05.1990, 33.

[2] See General Introduction, n 1.

[3] Council Directive 62/225 of 25 February 1964 on the abolition of restrictions on freedom of establishment and freedom to provide services in respect of reinsurance and retrocession.

[4] Council Directive 93/13 on unfair terms in consumer contract; *OJ* 1993 L 09, 21. 04. 1993 29–34.

Insurance Directives which attempt to realise the freedom of non-life and life insurance services; the 1992 'Third Generation' Insurance Directives which aim to complete the creation of the Single Insurance Market.

A word needs to be said about the reasons for the utilisation of directives rather than regulations in order to achieve a single insurance market in Europe. Whilst there was no choice between directives and regulations before the introduction of the 1986 European Single Act, Article 95 (ex Article 100A) of the Treaty of Rome allows the Council to adopt regulations for 'the approximation of the provisions laid down by law, regulation or administrative action in Member States which have as their *object the establishment and functioning of the internal market*'.[5] The use of directives rather than regulations for the establishment of a common market in Europe can be justified by the principles of mutual recognition and minimum harmonisation of national provision laid down by the European Court of Justice in the famous *Cassis de Dijon* case.[6] This conclusion is suggested by the impact of the *Cassis de Dijon* jurisprudence on the European Single Act of 1986.[7]

3. THE TREATY OF ROME

The Treaty of Rome establishing the European Economic Community contains two principles which are of particular importance for the establishment of the Single Insurance Market in Europe. These principles are: the right of European insurers (individuals or companies) to set up business either through an agency, a branch or a company in another Member State (ie, the 'right of establishment') and the right of European nationals (individuals or companies) to provide services in any Member State of the European Community without being established there (ie, the 'right to provide services'). Alongside the right of establishment and the right to provide services the Treaty of Rome provides a duty of harmonisation. Article 3(h) of the Treaty of Rome provides for 'the approximation of laws of Member States to the extent required for the proper functioning of the Common Market'. A harmonisation of Member States' laws seems necessary particularly in order to avoid unfair practices between European insurers (individuals or companies) in the Single Insurance Market.[8] Article 51, paragraph 2 (ex Article 61) of the Treaty of Rome is also of importance for the European insurance market. It provides that the liberalisation of insurance services connected with the movement of capital is to be realised in step with the progressive liberalisation of the movement of capital.

[5] See Craig and de Búrca, *EU Law* (Oxford, Oxford University Press, 1998) 1124 seq.

[6] Case 120/78 [1979] ECR 649, (1979) 3 CMLR 494. For commentaries see Masclet (1981) *Revue Trimestrelle de Droit Européen* pp 611–30; Capelli (1981) *Revue Marché Commun* 421–35; Dashwood (1981) *European Law Review* 268.

[7] For a clear illustration of this point see Weatherill and Beaumont, *EU Law* (London, Penguin, 1999) *565 et seq.*

[8] See Clifford Chance (ed), *Insurance Regulation in Europe* (London, LLP, 1993) 3.

(a) **Establishment**

(i) The Right of Establishment

The right of establishment is laid down in Articles 43 to 48 (*ex Articles 52–58)* of the Treaty of Rome. In *Reyners v Belgian State*,[9] the European Court of Justice stated that Article 43 of the Treaty of Rome, which defines the freedom of establishment, had direct effect after the end of the *transitional* period for the creation of a single market in Europe—ie, after 1 January 1970, and that restrictions which discriminate against persons seeking to exercise freedom of establishment could not be enforced, notwithstanding the absence of specific Directives. Consequently, insurance undertakings (natural or legal persons) cannot be discriminated against on the basis of the location of their central administration, registered offices or principal places of business. The Treaty of Rome indicates the companies which may be considered as EC nationals and thus benefit from the right of establishment.[10] They must have their central administrations, registered offices or principal places of business within the Community and be formed in accordance with the law of a Member State of the European Community. It is worth noting that the exclusion of 'non-profit-making' organisations from the scope of application of Article 48 of the Treaty of Rome has a negative impact in the UK insurance market where friendly societies are allowed to carry on insurance business.[11]

(ii) Provision of Insurance Services Through Permanent Presence in Host State

In *Commission v Germany*,[12] the European Court of Justice held that Articles 43 to 48 (ex Articles 52–58) of the Treaty of Rome apply to a permanent presence in a Member State which does not consist of an agency, branch or subsidiary and to a natural person with power to do business for an insurer established in another Member State.

In its Draft Interpretative Communication entitled 'Freedom to provide services and the general good in the insurance sector',[13] the European Commission rejects this broad interpretation of the term 'permanent presence' and makes clear that intermediaries can be regarded as branches only when they act as genuine extensions of insurance undertakings. According to the Commission, intermediaries are equated to branches if they are subject to the

[9] Case 2/74, *Reyners v Belgium* [1974] ECR 631, (1974) 2 CMLR 305.

[10] See Art 58.

[11] See s 101 on Sched 20 of the Friendly Societies Act 1993. See also Reg 3 of the Financial Services and Markets Act 2000 which makes certain modifications to the application of the Regulations to friendly societies that are not covered by the insurance directives.

[12] See Case 205/84 [1986] ECR 3755 (1987) 1 CMLR 69.

[13] See Document CAB XV/207/97.

management and supervision of the insurer they represent; are able to commit to the insurance undertaking; and have received a permanent brief.

(b) The Freedom of Services

Articles 49 to 55 (ex Articles 59–66) of the Treaty of Rome deal with the freedom to provide services.

It is clear from the text of Article 60 that the definition of 'services' under this provision encompasses any service supplied by a provider to a recipient who resides in another Member State.[14] However, in *Commission v Ireland*[15] the European Court of Justice held that these provisions do not apply to goods supplied in the context of the provision of a service.

In *Van Binsbergen v Bestuur van de Bedrijsverenigng voor de Metaalnijverheild*[16] the European Court of Justice stated that the imposition of a requirement of habitual residence or establishment in the host State could breach Article 49 of the Treaty of Rome; a requirement imposed on the provider is admitted only if it is binding upon any person established in the State where the service is provided and if it is justified for the 'general good'; and measures may be adopted by Member States only in order to avoid the evasion of the rules of the State where the service is provided.

It is well established case-law that not only the provider but also the recipient is a potential beneficiary of the freedom to provide services.[17] However, if one looks at the text of Articles 49 to 55 of the Treaty of Rome greater attention is focused on the provider of services.

It is worth noting that the Third Non Life and Life Insurance Directives impose a duty of prior notification on the insurer who intends to carry on business for the first time in another Member State.[18] The meaning of these rules, which undoubtedly make the exercise of the freedom of insurance services more difficult, has been clarified recently by the European Commission in its Draft Interpretative Communication on the Insurance Directives.[19] According to the European Commission, the notification procedure laid down in the Third Insurance Directives 'pursues a simple objective of exchange of information between supervisory authorities'. Some uncertainties remain at present with regard to the application of the provisions on freedom of services to situations where services do not cross borders between Member States but encounter obstacles within their own national territories. It is very much to be hoped that

[14] See Craig and de Búrca, *EU Law*, 2nd edn (Oxford, OUP, 1998) 762 *et seq*.
[15] See Case 45/87 [1988] ECR 4929, 4963.
[16] See Case 33/74 [1974] ECR 1299, (1975) I CMLR 298.
[17] See especially joined Cases 186/82 e 26/83 [1984] ECR 377, 403; Case 186/87 [1989] ECR 195, 221.
[18] See Arts 3 to 7 on Title II.
[19] See above n 13.

this fundamental issue which has been negligently disregarded by the European Commission will be addressed in the forthcoming discussion of the draft Interpretative Communication of Insurance Directives.

(c) Establishment v Services

A word needs to be said about the distinction between establishment and services. It is well known that the dividing line between these Treaty regimes is not easy to draw in any circumstance.[20] Moreover, the European Court of Justice has been reluctant to make a clear distinction between the right of establishment and the right to provide services within the European market. But some attempts to clarify this distinction have been recently made by the European Commission in its 'Interpretative Communication on Freedom to Provide Services and the General Good in the Second Banking Directive'[21] and in its Draft Interpretative Communication of Insurance Directives.[22] Whilst the Non Life and Life Insurance Directives distinguish between establishment and services no serious consequences are attached to the violation of the different notification procedures laid down for branches and for the provision of services. The European Commission in its Draft Interpretative Communication on Insurance Directives makes clear that the violation of these notification procedures would not affect the validity of the policies issued.

(d) Harmonisation

Harmonisation of the laws of Member States is to be achieved under Article 94 (ex Article 100) of the Treaty of Rome by adoption of Directives by the Council acting on proposals from the Commission.

Towards the end of the seventies the European Commission examined the attainability of harmonising the substantive law applying to insurance contracts,[23] but in the circumstances that obtained in those days, the aim of harmonising the law of contract proved to be excessively arduous, with the result that the European Commission decided in the meantime to opt for a solution that aimed to solve conflict of laws in its Second 'Generation' of Insurance Directives. Since 1985 the harmonisation realised by the insurance directives was restricted to those issues that were sufficient to warrant Member States'

[20] See Weatherill and Beaumont, *EU Law*, n 7 above, 671.

[21] OJC 209/6—ref. 97/C 209/04.

[22] See n 13 above.

[23] Proposal for a Council Directive on the co-ordination of laws, regulations and administrative provisions relating to insurance contracts, OJ C (1979) 190, 2. See also the so-called Schwartz Document—'Errichtung des gemeinsamen Markets für Schadensversicherungen' in (1980) 144 *Zeitschrift für das gesamte Handels und Wirtschaftsrecht (ZHR)* 447 and 450–51.

reciprocal confidence in each other's regulations. Finally, in 1993, under the influence of the discussions on subsidiarity, it withdrew its proposal.[24]

Renewed attempts to harmonise the substantive rules of the national legal systems are now supported by the Economic and Social Committee, which stated in a published opinion that 'a whole series of obstacles hampering completion of the single market in this field can be traced back to the absence of Community legislation on insurance contracts (a minimum level of harmonisation of substantive law).'[25] In the same vein, a resolution adopted by the European Parliament towards the end of 1998 takes the view

> that the harmonisation achieved in the sphere of general law through Council Directive 93/13/EEC of 5 April 1993 on unfair terms in consumer contracts [26] is not enough to present insurance undertakings wishing to provide services in a Member State other than that in which they are authorised from being unfairly required to comply with national legislation by reference to the general good and that the efforts which began ten years ago to approximate the most important provisions of the law of insurance contracts and conditions should therefore be resumed.[27]

4. THE 1993 UNFAIR CONTRACT TERMS DIRECTIVE

The Unfair Contract Terms Directive, which was introduced in 1993, aims to remove 'unfair terms' from consumer contracts, ie contracts made between natural persons and individuals or companies carrying on in business.

This Directive was implemented in the United Kingdom by the Unfair Terms in Consumer Contracts Regulations 1994,[28] with effect from 1 July 1995.[29]

The Directive defines unfair contract terms according to three criteria. First, a contract term is unfair if it has not been individually negotiated,[30] ie if the consumer has not been able to influence the content of the term. Secondly, if it is contrary to the requirement of good faith.[31] Thirdly, if it causes, to the detriment of the consumer, a significant imbalance in the parties' rights and obligations under the contract.[32]

The Directive provides that courts should determine whether or not the term is actually unfair when taking into consideration the prevailing circumstances at

[24] OJ C (1993) 228, 4 and 14.
[25] The opinion appears in OJ C (1998) 95, 72 *et seq*. The quotation here is from point 2.1.9. on p 77.
[26] OJ L (1993) 95, 29.
[27] Minutes of the plenary sitting of 22 October 1998 resolution on the draft Commission interpretative communication on freedom to provide services and the general good in the insurance sector. EP Doc A4-307/98 (SEC (97) 1824-C4-0049/98).
[28] SI 1994 No 3159.
[29] This was 6 months late.
[30] Reg 3(1).
[31] Reg 4(1).
[32] Reg 4(1).

the time the contract was made.[33] The Directive also provides that national courts cannot be concerned with any term which either defines the object of the consumer contract or deals with the adequacy of the price, as against services or goods supplied or sold.[34] Thus, as far as insurance is concerned, a court cannot assess the fairness of insuring clauses and exception clauses. Article 4, paragraph 2 excludes from the directive those terms of insurance contracts which 'clearly define or circumscribe . . . the risk.' Due to the difficulty of identifying the terms which define or circumscribe the risk in an insurance contract the insured will often be deprived of the Directive's protection. That may have serious consequences in countries such as the United Kingdom which exclude insurance contracts from their consumer protection legislation.[35]

5. REINSURANCE

A Directive was introduced in 1964 to abolish all restrictions on the establishment and provision of services relating to reinsurance in the European Community.[36] According to this Directive, EC-based reinsurers have the right to set up agencies, branches or subsidiaries and to manage undertakings, companies or firms within the meaning of Article 48, paragraph 2 (ex Article 58) of the Treaty of Rome in other Member States.

The Reinsurance Directive does not provide a right for reinsurers to establish branches in one Member State on the basis of an existing authorisation in another Member State. Nor can the right for reinsurers to establish themselves in another Member State if they do not comply with the local rules be derived from the Treaty provisions concerning establishment. Thus, it should be concluded that Member States normally require reinsurers to fulfil the requirements imposed on a local reinsurer.[37]

6. THE FIRST NON LIFE INSURANCE DIRECTIVE

(a) Scope

The First Non Life Insurance Directive, which was introduced in 1973, aims to abolish obstacles to the freedom of establishment in direct non-life business.[38]

[33] Reg 4(2).

[34] Reg 3(3).

[35] See Sched 1 of the Unfair Contract Terms Act 1977.

[36] Council Directive 62/225 of 25 February 1964 on the abolition of restrictions on freedom of establishment and freedom to provide services in respect of reinsurance and retrocession.

[37] However, it seems to me that Member States are not allowed to ask reinsurers to fulfil the conditions imposed to local reinsurers when this request constitutes a violation of the principle which prohibits the imposition of identical controls.

[38] Council Directive 73/239 of 24 July 1973 on the co-ordination of laws, regulations and administrative provisions relating to the taking up and pursuit of the business of direct insurance other than life assurance, as amended by Council Directive 76/580 of 29 June 1976 (of the same title).

The Directive covers the main areas of insurance such as marine, aviation, transport, fire, property, credit and suretyship, legal expenses and tourist assistance.[39]

Branches and agencies of insurers established outside the Community come within the scope of the Directive.[40]

(b) Authorisation Requirements

The Directive lays down a common regulatory structure for non-life insurers. Insurers with their head offices within the EC wishing to establish branches or agencies in other Member States are only requested to seek local authorisation.[41]

Article 7 provides that 'an authorisation shall be valid for the entire national territory unless, and in so far as national laws permit, the applicant seeks permission to carry on his business only in a part of the national territory.' Authorisation shall be given for a particular class of insurance.[42]

(c) The Definition of Establishment

As modified by the Second Non Life Insurance Directive, the definition of establishment also includes a permanent presence other than an agency or branch.[43] However, the extent to which an insurer may have a permanent representative to help provide services in another Member State without being considered as established there is unclear. It seems that in order to solve this problem insurers will need to look at the law of the Member State in which they intend to carry on their business.

7. THE FIRST LIFE INSURANCE DIRECTIVE

(a) Scope

The First Life Insurance Directive, which was adopted in 1979, introduces equivalent measures for life insurance.[44]

[39] Art 2 and Annex.
[40] Art 23.
[41] Arts 10 and 11.
[42] Art 6.
[43] Art 3 of the Second Council Directive on direct non-life insurance 1988.
[44] Council Directive 79/267 of 5 March 1979 on the co-ordination of laws, regulations and administrative provisions relating to the taking-up and pursuit of the business of direct life assurance.

The Directive covers various classes of long term business such as life assurance (including ancillary risks), annuities, permanent health insurance and pension funds.[45]

(b) Authorisation Requirements

The Directive requires Member States to introduce a common regulatory structure for life insurers. As in the case of non-life insurance, authorisation is given for a particular class of business.[46] Thus insurers wishing to expand their business into other classes of life insurance have to seek specific authorisation.

(c) The Simultaneous Operation of Life and Non-life Insurance

Article 8 of the Directive prohibits the future authorisation of composite insurers, ie insurers carrying on both life and non life business simultaneously.[47] Composites which had been established can only continue to write both life and non-life insurance if they have separate management for each activity.This prohibition constitutes a change in the law for England. However, for some other European Community States, which already imposed such a prohibition, this represents no change in the law.

8. THE CO-INSURANCE DIRECTIVE

(a) Scope

The Co-insurance Directive, which was introduced in 1978, aims to co-ordinate rules for Community co-insurance.[48]

As modified by the Second Non Life Directive, the Directive covers all the risks which are classified as 'large risks' in the Second Non Life Directive.[49]

The Directive only applies in three circumstances: i) where the risk is situated in a Member State, ii) where at least one of the co-insurers is established in a Member State different to that of the lead insurer, iii) and where the risk requires the participation of several insurers for adequate cover. The Directive also requires the lead insurer to be authorised under the First Non-Life Directive.

[45] Art 1.

[46] Art 7.

[47] For a fuller examination of the meaning of this provision see Donohue and Radmore (1993) 10 *International Insurance Law Review* 323 *et seq.*

[48] Council Directive 78/473 of 30 May 1978 on the co-ordination of laws, regulations and administrative provisions relating to Community co-insurance.

[49] For the meaning of this concept see below para 11(b).

(b) The Co-insurance Directive and the Insurance Cases

In the 1986 insurance cases[50] the European Court of Justice held that a lead insurer may be situated in a Member State different to that where the risk is situated. The Court of Justice also stated that the State where the risk is situated cannot require a separate authorisation to a lead insurer authorised in another Member State.

9. THE SECOND NON LIFE INSURANCE DIRECTIVE

(a) Scope

The Second Non Life Insurance Directive, which was adopted in 1988, introduces new measures towards achieving the freedom of non-life insurance services.[51]

The Directive generally applies to the same risks as the First Non-Life Insurance Directive.

(b) Large Risks and Mass Risks

As originally drafted, the Directive provided a distinction between large risks (essentially those of a commercial nature) and mass risks (risks of a consumer nature). In the case of large risks, it gave the right for insurance companies to provide services freely in the European Market. By contrast, in the case of mass risks it introduced the right for Member States to impose an authorisation requirement on insurers wishing to sell insurance into its territory by means of services.

The Second Non Insurance Life Directive has been amended by the Third Non Life Insurance Directive. For the purposes of provision of insurance by way of services, the Directive abolishes the distinction between large and mass risks.[52] It follows that an EU insurer who wishes to provide insurance services outside its own country can do so by obtaining documentation from its home authorities, and by communicating to the host authorities its intention to do so.

[50] Case 252/83 (1987) 2 CMLR 169; Case 205/84 [1986] ECR 3755, (1987) 2 CMLR 69; Case 206/84 [1986] ECR 3817, (1987) 2 CMLR 150; Case 220/83 [1986] ECR 3663, (1987) 2 CMLR 113.

[51] Council Directive 88/357 of 22 June 1988 on the co-ordination of laws, regulations and administrative provisions relating to direct insurance other than life insurance and laying down provisions to facilitate the effective exercise of freedom to provide services.

[52] Art 6 as modified by Art 4 of the Third Non-Life Directive.

(c) Member State Where the Risk is Situated

Article 2(d) of the Directive defines the Member State where the risk is situated as follows:

> the Member State in which the property is situated, where the insurance relates either to buildings or to buildings and their contents, in so far as the contents are covered by the same insurance policy, the Member State of registration, where the insurance relates to vehicles of any type, the Member State where the policyholder took out the policy in the case of policies of a duration of four months or less covering travel or holiday risks, whatever the class concerned.

(d) Supervisory System[53]

The Second Non Life Insurance Directive does not harmonise the distinct supervisory systems of the Member States of the European Union. The Member States have the option to preserve or insert rules, administrative provisions or regulations justified on policy-holder grounds. Inconsistencies between the substantial and normative systems continue to remain. In the case of the provision of services, the host Member State can demand a previous validation of, for example, general and special policy terms. This is contrary to large risks, for which the host country can just demand non-methodical notification of these requirements and other certificates.[54] This requirement cannot represent a prior requirement to an undertaking carrying on its activities in the host Member State. But, in both cases, the authorities of the host Member State are bound by the application of the principles of non-duplication and proportionality set forth by the Court of Justice in *Commission v Germany*.[55] The Court of Justice maintained that the freedom to provide services can only be restrained by rules in domestic legislation if the public interest is not already protected by the rules of the home Member State, and the conditions are objectively verified. An insurer faced with an unnecessary overlap of prescriptions can invoke these principles. For the host Member State, it will become more complicated to justify supplementary requirements, as soon as a higher level of harmonisation and co-ordination is demanded. At the same time, the insurance business will continue to put pressure on the authorities of Member States with a precise control system to take a more open-handed stance toward their activities. For example, an insurer established in Italy which is subject to substantial, detailed, provisions, may be requested to compete with a French insurer providing services in Italy. Competition from insurers in Member States with a more open-ended supervision policy will cause a change of approach.

[53] See Ottow (1992) *Common Market Law Review* 518–19.

[54] Art 18.

[55] *Commission v Germany* cited above, n 12, 9.

10. THE SECOND LIFE INSURANCE DIRECTIVE

(a) Scope

The Second Life Insurance Directive[56] introduces new measures towards achieving the freedom of services for life business.

The Directive applies to an EC insurer authorised under the First Life Insurance Directive, which through an establishment in a Member State provides services in another Member State where the policyholder has his habitual residence or its establishment.[57]

(b) Policyholders

As adopted in 1990, the Directive distinguished between policy holders who had taken the initiative in seeking the commitment and ordinary policy holders. This distinction, which closely followed the pattern of the Non Life Insurance Directive, aims to separate assureds who need protection and those who do not.

The Directive states that a policyholder is to be considered as having taken the initiative in two circumstances: i) where the contract was concluded in the insurer's home state or by each of the parties in their own home states and there had been no prior contact between the policyholder and the insurer or his agent in the Member State in which the policyholder resides, by means of advertising or any form of approach to the policyholder personally; ii) where the policyholder approaches an independent intermediary to request information or to obtain a policy from an insurer established in another Member State and had signed a statement requesting such information. If either of these circumstances apply, the insurer does not need to be authorised by the host authorities and may sell the policy to the assured, provided only that the host authorities are informed of the insurer's activities. By contrast, where the life contract is not taken out on the assured's own initiative, the insurer is required to be authorised by the regulatory authorities of the assured's home state.

The Second Life Insurance Directive has been amended by the Third Life Insurance Directive. For the purposes of provision of insurance by way of services, the distinction between ordinary policyholders and policyholders who had 'taken the initiative in seeking the commitment' is abolished.[58] An insurer who wishes to provide life insurance services outside its own territory is

[56] Council Directive 90/619 of November 1990 on the co-ordination of laws, regulations and administrative provisions relating to direct life assurance, laying down provisions to facilitate the effective exercise of freedom to provide services.

[57] Arts 2 and 3.

[58] Art 6 as modified by Art 3 of the Third Non Life Directive.

requested merely to communicate to the host regulatory authorities its intention to do so.

11. INSURANCE COMPANIES FROM THIRD COUNTRIES[59]

A Member State is not under an obligation to open up its market for an insurer from a non-EU country.[60] If the Member State, however, permits a non-EU undertaking to establish itself in its territory, it has a duty to make access by branches and agencies subject to a validated permission.[61] Ad hoc provisions, concerning especially the establishment of appropriate technical reserves and the prerequisite of an express solvency margin, apply to the allowance of such a permission.[62]

In the Directive of 8 November 1990 and the Second Life Assurance Directive, the Council has inserted[63] the option of mutual action by the Commission if EU insurers in a third country are not obtaining national treatment giving the same opportunities as are obtainable to national insurance undertakings.

Once a non-EU insurer is established in the EU, he can provide services under the regime of the Second Insurance Directives.

12. THE 'THIRD GENERATION' INSURANCE DIRECTIVES

The Third Non Life Insurance Directive and the Third Life Assurance Directive, which were adopted in 1992, aim to complete the Single Insurance Market. They contain at least three types of provisions.

First, there are provisions which alter the rules on the rights of establishment and the right to provide services contained in the previous two generations of Directives.

Secondly, there are rules which replace the previous authorisation system with a single authorisation applicable to both establishment and services.

[59] See Ottow, above n 6.

[60] Art 23(2) of the First Non-Life Insurance Directive. The First Life Assurance Directive follows the regime of the former.

[61] Art 23(1) of the First Non Life Insurance Directive.

[62] Title III of the First Non Life Insurance Directive.

[63] Council Directive of 8 November 1990 amending, particularly as regards motor vehicle liability insurance, Directive 73/239/EEC and Directive 88/357/EEC that concern the co-ordination of laws, regulations and administrative provisions relating to direct insurance other than life assurance, 90/618 EEC (OJ 1990, L330/45): Arts 4, 8 and 9 of the Second Life Assurance Directive. A special agreement is concluded between the EEC and the Swiss Confederation regarding insurance other than life assurance, signed on 10 October 1989. This agreement is an annexe to the Council decision on the conclusion of the Agreement between the Swiss Confederation and the EEC concerning direct insurance other than life assurance (OJ 1991, L 205/1) as quoted by Ottow, above n 6, at 527.

Thirdly, there are provisions which extend home Member State control on the insurance company's business throughout the Community whether conducted through branches or cross-border services.

13. THE THIRD NON LIFE INSURANCE DIRECTIVE

(a) Scope

The Third Non Life Directive[64] applies to the same forms of non-life insurance as the First and Second Non Life Insurance Directives.[65]

(b) The Single Authorisation System

The Directive lays down a system of authorisation similar to the single licence system in the banking and investment sectors. EU insurers are no longer required to seek authorisation in each Member State where they wish to sell insurance services. The authorisation provided by their home regulatory authorities will also be valid for the entire Community whether insurance business is carried on through a branch and whether the risks are mass risks.[66] However, when insurance business is carried on through subsidiaries insurers will have to seek separate authorisation.[67]

(c) The Extension of Home Member State Control

As a result of the introduction of single authorisation, the home authorities, ie the authorities of the Member State where the insurer's head office is situated, are solely responsible for the control of the insurer's finances.[68] They are also responsible for disciplining an insurer in the event of a breach of the host State's rules and are solely responsible for withdrawing authorisation.[69]

Residual powers are given to the host authorities in two circumstances: i) when the home authorities fail to act to prevent the insurer from infringing the host's rules and ii) when restrictions are imposed for the 'general good'.

It is maintained that the combination of the home country principle with the single insurance passport has led to a defective form of regulatory competition

[64] Third Council Directive 92/49 of 18 June 1992 on the co-ordination of laws, regulations and administrative provisions relating to direct insurance other than life assurance.

[65] Arts 1 and 2.

[66] Art 5.

[67] Art 10.

[68] Art 9.

[69] Art 14.

among EU supervisory authorities.[70] Under the present regime insurers do have an inducement to choose a 'home country' that they consider favourable. But the admissibility of a 'race of laxity' between Member States is quite restricted, because the main supervisory standards have already been harmonised.[71] Moreover, as pointed out above, host countries maintain residual authority to interpose when they perceive that the 'general good' reservation is activated.

14. THE THIRD LIFE INSURANCE DIRECTIVE

(a) Scope

The Third Life Insurance Directive[72] brought life insurance into line with non life insurance.

The Directive applies to the same forms of business insurance as the First Life Directive,[73] and introduces a system of authorisation similar to that introduced by the Third Non-Life Directive.

(b) The Single Authorisation System

The authorisation provided by the insurer's home State will be valid for the entire Community whether insurance business is carried on through a branch or the provision of cross-border services and regardless of the risk assured.[74] However, when insurance business is conducted through subsidiaries, insurers will need a separate authorisation.[75]

(c) The Extension of Home State Control

A home State's authorities are solely responsible for the control of insurers' finances and for withdrawing authorisation.[76] They have the right to carry out 'on the spot' verifications of branches established in other Member States.[77]

[70] See Hertig (1994) *International Review of Law and Economy* 177 *et seq.*

[71] *Ibid.*

[72] Third Council Directive 92/96 of 19 December 1992 on the co-ordination of laws, regulations and administrative provisions relating to direct life assurance.

[73] Art 2.

[74] Art 4.

[75] Art 9.

[76] Art 8.

[77] Art 9.

15. THE 'GENERAL GOOD' IN THE THIRD INSURANCE DIRECTIVES

A word needs to be said about the notion of 'general good' in EU insurance law. It is well known that this notion, which is a recurrent term in the Insurance Directives, has been developed by the European Court of Justice in order to widen the scope of the Treaty freedoms from mere non-discrimination principles to general prohibitions on all measures that constitute restrictions on the freedom of movement across borders.[78] As a result of the existence of the concept of the general good, insurers who benefit from a single licence must comply with host country's provisions adopted in the interest of the general good. With a view to facilitating the accomplishment of this task, the Insurance Directives request Member States to notify foreign financial institutions wishing to enter the market as to which rules apply in the general good. The European Court of Justice has refrained from giving a precise definition of the 'general good'. However, the conditions under which a Member State can invoke the general good are well established in the jurisprudence of the European Court of Justice and can be summarised as follows: non-harmonisation; justification by a general good motive; non discrimination on the grounds of nationality; non duplication; proportionality. In the long-awaited Draft Interpretative Communication for the Insurance Sector, the European Commission specifies the way in which the general good has to be applied and lays down the criteria against which any measure should be judged.[79] Furthermore, it examines a number of examples within the insurance market.[80]

16. THE EUROPEAN SUBSTANTIVE LAW FOR INTERMEDIARIES

The Council Directive 77/92 on *Measures to Facilitate the Effective Exercise of Freedom of Establishment and Freedom to Provide Services* aims to achieve freedom of establishment and services in respect of insurance intermediaries. It applies to three groups of intermediary: the UK designations are insurance brokers, employed and self-employed insurance agents and sub-agents.[81]

The Directive does not require Member States to lay down minimum qualifications upon intermediaries; but merely states that, where such qualifications are requested by a Member State, those qualifications cannot be used to exclude intermediaries appropriately qualified in other states of the European Union.[82]

[78] Tison (1998) *Legal issues of European Integration* 2.

[79] Draft Commission Interpretative Communication on Freedom to Provide Services and the General Good in the Insurance Sector in OJ C 365/7, 1997. For a commentary see Wolson (1998) *International Insurance Law Review* 268 *et seq*.

[80] See above n 7.

[81] Directive 77/92, Art 2.

[82] See Merkin and Rodger, *EC Insurance Law* (London and New York: Longman, 1997) 88.

The limits of this Directive are the lack of any EU qualifications or standards for intermediaries[83] and the absence of uniform rules on the relationship between the intermediary and the insurance company.[84]

17. ARE THE EC DIRECTIVES PRO-INSURED?

The introduction of pro-insured rules of jurisdiction in the Brussels Regulation and Lugano Convention raises the question of the existence of similar protective provisions in the substantive law introduced by EC Directives. In order to find an answer to this question a number of distinctions have to be drawn.

It is clear that pro-insured provisions are contained in the 1993 Unfair Contracts Terms Directive. The text and preamble to the Directive make clear that it is concerned with the protection of the insured.

By contrast, there is no doubt that the Reinsurance Directive, which attempts to liberalise the re-insurance market, contains merely neutral provisions.

As regards Insurance Directives, it cannot be assumed in general that the Directives favour the insured in the sense of being concerned predominantly with the interests of the insured. Certain provisions in the Directives are pro-insured, whilst others are pro-insurer.

The imposition of a duty on the policyholder to sign a statement in standard form recognising that the insurer was established in another state, and the introduction of a period of between 14 and 30 days in which the policyholder has the right to cancel the policy, are intended to be in the interests of the insured.

The introduction of a single authorisation system applicable both to establishment and services, the abolition of the Member States' right to impose material controls on policy terms and premium levels, and the restriction of the Member States' powers to protect their policyholders all operate in favour of the insurer.

The conclusion must be that, overall, the Insurance Directives produce a balanced package, taking into account the interests of both insured and insurer.

[83] *Ibid*, 88.

[84] See Claret, *Contrats d'assurance et conflits de loi* (Doctoral thesis, University of Lille, 1994) 165.

2

The Significance of the Substantive Law Background for Private International Law

THE SUBSTANTIVE law background is important both in terms of identifying the sort of jurisdiction and applicable law questions that will occur in Europe in insurance and reinsurance cases, and in terms of finding proper solutions to these problems.

1. IDENTIFYING THE PROBLEMS

(a) What Sort of Jurisdictional Problems Are There Going to be in Europe?

A European Union policyholder will normally have someone (insurer, broker and agent) within the European Union whom he or she can sue. In the common situation where the insurance policy is issued by an insurer domiciled in a European State, a claimant can proceed against the insurer in the State of the defendant's domicile.[1] Even if the policy is issued outside the European Union, by say a United States insurer, the claimant can normally proceed against the European agent of the insurer in the European Union State in which the agent is domiciled. Though in some cases, of course, the European Union agent of the United States insurer will be from the same State as the policyholder, which will mean that the claimant will be able to sue in his home State.

If the defendant is domiciled within the European Union, as will be seen later, the European provisions on jurisdiction contained in the Brussels Regulation and Lugano Convention will apply. These provisions make it easy to obtain jurisdiction against the defendant. The issue will be: in which European State or States is the claimant able to sue under the Brussels Regulation or Lugano Convention? Moreover, any judgment obtained will be enforceable throughout Europe under the enforcement rules of these Acts.

This does not mean that there will never be actions in insurance and reinsurance matters where the defendant is domiciled outside the European Union. For reasons of convenience a claimant can choose to sue both the agent in the

[1] See Art 8(1) of the Brussels Convention. For EFTA States see Art 8(1) of the Lugano Convention.

European Union and the United States insurer; and if the agent has gone into liquidation the claimant will have to sue the United States insurer. Nonetheless, in insurance and reinsurance cases, where trial is sought in Europe, it will be more usual to have a defendant domiciled within the European Union.

(b) Where Are There Going to be Choice of Law Problems in Europe?

A choice of law problem occurs when a case has pertinent connections with two or more States whose substantive law is different. It is clear that if you harmonise the substantive law of different countries you avoid or at least significantly reduce applicable law problems.[2]

There has been no world-wide attempt at the harmonisation of insurance and reinsurance laws of the sort undertaken recently by the United Nations Committee on Trade Law (UNCITRAL) in relation to leasing and factoring laws, which culminated in the Ottawa Conventions of 1988.

Even when the choice is between the insurance and reinsurance laws of two European Union States the issue of the applicable law can frequently arise because of the fact that insurance and reinsurance laws have only partially been harmonised within Europe.[3]

(i) The Timing of Implementation

The 15 European States which have implemented the Second and Third Insurance Directives have done so by legislation which takes effect from different dates, depending on the State in question.[4] This is of crucial importance because the Insurance Directives do not apply in a Member State to policies issued before the date on which that State's implementing legislation came into force. It follows that if a policy was issued in September 1994, the United Kingdom would apply to the policy its legislation implementing the rules of the Third Insurance Directives (the Insurance Company Act 1982) whereas other Community States would apply their non-Directive rules on insurance matters. This could result in a choice of law problem where the choice is, for example, between the English rules concerning material controls on policy terms and premium levels under the Insurance Companies Act 1982, and the Spanish more strict rules on policy terms and premium levels.

[2] See Fawcett (1984) *Northern Ireland Legal Quarterly* 141 *et seq.*

[3] See above ch 1, para 1.

[4] The implementation date of the Third Insurance Directives was 1 July 1994. Transitional arrangements for Spain operate until the end of 1996 and for Greece and Portugal operates until the end of 1998. For more information on this point see Merkin and Rodger, *EC Insurance Law*, n 82 above, 15.

(ii) Divergences in Implementing Statutes

Problems in relation to a lack of harmonisation are also created by the fact that there are, in some implementing statutes, noticeable divergences from the terms of the Second and Third Insurance Directives. But this raises aspects of European Union law which will be examined later in this chapter.

(iii) Matters Left to be Dealt With by the Application of Domestic Law

When it comes to the many issues that are not dealt with by the Insurance and Reinsurance Directives and the other European directives which apply to insurance matters and are left to be dealt with by the application of national law,[5] this will normally mean that rights and duties of the parties to an insurance or reinsurance contract and the third parties' rights and duties will have to come under existing rules of insurance and reinsurance contracts in the various European Union States, with the result that the issue of the applicable law may well arise.

(c) The Interaction of European Union Law and Private International Law: The Disappearance of Potential Applicable Law Problems

(i) Problems in Relation to Implementation of the Insurance Directives

A European Directive leaves implementation to national governments. In the area of insurance there have been problems over implementing statutes diverging from the terms of the Second and Third Insurance Directives.

(1) Divergences in Implementing Statutes

Some Member States have implemented the Second and Third Insurance Directives by setting out their provisions verbatim. Others have not done so and seem, at times, to have produced rules which diverge from those contained in the Directives. An example can be taken from the English legislation implementing the Second Life Insurance Directive. The Second Life Insurance Directive provides a minimum cancellation period of 14 days from receipt of the notice of cancellation. The English version is worded differently. Sections 75 to 77 of the Insurance Companies Act 1982 provide that the right of cancellation is exercisable by the policyholder within 10 days running from the date on which the policyholder is given a statutory notice of the right to cancel. This clearly restricts the defence granted by the Directive to the policyholder. Other Member States also appear to have diverged from the terms of the Insurance Directives in their implementing legislation. For example, the Belgian implementing legislation of

[5] See above ch 1, paras 5, 9, 10 and 11.

the Second Life Insurance Directive does not provide a definition of the locus where the commitment takes place.[6]

(2) The Effect of European Union law

At first glance, these problems of implementation could appear to give rise to differences in the substantive law of insurance and reinsurance of Member States, and accordingly to choice of law problems. But the effect of European law can be to eliminate differences in the substantive law of insurance; if so, no choice of law problem arises. Moreover, the Second and Third Insurance Directives contain some rules on the law applicable to insurance contracts covering risks situated in the territories of the Member States of the European Economic Community. Furthermore, the European law doctrine of direct effect is of assistance.[7] For it is clear that the Second and Third Insurance Directives do have direct horizontal effect (ie, they provide an individual with a right of action against other individuals). Finally, principles of interpretation and decisions of the European Court of Justice are of assistance in reducing choice of law problems.

Interpretation of National Law in the Light of the Insurance Directives

In applying domestic law, a national court is under a European law obligation to interpret it, as far as possible, in the light of the wording and scope of any relevant European Directive, 'whether the provisions in question were adopted before or after the Directive'.[8]

It follows that an English court would have to interpret the English version of the right of cancellation in the light of the Second Life Insurance Directive. If the English provision is interpreted in this light, it would appear to be the same as that contained in say the Dutch implementing legislation (the Dutch implemented the Directive verbatim). The result would be that the English court, rather than having a choice of law problem to solve, would merely have to ascertain the meaning of the right of cancellation under the Directive. This is a question of interpretation of the Directive, which may be referred to the European Court of Justice under Article 234 (ex Article 177) of the Treaty of Rome.[9] Nevertheless, a choice of law problem will remain if the English court comes to the conclusion that the meaning of the English version of the right of cancellation is clear.

What happens when an English court is faced with a foreign implementing statute which is worded differently from the Insurance Directives, for example the Italian Act of implementation of the Second Non Life and Life Insurance

[6] But see Art 2(e) of the Second Life Insurance Directive.

[7] For a clear illustration of this point see Frigessi di Rattalma, *Il contratto internazionale di assicurazione* (Padova, CEDAM, 1990) 111 *et seq.*

[8] Case C-106/89 *Marleasing SA v La Comercial Internacional de Alimentacion SA* [1990] ECR 1-4135. See also Case 14/83 *von Colson v Land Nordrhein-Westfalen* [1984] ECR 1891.

[9] See *Webb v EMO Air Cargo (UK) Ltd* [1992] 4 All ER 942 for the House of Lords's view of *Marleasing* and Art 177 references for clarification of the relevant Directive.

Directives? Under English private international law, foreign law is proved as a fact and evidence would be required as to how Italian courts would interpret the Italian Act of implementation of the Second Insurance Directives.[10] Of course, Italian courts are also under the same obligation to interpret national law in the light of the wording and scope of the Directive. The evidence seems to be that the Italian law, as interpreted in this way, now becomes the same as the English; there is accordingly no choice of law problem. If, however, the evidence is that the Italian courts consider their law as not in need of interpretation, and this law is different to English law, there would seem to be a choice of law problem.[11]

A Decision of the European Court of Justice

Differences in the substantive law of insurance and reinsurance contracts in Member States deriving from problems of implementation, or indeed deriving from different interpretations of ambiguous provisions, can be eliminated by decisions of the European Court of Justice. The European Court, after a reference from a national court under Article 234 (ex Article 177), or in the course of infringement proceedings brought by the Commission under Article 225 (ex Article 169), can maintain that a provision in a national implementation statute (or eventually a failure to implement) conflicts with European law. Such a ruling may then lead to a change in national law to correct the position. However, this seems unlikely to happen in relation to the English rule on the right of cancellation as the UK Securities and Investment Board generally does not follow this rule but allows a cancellation period of 14 days from receipt of the notice of cancellation that corresponds to the minimum cancellation period provided for in the Second Life Directive.[12]

(d) Conclusion

The conclusion in relation to harmonisation of the law of insurance and reinsurance is that few choice of law problems have been reduced within European Union. Therefore, a substantial number of cases, involving the issue of the

[10] For a clear and recent exposition of the role of foreign law in the English courts see Fentiman, *Foreign Law in English Courts* (Oxford, Clarendon, 1998).

[11] It appears that an English court cannot refer a question of interpretation of the Directive to the European Court of Justice when the ambiguity is in relation to *Italian* law because of the fact that foreign law is proved as a fact and expert evidence would be required as to how Italian courts interpret the relevant provisions. However, the wording of Art 234 (ex Art 177) of the Treaty of Rome may suggest a different conclusion as it grants the right to refer questions of its own motion to *every* 'court or tribunal of a Member State'. For a commentary on this provision see Lenaerts, Arts and Bray, *Procedural law of the European Union* (London, Sweet & Maxwell, 1999) 28 to 35.

[12] See Art 15 of the Second Life Directive. The UK Financial Services Act 1986 authorises the Securities and Investments Board to make the rules that have to be followed when a person who has entered into an investment agreement with an authorised person decides to rescind the agreement.

applicable law, will remain in the intra-European Union context. These must be resolved, in principle, through the application of the choice of law rules contained in the Second and Third Insurance Directives.

3

General Remarks on Insurance Conflict of Laws

1. THE MAJOR IMPORTANCE OF CHOICE OF LAW QUESTIONS IN INSURANCE LAW

SOMEWHAT SIMPLIFIED, we can maintain that there are two factors which give choice of laws questions central importance in insurance law: a) the large number of international contracts, ie contracts entered into by parties from different countries, and b) the central position of the insurance policy in all international legal business relations.

The first factor, the large number of international contracts, is not peculiar to insurance law. In maritime, the sale of goods, finance and a number of other sectors of trade, numerous and important contracts are entered into that cross-national borders. But the proportion of international contracts is certainly higher in the insurance sector than in most of the other trade. Especially striking are conditions in countries such as the United Kingdom, for example, where the operating insurance and reinsurance companies are much larger than what the nation's own needs for insurance and reinsurance contracts might otherwise suggest. In other countries such as Italy the home market is likely to be of more importance, though by no means wholly dominant. An important consideration is the increasing number of insurance and reinsurance contracts concluded online. Practically speaking, these contracts have no home market; their formation takes place at an international level.[1]

The other factor, the insurance policy's central role in all business legal relations, viewed together with the international mobility of insurers, is not peculiar to a particular country, even if it is much more evident in certain countries such as the United Kingdom rather than in others like Italy or France. Legally speaking, the insurance policy can be characterised as a negotiable instrument, but one of quite a special nature.[2] It is often of sizeable value, does not possess a high degree of mobility, and cannot be easily distinguished from the contract of insurance. A number of persons have legal interests bound up in the insurance policy and contract. In addition to the policyholder or policyholders we might have the third party beneficiaries, the banks or others who have advanced loans against the security of the policy to the insured upon his request. The list is far from complete, also included could be policyholder's successor or successors,

[1] See below ch 14.

[2] But see below ch 8, para 2.

members and beneficiaries of fraternal benefit associations where benefit certificates are issued by Fraternal Benefit Associations and Societies to their members. Legal relations in the case of typical negotiable instruments in situations like these would usually possess a natural bond to the State in which the particular promise or order the payment of a certain amount of money is made. For insurance policies, as well, the law of the place where the policy is issued seems to be appropriate in a number of instances: by imposing obligations on an insurer of a foreign State, a policy can be said to submit to this State's authorities in a number of ways. There will also arise a strong tie to the law of the place where the policy is issued in questions of liability for damages caused by the insurer to the policyholder. In the case of co-insurance where the contractual counter-parties of the insured are two or more insurance companies a persistent adherence to the law of the place where the policy is issued means an almost complete rupture of the law applicable to the policy. This is bound to lead to difficulties. When the insurance policy is delivered online by email, the law of the place where the insurance policy is issued is no solution at all, there is no such law.

2. POLICY CONSIDERATIONS: WHAT HAS TO BE ACHIEVED BY PRIVATE INTERNATIONAL LAW RULES IN THE FIELDS OF INSURANCE AND REINSURANCE?

If you aim to explore freely, unbound by existing positive law, what would be the most expedient choice of laws provisions in the insurance and reinsurance fields, you should first be sure of what you wish to achieve through the use of such provisions. The easiest of solutions, undoubtedly, would be if all judges were entitled to apply their owns laws, with which they are very familiar. One could then entirely pass over the private international law issues of insurance and reinsurance contracts. However, if a judge is requested to apply foreign law, it is necessary to seek positive arguments in favour of such effort.

(a) Providing a Range of Comparable Offers to Prospective Insureds

The argument that is likely to be recalled first is the following: prospective insureds should be able to choose from a range of offers from various Member States, and these offers should be comparable with each other. The input of information and advice demanded so that comparability can be achieved must be proportionate to the value of the policy. While it can be worthwhile to involve a specialist insurance consultant in the case of insurance cover against interruptions of business or industrial fires, in the case of a private third party indemnity or household contents policy this would be an unwarranted expense and cannot be imposed as a compulsory element of the comparability assessment.

Again, it would certainly be unsatisfactory if a case were to be decided according to different provisions depending on whether the case was brought before the courts of the country X, Y or Z. This could be perceived as being contrary to the nature and spirit of the law. One thinks of the parties' obligations and rights as something that is firmly and well established. Where the law of the forum applies as the principle of choice of law and there are a number of possible jurisdictions, obligations and rights can, however, as a result first be secured *ex post*, in that a case is brought before a certain jurisdiction. It is also possible that the same event, a damage incurred in an accident abroad, leads to several legal proceedings, for example where some victims sues the wrongdoer in the State X, others in State Y. If each court bases itself on its own laws, similar questions of liability arising from the same accident abroad may be resolved according to different provisions.

The conflict of laws rules undoubtedly have a relevant task here: to make sure that a dispute is resolved according to the identical material matter—to give a criterion as to which law shall apply even if the case it is not sufficient that private international law rules are laid down in each country. The conflict of laws provisions of the different countries should be the same, or at least very similar to one another. If State X decides liability according to the law where the accident occurred and State Y employs the law which is the most favourable to the victims, choice of forum will still be of relevance.

(b) Ensuring Compatibility with the Substantive Law of Insurance

The principle that a certain case must be decided by the same provisions regardless of where the litigation takes place, is not a very positive guidepost: it hinders private international law provisions that lead to a relationship being exposed to different laws in different jurisdictions. The principle, however, does not give any guidance for a positive option among several choice of law preferences, each pledging equal dealings.

A certain such positive contribution, however, is supplied by the principle according to which private international law rules should be formulated so as to support the considerations that the appropriate substantive law provisions try to realise. This principle can give clear guidance in a number of circumstances. As an example one may recall the choice of laws provisions concerning loans contained in life insurance policies. Today's life-insurance industry is highly capital intensive, and it appears clear that a fundamental part of the necessary capital should be raised on a fairly long-term basis. Thus, it is important for insureds that they obtain a promise by the insurer to make loans on the security of the policy to the insured upon his request. It is not sufficient that the insurance policy is protected in the insured's homeland. That the insured might travel from State to State, an internationally protected right for the insured is a necessity. This places certain demands upon private international law rules. A single specific law must be decisive. In other cases, considerations of the purpose behind a statute can give a significant contribution to the solution of a problem, although without singling out any specific private international law rule. When, for example, a legislator has laid down mandatory provisions concerning motor vehicle owner's liability for passengers and cargo, conflict of laws rules have to be set forth that give these mandatory law provisions a reasonable international scope, for example by not allowing choice of laws clauses that refer questions concerning the motor vehicle's liability to a law possessing softer requirements.

In a number of circumstances, however, considerations of scope will fall short because they do not open the way for an internationally uniform solution. Legal provisions very often constitute a balance between competing interests—in certain countries special relevance has perhaps been attached to one of these concerns, in another country a different interest can have come to the fore. Legal provisions regulating 'overall' limitations of liability furnish a very good example of this: State X considers the protection of the national insurance industry from burdensome tort liability as a fundamental quest. It therefore provides legal provisions regulating the limitation of liability creating low limits. In country Y one is more interested in protecting tort victims, and as a result law drafters cut off any chance of limitations of liability, or enact provisions calling for very high standards. In State X continued pursuance of considerations of statutory aim would demand the law of the place where the accident occurs to be the rule of choice of law, while in State Y the law of the place which grants the better protection to the victim would be the end result. We obtain, in a sense, ultimate results. We do not, however, get equal dealings, and none of the national conflict of laws provisions achieve international scope.

(c) Preventing Insurers From Achieving Unreasonable Competitive Advantages

A principle of a more particular nature, which is of relevance in an insurance connotation, is the following: private international law rules have to prevent insurers trading under certain rules of law and contractual conditions from achieving unreasonable competitive advantages. Insurance companies and insurance policies have, as is well known, seen a very rapid development during the last century, and a corresponding development has followed in the legal regulation of the insurance industry. The changes have been particularly sizeable in the decades following the Second World War.[3] The result: questions concerning the scope and legal nature earlier unknown. Key words such as co-insurance, group insurance, insurance markets, brokers, credit insurance, and consumer protection demonstrate the point made here. Legislative reactions to these new

[3] For an excellent account see Pfennigtorf, *Public Law of Insurance* in *International Encyclopedia of Comparative Law*, vol IX, (Tübingen, Boston, Lancaster, JCB Mohr, 1997) 7-24 to 7-36.

problems have involved steadily increasing demands for better-drafted contracts, more careful handling of serious and massive risks, greater demands upon the competence of the national supervision authorities, stricter rules and higher limits of liability. It would appear obvious that the national legislators at first make greater demands upon their own supervisory powers. But most of the reforms discussed are expensive and increase the insurer's requirements for capital and his running costs. A typical argument brought against such reform is naturally that they will weaken the ability of the insurers to compete on the international market where the law of supply and demand and competitive pricing still apply.[4] A possible recourse is the accomplishing of such reform on an international level. There remains, however, the possibility that certain States will choose to remain outside the international regulations. By choosing the law of one of these States the insurer can escape the application of the stricter rules and standards of the international regulations. Here, private international law rules can serve as an aid in the campaign against insurers which technically and legally can be said to be substandard: in the countries placing strict requirements on their insurers, the national provisions, to a greater or lesser extent, may be given application to insurance contracts and policies concluded abroad, by choosing the law of the place where the policyholder is habitually resident or even the law of the forum as the conflict of law provision.

(d) Empowering Insurers to Form Risk Pools Comprising Inhabitants of Different Member States of the European Union

Another principle which is of relevance in an insurance connotation is the following: insurers must be empowered to form risk pools comprising inhabitants of various Member States. The aim of strength in numbers that is at the heart of the insurance trade, should not be frustrated by national borders. The policies of the European risk pool should essentially be regulated by the same product-related provisions, in other terms by the same law of contract.

(e) Allowing Parties to Predict the Law Applicable to their Legal Relationship

Usually cited as a relevant factor to consider in the formulation of private international law rules is the desirability of the parties being able to predict which national law will apply to their legal relationship. The first requirement for the accomplishment of this desire is that the private international law provisions in the different countries be easy to employ and unequivocal. Where the private international law rules in the single countries relate one to different substantive law rules, it is a further requirement that it can be determined ahead of time

[4] *Ibid*, 7-50 to 7-54.

which country's private international law provisions are to be fundamental. A contract of insurance that appoints a certain country's law as governing law fully satisfies these requirements of predictability. At the other end of the scale you find systems entailing a constant use of the law of the forum joined with wide access to forum shopping.

The demand for predictability with regard to the applicable law is unquestionably of relevance in a number of situations. But it differs considerably depending upon the kind of legal relationship in question.

By way of example, take the insured's rights and liabilities under an insurance contract on the one hand and his liability for omission of material facts, false information, misrepresentation in a prospectus on the other. As regards the insurance contract, it is of greatest importance that the insured, from the time the contract is concluded and throughout the insurance period, can know precisely which law shall be the governing law. Uncertainties may arise, for example, concerning the right to cancel the insurance policy in cases of war, major force or other forms of alleged frustration. The parties should, in a number of circumstances, take positive action to maintain their rights under the contract: pay or elect not to pay the premium, cancel the insurance policy, etc. But their course of action should be rightful under the insurance contract; if it not, it will represent a breach of contract. This may give the other party the right to cancel, something that in time can mean the loss of a valuable insurance policy, and possibly a very burdensome liability for damages. A party should therefore undertake a very cautious examination of its contractual obligations and rights before it acts. The background law is then, in many circumstances, of fundamental relevance. Private international law provisions that are difficult to employ, for example, because they refer issues to judicial evaluation will be a burden here, especially as the parties' resolutions under a contract of insurance should often be made under considerable time pressure.

(f) Protecting the Interest of the Parties in Continuity of Cover

Account should be taken of the fact that all parties have an interest in continuity of cover in cases where 'Euro-mobile' policyholders, who live in various Member States in the course of their existences, wish to renew or extend their policies with the same insurer. While the current legal position means that contracts are governed by a different legal system once the policyholder has moved to another Member State, any future system should protect the interests of both parties in contractual continuity with the Single European Market.

3. POLICY ISSUES: THE CONNECTING FACTORS

(a) Introductory Remarks

First, you encounter an option of method. Shall you allow a unique or a number of connecting factors to be definitive, or shall you rely instead upon a comprehensive judicial assessment based on all the connecting factors present? The first method is the traditional one. It results in choice of laws provisions founded on connecting factors such as the place where the tort was committed, the place where the contract was concluded, the place where the insured is habitually resident or domiciled, etc. The second method is more recent, but already well founded. It is described as 'the proper law of contract' or 'the centre of gravity method'.[5]

This latter method has its noticeable benefits. It allows decisions that are both flexible and fair with regard to the specific circumstances of the case. However, one should not underestimate the legal uncertainties this method will give rise to several circumstances. The length to which this method leaves the decision to the court's appreciation implies there is not very much to cause the result in a specific dispute from varying depending on whether judge A or judge B makes the decision. It is true that even the highest masterly guidelines on the part of both judges will not stop their putting divergent stress on the single connecting elements.

As concerns insurance choice of law, however, there are some powerful arguments against the experience of operating with decisions founded entirely upon judicial consideration of the specific circumstances of the case. For the judge, who has seen the case lit up from all angles, and who may take the time he thinks is necessary to weigh up the different connecting factors, 'the proper law of the contract' method may appear to be a successful technique giving excellent outcomes. But only a small and presumably steadily diminishing number of these types of cases are brought before a court. As already stated above, the parties to friendly settlements of disputes usually adopt, as a starting point, what they consider to be their position before the law. In the relationship between the insurer and insured knowledge of the law may be of highest relevance, even before any dispute has arisen. I refer again to the case of a long-term insurance contract, and to the number of measures the parties should take to defend their interests and rights or to avoid responsibility during the insurance period; here it appears evident that they know where they stand legally. However, this again assumes that they may foresee which country's law will be definitive. If 'the proper law of the contract' method is to be retained such prognostication can be hard or even impossible.

[5] For an excellent account see Dicey and Morris, *The Conflict of Laws* by L Collins *et al*, 13th edn (London, Sweet & Maxwell, 1999) 1196–97.

(b) An Exposition of Certain Connecting Factors of Relevance in Insurance and Reinsurance Contexts

To be suitable, a connecting factor must be founded on a strong connection. A purely fortuitous connection with a State is not sufficient to substantiate the application of that State's law. The strength of a connection will depend on the type of risk covered by the insurance contract. Thus in actions involving rights and obligations deriving from a contract of insurance covering a land vehicle the place of the registration of the vehicle will be significant. On the other hand, if the actions involved rights and obligations deriving from an insurance contract covering risks related to 'goods in transit', the place of the registration of the goods would seem to have no relevance to the present action.

In the contractual relationships between insurers and insureds a number of divergent connecting elements might be important: the law of the place of performance, the law of the place where the contract was concluded, the law of the place where the premium is paid, the law of the place where the insured is habitually resident or domiciled, the law of the place of delivery of the policy, the law of the place of the acceptance of the policy, etc. Of most importance in practice, however, is the law the parties themselves have chosen, whether explicitly, through a clear choice of law clause in the contract, or implicitly, usually through arbitration or jurisdiction clauses. The problems arising in this connection will be discussed in chapters eight, nine, ten, eleven, twelve, thirteen and fourteen.

If you take conflict of laws as a set of provisions stating when a judge must build upon other rules of law than internal law, it follows that the law of the forum cannot be a choice of law alternative. If one is less judge-oriented, and instead one considers the problems through the eyes of the individual insurer and insured, the law of the forum is clearly a choice of law option: it suggests that the choice of law will first be determined with the filing of legal proceedings. However, neither the 1980 Rome Convention nor the Second and Third 'Generation' of Insurance Directives lead to this choice of law principle. But the provisions on mandatory rules and public policy exception in the Rome Convention and the Insurance Directives may lead to the application of the fundamental principles of the law of the forum.

4. SPECIFIC FEATURES OF CONFLICTS RULES IN INTERNATIONAL INSURANCE LAW

Being a part of private international law, conflicts rules in international insurance law demonstrate all legal characteristics typical for this branch of law. They raise problems of classification and renvoi which have to be settled according to general principles of private international law. Application of foreign law may be limited and even excluded by public order though such cases are very rare.

As a general principle of the conflict of laws, the autonomy of contracting parties is accepted by international insurance law. Thus, on entering into an insurance or reinsurance transaction the parties are generally free to choose the applicable law, but the parties' autonomy may be restricted by a mandatory conflicts rule set out by international conventions or by mandatory provisions of national law.[6]

At the same time conflicts rules of international law present specific features. They reflect both the character of insurance activity and the peculiarities of the functioning of each mode of insurance. In this context two important points have to be mentioned.

Though the activities of all modes of insurance have, in principle, the very same essence (replacement of services) and for this purpose the same legal instrument—a contract of insurance is used—the functioning of certain modes of insurance demonstrates peculiarities determining the character of applicable conflicts rules.

The first peculiarity of conflicts rules in international insurance law reflects the difference between non-life insurance and life-insurance contracts. The rights and obligations of the parties to a contract of non-life insurance are based on the contract and conflicts problems in this field are solved in accordance with the conflicts principles of contract law. On the contrary, the rights and obligations of the policyholder and third party beneficiary of a life-insurance contract are not entirely based on the contract and conflicts problems in this field are solved in accordance either with the conflicts principles of labour/family law and contract law.[7]

The second peculiarity of conflicts rules in international insurance law reflects the fact that the insurance products and services are crossing the territories of several States and conditions of insurance are to comply with the provisions in force in those different States. Therefore, each contract of insurance is practically governed by different legal systems and a set of conflicts rules is to be applied to that contract.

The system of conflicts rules practically applied in international insurance law includes two groups of conflicts of laws rules: special and general. This classification is of a great practical importance.

Special conflicts rules are used for solving conflicts problems arising from international insurance contracts covering risks situated within the territories of the Member States of the European Community. General conflicts rules operate when issues arise which are not covered by special conflicts rules.

The system of conflicts rules applied in international insurance law takes into

[6] See also below chs 8, 9, 10.
[7] See below ch 10, para 11.

account specific features of different insurance operations and the place of their performance. Such a system of conflicts rules is provided for by the 1980 Rome Convention on the law applicable to contractual obligations.[8] The same method of solving conflicts problems is used in the EC Insurance Directives.[9]

[8] See below ch 8.
[9] See below chs 9 and 10.

4

Admission of Insurance and Reinsurance Services and Products to the EU Market—Conflict of Laws Issues

1. INTRODUCTION

IN THIS chapter, the concern is with the general aspects of admission of insurance and reinsurance services and products to the EU Insurance Market. These may involve references to the access of insurers and brokers, distribution of and trading in insurance and reinsurance services and types of insurance and reinsurance transactions within the EU Market. I propose to deal separately with each of these types of issues, as they raise different choice of laws questions. The aim of the present chapter is to discuss the private international law questions arising from the distribution of and trading in insurance and reinsurance services within the Single Insurance Market. The starting point must be the general aspects of admission of insurance and reinsurance services to the EU Market through off-line transactions. These matters having been established, we can go on to consider the conflict of laws issues raised by the admission of insurance and reinsurance services to the EU Market through online transactions. Due to the fact that choice of laws rules for insurance contracts have been the subject of a significant harmonisation programme within the European Union, it is proposed not to deal with the private international law issues arising from insurance and reinsurance contracts in the present chapter. These will be the subject of the following chapters.

2. ADMISSION OF INSURANCE AND REINSURANCE SERVICES AND PRODUCTS

Unremarkably, the local law applies to the matter if and under which rules insurance and reinsurance services and products are admitted to selling in the local market. This does not need to be enunciated in a choice of law provision.[1]

[1] For further references see Kronke, *Capital Markets and Conflict of Laws* [2000] Hague Recueil 293, n 83 who refers specifically to the competence of the local law in relation to the selling of securities.

As already stated above, in the Member States of the European Union, community law and implementing national legislations have created a unified market for a large number of products and services including insurance products and services. Thus, access to one market requires eligibility for admittance to all other markets. In the occurrence of concomitant request of admittance the local law normally allows for co-ordination of agreement control to be implemented by the different regulators.

Although established on different assumptions and utilising dissimilar administrative and legal methods, the US regulators and markets are attempting to captivate trading by making admittance of European insurers easier.[2]

As insurers are usually not physical but legal persons the local law should look at the preliminary issue of whether the law whose creature it is recognises its being a public limited company, a stock corporation etc to the insurer's personal law, ie the governing law of the insurance company.[3] This is usually of crucial importance to establish whether an insurer from another country is eligible to trade its services and products and under which conditions. In some countries such as the Netherlands, this is the law according to which the company has been incorporated; in most of other European countries the law of the main place of business applies.[4] It has been pointed out correctly that the establishment of a multi-market such as the EU Insurance Market requires legal advisers to find solutions to meet the mandatory requisites of both the governing law of the company and the market where the product or service is provided.[5]

3. COMMUNICATION

Advanced insurance law legislations usually demands communication of information about the provider of insurance product and services, its financial position as well as the security as such essential to appreciate the future benefits and risks of insurance transactions.[6] More precisely, an insurer will have to supply that information, first, at the moment when it enters the market by advertising its products and services and, second, periodically while they are provided. A crescent number of legal systems demand that a listed company of insurance, ie an insurance company which belongs to the stock market by having its shares listed on the stock exchange, communicate on an ad hoc basis such information concerning its financial situation, its negotiations, its products, and so on, as could have an influence on the share's cost. Insurance law legislation,

[2] See Kronke, *Capital Markets and Conflict of Laws* [2000] Hague Recueil 693.

[3] On the governing law of insurance companies see recently Rammeloo, *Corporations in Private International Law: A European Perspective* (Oxford, Clarendon Press, 2000).

[4] *Ibid.*

[5] See Kronke, *Capital Markets and Conflict of Laws*, above n 1, 294.

[6] For an excellent account see Pfennigstorf, *Public Law of Insurance* in ch 3, n 3, 73.

however, varies essentially as to which elements of those obligations to communicate.[7]

For private international law purposes, the issue is critically made difficult by two circumstances. First, some legal systems, in ruling upon the communication requirements, make a distinction between different types of insurance company, their dimension, etc. Second, whereas some countries have chosen a unitary capital market communication regime founded on public distribution, others rule these issues in general in company law regulations, or they combine these two regimes.

Some authors maintain that provisions requiring continuous, periodic communication and founded in company law regulations or civil codes are mainly intended to deal with shareholders' interests and are thus to be characterised as company law, rather than market law.[8] Therefore, for example, the majority of Italian communication requirements would not be applicable to an insurance company traded in Italy, whose main place of business is in New Zealand or Mexico. Paired with the prevalent opinion that foreign capital markets legislation, being public policy regulation, cannot be applied by Italian courts, this examination would lead to odd outcomes: though traded in Italy, the foreign insurance company would not be requested to comply with any communication requirements in Italy at all.

Concluding that a foreign insurer whose products and services are traded on the English market should comply with that country's communication requirements it has to be pointed out, however, that there is room for modifications which take aspects of the international situations into account. This is particularly true in countries such as Italy and France which follow traditional conflict of laws doctrines.

4. OTHER ISSUES

In the course of an insurance transaction, omissions and actions other than those relating to communication requirements can raise questions of liability vis-à-vis insureds but also vis-à-vis intermediates and brokers. Therefore, the insurer's consultants such as an accountant or investment bank can make erroneous representations or withhold information relevant to the decision of the insured or its personal representatives. Depending on the circumstances, this will give rise to tortious liability and/or contractual liability and the applicable law will have to be determined through the general private international law provisions for torts and contracts. Furthermore, in many jurisdictions special consideration has to be given to the legislation regulating brokers and other

[7] *Ibid*, 73.

[8] See especially Ballarino, *Le Società per azioni: profili internazionalprivatistici* in Colombo and Portale (eds), *Trattato delle società per azioni* (Torino, UTET, 1990) 236; Grundmann (1990) *Rabels Zeitschrift für ausländisches und internationales Privatrecht* 283 to 300.

intermediaries' and other professionals' obligations in this regard. By the same token, the insurance company itself, its directors, officers and its shareholders can be in breach of their statutory obligations under the governing law of the company.

5. LIABILITY

Omissions of facts, false information, misrepresentation in a prospectus, result, in certain circumstances, in the insurer and others (eg lawyers, accountants, etc) and their representatives or intermediaries being held liable.

Under English law, the question of liability for incorrect information has been characterised as either tortious or contractual.[9]

Characterising the insured's claim as contractual or quasi-contractual works only where certain impediments such as the limits to third parties' beneficiaries, the doctrine of consideration, etc can be defeated and where the situation is actually similar to the relationship between a provider of financial services and his client seeking information on a programmed investment. Characterising the insured's claim as a tort can be dangerous in certain countries such as Italy because of the excessively high lower limit of culpability, inadequate state of vicarious liability, and so on.[10]

Moving to the conflict of laws issues, the tortious characterisation has been suggested largely on the basis that in contract, ie with freedom of choice, the insurer and its intermediaries could use their greater bargaining power to misuse that freedom to the detriment of the insured who is usually in a weaker bargaining position. But it is also true that characterising misrepresentation and omission in a registration statement or a prospectus as tort raises equally complex questions. First, because many civil law and common law countries have been moving away from the traditional and quite rigid connecting factor of the *lex loci delicti*, embracing rather flexible proper law of the tort approach.[11] Second, a choice of law provision based on the principle of ubiquity opens up a potentially applicable multitude of laws. As has been pointed out by others, under the principle of ubiquity not only the place of the wrongdoing but also the place where the harm takes place should be considered as connecting factors.[12] Imagine, an insurance company based in Australia engaging New Zealand and

[9] See Wood, *International Loans, Bonds and Securities Regulation* (London, LLP, 1995) No 17-37

[10] For similar remarks see Kronke n 1 above, 308.

[11] Art 132 Swiss Law on PIL, Arts 40–42 Einführungsegesetz zum Bürgerlichen Gesetzbuche as quoted by Kronke, *Capital Markets and Conflict of Laws*, n 1 above, at note 127.

[12] See Fawcett, *Product Liability in Private International Law: A European Perspective* [1993] I Hague Recueil 212 to 213 who refers to the 'alternative reference solution' in product liability cases. See more recently Wolf, *Grenzüberschereitende Umweltbeeintrachtigungen im Internationalen Privat-und Verfahrensrecht* in Wolfrun and Lagagenfield (eds), *Umweltschutz durch internationals Hafturesrecht* (Berlin, Beck, 1999) 355 to 384.

London based lawyers and accountants to draft a prospectus for the selling of its products and services on the insurance markets of Sydney, Auckland, Montreal, London, Rome and Paris. Due to a negligent misrepresentation of a material element by the Paris lawyers, an Italian insured (and its Belgian parent company) is harmed. Is it really necessary to choose between the laws of Italy, France, England, New Zealand or Australia? Or is it possible to reserve that choice to the judge or the claimant under the principle of the law most favourable to the injured party? Taking this question into consideration one has to keep in mind that not only the courts in Rome but also the courts in Paris may have jurisdiction under Article 5, No 3 of the Brussels Regulation.[13]

It seems that having the governing law of the insurance company (lex societatis) applicable to the liability of the insurer for incorrect communications can be justified in case of intra-companies litigations, ie if directors or officers of an insurance company misuse their powers and breach their fiduciary obligations owed to shareholders and insureds by persuading them to make investments on the basis of incomplete or incorrect communications.[14] Other than in these special cases, only a presumption of greater efficiency can validly point towards application of the governing law of the insurance company in this respect.

6. THE IMPACT OF NEW TECHNOLOGIES ON THE ADMISSION OF INSURANCE AND REINSURANCE PRODUCTS TO THE EC INSURANCE MARKET

As a matter of fact, the Internet is about to acquire a fundamental role for both the dissemination of reports, ad hoc communications, periodic filings etc and the distribution of insurance products and services. Inadequate finance of certain insurance markets will encourage insurers, brokers and intermediaries to convey their clients to foreign markets, thereby converting cross-border insurance and reinsurance transactions into a universal event.

However, the data publicised will often be incorrect, and there will be fraudulence and perhaps even influences over the prices of products and services sold online. Nevertheless, not everything is original, and under no circumstances should the Internet's influence on conflict of laws be over-estimated.[15] To the extent that it is basically a new communication tool, little will change in the law of tort as 'places' continue to be ascertainable: there will always be a place where the harm occurs. What has altered, however, is that it can be more complicated to find out the wrongdoer and also the number of places where harm

[13] Art 5 (3) provides that 'in matters relating to torts, delict or quasi-delict (*a person domiciled in a Member State may, in another Member State, be sued*) in the courts for the place where the harmful event occurred or may occur'.

[14] See also Ahrens (1988) *Praxis des Internationalen Privat- und Verfahrenrechts* 355 to 360.

[15] For these and further remarks see Kronke, '*Applicable law in Torts and Contracts in Cyberspace*' in Boele-Woelki and Kessedjian (eds), *Internet: Which Court Decides? Which Law Applies?* (The Hague, Kluwer Law International, 1998) 65 *et seq* criticising the discussion in Burnstein (1996) *Vanderbilt Journal of Transnational Law* 75, 97–100.

occurs may increase. However, this is not theoretically different to the traditional private international law provisions for non-contractual obligations.[16]

As far as determining the contract law applicable to insurance and reinsurance transactions on the Internet is concerned, the situation is not the same as the most relevant conventions and uniform choice of laws provisions for insurance contracts, in the extent to which they go beyond parties' choice of the applicable law, adopt concepts such as the differentiation between the 'active' and 'passive' consumer, or take for granted that the provider of products and services has aimed his offer at a specific market, etc.

Yet again, one should consider the Internet's function as a tool of communication and its potential for making markets separate. If a Rome, or London, or Paris established insurer, insurance broker or intermediary proposes online selling in insurance products or services created in the EU Market he is acting in a familiar environment: an Italian, English or French intermediary or insured enters into a contract with regard to a service on the respective US market.

Nevertheless, there are some questions which need to be considered further: a) disintermediation, b) delocalisation of insurance and reinsurance markets.

(a) Disintermediation

Intermediaries and brokers play a fundamental role in insurance and reinsurance transactions.[17] Leaving aspects of their expertise and their trustworthiness aside, insurance brokers and intermediaries, in the near future, might be passed over by insureds and insurers in order to make savings in respect of, for example, their costs and brokerages.[18] The Internet allows insurers to directly approach their clients, and insureds to directly communicate with insurers established abroad. Internet-based bulletin boards allow an insured to post interest in purchasing on the insurer's home page. Internet-based crossing systems permit physical and legal investors to match the purchase of insurance products and sale orders electronically.[19]

Those tasks are carried out by intermediaries and brokers. However, as certain legal systems require insurers and other financial issuers to make certain communications and to post certain explanations as to the legal character of the proposed transactions, this should also be guaranteed in transnational transactions, ie cases of insurers from one country soliciting clients from another country.

[16] Kronke, n 1 above, 66.

[17] See especially Hodgin, *Insurance Intermediaries Law and Regulation* (London, Lloyd's of London, 1992).

[18] *Ibid.*

[19] See below ch 14.

(b) Delocalisation of Insurance and Reinsurance Markets

Insurance markets are usually physical entities. However, there is a strong tendency, at least in Western Europe and the United States, to trade insurance products and services in markets which do not have a single physical location.[20] It is certainly true that some fictitious places can be identified with regard to these markets such as the corporate headquarters of some supporting associations of insurers or brokers. But one cannot rely on such places to establish the relevant market for conflict of laws purposes.[21] Undoubtedly, in these cases the establishment of the relevant market is much more complex than in the ordinary situations, ie when insurance products and services are traded on 'real' markets.[22] Unlike in the latter situations you must take into consideration here elements such as, for example, the place where the policy is delivered or where the third beneficiary of a life-insurance contract is habitually resident or domiciled.

7. FINAL REMARKS

At first glance, delocalisation and globalisation of insurance markets might be regarded as developments intended to remove private international law provisions over international insurance and reinsurance transactions on those markets.[23] For it is private international law's purpose to nationalise transnational situations in order to establish the applicable law.[24] Furthermore, delocalisation requires that, whenever market participants deem conflict of laws regulation of insurance and reinsurance transactions undue or detrimental to their interests, they shift their transactions to another accessible place.

[20] See below ch 14.

[21] See Kronke, *Capital Markets and Conflict of Laws*, n 1 above, 366.

[22] *Ibid*, 366.

[23] For the same conclusion see Kronke, *ibid*, 372 who refers to the delocalisation of financial markets.

[24] *Ibid*, 372.

PART II

Jurisdictional Recognition and Enforcement of Judgments Problems and Possible Solutions

Section I
Jurisdictional Problems and Possible Solutions: Preliminary Observations

In a case involving a foreign element the first thing that a judge must ascertain is whether the court possesses the necessary jurisdiction. This leads to the question whether a court of an EU Member State will hear and determine an issue upon which its decision is sought.[1] The jurisdiction of the courts of the EU Member States is complicated by the fact that there are two separate sets of jurisdiction provisions. The first is the EU/European Free Trade Association rules, the sources of which are the Brussels Regulation and the Lugano Convention.[2] The second is the traditional domestic provisions on jurisdiction. Accordingly, the national judges and tribunals must ascertain in the first place which instrument is relevant to the pending dispute. As far as the assertion of jurisdiction is concerned, the relevant provisions are almost identical. But a significant difference between the Brussels Regulation, on the one hand, and the Lugano Convention, on the other hand, is that the European Court of Justice has no jurisdiction to interpret the Lugano Convention. Moreover, invoking the incorrect provisions can give rise to a ground of appeal for the losing party to a dispute.

1. WHEN WILL THE BRUSSELS REGULATION AND LUGANO CONVENTION APPLY?

(a) The Brussels Regulation[3]

First, the Brussels Regulation, according to its preamble, only deals with the international jurisdiction of Member States of the European Union, and will not apply where there is no foreign element.

[1] Cheshire and North, *Private International Law*, PM North and JJ Fawcett, 13th edn (London, Edinburgh, Dublin, Butterworths) 179.

[2] The Brussels Regulation, which replaced the Brussels Convention of 1968, entered into force on 1 March 2002. The Regulation itself was preceded by a proposed major rewrite of the Brussels Convention (see COM/97/0609 Final, 1998, OJ C33/20) which was never brought into force because superseded by the Treaty of Amsterdam. The Lugano Convention is contained in [1988] OJ L391/9.

[3] Council Regulation (EC) No. 44/2001 of 22 December 2000; 2001 OJ L 12/1. See also the statement by the United Kingdom contained in 2001 C 13/1. For a commentary see Harris (2001) *Civil Justice Quarterly* 218 to 224.

Secondly, this Regulation does not have an effect on certain Conventions on jurisdiction or recognition or enforcement that Member States have in the past, or will in the future, enter into, or statutes implementing them.[4]

Thirdly, the matter should be within the scope of the Regulation, ie civil and commercial matters.[5]

Fourthly, when it comes to bases of jurisdiction, the defendant should be domiciled in a EU Member State (ie one of the 15 EU States). Even if he is not, jurisdiction can be assigned to the courts of a Member State by virtue of Article 22 (exclusive jurisdiction) or Article 23 (an agreement conferring jurisdiction on the courts of a EU Member State) of the Regulation.

(b) The Lugano Convention

The first three points made above apply identically to the Lugano Convention. The distinction arises in relation to the fourth point. When it comes to bases of jurisdiction, the Lugano Convention applies where the defendant is domiciled in an EFTA Member State (ie one of the three EFTA States).

Even if he is not, jurisdiction can be assigned to the courts of an EFTA Member State under Articles 17 or 17 of that Convention.

2. WHEN WILL THE TRADITIONAL PROVISIONS APPLY?

The traditional provisions on jurisdiction of the EC/EFTA Member States will apply where the Brussels Regulation and Lugano Convention do not apply. However, other international Conventions containing jurisdiction provisions will take precedence over the traditional provisions.

3. JURISDICTIONAL QUESTIONS

Though there are many relevant differences between the two sets of jurisdictional provisions, one can identify three fundamental issues which must be examined under both sets of provisions in order to establish whether a judge possesses jurisdiction. First, whether there is the basis of jurisdiction. Secondly, whether, even though there is the basis of jurisdiction, the judge will consider exercising that jurisdiction. Thirdly, whether there is a subject matter restriction in relation to jurisdiction. This is relevant in insurance and reinsurance cases, where there is a restriction in cases concerning foreign rights.

[4] Art 67 of the Brussels Regulation.
[5] Art 1 of the Brussels Regulation.

4. JURISDICTION AND APPLICABLE LAW

If a judge accepts jurisdiction, then the next thing to be determined is the applicable law to that case, ie which State's law applies. In the context of insurance the matter is further complicated since a judge of an EU/EFTA Member State will have to decide whether the substantive law contained in the statutes dealing with insurance and reinsurance matters is meant to be applied even though a foreign law governs. Nevertheless, it may be seen that conflict of laws entails a two stage process. The two stages of jurisdiction and applicable law are not entirely separate; a finding as to the applicable law is reached at the jurisdictional stage of the process.[6] But what is relevant to the conflicts lawyer is that this jurisdictional stage has to be considered. Appreciation of the two-stage process is not assisted by the fact that reported cases usually concern either jurisdiction or the applicable law, but not both.

It is crucial to emphasise the methodology at this initial stage. Several questions have arisen due to the fact that insurance lawyers are unfamiliar with the methodology of private international law. Private international lawyers, on the other hand, are likely to be confused by the intricacy of national and European insurance law.

5. INTERPRETING THE BRUSSELS REGULATION

There are a number of remarks to be formulated in relation to the interpretation of the Brussels Regulation. First, the case law of the European Court of Justice is the principal route in the interpretation of this instrument. The European Court of Justice has, so far, given more than 110 judgments on the interpretation of the Brussels Convention. The *acquis* on the Brussels Convention is also relevant to the interpretation of the Brussels Regulation, as the significant provisions are similar to those of the Brussels Convention.The European Court of Justice has been given jurisdiction to make preliminary rulings upon the Brussels Regulation and Brussels Convention as amended.[7] It should be pointed out that preliminary rulings requested of the European Court of Justice on the interpretation of the Brussels Regulation should be based on Article 68 of the EC

[6] See Fawcett (1991) *Current Legal Problems* 39.

[7] The European Court of Justice does not have interpretative jurisdiction over the 1988 Lugano Convention. But, annexed to the Lugano Convention is a declaration from the representatives of the EFTA States that, in interpreting the Lugano Convention, their courts take adequate account of the decisions of the European Court of Justice, and of the courts of the Member States of the European Union, in respect of the provisions of the Brussels Convention that are substantially reproduced in the Lugano Convention: see [1988] OJ L319/40. Moreover, it must also be pointed out that Art 1 of Protocol 2 provides that the courts of the Contracting States of the Lugano Convention are requested to take into consideration any principles laid down in any relevant decision of a court of any other Lugano Contracting State concerning the interpretation of the Convention.

Treaty, which refers to Article 234 of the EC Treaty and not on the 1971 Protocol on Interpretation.[8] It derives from this change of legal basis that only the courts against whose decisions there is no judicial remedy—which is the highest national courts of the EU Member States (with the exception of Denmark)—can demand a preliminary ruling.

Secondly, the Brussels and Lugano Conventions are each supplemented by a report, written by experts, which provides a background and explanation to the text.[9] These reports are of great relevance in the interpretation of the Conventions and are given relevant weight.[10] Similarly, the recitals to the rules of the Brussels Regulation provide a background and an explanation to the text.

Finally, the European Court of Justice has normally adopted a finalistic approach to the interpretation of the Conventions. That is, an interpretation is taken that advances the purposes and objectives of the Conventions, namely, the furtherance of a truly internal market through the adoption of common provisions of jurisdiction allowing for increased harmonisation of laws, providing greater legal stability, reducing discrimination and expediting the 'free movement' of decisions and judgments. As such, the European Court of Justice has usually given 'autonomous' meanings to different terms and concepts, as opposed to the meaning such a term can have under internal law.[11]

[8] See the 1971 Protocol to the Brussels Convention as contained in Sch 2 of the 1982 Act.

[9] The reports are: the Jenard Report [1979] OJ C59/1; the Schlosser Report [1979] OJ C59/71; the Evrigenis and Kerameus Report [1986] OJ C298/1; the Almeida Cruz, Desantes Real and Jenard Report [1990] OJ C139/35; the Jenard and Möller Report [1990] OJ C189/57.

[10] The English courts are entitled to consider the reports and to give them such weight as is appropriate in the circumstances. See, for example, s 3 of the 1982 Act.

[11] Autonomous meanings have been adopted inter alia in relation to 'civil and commercial matters' in Art 1 (see the cases *LTU GmbH v Eurocontrol* (29/76) [1976] ECR 1541; *Netherlands State v Rüffer (814/79)* [1980] ECR 3807); 'contract' in Art 5(1) (see the cases *Peters Bauunternehmung GmbH v Zuid Nederlandse Aannemers Vereneging (34/82)* [1983] ECR 987, 1002 (para. 9)); 'matters relating to tort, delict or quasi-delict' in Art 5(3) (see the cases *Kalfelis v Schroeder, Munchmeyer, Hengst & Co (1989/87)* [1988] ECR 5565).

5

The Special Rules in the Brussels Regulation and Lugano Convention for Insurance and Reinsurance Disputes

1. WHICH SET OF RULES WILL APPLY IN INSURANCE CASES?

IN ACTIONS related to insurance matters it will be the case that, although there is a foreign element, the claimant and defendant are both domiciled in the same State. For example, an English policyholder of a travel insurance policy covering any liability for bodily injury is injured in Australia, but sues the English insurer in England. Normally, questions of 'international jurisdiction' will not be raised in such a situation, ie where the parties are domiciled in the same Member State, and the Brussels Regulation and Lugano Convention will generally not apply.[12] Some uncertainties arise, however, if one of the provisions on jurisdiction other than Article 2, which allocates jurisdiction to the Member State in which the defendant is domiciled or on enforcement under the Regulation, is raised on the facts of the case.[13] For example, it seems that the Brussels Regulation and Lugano Convention would apply if another Member State had special jurisdiction under Article 10. Therefore, the same English policyholder could sue his English insurer in the courts of the State where the harmful event occurred if this is a Member State. Nevertheless, in this example no other provision in the Regulation is raised and the Brussels Regulation would seem to be inapplicable. The United Kingdom would therefore have to apply its national rules on jurisdiction. The most important question in insurance cases

[12] However questions surrounding the allocation of jurisdiction within the United Kingdom may arise in cases which, from the perspective of other Member States, do not involve issues of international jurisdiction since they are entirely internal to the United Kingdom but which, from the perspective of the English court, are cases with a foreign element because not all the relevant elements are connected with England. For a clear illustration of this point see Hill, *The Law Relating to International Commercial Disputes* (London, LLP, 1998) ch 6, para 6.1., who gives the example of a Scottish pedestrian injured in Northern Ireland by an English motorist. But the Brussels Regulation, which deals only with international jurisdiction, does not provide an answer to the question of which courts have jurisdiction.

[13] For the same conclusion with regards to the 1968 Brussels Convention see O'Malley and Layton, *European Civil Practice* (London, Sweet & Maxwell, 1989) para 13.11; Kaye, *Civil Jurisdiction and Enforcement of Foreign Judgments* (Abingdon, Oxon, Professional Books, 1987) 221–22; Collins, *The Civil Jurisdiction and Judgments Act 1982* (London, Sweet & Maxwell, 1983) 17.

is therefore going to be: is there a defendant domiciled within an European Union or an EFTA Member State?

(a) The Availability of a Defendant Domiciled in Europe

European Union policyholders, insureds and beneficiaries, will normally have someone domiciled within the European Union who can be sued, whether this be a branch, agency or other establishment of the insurer. The availability of a defendant domiciled in the European Union means that the Brussels Regulation or Lugano Convention is going to apply in a large number of insurance and reinsurance cases. In its judgment of 13 July 2000 in the case *Group Josi Reinsurance Company SA*[14] the European Court of Justice held that the rules of jurisdiction contained in Title II of the Brussels Convention apply independently of whether the claimant is located within the internal market or in a non-Contracting State. The ECJ's judgment consequently demonstrated its conclusion that the Brussels Convention does not demand a connecting link to different Contracting States. Rather, Article 2(1) of the Brussels Convention already comes into play where the connection to the internal market extends no further than the defendant's domicile. The European Court substantiated this result on the one hand by a literal interpretation of Article 2(1) of the Brussels Convention. On the other hand, the ECJ systematically maintains the irrelevance of the claimant's domicile in that it opposes the general rule contained in Article 2(1) of the Brussels Convention by the ad hoc rules of the 2nd to 5th Sections which are to be narrowly interpreted. Therefore, the claimant's residence only gains relevance in narrowly defined exceptional cases. What is most relevant here is that the judgment is in accord with the Regulation that takes the place of the Brussels Convention.

It is worth noting that the Brussels Regulation and Lugano Convention are not only relevant to European Union policyholders, insureds or beneficiaries, but to any policyholder, insured or beneficiary in the world who has entered into an insurance contract with a European Community insurer (ie, an insurer with a seat in a Member State).

(b) Multi-defendant Cases

Multi-defendant cases with a defendant domiciled in the European Union (for example a branch, an agency or other establishment of the insurer) and another defendant domiciled outside the European Union (for example the insurance company) are likely to become increasingly common. This is true especially in the reinsurance sector where the reinsurer is either domiciled in the United

14 [2000] All ER (EC) 653.

Kingdom and the insurer is often domiciled outside the European Union. In these situations national courts of the Member States will have to make use of the rules of the Brussels Regulation or Lugano Convention for the defendant domiciled within Europe (EU/EFTA) and national rules for the defendant domiciled outside the EC/EFTA.

2. JURISDICTION UNDER THE BRUSSELS REGULATION AND LUGANO CONVENTION

(a) **The Set of Special Rules for Insurance Matters**

The Brussels Regulation and Lugano Convention have special jurisdictional rules for matters relating to insurance as well as for those relating to individual contracts of employment[15] and consumer contracts.[16] The set of special jurisdictional rules for insurance matters is contained in Articles 8 to 14.

(i) The Purpose of the Set of Special Rules for Insurance Matters

It is generally accepted in the legal writings that the aim of the jurisdictional rules of the Brussels Regulation (Brussels Convention) and Lugano Convention in matters relating to insurance is to protect the party who, from a socio-economic point of view, is the weaker.[17] The weaker party may be the policy-holder, the insured or the third party beneficiary. The effect of these rules is that, regardless of whether he is the defendant or the claimant, the weaker party can plead the case in the courts of the State where he is domiciled. Moreover, the

[15] Arts 5(1) and 17(5).

[16] Arts 13 to 15.

[17] See generally Brulhart, *La compétence internationale en matière d'assurances dans l'espace judiciaire européen* (St Gallen/Lachen, Dike Verlag, 1997); Mari, *Il diritto processuale civile della Convenzione di Bruxelles—Il sistema della competenza* (Padova, CEDAM, 1999) 493; Benedetelli, *La giurisdizione internazionale in materia assicurativa secondo la Convenzione di Bruxelles* (1998) *Diritto del commercio internazionale*, 597; Hill, *The Law Relating to International Commercial Disputes*, para 5.8.3.; Gaudemet-Tallon, *Les Conventions de Bruxelles et de Lugano-Competence internationale, reconnaissance et execution des judgments en Europe*, 2nd edn (Paris, LDJ, 1996) 176; Blanco Morales Limones, *Commento alla Sez. 3* in AL Calvo Caracava, *Comentario al Convenio de Bruselas relativo a la competencia judicial y a la ejecucion de resoluciones judiciales en materia civil y mercantil* (Madrid, Aranzi, 1994) 201; Anton and Beaumont, *Civil jurisdiction in Scotland* (Edinburgh, Sweet & Maxwell, 1995) para 6.0.1.; O'Malley and Layton, *European Civil Practice*, para. 18. 02.; Hartley, *Civil jurisdiction and judgments: the application in England of the Convention on Jurisdiction and the Enforcement of Judgments in Civil and Commercial Matters under the Civil Jurisdiction and Judgments Act 1982* (London, Sweet & Maxwell, 1984) 59; Gothot and Holleaux, *La convention de Bruxelles du 27.9.1968—Competence judiciaire et effets des judgments dans la CEE* (Paris, Jupiter, 1985) n 120; Dashwood, Hacon, White, *A Guide to the Civil Jurisdiction and Judgments Convention* (Antwerp, Deventer, 1986) 103; Linke in Von Bulow, Bockstiegel, *Internationaler Rechtsverkehr in Zivil-und Handelsachen* (Munchen, Beck, 1977) 87 note 606; Droz, *Competence judiciaire et effets des judgments dans le marche' commun (Etudes de la Convention de Bruxelles du 27 september 1968)* (Paris, Dalloz, 1972) 80. See also recitals to Arts 8 to 14 of the Brussels Regulation: Com (1999) 348, final, 16.

requirements for jurisdiction agreements under Articles 13 and 14 of the Brussels Regulation and Lugano Convention are stricter than the requirements for jurisdiction agreement under Article 23 with the consequence that only in a restricted number of cases may such agreements be enforced against the policy-holder, the insured or the beneficiary.

It is the author's opinion that, despite the existence of some provisions in Articles 8 to 14 which favour the weaker party, the main goal of the jurisdictional rules relating to insurance is not the protection of the party who is considered to be in a 'weaker bargaining position'. As stated below, the Brussels Regulation and Lugano Convention lay down some protective rules in Section 4 of Chapter II concerning jurisdiction for consumer contracts that apply to policy-holders, insureds and third party beneficiaries who are in a weaker bargaining position.[18] Therefore it is most likely that the main purpose of the jurisdictional rules in matters relating to insurance was to provide a set of appropriate fora for trial. This is shown by the following articles: Articles 10, 11(1), (3) and 12(2). Article 10 provides that in respect of liability insurance or insurance of immovable property the insurer may be sued in the courts for the place where the harmful event occurred. Article 11(1) states that in respect of liability insurance the insurer may also be joined in proceedings which the injured party had brought against the insurer. Article 11(3) makes clear that the court which is competent to hear actions brought by the injured party directly against the insurer shall have jurisdiction over the policyholder or that the insured be joined as a party to the action. Article 12(2) provides that conterclaims shall be brought in the court in which the original claim is pending. It is clear that all these bases of jurisdiction require a strong connection with the forum. 'Appropriateness' under Articles 11(1), (3) and 12(2) seems to be referring not only to the connections that the parties and the dispute have with a particular Contracting State but also to matters of litigational convenience. This involves an examination of where the evidence is centred and of where the trial can best be conducted.[19]

(b) Jurisdiction in Matters Relating to Insurance

Article 8 provides that 'in matters relating to insurance, jurisdiction shall be determined by this section, without prejudice to the provisions of Articles 4 and 5(5)'. A similar rule is contained in Article 15(1) relating to jurisdiction over consumer contracts. Two problems arise from the text of Article 8: the first

[18] See below para 2.1.(b)(ii).

[19] For a criticism of the protective purpose of the jurisdiction rules in matters relating to insurance see Frigessi di Rattalma, *La giurisdizione internazione in materia assicurativa nel sistema della Convenzione di Bruxelles* (1993) *Assicurazione internazionale veicoli* 124; see also Sacerdoti, *La giurisdizione in materia di assicurazioni nella riforma del diritto internazionale privato e processuale italiano* (1996) *Diritto de economia delle assicurazioni* 15 to 27.

concerns the meaning of 'insurance'; and the second the scope of application of the general rules of the Brussels Regulation and Lugano Convention in matters relating to insurance. These problems will now be considered.

(i) The Meaning of 'Insurance'

Section 3 of Chapter II of the Brussels Regulation, which lays down jurisdictional rules in matters relating to insurance, does not provide a definition of the term 'insurance'. The recitals to Articles 8–14 of the Brussels Regulation do not clarify the meaning of the word 'insurance' for the purpose of the application of the Regulation. They merely state that the special rules of jurisdiction in insurance matters aim to protect the 'weaker party'.[20] But this is of little help in defining the term insurance. Strangely enough, this is an even more vague and ambiguous indication than that in the Schlosser Report to the Brussels Convention, which states that the special rules for insurance in the Brussels Convention do not apply to reinsurance contracts.[21] Due to the absence of the need for protection, it might be held that the special rules on jurisdiction in matters relating to insurance contracts do not apply to any action by or against an insurer, but only to actions in the context of a contract of insurance.[22] This conclusion is suggested by the language of Articles 9 to 12 of the Brussels Regulation and especially by the terms 'policy-holder', 'insured' and 'beneficiary' contained therein which refer to the contract of insurance. The language of these provisions also suggests that the exercise of subrogated rights by an insurer against a third party who is responsible for a loss has to be considered as a matter relating to insurance. On the other hand, the exercise of direct rights by an insurer against the same party could not be regarded as an insurance matter.[23] The wording of Articles 8 to 14 indicates that these rules apply to certain types of insurance contracts such as liability insurance, compulsory insurance, marine and aviation insurance and insurance of immovable property. Moreover, it is submitted that at least Article 9(1)(c) of the Brussels Regulation and Lugano Convention applies to co-insurance contracts.[24] Furthermore, Articles 8 to 14 apply to contracts of insurance covering risks situated *in* and *outside* the territories of the Member States of the European Union.[25] However, Article 14(4) which provides that the jurisdiction rules of Section 3 may be departed from by an agreement on jurisdiction concluded with a policy-holder who is *not*

[20] See the recitals to Art 8 of the Regulation: Com (1999) 348, final, 16.

[21] Schlosser Report, OJ 1979/117 (para 151). See also ECJ Case 412/98 *Group Josi Reinsurance Company SA v Universal General Insurance Company (UGIC)* [2000] ILPr 549 *et seq.*

[22] See Anton and Beaumont, *Civil Jurisdiction in Scotland*, n 17 above, para 6.07 who refer to Arts 7 to 12A of the Brussels Convention.

[23] *Cf* O'Malley and Layton, *European Civil Practice*, n 13 above, para 18.07.

[24] See Kaye, *Civil Jurisdiction and Enforcement of Judgement Convention*, n 13 above, 816 who refers to Article 8(3) of the Brussels Convention.

[25] *Cf* Benedettelli, *La giurisdizione internazionale in materia assicurativa*, n 17 above, 628 who refers to articles 7 to 12A of the Brussels Convention.

domiciled in a Contracting State suggests that these rules do not apply to insurance contracts covering risks situated *outside* the territories of the Member States of the European Union.

(ii) The Application of General Rules of the Brussels Regulation and Lugano Convention to Insurance Matters

A word needs to be said about the application of the general rules of the Brussels Regulation and Lugano Convention to matters relating to insurance. As already stated above, Article 8 preserves the operation of Articles 4 and 5(5). The preservation of Article 4 means that Articles 8 to 12 of the Brussels Regulation do not apply to a defendant who is not domiciled in a Member State of the European Union and where there is such a defendant Member States shall apply their traditional rules of jurisdiction, however exorbitant. The effect of the reference to Article 5(5) is to provide a basis of jurisdiction additional to those contained in Articles 8 to 14.

It is submitted that Article 5(5) applies where either the defendant is an insurer or insured.[26] This conclusion is derived from the fact that the identical provision of Article 5 of the Brussels Convention has been justified by the European Court of Justice on the ground that it allocates jurisdiction to a Member State with which the dispute has a close relationship.[27] Therefore, there are no reasons to restrict the scope of application of Article 5(5) of the Brussels Regulation to actions brought by insureds against insurers. Some problems might arise, however, in relation to actions brought by or against agents, brokers or underwriters who are independent of the insurer. That Article 5(5) requires the agent to be subordinated to the main company might suggest the conclusion that a Lloyd's agent, who has no authority on behalf of Lloyd's, should not be regarded as an agent for the purposes of Article 5(5). But Articles 21, 32 of the Council Directive 92/49 and Articles 8(1)(a), 10(2)(d) of the Council Directive 79/267 provide that the 'association of the Lloyd's agents' has to be regarded as an insurance company.[28]

It is the present author's opinion that the application of the general rules of the Brussels Regulation and Lugano Convention to matters relating to insurance cannot be decided only by looking at the words of Article 8; interpreters must adopt a purposive approach to the identification of the applicable rules of jurisdiction to insurance matters. As is well known, the European Court of Justice

[26] See Benedetelli, *La giurisdizione internazionale*, n 17 above, 631 who refers to Article 5(5) of the Brussels Convention.

[27] Case 21/76 *Handelskwekerij GJ Bier BV v Mines de Potasse d'Alsace SA* [1976] ECR 1736, at 1746. See also Case 12/76 *Tessili v Dunlop* [1976] ECR 1473, (1977) 1 CMLR 26; Case 33/78 *Etablissement Somafer v Saar-Ferngas AG* [1978] ECR 2183, (1979) 1 CMLR 490; Case 34/82 *Peters v Zuid Nederlandse Aaannemers Vereniging* [1983] ECR 987; Case 220/88 *Dumez France and Tracoba v Hessische Landesbank* [1990] ECR 49; see also the Jenard Report, *OJ* 1979, C 59, 22.

[28] See also Queen's Bench Division (Commercial Court) of London, judgment of 31 July 1992, *JR Charman and ME Brockbank v WOC Offshore BV*, [1993] 1 Lloyd's Law Reports 378.

adopts a purposive approach to the interpretation of the Brussels Convention. It looks at what the provisions say, but it looks at them with an eye to what they are aiming to achieve.[29] It is well established case law that national courts must approach the interpretation of the Brussels Convention as would the European Court of Justice.[30] A purposive approach to the interpretation of the jurisdictional rules of the Brussels Regulation and Lugano Convention relating to insurance matters suggests that these are not rules which, with two exceptions, apply exclusively to cases falling within their scope. There are, in fact, other bases of jurisdiction in the Brussels Regulation and Lugano Convention which may be of use for insurance contracts. It appears that Article 15, which provides jurisdiction rules over consumer contracts, applies to insurance contracts concluded by policyholders, insureds or third party beneficiaries who are in a weaker bargaining position.[31] This is suggested by the scope of the definition of consumer contract in Article 15 which encompasses *any* contract for the supply of services where the two conditions laid down in the text are fulfilled.[32] Furthermore, it appears that Articles 23(1)(c) and 24 of Section 7 relating to the prorogation of jurisdiction apply to jurisdiction agreements and jurisdictional clauses in insurance matters.[33] This conclusion is supported by the fact that these provisions apply to jurisdiction agreements and jurisdictional clauses related to consumer contracts. Again, Articles 25, 26 of Section 8 relating to the examination as to jurisdiction and admissibility as well as Articles 27, 28, 29 of Section 9 relating

[29] See Layton (1992) 11 CJQ pp 32–35. For a clear exposition of the principles of interpretation of the Brussels Regulation see Briggs and Rees, *Civil Jurisdiction and Judgments*, 3rd edn (Essex, Informa Publishing Group, 2001) para 2.2.1.

[30] See *Grupo Torras SA v Sheikh Fahad Mohammed al Sabah* [1995] ILPr 667; *Papanicolauou v Thielen* [1997] ILPr 37 (High Court, Ireland). For a clear illustration of this point see Hill, *The Law Relating to International Commercial Disputes*, 56 *et seq*.

[31] See Dicey and Morris, *The Conflict of Laws* by L Collins *et al*, 13th edn (London, Sweet & Maxwell, 1999) 372; Anton and Beaumont, *Civil Jurisdiction in Scotland*, n 17 above, 139; *cf* Gothot, Holleaux, *La Convention de Bruxelles*, n 17 above, fn 134; Benedettelli, *La giurisdizione internazionale*, n 17 above, 629.

[32] Art 15 reads as follows: '1. In matters relating to a contract concluded by a person, the consumer, for a purpose which can be regarded as being outside his trade or profession, jurisdiction shall be determined by this Section, without prejudice to Article 4 and point 5 of Article 5, if

(a) it is a contract for the sale of goods on instalment credit terms; or
(b) it is a contract for a loan repayable by instalments, or for any other form of credit, made to finance the sale of goods; or
(c) in all other cases, the contract has been concluded with a person who pursues commercial or professional activities in the Member State of the consumer's domicile or, by any means, directs such activities to that Member State or to several States including that Member State, and the contract falls within the scope of such activities.

2. Where a consumer enters into a contract with a party who is not domiciled in the Member State but has a branch, agency or other establishment in one of the Member States, that party shall, in disputes arising out of the operations of the branch, agency or establishment, be deemed to be domiciled in that State.

(1) This Section shall not apply to a contract of transport other than a contract which, for an inclusive price, provides for a combination of travel and accommodation.'

[33] See Briggs and Rees, n 29 above, 56–58; Dicey and Morris, n 31 above, 368; Mari, *Il diritto processuale civile*, n 17 above, 506, 703 et seq. O'Malley and Layton, *European Civil Practice*, para 18.03.

to lis pendens-related actions[34] and Article 31 of Section 10 relating to provisional and protective measures are not affected by the jurisdiction rules of Section 3 of Chapter II of the Brussels Regulation and Lugano Convention.[35]

(iii) Are the Jurisdictional Rules of Section 3 Applicable to Reinsurance Disputes?

As already stated above, the Schlosser Report to the Brussels Convention suggests that, since reinsurance contracts cannot be equated with insurance contracts, Articles 7 to 12A do not apply to reinsurance contracts.[36] The European Court of Justice left the question unanswered in *Overseas Union Insurance Ltd v New Hampshire Insurance Co* case.[37] However, in its written observations to the Court, the Commission took a position in favour of the submission of reinsurance contracts to the scope of application of Articles 8 to 12A and stated that

> it is difficult to see any fundamental difference between insurance and reinsurance which could justify exclusion of reinsurance contracts from the scope of Section 3 of Title II. As a more general matter, since the Convention is designed precisely to avoid and resolve conflicts of jurisdiction, any exclusion of such a substantial nature would need to be expressly stated in the text of the Convention, and not merely inferred.

But in the recent case *Group Josi Reinsurance Company SA v Universal General Insurance Company (UGIC)* the European Court of Justice held that the rules of jurisdiction in matters relating to insurance set out in Section 3 of Title II of the Brussels Convention do not cover disputes between the reinsurer and reinsured in connection with a reinsurance contract.[38] The European Court derives this conclusion mainly from the fact that

> the role of protecting the party deemed to be economically weaker and less experienced in legal matters than the other party to the contract which is fulfilled by those provisions (Articles 7 to 12A) implies . . . that the application of the rules of special jurisdiction laid down to that end by the Convention should not be extended to persons *such as reinsurers* for whom that protection is not justified.[39]

Therefore, Articles 7 to 12 A do not apply to the relationship between a reinsured and his reinsurer in connection with a reinsurance contract as

> both parties to the reinsurance contracts are professionals in the insurance sector, neither of whom can be presumed to be in a weaker position compared with the other party to the contract.

[34] See the English case *Overseas Union Insurance Ltd v New Hampshire Insurance Ltd* [1992] 2 All ER 138.

[35] See Benedettelli, *La giurisdizione internazionale*, n 17 above, 630.

[36] See the Schlosser Report, n 9 above, para 156.

[37] Case C-3551/89 [1991] ECR I-3317.

[38] See Case C-412/98 *Group Josi Reinsurance Company SA v Universal General Insurance Company (UGCI)* [2000] ILPr 549 *et seq*.

[39] My emphasis.

It appears that the same conclusion applies to Articles 8 to 14 of the Brussels Regulation as these provisions do not differ significantly from Articles 7 to 12A of the Brussels Convention. Moreover, the exclusion of reinsurance (ie, the relationship between a reinsured and his reinsurer) from the scope of application of Articles 8 to 14 of the Brussels Regulation can be derived by analogy from the fact that insurance contracts covering large risks are excluded from the scope of Section 3. Article 14(5) of the Brussels Regulation in fact provides that the provisions of Section 3 may be *departed* from by an *agreement on jurisdiction* which relates to a contract of insurance in so far as it covers one or more of the large risks set out in Article 14.

(iv) The Exclusion of Arbitration Proceedings

It is unclear whether the exclusion of arbitration proceedings provided by Article 1(d) of the Brussels Regulation and Lugano Convention affects the application of the provisions contained in Articles 8 to 14. The crucial question is whether the protecting provisions relating to insurance matters can be departed from by an arbitration clause in circumstances other than those indicated in Articles 13 and 14. According to Droz[40] and more recently Benedettelli,[41] who examined the question in relation to Articles 7 to 12A of the Brussels Convention, this question deserves a negative answer since the freedom to depart from the provisions of Section 3 by an arbitration clause would conflict with the objective of the protection of the weaker party pursued by these rules. However, it has already been submitted that the protection of the party in a weaker bargaining position (ie the insured, third party beneficiary, policyholder) is only an indirect effect arising from certain provisions of Section 3.[42] Therefore, it appears that the jurisdictional rules in matters relating to insurance can be departed from by an arbitration agreement in circumstances other than those indicated in Article 13 and 14 of the Brussels Regulation and Lugano Convention.

(c) **Actions Against Insurer: Article 9(1)**

Article 9(1) allows an insurer domiciled in a Contracting State to be sued:

(1) in the courts of the State where he is domiciled, or
(2) in another Contracting State, in the case of actions brought by the policyholder, the insured or a beneficiary, in the courts for the place where the claimant is domiciled,

or

[40] See Droz, *Compétence judiciaire*, n 17 above, 47 and 135 at note 2.
[41] See Benedettelli, *La giurisdizione internazionale*, n 17 above, 623.
[42] See above para 2.1.(a)(i).

(3) if he is a co-insurer in the courts of a Contracting State in which proceedings are brought against the leading insurer.

Article 9(1)(1) normally allocates jurisdiction to just one European State, that of the defendant's domicile. However, due to the absence of a uniform definition of domicile in the European Union the claimant (policy-holder, insured, beneficiary) may have a choice of fora even when suing one insurer. For example, the case may involve an insurance company. An insurance company is domiciled where it has its seat.[43] The defendant may have the choice of suing the insurance company in Italy, where the defendant is domiciled under the Italian definition of a seat,[44] or in England, where the defendant is domiciled under the differing English definition of a seat.[45] In insurance and reinsurance cases the effect of the substantive law is to present the claimant with a choice of defendant and, because they may be domiciled in different European States, with a choice of European States in which he can sue under Article 9(1)(1). It follows that the claimant may have the choice of suing in Germany the insurer, domiciled in Germany, or suing in Italy the branch or the agency, domiciled in Italy.[46]

For the purposes of Article 9(1)(2) the word 'policyholder' has to be interpreted as meaning the party to the contract of insurance other than the insurer. The domicile of the policy-holder which is relevant is the domicile existing at the time when the proceedings are brought.[47] Where the policy-holder is not domiciled in a Contracting State Article 9(1)(2) does not apply.[48]

(d) Actions Against Insurer: Article 9(2)

Article 9(2) provides that

> an insurer who is not domiciled in a Member State but has a branch, agency or other establishment in one of the Member States shall, in disputes arising out of the operations of the branch, agency or establishment, be deemed to be domiciled in that State.

It is clear that Article 9(2) does not provide a special basis of jurisdiction, but is a deeming provision. The effect of this paragraph is to bring an insurer who is not domiciled in a Member State but has a branch, agency or other establishment in a Member State of the European Union within the scope of Article 5(5), which in principle applies only to defendants domiciled in a Member State. However, it appears that this provision does not assimilate the position of this insurer with the position of an insurer domiciled in the Member State where the

43 Art 53
44 See O'Malley and Layton, *European Civil Practice*, n 13 above, para 51.25.
45 *Ibid*, para 50. 25.
46 However, Art 5(5) has a special forum as regards 'a dispute arising out of the operations of a branch, agency or other establishment'.
47 See O'Malley and Layton, *European Civil Practice*, n 13 above, para 50. 25.
48 *Lassin v Payne* [1995] ILPr 17 (Paris, Court of Appeal).

branch, agency or other establishment is situated. Therefore, an insurer who is not domiciled in a Member State but has a branch, agency or other establishment in a Member State cannot be sued in the courts of any place permitted by the national law of the State where the branch, agency or other establishment is situated.[49]

Although a different conclusion can be derived from the text of Article 9(2), it appears that this provision applies not only when the action is brought under Article 9(1) but also when it is brought under Articles 10 and 11(1), (3). This interpretation is suggested by the fact that the purpose of Articles 10, 11(1) and (3) is to allocate jurisdiction to the Member State with which the dispute has a particularly close relationship.[50]

(e) Actions Against Insurer in Matters Relating to Liability Insurance or Insurance of Immovable Property

Article 10 states that

> in respect of liability insurance or insurance of immovable property, the insurer may in addition be sued in the courts for the place where the harmful event occurred. The same applies if movable and immovable property are covered by the same insurance policy and both are adversely effected by the same contingency.

According to the Jenard Report,[51] the identical provision of Article 9 of the Brussels Convention allows an insurer to be sued in a State other than that in which he is domiciled, in the courts for the place where the harmful event occurred. However, it can be argued from the purpose of this provision, which is to allocate jurisdiction to the courts of the Member State with which the dispute has a particularly close relationship, that Article 9 (Article 10 of the Brussels Regulation) has the effect of allowing an insurer to be sued in the State of his domicile in the courts for the place where the harmful event occurred.[52] The purpose of this provision also suggests that the expressions 'liability insurance or insurance of immovable property' are to be given such a wide interpretation as to encompass any type of liability insurance. Therefore, Article 10 will apply to liability in tort, liability for the insured's breach of contract, liability for lawyers' fees in connection with litigation or liability for doctors' fees.[53]

[49] *Cf* O'Malley and Layton, *European Civil Practice*, n 13 above, para 18.20.

[50] See above para 2(a)(i).

[51] See the Jenard Report, n 54 below, para A1.141.

[52] See O'Malley and Layton, *European Civil Practice*, n 13 above, para 18. 26-27-28.

[53] But see O'Malley and Layton, *European Civil Practice*, n 13 above, para 18.25 who suggest that Art 9 of the Brussels Convention does not apply to liability for lawyers' fees in connection with litigation and liability for doctors' fees.

(f) Third Party Proceedings Against the Insurer

Article 11 also deals with liability insurance. The first paragraph provides that in respect of liability insurance 'the insurer may also, if the law of the court permits it, be joined in proceedings which the injured party has brought against the insured'. It is clear that the purpose of this provision is the prevention of conflicting judgments which could arise if the insurer and insured are sued in different countries because of the strict relationship existing between these actions.[54] Article 11(1) is likely to be of greatest importance in road accident cases since the person liable normally holds an insurance policy covering all risks related to the use of a motor vehicle.[55] But the insurer may be joined in *any* proceeding that the injured party has brought against the insured if the law of the forum allows it. Therefore, where the victim of a road traffic accident sues the driver in the courts of a Member State which would not have jurisdiction over the driver's insurer by virtue of Article 9, the effect of Article 11(1) is to allow the driver to join the insurer as third party, but only if the 'court seised of the matter has jurisdiction in such a case under its own law'.[56]

(i) Injured Party's Direct Action Against the Insurer

The second paragraph of Article 11 states that the provisions of Articles 8, 9 and 10 'shall apply to actions brought by the injured party directly against the insurer, where such direct actions are permitted'. According to the Paris Court of Appeal,[57] a jurisdiction agreement between insured and insurer does not bind the third party in his direct action against the insurer. The French Court draws this conclusion from the fact that the victim who was exercising a direct action could not be subject to a jurisdiction clause which, by definition, he had not been able to negotiate, and therefore which he was not aware of. Like Article 11(1), Article 11(2) appears to be of particular relevance in road traffic accidents cases. It allows victims of road traffic accidents to sue the insurer of the person who injured them in one of the courts of the Member States referred to in Articles 5(5), 8 and 9. However, it does not enable the victim to bring an action in the courts of the Member State where he is domiciled or in the courts of the Member State where the insured is domiciled.[58] This choice of the drafters of the Brussels Regulation and Lugano Convention is questionable and truly conflicts with the purpose of this provision which is the protection of the victims. Nevertheless, it

[54] See The Jenard Report, OJ 1979 C59/31 on the identical provision of Art 10(1) of the Brussels Convention.

[55] See below ch 9.

[56] See the Jenard Report, OJ 1979 C59/32 which refers to Art 10(1) of the Brussels Convention.

[57] Societe Lutz et autre *v* Societe Frasgo et autres, D (1991) SC 285 Paris Court of Appeal, Fifth Chamber, 12 November 1991 as reported in Kaye (ed), *European case law in the judgment convention* (Chichester, Wiley, 1998) 434.

[58] See O'Malley and Layton, *European Civil Practice*, n 13 above, para 18.38.

is coherent with the other provisions of Section 3 especially with Article 9(1)(b) which does not take into account the domicile of the insured or third party beneficiary where the insured or third party beneficiary is not the same person as the policy-holder.[59]

(ii) Direct Actions: Article 11(3)

Where the insurer is sued by the injured party under Article 11(2), then, if the law applicable to the direct action of the victim allows it, he may join the policy-holder or the insured as a party to the action. By commenting the identical provision of Article 10(3) of the Brussels Convention the Jenard Report suggests that the purpose of this rule is the prevention of different courts from giving judgments which are conflicting or irreconcilable and the protection of insurers from fraud.[60]

(g) Actions by Insurers

(i) The Insurer or Reinsurer as Claimant

With regard to proceedings relating to insurance contracts in which the defendant is not the insurer, the general rule is that the courts of the defendant's domicile have jurisdiction. Article 12(1) states that

> without prejudice to the provisions of the third paragraph of Article 10, an insurer may bring proceedings only in the courts of the Member State in which the defendant is domiciled, irrespective of whether he is the policy-holder, the insured or a beneficiary.

It is the defendant's domicile at the time when the proceedings are brought that should be taken into consideration for the application of this provision. In *Jordan Grand Prix Ltd v Baltic Group and Others*[61] the House of Lords maintained that the identical provision of Article 11 of the Brussels Convention applies to *all* insurers wherever domiciled. Accordingly, the insurer in the case, a company from Lithuania, a non-Contracting State, was prevented from adding Irish parties to its counterclaim in proceedings brought against it in England by an English insurer.

Article 11(1) normally allocates jurisdiction to just one Member State, that of the defendant's domicile. Nevertheless, the claimant may have a choice of fora even when suing just one defendant due to the absence of a definition of domicile in the Brussels Regulation and Lugano Convention. Especially in cases concerning insurance contracts covering large risks, which generally involve a

[59] See above para 2.1.(d).
[60] Jenard Report, n 54 above, para A1.146.
[61] [1999] 2 AC 127.

corporate defendant, the claimant-insurer may, for example, have the choice of suing the insured in Italy where the defendant is domiciled under the Italian definition of a seat[62] or in Switzerland where the defendant is domiciled under the different Swiss definition of a seat.[63]

It is worth noting that, despite the wording of Article 12, this provision admits some exceptions other than Article 11(3). The insurer may counterclaim under the second paragraph of Article 12. Moreover, where the insurer enters into a jurisdiction agreement with the defendant, both parties may bring proceedings in the chosen forum, provided the agreement complies with Article 13. Furthermore, if the defendant is domiciled in a Member State and has a branch, agency or other establishment in another Member State, he may be sued in the courts of the place in which the branch, agency or other establishment is situated whether or not the dispute arises out of the operations of the branch, agency or other establishment. Finally, Article 6(2) and (3) may apply when the action is brought by an insurer against the insured, the policyholder or a third party beneficiary.

(ii) The Right of the Insurer to Bring Counterclaims

Article 12(2) states that 'the provisions of this section should not affect the right to bring a counterclaim in the court in which, in accordance with this Section, the original claim is pending'. In *Jordan Grand Prix LTD v Baltic Insurance Group and Others*[64] the House of Lords held that the rules of Article 11 (Article 12 of the Brussels Regulation) are designed not to affect the right to bring a counterclaim in the court in which the original claim is pending but 'counterclaim' must there be construed as meaning a counterclaim against the original claimant. It is submitted that Article 12(2) must be interpreted together with Article 6(3).[65]

3. THE OBJECTIVES OF THE SPECIAL RULES ON JURISDICTION AGREEMENTS IN INSURANCE MATTERS

It appears that the purpose of Article 13 which contains special rules on jurisdiction agreements in insurance matters is to prevent the parties from restricting the choice of fora granted to the policy-holder by Articles 8 to 12 and to prevent the insurer from avoiding the restrictions imposed by Article 12.[66] But

[62] See O'Malley and Layton, *European Civil Practice*, n 13 above, para 51.25.
[63] *Ibid*, para 50.25.
[64] See above n 61.
[65] Jenard Report, n 54 above, para A1.147 below.
[66] See with regard to the identical provision of Art 12 of the Brussels Convention Jenard, n 54 above, para. A1.148–A1.149 below; Schlosser Report, paras 137–140 (paras A1.421–A1.433, n 54 above); Collins, *The Civil Jurisdiction and Judgments Act*, n 13 above, 72–74; Dashwood/Halcon/White, *A Guide to the Civil Jurisdiction and Judgments Convention*, n 17 above, 28, 106–8;

the purpose of Article 13 is also to take account of the needs of the British insurance market where many policy-holders are not domiciled in Member States.[67]

(a) The Requirements of the Jurisdiction Agreements

Article 13 states that the provisions of Articles 8 to 12 may be departed from only by an agreement on jurisdiction which satisfies one of the conditions set out in paragraphs 1 to 5. The following sub-paragraphs will analyse these requirements in detail.

(i) Jurisdiction Agreements Entered into after the Dispute has Arisen

Article 13(1) states that a jurisdiction clause 'which is entered into after the dispute has arisen' is allowed. A similar rule is contained in Article 15(1) relating to jurisdiction over consumer contracts. By commenting on the identical provision of Article 12(1) of the Brussels Convention the Jenard Report suggests that a 'dispute' has 'arisen' when 'the parties disagree on a specific point and legal proceedings are imminent *or* contemplated'.[68] According to O'Malley and Layton, the proceedings must be '*both* imminent *and* contemplated'.[69] This interpretation is supported by the fact that there is no need of a jurisdiction agreement or a jurisdiction clause until the dispute becomes one which will apparently require litigation to resolve it.[70]

(ii) Jurisdiction Agreements in Favour of the Insured

According to Article 13(2) parties can enter into a jurisdiction agreement 'which allows the policy-holder, the insured or a beneficiary to bring proceedings in courts other than those indicated in this Section'. It is clear that the aim of this provision is to protect the party who is supposed to be in a weaker bargaining position (ie, the policy-holder, insured or third party beneficiary).[71] However, it is uncertain whether this provision can achieve a higher protection for the policyholder, insured or third party beneficiary. It appears, in fact, that jurisdiction

Hartley, *Civil Jurisdiction and judgments*, n 17 above, 61–62; Kaye, *Civil Jurisdiction and Enforcement of Judgments*, n 17 above, pp 817–21; Anton and Beaumont, *Civil Jurisdiction in Scotland*, n 17 above, paras 6.16-6.17; Droz, *Compétence judiciaire*, n 17 above, paras 128–30; Pocar, *La Convenzione di Bruxelles sulla giurisdizione e l'esecuzione delle sentenze* (Milan, Guiffré, 1995) 165; O'Malley and Layton, *European Civil Practice*, n 17 above, para 18.50; Hill, *The Law Relating to International Commercial Disputes*, n 12 above, para 5.8.15.

[67] See the Schlosser Report, n 9 above, para. 140 which refers to the purpose of Art 12 of the Brussels Convention as modified by the Accession Convention of the United Kingdom.

[68] See the Jenard Report, n 54 above, para A1.148 below.

[69] For a clear exposition of the different opinions on this subject see O'Malley and Layton, *European Civil Practice*, n 13 above, para 18.55, note 45.

[70] See O'Malley and Layton, *European Civil Practice*, n 13 above, para 18.55.

[71] See, inter alia, Hill, *The Law Relating to International Commercial Disputes*, 160.

agreements or jurisdiction clauses which widen the choice of fora available to the insured under Articles 8 to 11 are unlikely to be concluded in the real world because most insurers would probably deny their consent as there is no lack of protection for policyholders, insureds, or third party beneficiaries in the jurisdictional rules of Section 3.

(iii) Jurisdiction Agreements Entered Into Between Parties who are Domiciled or Habitually Resident in the Same Member State

Article 13(3) provides that Articles 8 to 12 may be departed from with an agreement on jurisdiction

> which is concluded between a policy-holder and an insurer, both of whom are domiciled in the same Member State, and which has the effect of conferring jurisdiction on the courts of that State even if the harmful event were to occur abroad, provided that such an agreement is not contrary to the law of that State.

It appears that Article 13(3) does not favour the insured who is supposed to be in a weaker bargaining position but operates in favour of both the insured and insurer. The courts of the State where the parties are domiciled, in fact, are very appropriate ones for trial: 'appropriateness' appears to be referring not only to the connections that the parties to the dispute have with the Member State of their domicile but also to matters of litigational convenience. This interpretation is confirmed by the commentary to the identical provision of Article 12(3) of the Brussels Convention in the Jenard Report which suggests that this paragraph had been inserted to enable the scope of Article 11(1) to be limited.[72]

(iv) Jurisdiction Agreements Entered Into with a Party Who is Not Domiciled in a Member State

Article 13(4) states that the rules of Section 3 may be departed from with an agreement on jurisdiction 'which is concluded with a policy-holder who is not domiciled in a Member State, except in so far as the insurance is compulsory or relates to immovable property in a Member State'. Subject to the exceptions of compulsory insurance and immovable property, Article 13(4) allows the parties to an insurance contract to confer exclusive jurisdiction on the courts of a Member State which would not have it under Articles 8 to 12, or whose jurisdiction under those provisions would not be otherwise exclusive.[73] It is well known that the identical provision of Article 12(4) of the Brussels Convention had been included in the original text of the Brussels Convention by the 1978 United Kingdom Accession Convention in order to take account of the peculiarities of the British insurance market where a large number of insurance contracts are negotiated with policy-holders who are not domiciled in a Member

[72] See O'Malley and Layton, *European Civil Practice*, n 13 above, para 18.57.

[73] See O'Malley and Layton, *European Civil Practice*, n 13 above, para 18.60.

State.[74] It is submitted that a policy-holder who is not domiciled in a Member State does not normally have strong connections with the courts of Member States and, therefore, he does not usually have an interest in bringing proceedings in the courts of a particular State.[75]

(v) Jurisdiction Clauses Inserted into Contracts of Insurance Covering Large Risks

The last paragraph of Article 13 provides that an agreement on jurisdiction 'which relates to a contract of insurance in so far as it covers one or more of the risks set out in Article 14' is permissible. It appears that the phrase 'in so far as' must be given a literal interpretation, thus that a jurisdiction agreement is valid only to the extent that it covers the risks referred to in Article 14.[76] As a result of this interpretation actions concerning an insurance contract which covers some risks within the scope of Article 14 and other risks falling outside its scope can be taken in more than one jurisdiction. The rationale for refusing a wider interpretation of Article 13(5) is that it would undermine the policy of Section 3, which is to restrict the exceptions to the general rule that actions must be brought against a policy-holder or an insured only in the courts of his domicile.[77] Article 14 lays down a very detailed list of the risks referred to in Article 13(5). It provides that these are:

> 1. Any loss of or damage to a) sea-going ships, installations situated off-shore or on the high seas, or aircraft, arising from perils which relate to their use for commercial purposes, b) goods in transit other than passengers' baggage where the transit consists of or includes carriage by such ships or aircraft; 2. Any liability, other than for bodily injury to passengers or loss of or damage to their baggage, a) arising out of the use or operation of ships, installations or aircraft as referred to in (1)(a) above in so far as the law of the Contracting State in which such aircraft are registered does not prohibit agreements on jurisdiction regarding insurance of such risks, b) for loss or damage caused by goods in transit as described in (1)(b) above; 3. Any financial loss connected with the use or operation of ships, installations or aircraft as referred to in (1)(a) above, in particular loss of freight or charter-hire; 4. Any risk or interest connected with any of those referred to in (1) to (3) above.

As is clear from the text of Article 14, this provision includes marine and aviation risks. This is not surprising if you consider that the text of this provision is the 'political result' of the negotiations for the accession of the United Kingdom to the Brussels Convention.[78] Thus the historical background of the

[74] See the Jenard Report, n 54 above, para 142.

[75] See Kaye, *Civil Jurisdiction*, n 13 above, 819.

[76] See Mr Justice Hirst in the English case *Charman v WOC Offshore BV* [1993] 1 Lloyd's Rep 378, 384.

[77] See Anton and Beaumont, *Civil Jurisdiction in Scotland*, n 17 above, para 6.18 who refers to Art 12 of the Brussels Convention.

[78] See above note n 62.

provision must be taken into account for the interpretation of the expressions used in Article 14. It is arguable from the history and the text of Article 14 that this provision must be interpreted as encompassing *any* type of marine and aviation risk. Moreover, Article 14 should not be read as encompassing *any* type of large risk.[79]

[79] See Art 14(5). But a different conclusion was suggested by Art 12A of the Brussels Convention. For a commentary on this provision see Hill, *Law Relating to International Commercial Disputes*, n 12 above, 161; Kaye, *Civil Jurisdiction and Enforcement*, n 13 above, 820–21; Anton and Beaumont, *Civil Jurisdiction in Scotland*, n 17 above, 133–35; O'Malley and Layton, *European Civil Practice*, n 13 above, para 18.64; Mari, *Il diritto processuale civile*, n 17 above, 507–8; Celle, *Il contratto di assicurazione grandi rischi* (Padova, Cedam, 2000) 284–86; Benedettelli, *La giurisdizione internazionale in materia assicurativa*, n 17 above, 927 *et seq*; Fuentes Camacho, *Los contratos de seguro y el Derecho Internacional Privado en la Unión Europea* (Madrid, Civitas, 1999) 59.

Section II
Cross-border Co-operation Regarding Litigation in Insurance and Reinsurance Matters: Preliminary Observations

In the field of insurance and reinsurance litigations, two approaches to cross-border co-operation should be distinguished: passive co-operation and active co-operation.

Passive co-operation means that the judicial authorities of one State recognise judicial events which have taken place in another jurisdiction. One of the most salient examples is the effect of '*lis alibi pendens*'. The courts of one State are deprived of their jurisdiction, or they are entitled to take a discretionary decision to decline jurisdiction, if the identical law is pending abroad. By contrast, active co-operation implies that the State in which the proceedings are not conducted is requested to commit official acts in furtherance of foreign proceedings. The most conspicuous example is the taking of evidence, which could not be taken in the country of the court seized with the lawsuit because, for example, the witness to be examined refuses to travel to the respective foreign country.

1. *LIS ALIBI PENDENS*

Insurance and reinsurance litigations in an international setting is likely to involve multiple causes of action and parties. Following from this is the strong likelihood that courts and tribunals in different States may have jurisdiction. To avoid a multiplicity of actions, with the concomitant increased risk of conflicting judgments, the new Judgments Regulation control multiple actions in Contracting States by a form of *lis alibi pendens* covering identical actions (Article 27) and related actions (Article 28).

2. IDENTICAL ACTIONS

Where a number of actions proceed in different Member States between the same parties and with the same cause of action, Article 27 of the Brussels Regulation requires the court second seized[1] to stay their proceedings until the jurisdiction of the court first seized is established.[2] If the court has jurisdiction, the court seized thereafter must decline jurisdiction. These obligations of a court subsequently seized are mandatory, not discretionary.

[1] Determined in accordance with local law; see *Zelger v Salinitri* [1984] ECR 2397.

[2] Art 27 will apply whether or not any of the parties are domiciled in a Member State. See on the identical provision of Art 21 of the Brussels Convention the case *Overseas Union Ins Ltd v New Hampshire Ins Co* [1991] ECR I-3317.

Article 27 requires that the parties be identical, regardless of their procedural status as claimants or defendants. To the extent that only some of the parties are identical in two separate actions, the court second seized must stay its proceedings only as against those parties.[3] This entails a possible fragmentation of proceedings.[4]

For separate actions to have the 'same' cause of actions, the basis of the actions must rely on the same facts and rules of law, and the actions must have the same end, or objective, in view. These elements have to be interpreted autonomously; that is independently of the specific features of national law in any Member State.[5] For instance, separate actions based on the same facts, one alleging liability for breach of contract or misrepresentation, and the other seeking a declaration denying any duty or standard of care, are actions having 'the same cause of action' for the purposes of Article 27.

As a result of the *lis alibi pendens* rule of Article 27 there may be strong competition to commence the first proceedings, whether an action for damages or for a negative declaration denying responsibility. For example, an insurance broker may begin an anticipatory lawsuit to deny any contractual relationship or duty of care toward the policyholder, in anticipation of the latter's action for misrepresentation.

3. RELATED ACTIONS

Related actions defined as being 'so closely connected that it is expedient to hear and determine them together to avoid the risk of irreconcilable judgments', it is sufficient that there exists a risk of conflicting decisions, but not necessarily leading to mutually exclusive legal consequences.[6] Therefore where separate actions based on the same facts include parties, some of which are the same and some of which are not, Article 28 allows, but does not require, a court to stay its proceedings in favour of the court first seized in the related proceedings. If the same court has jurisdiction over both actions, that court may consolidate the action.

4. RECOGNITION AND ENFORCEMENT OF JUDGMENTS: PRELIMINARY OBSERVATIONS

Jurisdiction and choice of law are just the first two stages of a private international law case. There is also a third stage, viz that of the recognition and enforcement of the judgment. It can be possible to enforce the judgment in the State in which the action was taken, but where this is not allowed it is required

[3] *The Tatry* [1994] ECR I-5439.
[4] *Ibid.*
[5] *Gubbish v Palumbo* [1987] ECR 4861.
[6] *The Tatry*, n 3 above.

to recognise and implement the judgment in some different State in which the defendant has property.

The rules on recognition and enforcement of foreign judgments apply to all judgments. Judgments in relation to insurance and reinsurance contracts are not subject to special provisions. Most of the rules do not cause particular problems for judgments in relation to insurance and reinsurance contracts.

We will not try to deal with every single aspect of the issues raised by the recognition and enforcement of foreign judgments. We will rather concentrate our attention on those questions which are particularly important in relation to insurance and reinsurance contracts.

5. INTRODUCTION

Under English law as well as under the laws of several EU Member States, the recognition and enforcement of foreign judgments is complicated by the fact that there is a large diversity of different sets of provisions dealing with this topic. A fundamental differentiation can be drawn though between recognition and enforcement under the EU/EFTA States provisions, and recognition and enforcement under the traditional municipal rules. In the following paragraphs, the concern is with the recognition and enforcement under the EU/EFTA States rules. It is submitted as a preliminary comment that insurance and reinsurance related cases give rise to few unusual questions as regards recognition and enforcement of foreign judgments, thus the relative briefness of the following chapter.

6

Recognition and Enforcement of Judgments in Insurance and Reinsurance Matters

1. WHEN WILL THE BRUSSELS REGULATION AND THE LUGANO CONVENTION APPLY?

(a) The Brussels Regulation

The Brussels Regulation on Jurisdiction and the Recognition and Enforcement of Judgments in Civil and Commercial Matters of 2000, contains one of the main systems of rules for the recognition and enforcement of foreign judgments. However, since the Regulation does not cover all foreign judgments its scope will have to be determined precisely and the systems that apply to judgments that fall outside its scope will be examined later on in this chapter. The Brussels Regulation contains separate rules on recognition and enforcement. They will be examined as far as they apply to insurance and reinsurance related cases.

The new Regulation's aim is that judgments should circulate freely within the European Union, so as not to cause any disturbance to economic and social life. To obtain this, the Regulation provides an almost automatic recognition mechanism and a rather procedural enforcement mechanism. These have only become possible as a result of the harmonisation of the bases on which the courts accept jurisdiction in the first place. The supervisions could only be weakened at the recognition and enforcement stage, as severe and uniform checks have been inserted at the jurisdictional stage.

(b) The Lugano Convention

Judgments granted in EFTA Member States will be recognised and enforced under the Lugano Convention. The rules on recognition and enforcement which are contained in this Convention are, in most regards, identical to those contained in the new Brussels Regulation.

2. THE SCOPE OF THE BRUSSELS REGULATION

(a) A Judgment Given in a Member State

According to the Regulation,[7] its provisions on recognition and enforcement will apply to the exclusion of all other provisions where the judgment concerned has been given in a Member State. Article 32 defines the term judgment widely as 'any judgment given by a Court or Tribunal in a Member State'.[8] Courts at all levels are encompassed by this rule and the use of the wording 'any judgment' indicates that the provisions will apply irrespective of the type of judgment, order, decree, decision, etc. There is no prerequisite that the judgment is a final one.[9] As far as insurance and reinsurance cases are concerned, an interim order can come within Article 32, as can an injunction.

(b) The Type of Jurisdiction Provision is Irrelevant

As long as recognition and enforcement is sought in relation to a judgment which has been rendered by a tribunal or a court in a Member State, the Regulation applies irrespective of the basis on which that tribunal or court accepts jurisdiction. It is by no means essential that the tribunal or the court accepts jurisdiction on the basis of a jurisdictional provision which is contained in the Brussels Regulation. It could have accepted jurisdiction on the basis of a traditional municipal provision.

(c) The Judgment is Given in Respect of a Civil and Commercial Issue

This is the point where the scope of the new Regulation is restricted. The Regulation's provisions on recognition and enforcement will only be applicable if the judgment is given is respect of an issue coming within the scope of the Regulation. The Regulation's definition of civil and commercial matters does not have to be restated here, it is enough to state that the identical notion applies in relation to jurisdiction and recognition and enforcement. This issue is always raised at the recognition and enforcement stage and the court that is demanded to recognise and enforce a judgment must take a new look at the issue. Regardless of the result at the jurisdictional stage, it should examine whether or not the question falls within the scope of the Regulation. Only an affirmative

[7] Arts 33 to 38.

[8] See Bariatti (2001) *Diritto internazionale privato e processuale* 5 to 22.

[9] See the case 143/78 *De Cavel v De Cavel* [1979] ECR 1055 which refers to Art 25 of the Brussels Convention.

response will guide the application of the Regulation's provisions on recognition and enforcement.

3. RECOGNITION OF THE FOREIGN JUDGMENT

(a) An Indispensable First Stage

No foreign judgment can be implemented until it has been recognised. Recognition is a fundamental first step towards the implementation of the foreign judgment. Enforcement will not always follow notwithstanding. If the judgment is simply to be used as a defence in a new lawsuit its recognition will be adequate. And lastly, recognition may also function on its own, for example to determine a title of property.

(b) The Rebuttable Presumption in Favour of Recognition

Article 33 of the Regulation provides that 'a judgment given in a Member State shall be recognised in the other Member States without any procedure being requested'. No prerequisites and procedures are attached to this provision. A foreign judgment should automatically be given the identical effects in the recognising State as it has in the State in which it was rendered.[10] But the automatic recognition is in reality a rebuttable presumption that judgments are to be recognised.[11] This should be the obvious result of the fact that the Regulation also indicates a number of defences against the recognition of foreign judgments. The existence of any of these defences will rebut the presumption and block the recognition of the foreign judgments.[12]

(i) Defences Against Recognition

(1) The Scope of the Public Policy Defence to Enforcement of Prorogation Clauses Inserted into Insurance and Reinsurance Contracts

Could the enforcement of a derogation clause inserted into a contract of insurance or reinsurance deprive the claimant of rights that a forum statute declares not waivable? In its 1982 opinion in *The Hollandia*[13] the House of Lords maintained that a clause in a contract of carriage limiting suit to a court in the Netherlands was unenforceable because it would result in waiver of rights that

[10] See the case 145/86 *Hoffmann v Krieg* [1988] ECR 645 which refers to Art 26 of the Brussels Convention.

[11] See the opinion of the Advocate General in Case 42/76 *De Wolf v Cox* [1976] ECR 1759, (1977) 2 CMLR 43.

[12] See, for example, Art 34.

[13] [1983] 1 AC 565.

the English Carriage of Goods by Sea Act declared not waivable. However, it is unlikely that the English courts would take the same approach in an analogous case concerning the enforcement of a derogation clause contained in an insurance or reinsurance contract as Article 35(3) of the Brussels Regulation provides that 'the test of public policy . . . may not be applied to the rules relating to jurisdiction'. But there are few other examples of situations in which public policy or 'ordre public' can be invoked in insurance and reinsurance cases.[14]

(2) Natural Justice

The impact of the absence of proper appraisal of the legal proceedings, etc[15] was examined above in relation to the scope of the Regulation. The defendant should have received precise appraisal and he should have been given the opportunity and time to plead for himself in court. This provision applies to any kind of legal proceedings. There is no necessity to adjoin anything else at this stage and this defence does not raise any particular questions in relation to insurance and reinsurance cases.

(3) Irreconcilable Judgment in the Recognising State

A judgment which has been rendered in the State in which recognition is sought functions as a defence against the recognition of a foreign judgment.[16] Such a judgment can be rendered before or even after the foreign judgment. On the top of that, the two judgments should be irreconcilable. This latter prerequisite has been introduced to clarify that they must result in legal consequences which are mutually exclusive.[17]

This defence may be applied in insurance cases in the situation where the insurer that has been successful in a declaratory action to invalidate the insurance policy at the end of the grace period in the policyholder's State of domicile seeks to have that judgment recognised in the State in which his headquarters are based and is confronted in that State with a domestic judgment (obtained by the insured in the declaratory action) that states that the insurance policy has to be considered as valid following the grace period. The consequence is that these two judgments are mutually exclusive and the foreign declaratory judgment will not be recognised.

(4) An Irreconcilable Judgment in a Non-Member State

A foreign judgment will also not be recognised if it is irreconcilable with a judgment given by a court in another Member State or in a non-Member State. There are two prerequisites for this defence to apply.[18] The judgment in a non-

[14] See below ch 8, para 12.
[15] Art 34(2) of the Brussels Regulation.
[16] Art 34(3) of the Brussels Regulation.
[17] See the case 145/86 *Hoffmann v Krieg* [1988] ECR 645 which refers to the identical provision of Art 27(3) of the Brussels Convention.
[18] Art 34(4).

Member State must be an earlier judgment and the two judgments should be irreconcilable in the sense that they must lead to legal consequences which are mutually exclusive.

(5) Judgments Conflicting with the Provisions of Section 3

Article 35(1) provides that a judgment shall not be recognised whenever it conflicts with the provisions of Section 3. However, Article 58 states that

> a settlement which has been approved by a court in the course of proceedings and is enforceable in the State in which it was concluded shall be enforceable in the State addressed under the same conditions as an authentic instrument.

With regards to the enforcement of authentic instruments, Article 57 provides that this may be refused *only* if it is contrary to public policy in the State addressed.

4. HOW PROBLEMS ARISE IN INSURANCE AND REINSURANCE CASES

(a) Recognition and Enforcement by EU National Courts of Judgments Rendered by Other EU National Courts

(i) Against the UK Defendant

Suppose a Belgian policyholder has brought the action against his UK insurer in Belgium, and has obtained a judgment in its favour. Suppose also that the defendant lacks sufficient assets in Belgium to satisfy the judgment: the Belgian policyholder will then seek to have the judgment enforced in England, where the defendant's assets are located. Or suppose the Belgian policyholder litigated the compensation claim in England, but discovered that the UK party was sheltering most of its assets in Germany. The Belgian claimant would then turn to the German courts to enforce the English judgment. Because Belgium and Germany are both party to the Brussels Regulation, that Act's provisions will take priority.

As to enforcement, Article 38 provides that a judgment that is enforceable in the rendering Member State 'shall be enforced in another Contracting State when on the application of any interested party, it has been declared enforceable there (in the other Member State)'. The application for enforcement must be ruled on 'without delay', and can be refused only for one of the reasons indicated for refusing recognition to a Member State's judgment.[19] Article 58 of the Brussels Regulation provides that

> a settlement which has been approved by a court in the course of proceedings and is enforceable in the State in which it was concluded shall be enforceable in the State addressed under the same conditions as an authentic instrument.

[19] See Art 34 of the Brussels Convention.

With regards to the enforcement of authentic instruments, Article 57 provides that this may be refused *only* if it is contrary to public policy in the State addressed.

Therefore, if the English court awards the Belgian policyholder damages, and if there are insufficient assets to satisfy the judgment in England, the Belgian policyholder may pursue enforcement of the judgment in Germany. The German court will have to verify that the judgment was not rendered in violation of any of the Act's bases for non-recognition and enforcement; the German court must then order the enforcement of the English court's order. But the enforcing court cannot review the English judgment 'as to substance', not can it revisit the factual basis on which the rendering court asserted jurisdiction.[20]

(ii) Against a Defendant From a Non-Member State

The same principles apply when a Member State has rendered a judgment against a defendant from a non-Member State, even if the rendering court exercised jurisdiction in a manner incompatible with the Regulation's restrictions on the judicial competence of Member States. Those limits apply to actions between persons who are domiciled in Member States, and do not bind the national courts of Member States in their judicial competence over non-domiciliaries. It follows that if an English court were to exercise jurisdiction over an insurer domiciled in the United States on the basis of its domestic jurisdictional rules, other courts in the European Union must recognise and enforce that judgment.[21]

The practical implications of this may be important. Suppose, for example, that the US defendant has assets in England, but not in France. The French court acting under Article 14 of the French Civil Code may assert jurisdiction over alleged damage occurring outside France, while an English court's competence would most likely be restricted to adjudicating claims regarding damage which occurred in England. The French policyholder could nonetheless decide to bring an action in France, knowing that the English courts must execute the ensuing French judgement, even though the English court would not itself have awarded damages in such circumstances.

(b) Recognition and Enforcement by EU National Courts of Judgments Rendered by Courts of a Non-Member State Against the UK Defendant

The analysis above has concerned the recognition and enforcement by EU courts of judgments rendered by other EU courts. Suppose, on the other hand,

[20] See Arts 28 to 34 of the Brussels Convention.

[21] See Art 4(1) of the Brussels Convention which preserves contracting States' domestic jurisdictional rules as applied to EU non-domiciliaries.

that the Belgian policyholder elected to sue both the English broker and the US insurer in the United States, and, having obtained a favourable judgment, sought its enforcement in England or Belgium against the English defendant. As the Brussels Regulation and Lugano Convention do not deal with the recognition in Member States of judgments rendered in non Member States that question is governed by the traditional rules on enforcement of foreign judgments of each EU State in which recognition is sought.

7

Forum Shopping

1. INTRODUCTION

ANOTHER QUESTION that needs to be considered is that of 'forum shopping'. This refers to the choice by the plaintiff of one forum rather than another as the place in which to bring the action because he thinks there will be some advantages for him in suing in that country rather than elsewhere.[1] The incentive to forum shop is often provided by differences in the substantive laws of different States. However the incentive to forum shop is also provided by differences in the procedural provisions of different countries. If the claimant is encouraged to proceed in a foreign jurisdiction for a procedural advantage it is a question of bringing the action in a court of the State which provides that advantage, since that court will apply its own procedural provisions.[2] But if the claimant is forum shopping for a substantive law advantage the position is not so simple. If, for example, a claimant from England wants to achieve the benefit of the German substantive law of life insurance he will have to go to a country which will apply German law. Differences in choice of law provisions in different countries mean that proceedings in one country rather than in another can produce the desired inducement.[3] For, self evidently, if every country were to have the same choice of law provisions there would be no reason to forum shop for substantive law advantage.[4]

Forum shopping occurs when a number of States have broad provisions on jurisdiction; this grants the claimant a wide choice of alternative fora for trial.[5]

2. REASONS TO FORUM SHOP

A decision to proceed in a foreign jurisdiction can, of course, be made for valid reasons. It may, for example, be that one party desires litigation to be conducted in one language rather than another; for, self evidently, there are major

[1] See especially Diamond, *Harmonisation of private international law relating to contractual obligations* [1986] II Hague Recueil 233 *et seq*; Fawcett, *Product Liability in Private International Law: A European Perspective* [1993] I Hague Recueil 96 *et seq*; Fawcett (1984) *Northern Ireland Legal Quarterly* 141 *et seq*.

[2] See Fawcett, *Product Liability in Private International Law*, above n 1, 96.

[3] See *ibid*, 97.

[4] *Ibid*, 97.

[5] *Ibid*, 96.

disadvantages in translation in relation to legal questions.[6] Again, the claimant may think that the judges of a certain forum are more experienced in his type of claim or that litigation is faster.[7] However forum shopping is objectionable when it involves proceedings in one jurisdiction when an appropriate forum is available for trial.[8] This can lead to unfairness to the defendant.[9] This may take two forms. First, the defendant can be greatly troubled in having to defend in a forum with which the parties have weak connections or no connection at all.[10] The defendant has no such reason to complain if the forum is one which has a strong link with the parties and the dispute.[11] Secondly, any advantage that the claimant achieves from trial in his elected forum will be to the disadvantage of the defendant. The claimant who forum shops can, for example, win an action which he would otherwise have lost or he can obtain higher compensation for the damage suffered.[12]

3. FORUM SHOPPING WITHIN THE EUROPEAN UNION IN INSURANCE CASES

(a) **What Advantages Will a Claimant Obtain?**

By forum shopping in the European Union, a claimant can achieve advantages, such as less media coverage. More importantly, he can achieve procedural or substantive law advantages or both.[13]

(i) Procedural Advantages

There are differences in the procedural provisions used in the different European Union States. This encourages forum shopping in any civil and commercial matter, though some of the differences are particularly important in relation to insurance and reinsurance. The following sub-paragraphs will give some examples of these differences in procedural provisions.

(1) Documentary Evidence

Under English law and that of a number of other European Union States a party who produces a document as evidence has to prove to the judge that it is authentic.[14]

[6] See Diamond, *Harmonisation of private international law*, n 1 above, 150 *et seq.*
[7] *Ibid*, 150 *et seq.*
[8] Fawcett, *Product Liability in Private International Law*, n 1 above, 97.
[9] See Fawcett (1984) 35 *Northern Ireland Law Quarterly* 144–45.
[10] See Fawcett, *Product Liability of Private International Law*, n 1 above, 97.
[11] *Ibid*, 97.
[12] *Ibid*, 97.
[13] *Ibid*, 97–98.
[14] See D Campbell, *England* in D Campbell and C Campbell (eds), *International Civil Procedures* (London, Lloyd's of London Press, 1999) 152.

This rule is more inconvenient for the claimant than the French rule which provides that documentary proof is only needed for those obligations exceeding FF 5,000, and which are of a non-mercantile kind.[15]

(2) Testimonial Evidence

In a number of European Union States the judge can hear testimonial evidence. However, it is rare to hear any testimonial evidence in a French court during civil and commercial matters. Further, when testimonial evidence is introduced, it will usually be in the form of a written affidavit rather than oral testimony.[16]

(3) Party Testimony

Under French law and that of a number of other European Union States parties cannot testify in litigation. They can appear in court and be heard at the court's discretion, but they cannot testify under oath and their statement is regarded with suspicion. This affects its weight. In practice the appearance of the parties is rather uncommon.[17]

A claimant would be better advised to seek trial in European Union States such as England which allows any party to request further information relating to any matter in question between the applicant and the other party in the cause or matter, which are necessary for disposing fairly of the cause or matter or for saving costs.[18]

(4) Costs[19]

In all European Union States the judge has a discretionary power to order legal costs to be paid by the unsuccessful party. But a winning claimant looks to do badly in some civil law countries such as Belgium in so far as lawyers' fees are not included in the costs to be paid by the unsuccessful party.[20] In Spain the judge's discretion is restricted to ordering that no more than one-third of the claimed amount is to be paid by the unsuccessful party.[21]

(5) Payment into court[22]

Under the law of some Member States of the European Union a defendant may make a payment into court of a sum of money by way of a settlement. The payment may be made prior to or during trial or judgment. If the claimant refuses

[15] Art 1341 of the French Civil Code.

[16] See C Lécuyer-Thieffry, *France* in D Campbell and C Campbell (eds), *International Civil Procedures*, n 14 above, 263.

[17] *Ibid*, 264.

[18] Civil Procedure Rules, Pt 18.

[19] Fawcett, *Product Liability in Private International Law*, n 1 above, 99.

[20] See McIntosh and Holmes, *International Civil Procedures in EC Countries: An Industry Report* (London, Lloyd's of London Press, 1991) 50. A fixed sum is however, paid to compensate for time spent in preparing the case.

[21] *Ibid*, 290–91.

[22] *Ibid*, 15.

to accept this sum and is subsequently awarded a lesser amount, or loses altogether, he should pay all costs from the point of payment into court onward.

This procedure puts pressure on a claimant to settle an action. A claimant would be better advised to bring action in European States such as Germany, Belgium or the Netherlands, which do not allow payment into court, rather than in England, which allows this.[23]

(6) Delay

Making comparisons as to the time gap between the issue of proceedings and a judgment being obtained is difficult in relation to European Union States. Nonetheless, it appears that a claimant who desires a quick judgment is better advised to start proceedings in Germany, where the period is usually around six months, than to Italy, where the period may be up to five years.[24]

(ii) Substantive law advantages

(1) Differences in the Substantive Law and Choice of Law in Insurance Contracts

The lack of complete harmonisation of substantive insurance law and choice of law rules for non-life and compulsory insurance contracts in Europe, with consequent choice of law problems, means that there are still substantive law advantages to be gained from forum shopping.[25] The following are examples of such advantages.

Payment of the Premium

Probably one of the most common reasons for forum shopping from the insured's point of view is the expectation of gaining better protection against late payment or non-payment of the premium. The lack of measures of harmonisation of the rules on the premium in the Insurance Directives leaves open, in theory at least, the possibility of forum shopping for the payment of the premium. But, in practice, forum shopping in order to achieve better conditions for payment of the premium is not going to be common in Europe. There are many similarities in the laws of different European Union States as to the conditions for payment of the premium. Nonetheless, there are some differences in relation to the consequences of late payment or non-payment and to that extent this could lead to forum shopping. For example, some common law countries such as England do not protect the assured against forfeiture for late payment.[26]

[23] Fawcett, *Product Liability in Private International Law*, n 1 above, 100.

[24] See McIntosh and Holmes, n 20 above, 5–6, 11–12.

[25] For more information on the lack of harmonisation of the substantive insurance law in Europe see above ch 1. For a more detailed exposition of the lack of harmonisation of the choice of law rules for non life and compulsory insurance contracts see below ch 12, paras 1 and 2.

[26] See Merkin and Rodger, *EC Insurance Law* (London and New York, Longman, 1997) 41.

Reduction of Risk

Claimants in a multi-claimant case will gain an advantage from obtaining trial in a State which will apply Italian law rather than English in that English law does not recognise the right to ask for a reduction in the premium where the risk has diminished. Under English law once the risk has commenced, any reduction in it does not entitle the assured to any return of premium, on the basis that there can be restitution only for a total failure of consideration, ie, where the risk has never been run at all.[27]

Mitigation of Loss

On the other hand, if the issue in the case is that of the mitigation of loss a claimant/insurer is best advised to obtain trial in a European Union State which applies English law rather than Italian law, since the latter requires an assured to take steps to avoid or mitigate the loss whereas English law does not.[28] However, this is not true if the issue concerns mitigation of loss in a marine insurance contract. It is a well-established practice in marine insurance for the policy to contain a 'suing and labouring' clause, whereby the assured falls under a duty to take reasonable steps to prevent or mitigate loss, and the insurer is under a corresponding obligation to indemnify the assured for the reasonable costs incurred in doing so in addition to any sums due under the policy itself.[29]

(b) The Opportunity to Forum Shop

One of the features of European jurisdiction under the Brussels Regulation and Lugano Convention is the excessively wide choice of fora given to the insured/claimant in insurance and reinsurance cases. This provides ample opportunity for an insured, who wishes to forum shop, to do so. For self evidently forum shopping does depend on good legal advice as to the chances of suing in another European State.[30] With uniform provisions on jurisdiction in Europe it is possible for a legal adviser in one European State to do so.[31] At the same time, the claimant can proceed in the most advantageous forum without having to worry about problems of enforcement of the judgment in Europe since the Brussels Regulation and Lugano Convention provide that a judgment obtained in one European State shall be enforced, subject to few exceptions, in any other Member State.[32]

[27] *Tyrie v Fletcher* (1774) 2 Cowp 666, codified in the Marine Insurance Act 1906, s 84. For a clear illustration of this point see Merkin and Rodger, n 26 above, 41.

[28] See Merkin and Rodger, n 26 above, 41.

[29] *Ibid*, 41.

[30] See Fawcett, *Product Liability in Private International Law*, n 1 above, 105.

[31] *Ibid*, 105.

[32] *Ibid*, 105.

(c) Is There Anything Wrong with Forum Shopping within Europe?

The jurisdictional rules of the Brussels Regulation and Lugano Convention in insurance and reinsurance matters allow the insured to proceed in a foreign jurisdiction. The insurer/defendant may legitimately complain of forum shopping if, for example, he is subject to trial in a fortuitous and unforeseeable place where the harmful event occurred. The extent of the unfairness to the insurer/defendant, in terms of litigational inconvenience, will, to some extent, be limited. The insurer is only being asked to defend in another European country, not in the United States or Australia. Nonetheless, it can be a real inconvenience for an English insurer to have to resist in, for example, Italy. Moreover, the unfairness to the insurer/defendant, in terms of the balance between the interests of the two parties being tilted in favour of the insured/claimant, cannot be justified by the substantive insurance law under the Insurance Directives since this does not, overall, favour the insured in the sense of being concerned predominantly with the interests of the insured.[33] It is difficult to justify to an insurer/defendant why, for example, an insured/claimant who is faced with the limit on a insurer's total liability for damage under Italian law, the law applicable to the insurance contract in what may be the natural forum, is allowed to bypass this limit by proceeding in an inconvenient forum.

(d) How can the Insured/Claimant be Discouraged from Forum Shopping?

In order to answer this question you must keep in mind that in insurance cases you have great inducements to forum shop in Europe: relevant differences in procedural provisions and in the substantive law, uniform jurisdictional provisions which give the insured/claimant a wide choice of fora, and the incomplete harmonisation of choice of law rules for non-life insurance and compulsory insurance contracts.

Bearing this in mind, it appears that the insured can be discouraged from forum shopping by adopting a combination of the following measures.

(i) Harmonisation of Procedural Provisions

Harmonisation of procedural provisions in Europe would discourage the insured/policyholder/third party from forum shopping for procedural advantages. The need for uniform jurisdictional provisions in the European Union has been satisfied by the introduction of the Brussels Regulation and Lugano Convention. But this must be just the first step in the process of harmonisation of the law of international commercial litigation.[34] The harmonisation of pro-

[33] See above ch 1, para 13.

[34] See Fawcett, *Product Liability in Private International Law*, n 1 above, 106.

cedural provisions is necessary for the protection of consumers.[35] Consumers will not obtain equal protection throughout the European Union and competition will be distorted if insurers in one European Union State are exposed to pro-claimant procedural provisions whereas insurers in another European Union State are not.

It is clear that a complete harmonisation, involving all procedural provisions, is not possible, but some measure of agreement on the main issues which induce forum shopping, such as rules on documentary evidence, testimonial evidence, party testimony, costs, payment into court and structured settlements is feasible.[36] In order to discourage forum shopping for substantive law advantages, this would have to be accompanied by increased harmonisation of the substantive insurance law and/or by harmonised choice of law rules.

(ii) Harmonisation of the Substantive Insurance Law

This would destroy the motivation for forum shopping for substantive law advantages. It may be possible, in the future, to provide increased harmonisation in relation to such issues as the consequences of late payment or non-payment of the premium, reduction of risk, mitigation of loss. But, the room for further harmonisation of substantive insurance law is limited, given that insurance as a whole encompasses traditional national provisions on contract and tort. What would be needed is a revival of one of the proposals for a Council Directive on the co-ordination of laws, regulations and administrative provisions relating to insurance contracts. At the same time, this would have to be accompanied by harmonised rules on such general matters as damages and limitation periods.

(iii) Narrow Jurisdictional Provisions

The narrower the rules on jurisdiction the less chance there is for forum shopping, either for procedural or substantive law advantages.[37] It has already been suggested that Article 9 of the Brussels Regulation which deals with actions against insurers should be re-worded so that an insurer domiciled in a Member State may be sued only in the courts of the state where he is domiciled or if he is a co-insurer, in the courts of the Member State in which proceedings are brought against the leading insurer. This rule would be much narrower than the present rule contained in Article 9 of the Brussels Regulation and Lugano Convention, yet it would still give the insured/claimant some choice. Jurisdiction would be allocated to an appropriate forum and the insurer/defendant could have no complaint if sued in such places.

[35] *Ibid*, 106.

[36] See McIntosh and Holmes, n 20 above, 19–21; Fawcett, *Product Liability in Private International Law*, n 1 above, 107.

[37] See Fawcett, *Product Liability in Private International Law*, n 1 above, 108.

PART III

The Law Applicable to Insurance and Reinsurance Contracts Under the 1980 Rome Convention and the EC Insurance Directives

Preliminary Observations

1. CHOICE OF LAW PROVISIONS

When a judge has reached a decision as to jurisdiction, he/she should proceed to the further stage of establishing the law applicable to that situation, ie which State's substantive law applies. This is of crucial relevance. To explain this, you may take the example of misleading or false publicity. The claimant complains that false or misleading information has been given about his product. Under Italian substantive law, there is an actionable tort of false publicity, whereas under English law there is not. It follows that the claimant will recover damages if Italian law is applied, but will not do so if English law is applied. In order to ascertain whether English substantive law or that of a foreign State applies, recourse should be made to private international law rules. Private international law provisions are formulated in terms of legal categories, such as contract and succession, and connecting elements, such as the place where the policyholder is habitually resident or where the contract was concluded.[1] To take an example, there is a conflict of laws provision that creation of a commercial company is governed by the law of the place where the company has its headquarters. The legal category is the company, the connecting element is the place where the company has its headquarters.[2] There are discrete choices of law provisions for different legal categories. The private international law rules for contracts are very different from those for non-contractual obligations, and both of these are different from those of succession. The starting point in the process of determining the applicable law is, thus, to characterise the cause of action, ie to allocate the issue raised in a certain case to its correct juridical category.[3] When this is done, one can proceed to apply the proper private international law provisions. It is not only essential to characterise the cause of action, it is also essential to characterise the specific question arising before the judge. The importance of the issue may be appreciated by looking at the private international law rules for contracts. If the question is that of material validity of a

[1] Dicey and Morris, *The Conflict of Laws* by L Collins *et al*, 13th edn (London, Sweet & Maxwell, 1999) 34.

[2] *Ibid*.

[3] Cheshire and North, *Private International Law*, PM North and JJ Fawcett, 13th edn (London, Edinburgh, Dublin, Butterworths) 44.

contract, a different private international law rule applies from that where the issue is that of formal validity of contract. Application of the correct private international law rule allows the judges to determine the applicable substantive law.

In insurance and reinsurance cases, the process of characterisation may raise some problems. Is there an existing category of private international law provisions within which the issues of creation, scope and termination of rights arising from insurance and reinsurance transactions fit? It is questionable whether all these issues fit properly within the category of contract. With insurance and reinsurance contracts, which issues are contractual, and therefore for the contract choice of law rules that deal with torts? Moving on to causes of action, how is breach of the third party beneficiary's rights to be classified? All of these issues will be analysed in the following chapters.

At last, a word needs to be said about the English choice of laws provisions. There is no single source. The tort choice of laws rules are largely based on statutory law. The choice of laws provisions for contracts are now largely Europeanised, and are contained in the Rome Convention on the law applicable to contractual obligations of 1980, implemented in the United Kingdom by the Contracts (Applicable Law) Act of 1990. The fact that we are concerned here with harmonised European law put an extra dimension to the question of characterisation. In contrast, tort choice of law provisions have not been Europeanised yet. After recent reform, this is now mostly put on a statutory basis. Statutes, case law, EC (EU) Conventions/Regulations on private international law are common sources of rules on conflict of laws. But two further possible sources of private international law provisions are special to insurance contracts. These are the EC Insurance Directives. These need to be examined in detail as they contain direct and indirect choice of laws provisions for insurance contracts covering risks situated in the territories of the Member States of the European Community. This will be done in Parts III, IV and V.

2. MANDATORY PROVISIONS OF THE FORUM

The Law Commission have defined mandatory provisions of the forum as substantive provisions that:

> are regarded so important that as a matter of construction or policy they must apply in any action before a court of the forum, even where the issues are in principle governed by foreign law selected by a choice of law rule.[4]

The statutory choice of law provisions in relation to torts and contracts both lay down rules securing the mandatory provisions of the forum. The notion is most established in contract cases and, in chapters 8 and 9, which are concerned with

[4] Law Commission Working Paper No 87 (1984) para 4.5.

the applicable law in relation to insurance contracts covering risks situated in the territories of the Member States of the European Community, the complex issue of the recognition of mandatory provisions will be examined in detail. This concept is especially likely to become relevant in insurance cases because of the links between insurance law and public law and because of the fact that the substantive law is territorially restricted in its scope, security only being granted in respect of local rights.

8

The 1980 Rome Convention and the Law Applicable to Insurance and Reinsurance Contracts

1. WHICH SET OF RULES WILL APPLY TO INSURANCE AND REINSURANCE CONTRACTS?

THE ROME Convention is concerned to determine the law applicable to contracts of insurance covering risks situated outside the territory of a Member State of the European Community. Article 1, paragraph 3 provides that 'the rules of this Convention do not apply to contracts of insurance which cover risks situated in the territories of the Member States of the European Economic Community'. However, the rules of the Rome Convention apply to reinsurance contracts which cover risks situated in the territories of a Member State of the European Community. Article 1, paragraph 4 states that paragraph 3 does not apply to contracts of reinsurance.

Furthermore, the Rome Convention applies in cases where the matter is within its scope. Therefore, it follows that the traditional choice of law rules of the Contracting States shall apply only to the matters excluded by Article 1, paragraph 2. These concern, inter alia, the questions involving the legal capacity of a natural person, arbitration agreements, the question of whether an agent is able to bind a principal, or an organ to bind a company or body corporate or unincorporate, to a third party.[5] However, in some civil law countries such as Italy the rules in the Convention apply to any contractual matter whether or not encompassed by the scope of the Rome Convention. As a result of Article 57 of the 1995 Italian statute of private international law,[6] the Rome Convention applies in Italy to any contractual obligation which is not covered by other international conventions or EC Directives. Reference has been made to the text of the Rome Convention as it has been implemented by the law of June 19, 1984, n. 975. Nevertheless, due to the implementation of the EC Insurance Directives in the Italian legal system, Italian courts cannot apply the rules in the

[5] Art 1, para 2.

[6] Art 57 reads as follow 'Le obbligazioni contrattuali sono in ogni caso regolate dalla Convenzione di Roma del 10 giugno 1980 sulla legge applicabile alle obbligazioni contrattuali, resa esecutiva con la legge 18 dicembre 1984, n. 975. senza pregiudizio delle altre convenzioni internazionali, in quanto applicabili'.

Convention to insurance contracts covering risks situated in the territories of a Member State of the European Community.

Article 2 of the Rome Convention provides that 'any law specified by this Convention shall be applied whether or not it is the law of a Contracting State'. It follows that the courts of the Contracting States shall apply the rules in the Convention to intra-community and extra-community disputes concerning insurance and reinsurance contracts whenever the conditions for the application of these rules occur.

2. THE DEFINITION OF 'RISK' IN THE ROME CONVENTION

The Rome Convention does not lay down criteria which can be used directly to determine whether a risk is situated in the territories of a Member State of the European Community. Article 1, paragraph 3 provides that 'in order to determine whether a risk is situated in these territories the court shall apply its internal law'. This provision raises two questions which are worth discussing.

The first question is whether Article 1, paragraph 3 allows national courts to use the choice of law rules of the *forum* in order to localise a risk in the territory of a Member State of the European Community. Some uncertainty in this regard comes about because of Article 15 of the Rome Convention which provides that:

> the application of the law of any country specified by this Convention means the application of the rules of law in force in that country *other* than its rules of private international law.[7]

This provision suggests prima facie that national courts cannot refer to the criteria contained in their private international law rules in order to determine whether a risk is situated in the territories of a Member State of the European Community. However, this would be a false conclusion, as Article 15 of the Rome Convention deals with the different question of the law applicable to the contract. Therefore, national courts can, and should, refer to their choice of law rules in order to determine whether a risk is situated in the territories of a Member State of the European Community.[8] Furthermore, this conclusion is suggested by the wording of Article 1, paragraph 3 which does not distinguish between substantive law and private international law.

The second question concerns the use of the specific criteria contained in the Insurance Directives for the localisation of the risk when the risk covered by an insurance contract is not situated in the territory of a Member State of the European Community. It can be deduced from the main purpose of the private international law rules in the Insurance Directives, which is the elimination of unfair practices in the Single Insurance Market, that the specific rules dealing with the criteria for the determination of the risk do not apply when the risk is

[7] Emphasis added.

[8] See Pocar (1987) *Rivista di diritto internazionale privato e processuale* 420 *et seq.*

not situated in the territory of a Member State of the European Community.[9] However, this would be a false conclusion as the implementation of the Insurance Directives in all the Member States of the European Community makes the rules contained in the Directives part of the domestic laws of the Member States. Therefore, the specific rules concerning the determination of the risk in the Insurance Directives are of relevance when the risk covered by the contract is situated outside the territory of a Member State of the Community. Moreover, this conclusion is supported by the text of Article 1, paragraph 3 which prescribes the application of the 'internal law' of the forum, regardless of whether some provisions of the 'internal law' are derived from the implementation of European Directives.

3. THE LAW APPLICABLE TO THE INSURANCE POLICY

It is well known that one of the peculiarities of insurance contracts, especially of life insurance contracts, derives from the fact that they create a type of property (the insurance policy) that, like any other property, can be sold, mortgaged, settled, seized in execution or confiscated. From a private international law perspective this raises two fundamental questions: a) the question of the juridical character of the insurance policy, ie the question of the classification (characterisation) of the insurance policy; b) the difference between the applicable law to the contract of insurance and the law governing title to the rights of the policyholder.[10]

It is unclear whether the insurance policy shall be characterised as a 'negotiable instrument' and, therefore, whether it is within the scope of the Rome Convention.[11] Some uncertainty arises from the fact that the Rome Convention does not define the term 'negotiable instrument' either in Article 1(2)(c), which provides the exclusion of the obligations arising from negotiable instruments nor in other provisions. Article 1(2)(c) tersely provides that the rules of the Rome Convention do not apply to

> obligations arising under bills of exchange, cheques and promissory notes and other negotiable instruments to the extent that the obligations under such negotiable instruments arise out of their negotiable character.

The Giuliano and Lagarde Report suggests that the judge must define the term 'negotiable instruments' *ex lege fori* (according to the law of the forum) because an independent definition of the term 'negotiable instruments' can effect proprietary rights in goods and those rights must not be regarded as the proper

[9] For a clear illustration of the purpose of the private international law rules in the Insurance Directives see Smulders and Glazener (1992) 3 *Common Market Law Review* 777.

[10] See Unger (1964) *International and Comparative Law Quarterly* 483, 492–98.

[11] For a discussion of this point see Celle (1995) *Diritto del commercio internazionale* 695–98.

subject matter of the Rome Convention.[12] If you look at the definition of negotiable instrument in English law it appears that insurance policies cannot be characterised as negotiable instruments and, therefore, they are not excluded from the scope of application of the Rome Convention. Unlike bills of exchange, cheques and promissory notes, insurance policies are not legal instruments which

> by customs of trade (or under statute) passes from hand to hand by delivery, and the holder of which for the time being, if he is a bona fide holder, for value without notice, has a good title, notwithstanding any defect of title in the person from whom he took it.[13]

Furthermore, the English law does not provide a clear distinction between the insurance policy and the contract of insurance.[14] It follows that the law applicable to the insurance policy must be ascertained according to the same choice of law rules as the insurance contract.

4. THE EXPRESS CHOICE OF THE LAW APPLICABLE TO INSURANCE AND REINSURANCE CONTRACTS

Insurance and reinsurance contracts shall be governed by the law chosen by the parties. Article 3, paragraph 1 provides that the choice 'must be express or demonstrated with reasonable certainty by the terms of the contract or the circumstances of the case'.

As a result of Article 3, paragraph 1 the choice of the applicable law can be made in writing or orally. However, it is clear that the choice is generally a written one because of the difficulties in producing the evidence of an oral agreement.[15] Especially in the sectors of marine insurance and reinsurance it is well established practice to insert express choice of law clauses into insurance policies with the intention of avoiding any future dispute over the governing law of the contract.[16] An express choice of law is present if the insurance or reinsurance contract stipulates that it is 'governed by' a particular law or that it is 'subject to' a particular law.[17] An implied choice of law is present if a reinsurance con-

[12] See the Giuliano and Lagarde Report (1980) OJ C281 of 31 October 1980, 571.

[13] See *Simmons v London Joint Stock Bank* [1891] AC 201.

[14] See Lowry, *Insurance law: doctrines and principles* (Oxford, Hart, 1999) 13.

[15] Kaye, *The New Private International Law of Contract of the European Community* (Aldershot, Dartmouth, 1993) 148.

[16] See Lewis and Woloniecki in *Conflict of Laws in the Interpretation of insurance and reinsurance contracts: the proceedings of a seminar organised by the IBA Section on Business Law's Insurance Committee, The Hague, Netherlands, March 1998* (London, International Bar Association, 1998) 84 *et seq*; Celle, *I contratti di assicurazione grandi rischi nel diritto internazionale privato* (Padova, CEDAM, 2000) 169 *et seq*.

[17] See the English cases *Armadora Occidental SA v Horace Mann Insurance Co* [1977] 1 WLR 520, affd *ibid* 1095 (CA) ('follow London' clause). See also *Cantieri Navali Riuniti SpA NV v Omne Justitia* [1985] 2 Lloyd's Rep 428 (CA); *EI du Pont de Nemours v Agnew* [1987] 2 Lloyd's Rep 585 (CA). See also *Chase v Ram Technical Services Ltd* [2000] 2 Lloyd's Rep 418.

tract which embodies some terms of an underlying contract of insurance states that these terms should be interpreted 'back to back' or 'as original' or 'as more fully described in the original policy wording'.[18] Moreover, the utilisation of a 'standard form which is known to be governed by a particular system of law'[19] can be taken to prove the choice of that country's law as the governing law. Again, a clause, embodied in a re-insurance contract, which provides that the courts of a certain country are to have jurisdiction to resolve a dispute arising out of the contract can reasonably demonstrate a choice of the law of that country as the applicable law.[20] In *American Motorists Insurance Co (AMICO) v Cellstar Corporation and Cellstar (UK) Limited*,[21] Steel J argued the existence of a choice of the Texas law as the governing law of an insurance contract covering risks situated both within and without the territories of the Member States of the European Community from the following matters: 'the described assured was a parent company with an address in Texas which was its principle place of business', 'the assured engaged a Texas agent to broke the policy', 'the policy was issued by an insurance company that was authorised to do business in Texas', 'the policy was issued in Texas'. But the choice of the governing law of the original contract of insurance as the law applicable to the re-insurance contract cannot be drawn if the re-insurance contract is drafted in a standard form which indicates ineluctably a choice of a different country's law.[22]

According to Article 3, paragraph 2, the *parties* can at any time decide to subject the contract to a law other than that which previously governed it. Article 3, paragraph 2 has raised three questions in the legal literature which are worth discussing in the context of insurance and reinsurance contracts.

The first question is whether this provision demands a choice be made at the very inception of the contract. 'Floating choices' to be nominated subsequently by one party either absolutely or amongst specific systems of law were not tolerated in England prior to the adoption of the Rome Convention.[23] The reason for this was that no contract can begin life without a governing law.[24] It appears

[18] See especially the English case *Gan Insurance Co Ltd v Tai Ping Insurance Co Ltd* [1999] EWCA Civ 1524.

[19] See the Giuliano and Lagarde Report, 17. See also the English case *Tiernan v Magen Insurance Co Ltd* [2000] ILPr 517 where it was maintained that where a re-insurance contract was placed on a Lloyd's market in the normal way, the contract was on a Lloyd' form and contained London market clauses, such elements were sufficient to prove with reasonable certainty a choice of English law for the purposes of Art 3, para 1 of the Rome Convention.

[20] See the Giuliano and Lagarde Report, n 12 above, 17. See also the English case *Royal Exchange Insurance Corp v Vega* [1902] 2 KB 384 (CA). For a commentary see Dicey and Morris, *The Conflict of Laws* by Collins *et al*, 13th edn (London, Sweet & Maxwell, 1999) 1378.

[21] Unreported.

[22] See the English case *Forsikringsaktieselskapet Vesta v Butcher* [1986] 2 All ER 488, [1986] Lloyd's Rep 179; on appeal sub nom *Forsikringsaktieselskapet Vesta v Butcher, Bain Dawles Ltd and Aquacultural Insurance Services Ltd* [1989] AC 852; affd [1989] AC 852, [1989] 11 LS Gaz R 42, HL. For a clear illustration of this point see Dicey and Morris, above, 1377. See also *Groupama Navigation et Transports v Catatumbo CA Seguros* [2000] 2 Lloyd's Rep 350 (CA).

[23] See *The Iran Vojdan* [1984] 2 Lloyd's Rep 380 at 385 *per* Bingham J; for a clear illustration of this point see Nygh, *Autonomy in International Contracts* (Oxford, Clarendon, 1999) 320.

[24] Nygh, *ibid*, 320.

from the words of Article 3, paragraph 2 that the Rome Convention also demands a choice be made at the beginning. According to Article 3, paragraph 2, the parties, in fact, can agree to subject the contract only to a law *other than that which previously governed it*. However, it is clear that despite the words of this provision there are good arguments in favour of the freedom of the parties to decide the applicable law at any time. As Boggiano[25] points out, in the absence of an express choice, the identification of the governing law will not be made until the judge determines it. Thus, it appears that the governing law of the insurance or reinsurance contract can be determined later with retrospective effect subject to considerations of fairness. Nevertheless, it is true that considerations of fairness might not always be easy to ascertain especially in consumer-insurance and most types of life-insurance contracts where the contractual parties are not in the same bargaining position.

The second question which deserves attention regards the protection of the vested rights and interests of third parties. With regards to this, Article 3, paragraph 2 provides that 'any variation by the parties of the law to be applied made after the conclusion of the contract shall not . . . affect the rights of third parties'. It is clear that this provision grants protection to the vested right of third parties.[26] However, it seems that the exclusive reference to the 'rights' in the text leaves no room for a wider interpretation encompassing the interests of third parties.[27] It follows that the interests of the third party beneficiary of a life-insurance contract cannot limit the 'retroactive effects' of a subsequent choice of law agreement.

The last question regards consent to the choice of law. It might happen, in fact, that the assured may be given cover under a policy which embodies a choice of law before coming into possession of the policy. Some questions, therefore, may arise as to the existence and validity of the consent of the parties to the choice of the applicable law.[28] Article 3, paragraph 4 provides that 'the existence and validity of the consent of the parties as to the choice of the applicable law shall be determined in accordance with the provisions of Articles 8, 9 and 11'. According to Article 8(2), a party who alleges he did not consent to the choice of law clause can rely upon the law of his habitual residence if it appears from the circumstances that it would not be reasonable to apply the chosen law. As Nygh[29] points out correctly, the application of the law of habitual residence is preferable to the law of the forum because it does not conflict with the reasonable expectations of the parties. It is clear, in fact, that the forum may be chosen

[25] Boggiano, *International Standard Contracts. The Price of Fairness* (Oxford, OUP, 1991) 104–6 at note 132.

[26] Kaye, *The New Private International Law of Contracts in the European Community* (Aldershot, Dartmouth, 1993) 158.

[27] *Cf*, Nygh, *Autonomy in International Contracts*, n 23 above, 321.

[28] See Morse in Facilides and Jessurun d'Oliveira (eds), *International Insurance Contracts in the EC* (Deventer, Kluwer Law and Taxation, 1993) 28.

[29] Nygh, *Autonomy in International Contracts*, n 23 above, 318.

by a claimant resident in a country where silence in some circumstances may be token consent.[30]

5. DOES THE *LEX MERCATORIA* APPLY TO REINSURANCE CONTRACTS AND INSURANCE CONTRACTS COVERING RISKS SITUATED OUTSIDE THE TERRITORIES OF THE MEMBER STATES OF THE EUROPEAN COMMUNITY?

(a) The Notion of *Lex Mercatoria*

The *lex mercatoria* has been triumphantly described as

> a system of law that does not rest exclusively on the institutions and local customs of any particular country, but consists of certain principles of equity and usages of trade which general convenience and a common sense of justice have established to regulate [international commercial activity],

as the

> rules of law which are common to all or most of the States engaged in international trade . . . and where such common rules are not ascertainable . . . the rule . . . which appears to the arbitrator to be the most appropriate and equitable . . . considering the laws of several legal systems,

or as

> a set of general principle and customary rules spontaneously referred to or elaborated in the framework of international trade, without reference to a particular national system of law.

These inconsistencies in the definition of the *lex mercatoria* exemplify the intensity of the discussions on the admissibility of *lex mercatoria* as law. Beyond those who questioned the existence of such transnational provisions, there seem to be two differing schools of thought. Positivists refuse to accept *lex mercatoria* as a legitimate source of law on the basis that by definition, it should be possible to implement law by a sovereign with the authority to prescribe force in support of its own decisions. The adversaries of the *lex mercatoria* also maintain that it does not provide a sufficiently substantial and concrete system: as such, it cannot be regarded as a legal order and is not suitable as a settlement for legal controversies.

Others take a more practical approach and maintain that because arbiters apply *lex mercatoria* to resolve disputes and parties take that law into account in drafting international contracts, the *lex mercatoria* is, at some level, law. At the other extreme, Lord Justice Mustill goes as far as to maintain that 'the rules of the *lex mercatoria* have a normative value which is independent of any one national system. The *lex mercatoria* constitutes an autonomous legal order'.

[30] *Ibid*, 318.

(b) The Applicability of the *Lex Mercatoria*

Professor Berthold Goldman maintains that the applicability of the *lex mercatoria* can result from (a) clauses in international contracts and (b) provisions validly applied by international awards.

The concern is here with the clauses in international insurance and reinsurance contracts which provide the application of the *lex mercatoria*, ie the application of transnational rules and customs elaborated in the framework of international insurance trade. These may involve references to the applicability of the *lex mercatoria* to insurance and reinsurance contracts under the 1980 Rome Convention.

Under Article 3, paragraph 1 the parties can choose the applicable law, and this probably relates to the law of the country. A problem arises, however, in situations where the parties indicate that the *lex mercatoria* must apply to all disputes between them or expressly exclude the application of every internal law, and provide for the application of internationally accepted principles of law governing contractual obligations. Such choices allude not to the internal law of any country but rather to a type of transnational law, to be determined by arbitrators. Such choices would therefore seem to be outside the parties' freedom to determine the applicable law. Similar conclusions apply to the cases where contractual clauses do not exclude the applicability of municipal law, but call for its combination with the *lex mercatoria*, referring either to the general principles of the *lex mercatoria* and of international law, or the usage of international trade or to both. For example, the applicable law clause in a insurance contract referring to the principles of Italian law in so far as they are in accord with the principles of international law, and lacking such conformity, to the general principles of law. In these cases the judge has to refer only to the Italian law as the governing law of the contract no matter whether its principles and rules can be considered to be in accord with the 'internationally accepted principles of law governing contractual obligations'[31] or the *lex mercatoria*.

6. DÉPEÇAGE OF INSURANCE AND REINSURANCE CONTRACTS

Parties can split issues away from the proper law of an insurance or reinsurance contract (*lex causae*) and subject them to different laws. It is worth noting that the possibility of *dépeçage* has long been established in common law countries.[32] However, for some other European States such as Italy this represents a change in the law.[33]

[31] *Deutsche Schachtbau- und Tiefbohrgesellschaft mbH v R'As al-Khaimah National Oil Co* [1990] 1 AC 295 (CA).

[32] *Kahler v Midland Bank Ltd* [1950] AC 24 to 42 *per* Lord McDermott, *Tomkison v First Pennsylvania Banking and Trust Co.* [1961] AC 1007.

[33] See inter alia Villani, *La Convenzione di Roma sulla legge applicabile ai contratti* (Bari, Cacucci, 1997) 150 *et seq*.

The Rome Convention in Article 3, paragraph 1 allows *dépeçage of a* 'severable part of the contract'.[34] According to the Giuliano and Lagarde Report,[35] the severance of the contract would only be allowed

> for a part of a contract which is independent and separable, in terms of the contract and not of the dispute, where that part has a closer connection with another country (for example, contracts for joint venture, complex contracts).

Therefore, the form, the capacity, the definition-of-loss clause or the payment of an insurance premium can be subject to different laws.

According to Article 3, paragraph 1, *dépeçage* of the contract must be express or demonstrated with reasonable certainty by the terms of the contract or the circumstances of the case. Therefore, in the absence of express or clear indications by the parties or in the text of the contract, the court shall presume that the insurance or reinsurance contract is governed by one law only.[36] It is worth noting that *dépeçage* has particular importance in reinsurance contracts, where the clauses of underlying contracts are often embodied with the objective that the contracts be interpreted 'back to back'.[37] *Dépeçage* is also relevant to marine insurance contracts, where the terms of foreign polices are often incorporated with the intention that these clauses be interpreted according to their original meaning.[38] In contrast, *dépeçage* does not have particular importance in life-insurance and motor insurance contracts, where there are usually no foreign terms. It goes without saying that the parties to the contract might expressly provide that all the terms are to be governed by the law applicable to the insurance or reinsurance contract and thus preclude such an interpretation.[39]

It is unclear whether the parties shall make more than one choice. According to Article 3, paragraph 1, the parties can select the 'law applicable to the whole or a part only of the contract'. Although these words suggest that the parties shall make one choice only, Dicey and Morris[40] maintain that the Rome Convention intends 'to allow the parties the choice of more than one law to govern different parts'.

[34] See Morse (1982) 2 *Yearbook of European Law* 107, 117–19.

[35] The Giuliano and Lagarde Report, n 12 above, 17.

[36] See the explanation given in the non-Convention case *Jones v Steam Navigation Co* (1924) 2 KB 730, at 733 'it is not probable that parties would intend that some parts of the contract should be governed by the law of one country and other parts by the law of another country.'

[37] See Merkin and Rodger, *EC Insurance Law* (London and New York, Longman, 1997) 143.

[38] See Celle (1998) *Diritto del commercio internazionale*, 649 et seq.

[39] See Merkin and Rodger, *EC Insurance Law*, n 37 above, 143.

[40] Dicey and Morris, n 1 above, 1213. See also Lagarde (1991) *Revue critique de droit international privé*, 309.

7. THE LAW APPLICABLE TO INSURANCE AND REINSURANCE CONTRACTS IN THE ABSENCE OF AN EXPRESS CHOICE

A choice of the law applicable to insurance and reinsurance contracts can be demonstrated by the terms of the contract or the circumstances of the case. Article 3, paragraph 1 demands that a choice of law must be demonstrated 'with reasonable certainty'. According to the Giuliano and Lagarde Report,[41] this provision 'does not permit the court to infer a choice of law that the parties might have made where they had no clear intention of making such a choice'. The judge cannot impute an intention to parties who have never thought about choice of law but must ascertain their actual intention.

The Giuliano and Lagarde Report[42] suggests that a choice of law may be derived, inter alia, from the adoption of a standard form for the contract 'which is known to be governed by a particular system of law even though there is no express statement to this effect, such as a Lloyd's policy of marine insurance'. A choice of law may be derived also from a previous course of dealing between the parties under contracts containing an express choice of law.[43] This may, for instance, be the case in an insurance contract concluded by a broker or an agent acting on behalf of a trader. It is possible, in fact, that

> a previous course of dealing between the parties under contracts containing an express choice of law may leave the court in no doubt that the contract in question is to be governed by the law previously chosen where the choice of law clause has been omitted in circumstances which do not indicate a deliberate change of policy by the parties.[44]

A choice of forum clause is a third example of such an implied choice.[45] English law at least has a tendency to accept that whoever chooses the forum, chooses the law of the forum as the governing law.[46] A fourth example is found in the case where there is an arbitration clause indicating the place of arbitration. This may, for instance, be the case in a reinsurance contract. Another good example of such a choice of law by the parties is a reference to particular rules of a legal system.

A choice of law cannot be derived, however, from the fact that an insurance or reinsurance contract has been drawn up in a particular language. The use of a particular language for an insurance or reinsurance contract, in fact, may be justified for different reasons: such as the familiarity of the parties with the language chosen, the popularity of that language in the place where the contract is concluded, the popularity of that language in the insurance and reinsurance sectors and so on. That is generally true for marine insurance and reinsurance

[41] The Giuliano and Lagarde Report, n 12 above 17.
[42] *Ibid*, 17.
[43] *Ibid*, 17.
[44] *Ibid*, 17.
[45] See *Egon Oldendorff v Libera Corpn* [1995] 2 Lloyd's Rep 64.
[46] See Cheshire and North, n 3 above, 562.

contracts which are often drafted in English because most of them are concluded in London and because English is the most popular language in international commercial transactions.

8. THE LAW APPLICABLE TO INSURANCE AND REINSURANCE CONTRACTS IN THE ABSENCE OF A CHOICE

Article 4 of the Rome Convention deals with the problem of the applicable law in the absence of choice. Article 4, par. 1 provides that

> to the extent that the law applicable to the contract has not been chosen in accordance with Article 3, the contract shall be governed by the law of the country with which it is most closely connected.

The presumption of the characteristic performance, which is used to ascertain the closest connection is rebuttable.[47] It is arguable from the text of Article 4, paragraph 1 that the judge must apply the law of the country with which the contract is most closely connected not only when the parties have not chosen the law applicable to their contract but also where the choice of law does not concern the whole contract or the choice is void under Article 3, paragraph 4.

Some difficulties may arise in these cases where the judge must determine the law of the country with which the contract of insurance or reinsurance is most closely connected. It seems that the court must look at the insurance contract 'as a whole weighing all the relevant factors'.[48] It appears also that the factors must be evaluated objectively. The intentions of the contractual parties, which are essential to the application of Article 3, are of no importance here. There are a few good examples of factors the court should take into consideration in ascertaining the law of the country with which the insurance or reinsurance contract is most closely connected. The law of the place of the habitual residence of the assured is the first example. It is clear that the country of the habitual residence of the assured could rely on the fact that the vast majority of life-insurance contracts are concluded by assureds who are eager to insure themselves against events that might happen in their country of residence. On the other hand, it is clear that there is no reason to apply the law of the country of the habitual residence of the assured, as the law with which the contract has its closest connection, if the assured uses the policy to cover himself against events which might happen in a third country. A second example is the law of the place where the risk is situated. As already stated, the EC Insurance Directives refer to the place of the risk as a criterion for the determination of the governing law. Moreover, the criterion of the risk has been used by the drafters of the Rome Convention in Article 1, paragraph 3 to distinguish the contracts of insurance which are

[47] Arts 4(2) and 4(5) of the Rome Convention; see also the Giuliano and Lagarde Report, n 12 above, at 19–23.

[48] Cheshire and North, n 3 above, 569.

covered by the Convention from those excluded from its scope. Thus, there is no reason to prevent the application of the law of the place where the risk is situated. The law of the place where the broker or the agent acting on behalf of the insured has his principal place of business is a third example of factors the court should take into consideration in ascertaining the law of the country with which the insurance contract is most closely connected. Especially in the marine insurance and reinsurance sectors it is quite common for contracts to be concluded between insurance companies and brokers or agents acting on behalf of the insured.[49] Due to the fact that the broker usually has the power to choose the insured's counter-party and the type of insurance policy, it is clear that the law of his place of business may be closely connected with the contract. A 'follow London' clause in an insurance policy is a fourth and final example of factors the court should take into consideration in English law, even where the same policy contained a 'New York suable' clause aiming to give the assured a choice between English and American law.[50] On the contrary, the mere fact that an insurance or reinsurance contract is concluded in a particular place is not sufficient to make the law of that place connected with the contract. As has been pointed out correctly in the English case *Amin Rasheed Shipping Corp v Kuwait Insurance Co*[51]

> in these days of modern methods of communications where the international contracts are so frequently negotiated by telex whether what turns out to be the final offer is accepted in the country where one telex is situated or in the country where the other telex is installed is often a mere matter of chance. In the result the *lex contractus* has lost much of the significance in determining the proper law of the contract that it had close on 50 years ago.[52]

9. THE CHARACTERISTIC PERFORMANCE OF INSURANCE AND REINSURANCE CONTRACTS

Article 4(2) lays down the presumption that the contract is most closely connected with the country where the party who is to effect the performance which is characteristic of the contract has his habitual residence or, in the case of a body corporate or unincorporate, its central administration.[53] Despite the sim-

[49] See Celle (1998) *Diritto del commercio internazionale*, 673.

[50] See Tetley, *International conflict of laws* (Montreal, Blais, 1994) 360 note 122.

[51] [1984] AC 50 at p 60 as quoted by Celle, above n 49, note 134.

[52] For a clear exposition of the role of the place of the conclusion of the contract a connecting criterion in the traditional choice of law rules for insurance and reinsurance contracts see Rabel, *The Conflict of Laws: A Comparative study*, vol III (Ann Arbor, University of Michigan Press, 1947) 319 *et seq*.

[53] See Carillo Pozo, *El contrato internacional: la prestación característica* (Colectiones España, 1994); Magagni, *La prestazione caratteristica nella Convenzione di Roma del 19 giugno 1980* (Milano, Giuffrè, 1989); Cheshire and North, n 3 above, 569–74; Dicey and Morris, n 1 above, 1233–34; Hill, *The Law Relating to International Commercial Disputes* (London, LLP, 1998) 450–53; Juenger, *The EEC Convention on the Law Applicable to Contractual Obligations: An*

plicity of this rule, which introduces a rigid mechanism for the determination of the applicable law, a number of questions arise from the concept of characteristic performance. First, it must be pointed out that the presumption applies well to simple contracts, such as sale of goods, but it will not be easy to distinguish a single characteristic performance in a contract that is of a more complicated character,[54] particularly if it involves as insurance and reinsurance contracts do, mutual obligations of confidence and collaboration. Secondly, it is questionable whether there is always such a close link between the contract and the place of habitual residence of the person who is to effect the characteristic performance. The Rome Convention does not contain a definition of 'characteristic performance' either in Article 4 or in other provisions. It is worth noting that a different approach has been adopted in the 1987 Swiss statute of private international law. Although this statute does not define the concept of 'characteristic performance', it provides, a set of sub-rules which indicate the characteristic performance for a large number of contracts.[55]

Legal writers are very divided as to the identification of the characteristic performance. References have been made to the 'essence of the obligation', 'socio-economic function', and 'centre of gravity' of the contract. It goes without saying that this lack of objectivity has generated different opinions with regard to the characteristic performance of insurance and reinsurance contracts.

The Giuliano and Lagarde Report[56] suggests that the characteristic performance of an insurance contract rests with the insurer because it is the insurer who provides 'insurance services'. Dicey and Morris argue on the basis of analogy with an ordinary insurance contract that the party who is to effect the performance that is characteristic of a reinsurance contract is the re-insurer.[57] But if this is true, then the characteristic performance will be that of the insurer or re-insurer even though, in the event of the happening of a risk encompassed by the policy, the insurer's performance or re-insurer's performance will be the payment of money, something that the Report states cannot be characteristic performance.[58] In sharp contrast with this view, authors such as Clarke,[59]

American Assessment in North (ed), *Contract Conflict: the Rome Convention on the Choice of Law for Contracts* (London, Sweet & Maxwell, 2001) 300–2; Plender, *The European Contracts Convention: The EEC Convention on the Law Applicable to Contractual Obligations: A Comparative Study* (Amsterdam and Oxford, North Holland, 1982), paras 6.09–6.18.

[54] See Juenger, *ibid* in North (ed), *Contract Conflicts*, note 295, 301.

[55] See Art 117(3)

[56] The Giuliano and Lagarde Report, n 12 above 20; see also Plender, *The European Contracts Convention*, n 53 above, 111; Forlati Picchio, *La legge applicabile al contratti di assicurazione* in Treves (ed), *Verso una disciplina comunitaria della legge applicabile alle obbligazioni contrattuali* (Padova, CEDAM, 1983) 155; O'Dowd (1991) *British Insurance Law Association Journal* 16; Kaye, *The new private international law* (Aldershot, Dartmouth, 1993) 140.

[57] Dicey and Morris, n 1 above, 1380 and note 89. See also the English case *Tiernan v Magen Insurance Co Ltd* [2000] ILPr 517, 523, where it was maintained that the characteristic performance of a re-insurance contract was that of the re-insurer.

[58] See the Giuliano and Lagarde Report, n 12 above 20. For these remarks see Dicey and Morris, n 1 above, 1345.

[59] Clarke (1984) *Journal of Business Law* 545 at 561.

Merkin[60] and Villani[61] maintain that due to the subjectivity and inconsistency pervading the concept of characteristic performance no characteristic performance can be identified for insurance and reinsurance contracts. This conclusion is certainly true for co-insurance contracts which are concluded between an insured and two or more insurance companies. In these cases, in fact, the recourse to the presumption of the characteristic performance would not lead to the application of one law but every law of the places where each co-insurer has its central administration. According to Vischer, where there are two performances both requiring the payment of money, as in the contract of insurance, the performance of the party carrying the greater risk is decisive: the insurer 'appears to be socially deeper involved'[62] in the contract. But Lipstein[63] argues that risk-bearing is a 'very occasional' and 'incongruous' indicator of the characteristic performance. Moreover, it is not clear which is the risk that the court should take into consideration to determine the characteristic performance. Some uncertainties in this respect may arise when the insurance contract is concluded by an insurance company writing life insurance contracts. Should the court in these situations refer to the mortality or the investment risk? In *Amin Rasheed Corporation v Kuwait Insurance Co*,[64] a case decided prior to the Rome Convention entering into force, the Court of Appeal held that the principal performances under a contract of insurance are the payment of the premium and the settlement of claims. Therefore, it is arguable from the fact that the person who pays the premium is the assured, that the characteristic performance should be reallocated to the assured in some cases.

It might appear from this summary of views on the characteristic performance of insurance and reinsurance contracts that there is room for different approaches in the courts of the Contracting States towards the interpretation of this rule. A restriction on any such freedom in the courts can be found, however, in the text of Article 18 of the Rome Convention.This provides that:

> in the interpretation and application of the preceding uniform rules, regard shall be had to their *international character* and to the desirability of achieving *uniformity* in their interpretation and application.[65]

This means that, when interpreting the concept of characteristic performance, a court of a Contracting State should also have regard to the practice of the courts

[60] Merkin, *Insurance Contract Law*, 1987, vol 2 (Kingston upon Thames, Kluwer, 1995) para D.4. 2–24.

[61] Villani, *La convenzione di Roma sulla legge applicabile ai contratti* (Bari, Cacucci, 1997) 98.

[62] Reproduced as quoted in D'Oliveira (1977) 25 *American Journal of Comparative Law* 303 at 314; see also Celle, *I contratti di assicurazione grandi rischi nel diritto internazionale privato* (Padova, CEDAM, 2000) 200.

[63] Lipstein, (1981) 3 *New York Journal of International Law and Business*, 402 at 407. For similar remarks see also the Law Commission and the Scottish Law Commission, *Private International Law Report on the Choice of Law Rules in the Draft Non-Life Insurance Service Directive*, April 1979, 66.

[64] [1984] AC 50 62–63, *per* Lord Diplock.

[65] My emphasis.

of other Contracting States. Nevertheless, it is clear that a reference to foreign practice is not always possible or easy, because of the differences in language and the objective difficulties in finding foreign authorities.[66]

10. THE ROME CONVENTION AND THE LAW APPLICABLE TO CO-INSURANCE CONTRACTS

It is quite common, especially in the sector of marine insurance, that contractual counter-parties of the insured are two or more insurance companies acting in the sector.[67] It is submitted that the law applicable to such contracts concluded between two or more insurers and the insured (co-insurance contracts) must be determined according to the choice of law rules of the Rome Convention.[68] However, due to the fact that Article 1, paragraph 3 excludes from the scope of the Rome Convention *any type* of direct insurance contract covering risks situated in the territories of the Member States of the European Communities, it is clear that the rules in the Convention only apply to co-insurance contracts covering risks localised outside the territories of the Member States of the European Communities. The choice of law provisions of the Non-Life and Life Insurance Directives apply, depending on the circumstances, to the co-insurance contracts covering risks situated in the territories of the Member States of the European Communities.

It is unclear whether the governing law of the insurance contract will apply to the relationship between co-insurers.[69] Some uncertainties arise from the fact that agreements between co-insurers do not always concern the conclusion of a single contract but may concern an indeterminate number of contracts with different counter-parties.[70] When the scope of a co-insurer's agreement is not the conclusion of a specific contract of insurance it is hard to maintain that such an agreement has to be interpreted as a clause of the insurance contract in which it is embodied and therefore has to be submitted to the same law as governs that contract. This is true despite the fact that co-insurers's agreements are *usually* embodied in the text of a specific contract of insurance. Therefore, the court should apply the governing law of the insurance contract only to the co-insurers's agreement concerning the conclusion of a specific contract of insurance whether or not it is embodied in the text of the contract. If a co-insurers's

[66] For an illuminating exposition of the questions that arise from the application of foreign law with special reference to the problems related to the use of foreign law in the English courts see Fentiman, *Foreign law in English courts: pleading, proof, and choice of law* (Oxford, Clarendon, 1998).

[67] See Righetti, *Trattato di diritto marittimo* (Milano, Giuffré, 1994) 1110.

[68] See Araniz (1987) *Revista española de seguros* 70 *et seq*; Fuentes Camacho, *Los Contratos de Seguro y el Derecho Internacional Privado en la Unión Europea* (Madrid, Citivas, 1999) 142 *et seq*.

[69] See Celle, *I contratti di assicurazione grandi rischi nel diritto internazionale privato*, n 16 above, 706.

[70] *Ibid*, 706.

agreement is concerned not with the conclusion of a single contract but an indeterminate number of contracts of insurance the court must ascertain the proper law of the co-insurers's agreement by applying the rules in the Convention directly to it.[71]

11. THE LAW APPLICABLE TO INSURANCE CONTRACTS CONCLUDED BY CONSUMERS

Article 5 of the Rome Convention applies to

> a contract the object of which is the supply of goods or services to a person ('the consumer') for a purpose which can be regarded as being outside his trade or profession, or a contract for the provision of credit for that object.[72]

Since Article 5 applies to contracts for the supply of services, it can apply to contracts of insurance where insurance is provided to the insured for a purpose that can be regarded as being outside his trade or profession.[73] It is clear that some life and non-life insurance contracts might, therefore, fall within its scope. However, it goes without saying that this article does not apply to reinsurance and co-assurance contracts in which parties are in the same bargaining position. Article 5 applies only when the four conditions set out therein are satisfied.

First, the insurance service must be supplied for a purpose which can be regarded as outside the insured's trade or profession. It is arguable from the text of Article 5, paragraph 1 that this provision will still apply if the insured is acting partly within its trade or profession but not 'primarily' so. Nevertheless, according to the Giuliano and Lagarde Report,[74] Article 5 will not apply if the insurer who supplies the services reasonably believes that the insured was acting within its trade or profession when, in fact, he was not.

Secondly, the consumer protection provisions will not apply when the insurance services are to be supplied *exclusively* outside the country of the insured's habitual residence.[75] However, it is clear that Article 5 applies if the insurance services are to be supplied *partially* outside the country of the insured's habitual residence.[76] It has been questioned whether services are supplied by the insurer

[71] For the same conclusion Celle, *ibid*, 706.

[72] See H Bureau, *Le droit de la consommation transfrontière* (Doctoral thesis, Montpellier, 1998); Weber-Stecher, *Internationales Konsumvertragsrecht* (Berlin, Beck, 1997); Erauw in Šarcevic (ed), *International Contracts and Conflict of Laws* (London, Graham & Trotman, 1990) 82–85; Hartley, *Consumer protection provisions in the EEC Convention* in North (ed), *Contract Conflicts* (Amsterdam and Oxford, North Holland, 1982) 111 *et seq*; Morse (1992) 41 *International and Comparative Law Quarterly* 1, 2–11; Plender, *The European Contracts Convention*, n 53 above, paras 7.01–7.24; Kaye, *The new Private International Law of Contracts* (Aldershot, Dartmouth, 1993) 203–20.

[73] Merkin and Rodger, *EC Insurance Law* (London and New York, Longman, 1997) 146.

[74] The Giuliano and Lagarde Report, n 12 above, 23.

[75] Art 5(4)(b).

[76] Merkin and Rodger, *EC Insurance Law*, n 73 above, 146.

exclusively in such a country, for example, when a visitor to the United States obtains health cover from an English insurer the cover extends only to events occurring in the United States.[77] It appears that Article 5 does not apply in such a case and therefore the efficacy of any choice of law must be governed by Article 3. The application of the law of the country of the insured's habitual residence, in fact, would conflict with the purpose of Article 5(4)(b) which is to circumscribe the sphere of application of this law to services connected with the country of the insured's habitual residence.

Thirdly, Article 5 will not apply if in the country of the insured's habitual residence the conclusion of the contract was not preceded by a specific invitation addressed to him or by advertising. As paragraph 2(a) states:

> notwithstanding the provisions of Article 3, a choice of law made by the parties shall not have the result of depriving the consumer of the protection afforded to him by the mandatory rules of the law of the country in which he has his habitual residence: if in that country the conclusion of the contract was preceded by a specific invitation addressed to him or by advertising, and he had taken in that country all the steps necessary on his part for the conclusion of the contract.

According to the Giuliano and Lagarde Report,[78] the invitation must have been directed at that country. Therefore, if a policyholder living in England replies to an advertisement in an Australian publication, even if the publication is sold in England, the consumer protection provisions will apply only if the publication was a special edition intended for the Member States of the European Union. It is unclear whether the supplier of an insurance service must have intended to advertise to the insured in the latter's country of habitual residence.[79] The Giuliano and Lagarde Report[80] suggests that such an intention is essential. Moreover, the Report[81] clarifies that the invitation shall be made directly, via company literature or through middlemen. It appears that the 'steps' necessary for the conclusion of an insurance contract may include the completion of the proposed form,[82] writing or any action taken in consequence of an offer or advertisement.[83]

Finally, the consumer protection provisions will not apply if the other party or his agent did not receive the consumer's order in the country of the consumer's habitual residence. The word 'agent' is likely to cover all persons acting on behalf of the trader,[84] thus it is not essential that the legal relationship

[77] Morse, 'Party Autonomy in International Insurance Contract Law' in Richert Facilides and Jessurun d'Oliveira (eds), *International Insurance Contract Law in the EC* (Deventer, Kluwer Law and Taxation Publishers, 1993) 35.

[78] See the Giuliano and Lagarde Report, n 12 above, 23–24.

[79] See Morse, n 77 above, note 75, 33.

[80] The Giuliano and Lagarde Report, n 12 above, at 24.

[81] *Ibid*, at 24.

[82] See Merkin and Rodger, *EC Insurance Law*, n 37 above 147.

[83] See the Giuliano and Lagarde Report, n 12 above, 24.

[84] The Giuliano and Lagarde Report, n 12 above, 24.

of principal and agent exist.[85] It covers branches[86] and it can extend to brokers.

It is worth noting that the protective provisions of Article 5 can apply to a contract concluded by an insured-consumer even if he is not resident in a Contracting State. This conclusion can be derived from the universal scope of the Rome Convention. According to Article 2 (Application of law of non-Contracting States) 'any law indicated by this Convention shall be applied whether or not it is the law of a Contracting State'.[87]

With respect to parties of unequal bargaining power, Article 5 states that a choice of law cannot, as a rule, deprive a consumer of the protection of mandatory rules of the country of his habitual residence. Article 5 does not clarify the meaning of the words 'mandatory rules', thereby referring back to the definition in Article 3, paragraph 3 of the Convention, that is, rules which cannot be derogated from by contract. It can be observed that Article 5 does not demand these rules to be mandatory in the sense that they apply irrespective of the law chosen by the parties or objectively designed at by the court. If a choice of law has not been made, the law applicable to the contract shall be the law of the consumer's habitual residence.[88]

12. THE LAW APPLICABLE TO MULTIPLE RISK POLICIES

A word needs to be said about the governing law of multiple risk policies, ie which insure against risks located in several Non-Member States of the European Community. A single policy may, for example, insure dwelling houses located in Australia, New Zealand and the United States of America. These states may require that any fire insurance policy on buildings situated within their territory be in a certain statutory form. If so, the single policy will normally include the special statutory requirements of the several states concerned. Most courts would be likely to deal with such a case, at least with respect to most issues, as if it concerned three policies, each insuring an individual risk.[89] Accordingly, if the house located in Australia was damaged by fire, it is thought that the judge would presumably ascertain the duties and obligations of the parties under the policy, at least with respect to most issues, in accordance with Australian law. In any event, that part of the policy which embodies the special statutory form of a state would be formulated in accordance with the rules of construction of that state.

[85] See Morse, n 77 above, note 75, 34.

[86] *Ibid*, 34.

[87] See Forlati Picchio (1983) *Diritto communitario e degli scambi internazionali*, 54.

[88] Art 5(3).

[89] See the non-Convention case of *Forsikringsaktieselskapet Vesta v Butcher* [1986] 2 All ER 488; on appeal sub nom *Forsikringsaktieselskapet Vesta v Butcher, Bain Dawles Ltd and Aquacultural Insurance Services Ltd* [1989] AC 852; affd [1989] AC 852, [1989] 11 LS Gaz R 42, HL.

13. EVASION OF LAW

A form of abuse of party autonomy occurs when the insurer and insured intentionally change or insert new connecting factors in order to substantiate their choice of a foreign law that is more favourable. In such circumstances, the court may refuse to apply a foreign law designated by them on the grounds of evasion of the law (*fraude à la loi*).

Today the evasion of law clause is sometimes considered as a traditional correcting factor which is no longer necessary. As a result, such clauses are not always embodied into the most recent provisions of private international law.[90] According to von Overbeck, they are unnecessary because the same goal is now pursued by other means.[91] In such cases, courts and tribunals may refuse to respect the parties' choice of law on the ground of the lack of good faith.

Other traditional cases of evasion of law are now treated as a special category of evasion of the mandatory provisions. For example, if the parties intentionally conclude a contract of insurance in the United Kingdom instead of Italy in order to evade the requirements and conditions for insurance in regard to the form of the transaction, Italian courts will not take into consideration the place where the insurance contract is concluded but will apply the mandatory rules of Italian law on the formal requirements for such transactions.

The institution of evasion of law was not particularly well developed in English law:[92] nonetheless, English courts do not hesitate to refuse a choice of law clause if that law was designated for the objective of evading mandatory rules. According to North,[93] commercial actors normally have a good reason for choosing a certain law to govern their contract. This is undoubtedly true for operators in the fields of insurance and reinsurance. Therefore he suggests courts confirm the choice of the parties unless there is a good reason to refuse it. In his opinion, two reasons that are sufficient to justify judicial intervention with the parties' choice of law are lack of good faith and evasion of mandatory provisions.[94] The issue of evasion, however, is just one aspect of the intricate system of mandatory rules, the most relevant mechanism restricting party autonomy.

[90] This does not mean that the evasion of law clauses cannot be found in modern statute of private international law. For further references see Šarčević, *Choice of law issues* in Šarčević and Volken (eds), *International Contracts and Payments* (London, Graham & Trotman, 1991) 117–18.

[91] Von Overbeck, *La contribution de la Conférence de La Haye au development du droit international privé* [1992] Hague Recueil 208.

[92] Fawcett (1990) *Cambridge Law Journal* 44–45.

[93] North, *Reform but not Revolution* [1990] Hague Recueil 167.

[94] *Ibid.*

14. THE APPLICATION OF MANDATORY RULES TO INSURANCE AND REINSURANCE CONTRACTS

It is well known that common law, and especially civil law systems, lay down legal rules (known as 'mandatory rules') which cannot be derogated from by contract.[95] In English law, some international mandatory rules, ie rules which apply despite the parties' choice of the law applicable to the contract, have been introduced to avoid unfairness and protect national interests.[96] Section 27 of the Unfair Contract Terms Act 1977 provides that the Act has effect if the choice of law appears 'to have been imposed wholly or mainly for the purpose of enabling the party imposing it to evade the operation of this Act'. According to the House of Lords in *The Hollandia*[97] the Carriage of Goods by Sea Act 1971 contains an anti-evasion provision implementing the Hague-Visby Rules. However, none of these provisions are relevant in the context of insurance. But the Financial Services Act 1986 provides some international mandatory rules which apply to insurance contracts.[98] This Act authorised the Securities and Investments Board to make the rules that are to be followed when a person who has entered into an investment agreement with an authorised person decides to rescind the agreement (ie cancellation rules).[99] International mandatory rules are of greater relevance to direct insurance than to reinsurance because of the absence in the reinsurance contracts of a party in a weaker bargaining position. In the field of direct insurance these provisions are particularly relevant to life insurance and motor insurance contracts. The Rome Convention provides that mandatory rules shall apply in three well defined sets of circumstances.[100]

First, as a result of Article 3, paragraph 3 where all the elements (excluding the parties' choice of law) relevant to the situation are connected with one country only, but the parties have chosen the law of a different country, the parties' choice of law 'shall not . . . prejudice the application' of the former country's mandatory rules. Some continental commentators[101] have held that Article 3, paragraph 3 does not demand the mandatory rules being applied in all cases. According to Frigessi di Rattalma who maintained this thesis by examining the impact of Article 3, paragraph 3 on insurance contracts, the choice of law made

[95] See Bonomi, *Le norme imperative nel diritto internazionale privato: Considerazioni sulla Convenzione europea sulla legge applicabile alle obbligazioni contrattuali* (Zurich, Schulthess, 1998); Cambó, *Contracto internacional y Derecho imperativo extranjero* (Madrid, Aranzadi, 1992).

[96] See Fawcett (1990) 49 1 *Cambridge Law Journal* 44; Hartley, *Mandatory Rules in International Contracts: The Common Law Approach* [1997] Hague Recueil 266, 345.

[97] [1983] 1 AC 565.

[98] See MacNeil (1995) 44 *International and Comparative Law Quarterly* 39.

[99] *Ibid*, 39 *et seq*.

[100] But see also above para 11 for a discussion on the application of the mandatory rules to consumer transactions.

[101] Treves in Jayme and Picchio Forlati, *Giurisdizione e legge applicabile ai contratti nella CEE* (Padova, CEDAM, 1990) 30; Frigessi di Rattalma, *Il contratto internazionale di assicurazione* (Padova, CEDAM, 1990) 178 *et seq*.

by the parties cannot deprive the insured of the protection afforded to him by the mandatory rules of the country most closely connected with the contract. This conclusion seems to be suggested by the Italian version of Article 3, paragraph 3 which does not refer to the 'application' of the mandatory provisions but only states that the choice of a foreign law cannot override the mandatory rules of the country which is most closely connected with the contract. However, the same conclusion cannot be derived from the English version of Article 3, paragraph 3. The words 'prejudice the *application*' in Article 3, paragraph 3 indicate that the mandatory rules referred to in this provision must apply in *any* circumstance in which the parties have chosen a foreign law and *all* the elements relevant to the contract are connected with *one country only*.[102]

Secondly, as a result of Article 7, paragraph 1 where the insurance or reinsurance contract has a close connection with another country from that whose law is applicable, the judge may give effect to the former country's mandatory rules, but only in so far as the former country's law demands the rules be applied whatever the governing law of the contract. In deciding whether to apply these rules the court must have regard mainly to the nature, purpose and consequences of their application or non-application. However, it must be stressed that there is no general rule to determine whether a provision is internationally mandatory. The Giuliano and Lagarde Report[103] suggests that a real link between the contract as a whole and the other country is essential. According to this Report, such a real connection exists when the contract is to be performed in that other country or when one party is resident or has its main place of business in that country. As the criteria to be applied by the judge to define a 'close connection' are not free from ambiguities there is room for different interpretations by the national courts and forum shopping by the parties.[104] Because of these ambiguities Article 22(1)(a) of the Rome Convention provides that any Contracting State may reserve the right not to apply Article 7(1). Germany, Ireland, Luxembourg and the United Kingdom have entered such a reservation and therefore Article 7, paragraph 1 shall not have the force of law in these countries.

Finally, as a result of Article 7, paragraph 2, the rules of the law of the forum are mandatory irrespective of the law otherwise applicable to the contract. This Article provides that 'nothing in this Convention shall restrict the application of the rules of the law of the forum in a situation where they are mandatory . . .'. The Giuliano and Lagarde Report[105] states that this provision 'merely deals with the application of mandatory rules in a different way from paragraph 1' and was included mainly to appease certain states concerned by the implications of the Rome Convention on this subject. But Article 7, paragraph 2 is different from Article 7, paragraph 1 because it does not require a particular connection

[102] See especially Cheshire and North, n 3 above, 576.
[103] See the Giuliano and Lagarde Report, n 12 above, 27.
[104] See Cheshire and North, n 3 above, 584.
[105] See the Giuliano and Lagarde Report, n 12 above, 27.

between the law of the forum and the case. Thus it grants the judge a wider discretion to take into account mandatory rules. However it is not sufficient merely to show that the forum has a mandatory provision (ie a provision that cannot be derogated from by contract). It has to demonstrated that what is involved is 'a situation where [the provisions] are mandatory irrespective of the law otherwise applicable to the contract'.[106]

15. PUBLIC POLICY QUESTIONS

In addition to the provisions concerning mandatory rules, Article 16 allows the judge to refuse the application of any rule of the governing law if this would be 'manifestly incompatible' with the public policy of the forum.[107] Carter defines public policy as an 'escape route, from the application of the relevant choice of law rule, or from recognition of a foreign judgment which would otherwise be entitled to it'.[108] The words 'manifestly incompatible' in Article 16 suggest that the conflict between the fundamental principles of justice of the forum (ie the public policy) and a rule of the applicable law must be so obvious that any investigation would be superfluous.

There are a few good examples of situations in which public policy or *ordre public* may be invoked in insurance and reinsurance cases. Insurance on the property of an alien enemy national in time of armed conflict, though valid under its foreign applicable law, should be unenforceable due to the fact that a contract involving a trading relationship with an alien enemy is illegal as it will aid the enemy.[109] A second example is found in the situation where the insurance or reinsurance contract constitutes the commission of an unlawful act or seeks to indemnify someone for doing so. It appears that the court should apply this principle even if the insurance or reinsurance contract is governed by a foreign law which would consider the insurance as valid.[110] The rule that a contract, whether lawful by its governing law or not, is invalid if performance of it is illegal according to the law of the place where the insurance or reinsurance contract is to be performed is a third and final example of a situation in which public policy can be invoked in insurance and reinsurance cases.[111]

[106] See Cheshire and North, n 3 above, 579.

[107] See Philip (1978) Hague Recueil 1 at 55 *et seq*; Mosconi, *Exceptions to the operation of choice of law rules* [1989] V Hague Recueil 9; Plender, *The European Contracts Convention*, n 53 above, paras 9.13–19.15; Kaye, *The European Private International Law*, n 15 above, 345–50; Dicey and Morris, n 1 above, 1277–84;Villani, *La convenzione di Roma*, n 61 above, 188 *et seq*.

[108] See Carter, (1993) 42 *International and Comparative Law Quarterly* 1.

[109] See Morse in Rubino-Sammartano and Morse (eds), *Public Policy in Transnational Relationships* (New York, Transnational Publications, 1991) 85.

[110] *Ibid*, 85

[111] *Ibid*, 86.

16. THE SPHERE OF THE *LEX CONTRACTUS 'RATIONE MATERIAE'*: ARTICLE 10(1)

Article 10, paragraph 1 concerns the scope of the law applicable to insurance and reinsurance contracts under Articles 3 (choice of law), 4 (applicable law in the absence of choice), 5 (consumer contracts choice of law and applicable law in the absence of choice), 6 (employment contracts choice of law and applicable law in the absence thereof) and 12 (law applicable between voluntary assignor and assignee of rights). It provides that:

> the law applicable to a contract by virtue of Articles 3 to 6 and 12 of this Convention shall govern in particular:
> (a) interpretation;
> (b) performance;
> (c) within the limits of the powers conferred on the court by its procedural law, the consequences of breach, including the assessment of damages in so far as it is governed by rules of law;
> (d) the various ways of extinguishing obligations and prescription and limitation of actions;
> (e) the consequences of nullity of the contract;[112]

It is arguable from the use of the words 'in particular' that the list of matters in Article 10 is not to be considered as exhaustive, but, nevertheless, the matters inserted in the list are able to be regarded as governed by the applicable law.[113] Though not included in the list in Article 10 the modification of the obligations arising from the contract must be regarded as governed by the applicable law.[114] Thus the need for a preliminary agreement between the parties to modify the duties and rights arising from an insurance contract must be ascertained according to the law governing the contract.[115]

[112] See Plender, *The European contracts convention: the Rome Convention on the Choice of Law for Contracts* (London, Sweet & Maxwell, 1991) paras 11.01–11.17; Kaye, *The New Private International Law of Contracts*, n 72 above, 297–310; Lagarde in North (ed), *Contract Conflicts* (Amsterdam and Oxford, North Holland, 1982) 49 *et seq*; Villani, *La convenzione di Roma*, n 61 above, 101 *et seq*; Cheshire and North, n 3 above, 595.

[113] See especially Kaye, *The New Private International Law of Contracts*, n 72 above, 297.

[114] See Plender, *The European Contracts Convention*, n 112 above, 170; see also Vecchi, *Article 10* in Bianca and Giardina (eds) (1994) *Le Nuove Leggi Civili Commentate* 1037 *et seq*.

[115] See Claret, *Contrats d'assurance et conflits de loi en droit communautaire* (Doctoral thesis, Université de Lille, 1994) 230.

17. THE LAW APPLICABLE TO THE FORMATION AND THE VALIDITY OF THE INSURANCE AND REINSURANCE CONTRACTS

According to Article 8(1)

> the existence and validity of a contract, or of any term of a contract, shall be determined by the law which would govern it under this Convention if the contract or term were valid.[116]

The borderline between questions relating to the formation of a contract and questions relating to its validity is a disputed one.[117] Since both the formation and the validity of insurance and reinsurance contracts are governed by the same law the distinction has no practical relevance under the Rome Convention. Nevertheless, for reasons of convenience the term 'existence' will be restricted to the question whether the insurer and insured have reached an agreement, therefore encompassing offer and acceptance and the requirement of consensus. The term 'validity' encompasses issues such as actual consent *in idem* (including vitiating factors such as fraud, error and duress), cause, consideration, certainty and illegality.

18. ARTICLE 8 OF THE ROME CONVENTION: THE FORMATION OF THE INSURANCE CONTRACT

Article 8 provides that issues relating to the formation of insurance and reinsurance contracts (with the exception of formal validity and capacity) are governed by the law that would govern them if they were valid (the 'putative proper law'), albeit that under certain circumstances Article 8(2) allows a party to rely on the law of the country where he has his habitual residence.

In relation to the formation of insurance contracts, the main concern seems to be that the insured will become bound as a consequence of rules of the law governing the contract which he reasonably did not expect to be applicable. A good example is that of the situation where a natural person does not respond to an offer made by an agent or an insurance company. If under the law governing the insurance contract the party's silence would be construed as an acceptance of the offer, reference to the law governing the contract would lead to the result that this person would be bound. This would be so even in cases where under the law of the country where that party is resident his silence would be interpreted as a rejection of the offer. It appears that in such cases a party must, under certain circumstances, not be held bound despite the fact that under the law governing the contract a valid contract would have come into existence.

[116] See Cheshire and North, n 3 above, 587–89; Ferry (C), *La validité des contrats en droit international privé* (Paris, LGDJ, 1988).

[117] Cheshire and North, n 3 above 587

The same reasoning should apply to situations where one party sends a confirmation to the other party (for example, the broker, agent or insurer), which purports to alter the terms of the insurance or reinsurance contract. Under the legal systems of some Contracting States, the other party is bound by the terms of the confirmation if he does not expressly reject it. Other issues in respect of which it has been argued that special treatment is needed are the applicability of standard conditions, binding force of offers and reality of consent. As a consequence thereof Article 8(2) provides that a party may, if it would not be reasonable to determine the effect of his conduct in accordance with the law governing the contract, rely upon the law of the country where he resides in order to demonstrate that he did not consent. As the Giuliano and Lagarde Report points out, this rule has been drafted particularly with a view to consent by silence.[118]

It should therefore be concluded that the 'putative proper law' applies to the question whether an agreement between the insurer and insured or between the insured and an agent of the insurer has come into effect. Moreover, this law governs issues such as whether a party's declaration must be construed as a real offer or merely as an invitation to treat, whether an offer is revocable, whether and when an offer has been accepted, whether there is consensus and whether one party is bound by standard terms and conditions used by his counter-party.

19. ARTICLE 8 OF THE ROME CONVENTION: THE VALIDITY OF THE INSURANCE CONTRACT

The law that would govern the insurance or reinsurance contract if it was valid applies to the question whether this contract can be annulled on the basis that it has been entered into under the influence of fraud, error, duress or other vitiating factors. Where the application of the 'putative proper law' of the contract would lead to results which are contrary to the public policy of the forum, the forum may apply its own provisions pursuant to Article 16 of the Rome Convention.[119]

The law that would govern the insurance contract if it was valid also applies to the question whether a false statement made by the insured to the company bars recovery upon the policy, whether in the case of destruction or loss the insured's recovery will be limited to the actual value of the object despite the fact that it was insured for a larger amount. Likewise the question whether a contract of insurance or reinsurance must have a '*causa*' or consideration and what constitutes such *causa* or consideration is governed by the 'putative proper law'.

[118] The Giuliano and Lagarde Report, n 12 above, 28

[119] See above, para 15.

20. THE LAW OF THE PLACE OF PERFORMANCE (*LEX LOCI SOLUTIONIS*) AND INSURANCE AND REINSURANCE CONTRACTS

The mandatory rules and the public policy exception are not the only restrictions to the application of the governing law of insurance and reinsurance contracts. Article 10(2) provides that

> in relation to the manner of performance and the steps to be taken in the event of defective performance regard shall be had to the law of the country in which performance takes place.

A slightly different provision is contained in the Swiss Statute of Private International Law. According to Article 125 of the 1987 Swiss Statute, the manner of performance and the steps to be taken in the event of defective performance *must be governed* by the law of the country in which performance takes place. Article 10(2) has raised two questions in the legal literature which are worth discussing in the context of insurance contracts.

The first question concerns the meaning of the words 'manner of performance' and 'steps'. According to the Giuliano and Lagarde Report,[120] it is for the 'lex fori' to establish their meaning, and this might include inter alia public holidays, the manner in which goods are to be examined, and steps to be taken if goods are refused. Cheshire and North[121] point out correctly that the words 'manner of performance' must be interpreted as encompassing the minor details of performance, such as the currency of payment, and the date at which lay days begin to run. Therefore, it appears that the governing law of the contract applies almost to any aspect of the performance of insurance and reinsurance contracts. However the importance of the law of the place of performance (*lex loci solutionis*) should not be underestimated. Especially in the sectors of life insurance and compulsory insurance it is often crucial for the resolution of a dispute to determine the date at which lay days begin to run.

The second question which deserves attention is the meaning of the expression 'regard shall be had to the law'. The Giuliano and Lagarde Report[122] states that the judge shall consider whether such law has relevance to the manner in which the contract must be performed and has discretion whether to apply it in whole or in part. This interpretation is suggested by the word 'regard' in the text of Article 10(2).[123] In deciding whether to apply the law of the place of performance it is clear that the judge shall examine mainly the circumstances of the case and the consequences arising from the application of that law. However, it

[120] See the Giuliano and Lagarde Report, n 12 above, 33.

[121] Cheshire and North, n 3 above, 495–96.

[122] See the Giuliano and Lagarde Report, n 12 above, 33.

[123] See Cheshire and North, n 3 above, 515; Plender, *The European Contracts Convention*, n 53 above, 173; Gaudemet Tallon (1981) Revue Trimestrelle de Droit Européen 267; *Cf*, Vecchi, *Articolo 10* in Bianca and Giardina (eds) (1994) *Le Nuove Leggi Civili Commentate*, 1048.

is plain that the judge cannot decide to apply the law of the country in which performance takes place exclusively on the basis of the interests of the contracting party who is in a weaker bargaining position (ie generally the insured). The discretion of the judge, in fact, must be restricted to the evaluation of the relevance of the law of performance to the manner in which the insurance or reinsurance contract must be performed.[124] Moreover, it appears that the application of the law of the place of performance exclusively on the basis of the interests of the insured would be against the fact that Article 10(2) is not a protective rule but a rule which applies in any situation involving a choice between the laws of different countries. Therefore, the judge must apply, for example, the provision of the law of the place of performance on the date at which lay days begin to run to a life-insurance contract if it is a well-established practice in the place where the contract has been concluded to refer to that rule for the performance of the obligations of that type of contract.

21. THE LAW APPLICABLE TO THE INTERPRETATION OF INSURANCE AND REINSURANCE CONTRACTS

As already stated above, Article 10(1)(a) provides that the interpretation of the contract is governed by the law governing the contract.[125] It is disputed whether this rule should apply in all circumstances or be limited by certain exceptions in the context of marine insurance and reinsurance contracts.[126] As it is well known, it is very common for the parties to marine insurance and reinsurance contracts to insert foreign terms in the text of their contract or to refer to international commercial usages.[127] In these cases, it appears that the court cannot refer only to the governing law for the interpretation of these contracts, but must consider the meaning of the foreign terms in the original language. That does not mean, of course, that the judge shall interpret the English terms inserted in a French contract of marine insurance according to the English case law if it appears from the whole of the circumstances that the intention of the parties was to give them a different meaning. However, such an intention of the contractual parties cannot be presumed but must be ascertained unequivocally in the specific case.

[124] See the Giuliano and Lagarde Report, n 12 above, 33.
[125] See above, para 16.
[126] Celle (1995) *Il diritto marittimo*, 708.
[127] See Celle, *I contratti di assicurazione grandi rischi nel diritto internazionale privato*, n 16 above, 176 *et seq*.

22. THE SPHERE OF THE LAW APPLICABLE TO THE INSURANCE CONTRACT '*RATIONE PERSONAE*'

Some observations worthy of comment concern the scope of the law applicable to the insurance contract '*ratione personae*' (ie the persons to which this law applies).

It appears that the governing law of insurance contract generally applies to the relationship between insurer and policy-holder. There is no doubt, in fact, that the law applicable to this relationship must be ascertained according to the rules of the Rome Convention. Therefore, it is clear that in the absence of a different choice by the parties the governing law of the relationship between the insurer and policy-holder usually coincides with the law applicable to the insurance contract (ie the governing law of the relation between the original contractual parties).[128]

In contrast, it seems that the relationship between the contractual counter-party of the insurer and the insured is not always covered by the law applicable to the insurance contract. As has already been pointed out on many occasions, it is possible that the counter-party of the insurer is not the insured (ie the beneficiary of the contract). Especially in the sectors of marine insurance and reinsurance, it is quite common that the contractual counter-party of the insurer is not the insured but another person such as a broker or an agent who acts on behalf of the beneficiary of the contract. Moreover, in the field of life-insurance the beneficiary of the contract may not coincide with the contractual counter party of the insurer. In all these situations, if there was a previous contractual agreement between the third party beneficiary of the insurance contract and the person acting on behalf of the insured, it is obvious that the relationship between these two persons must be governed by the law applicable to the contract of agency.[129]

23. THE LAW APPLICABLE TO THE FORM OF INSURANCE AND REINSURANCE CONTRACTS

Article 9 lays down a system of alternative laws governing formal validity of the contract, with the objective of promoting validity of the contract and preventing parties from being surprised by unforeseen formalities of the governing law of the contract where the law of the place of conclusion does not contain such requirements.[130] It is worth noting that this liberal regime, which is in accordance with most of the national systems of private international law of the

[128] Celle, *I contratti di assicurazione grandi rischi nel diritto internazionale privato*, 698.
[129] *Ibid*, 699.
[130] See the Giuliano and Lagarde Report, n 12 above, 29 to 30; Kaye, *The New Private International Law of Contracts*, n 73 above, 281–95.

Contracting States, does not apply to consumer contracts. According to Article 9, paragraph 5, the provisions of Article 9 paragraphs 1 to 4 shall not apply to a contract to which Article 5 applies, concluded in the circumstances indicated in Article 5, paragraph 2. The formal validity of such a contract is governed by the law of the country in which the consumer has his habitual residence. As a result of Article 9, paragraph 1, an insurance or reinsurance contract concluded between persons who are in the same country is formally valid if it satisfies the formal requirements for insurance and reinsurance contracts of the governing law or the law of the country where it is concluded. But a different rule applies to insurance and reinsurance contracts concluded between persons who are in different countries. Article 9, paragraph 2 states that a contract concluded between persons who are in different countries is formally valid if it satisfies the formal requirements of the governing law (*lex causae*) or the law of one of those countries. In the insurance and reinsurance sectors, where an insurance or reinsurance contract is concluded by an agent, the country in which the agent acts is the relevant country for the purposes of paragraphs 1 and 2. Therefore, if the insurer is in England and the insured in Italy, and the former sends his agent to conclude the contract in Italy, the contract is concluded between parties in Italy; conversely, where insurer and insured are in England, but their agents conclude the contract on their behalf in Italy and Germany respectively, the contract is concluded by parties who are in different countries. Obviously, it is not sufficient for the agent to pass on the insured's offer to the insurer for acceptance, or to transmit the insurer's offer to the insured for acceptance: the agent should be capable of acting so as to bind the insurer for Article 9(3) to operate.[131]

As a result of Article 9, paragraph 4, an act relating to an insurance or reinsurance contract is formally valid if it satisfies the formal requirements of the law which governs or would govern the contract or the law of the country where the act was done. It appears that this rule applies to *any* act relating to insurance or reinsurance contracts, which might be required to be in a particular form for it to have legal effect: for example, the making of an offer, where the offeror is bound for a fixed or reasonable time, as under Article 1328 *et seq* of the 1942 Italian Civil Code; the notice of contractual termination; the declaration of rescission or repudiation.[132] This conclusion can be derived from the text of Article 9, paragraph 4 which does not restrict the scope of this provision to a certain category of acts.

It appears that Article 9(6) can not apply to insurance and reinsurance contracts. This conclusion is suggested by the text of this provision which refers to 'a contract the subject matter of which is a right in immovable property or a right to use immovable property'.[133] Therefore, an insurance or reinsurance

[131] Kaye, *ibid*, 288.

[132] Frigessi di Rattalma, *Il contratto internazionale di assicurazione*, n 101 above, 236.

[133] Art 9(6) reads as follow: 'Notwithstanding paras 1 to 4 of this Article, a contract the subject matter of which is a right in immovable property or a right to use immovable property shall be subject to the mandatory requirements of form of the law of the country where the property is situated

contract covering a risk related to immovable property is formally valid only if it satisfies the general requirements concerning the form laid down in Article 9, paragraphs 1 to 3.

24. THE IMPACT OF ARTICLES 9 (FORM) AND 14 (BURDEN OF PROOF) ON THE NATIONAL RULES OF INSURANCE CONTRACTS: EXAMPLE OF IMPACT ON CIVIL LAW SYSTEMS

A word needs to be said about the impact of Articles 9 and 14 on the domestic provisions for insurance contracts. Article 14, paragraph 2 provides that

> a contract or an act intended to have legal effect may be proved by any mode of proof recognised by the law of the forum or by any of the laws referred to in Article 9 under which that contract or act is formally valid, provided that such mode of proof can be administered by the forum.

It is worth noting that this provision, together with Article 9 had a relevant impact on the regulation of the form of insurance contracts laid down by some civil law countries such as Italy. According to the Italian system of private law a distinction has to be made between the form '*ad substantiam*' (ie the requirements concerning the form of the contract which must be fulfilled for the validity of the insurance contract) and the form '*ad probationem*' (ie the requirements regarding the form of the contract which must be fulfilled to prove the existence of the insurance contract). As a result of Articles 9 and 14(2) this distinction is not relevant any longer and the Italian courts must allow the parties to prove the insurance contract by any mode of proof (including by witnesses) if one of the applicable laws indicated in Article 9 allows them to do so. That is true despite the fact that Article 1888, paragraph 1 of the Italian civil code states that an insurance contract shall be proved only in writing.[134]

Due to the fact the English law does not impose any special requirement which must be fulfilled by the parties to prove the existence of an insurance contract, Articles 9 and 14 have no relevant impact on the English common law concerning the form of insurance and reinsurance contracts.

25. THE LAW APPLICABLE TO THE 'DIRECT ACTION' OF THE VICTIM AGAINST THE INSURER OF THE PERSON LIABLE

The Rome Convention gives no help to answer the question of the law applicable to the 'direct action' of the victim against the insurer of the person liable.

if by that law those requirements are imposed irrespective of the country where the contract is concluded and irrespective of the law governing the contract'.

[134] See Celle (1995) *Il diritto marittimo*, 694.

Article 12[135] which contains a provision on voluntary assignment of rights cannot support either the insertion nor the exclusion of the 'direct action' of the victim from the scope of the law governing the contract.[136] Therefore, the judge must ascertain the law applicable to the direct action of the victim against the insurer by looking at the characterisation of the 'direct action' of the victim under the law of the forum. If you look, for example, at French law where this action is not restricted to the motor insurance sector, as in most of the European systems of law, it appears that there is room for the application of the *lex loci delicti* and the governing law of the insurance contract.[137] However, it is unclear whether the judge shall apply the law governing the contract and the *lex loci delicti* simultaneously to different aspects of the 'direct action' of the victim[138] or shall make a choice between these laws.[139] In English law, there is no conclusive authority on the proper choice of law provision applicable in such cases, though the issue has received some examination in Australia and by the Law Commission.[140] The Australian authorities seem to treat the law applicable to the contract as governing the availability of the direct action of the victim against the insurer of the person liable.

26. THE APPLICABLE LAW TO THE SUBROGATION OF THE INSURER

Where the insured has a contractual claim upon another person, and the insurer has a duty to satisfy the insured, or has in fact satisfied the insured in the discharge of that duty, the law which governs the insurer's duty to satisfy the insured shall determine whether the insurer is entitled to exercise against the debtor of the insured the rights which the insured had against his debtor under the law governing their relationship and, if so, whether he may do so in full or only to a limited extent.[141] The same rule applies where several insurers are subject to the same contractual claim and one of them has satisfied the insured.[142]

According to the Giuliano and Lagarde Report,[143] this provision must be

[135] Article 12 states that: 'the mutual obligations of assignor and assignee under a voluntary assignment of a right against another person ("the debtor") shall be governed by the law which under this Convention applies to the contract between the assignor and assignee. 2.The law governing the right to which the assignment relates shall determine its assignability, the relationship between the assignee and the debtor, the conditions under which the assignment can be invoked against the debtor and any question whether the debtor's obligations have been discharged'.

[136] See especially Frigessi di Rattalma, *Il contratto internazionale di assicurazione*, n 101 above, 241–45.

[137] Claret, *Contrats d'assurance et conflits de loi*, n 115 above, 240–43.

[138] See Claret, n 115 above, 242.

[139] See Frigessi di Rattalma, n 101 above, 242 *et seq*.

[140] For a clear illustration of this point see Dicey and Morris, n 1 above, 1525–27; see also Kaye, *Civil Jurisdiction and Enforcement of Foreign Judgments* (1987) 809.

[141] Art 13(1).

[142] Art 13(2) of the Rome Convention.

[143] See the Giuliano and Lagarde Report, n 12 above, p 34. See also Gaudemet Tallon (1981) *Revue Trimestrelle de Droit Européen* 275; Foyer (1991) *Journal de droit international* 624, note 71.

interpreted literally and, therefore, applies only if the insured has a contractual claim upon another person. When the insured has a non-contractual claim the judge shall apply the law which governs the insurer's duty to satisfy the insured to the subrogation of the insurer if the choice of law rules of the forum provide so.[144]

It has been questioned whether Article 13 of the Rome Convention applies to the relation between the insured's debtor and the insurer.[145] Dubuisson holds that the subrogation of the insurer is a consequence deriving from the payment of the insurer to the insured, and maintains that the law which governs the insurer's duty to satisfy the insured must apply to the content of the subrogated rights and the exceptions of the insured's debtor against the insurer. However, it appears that this would be unfair to the insured's debtor in the sense that he is not protected from the application of an unforeseeable law. Moreover, it is quite unacceptable to request the insurer's debtor to rely on the remedies available in a legal system other than that which regulates his relationship with the creditor. It follows that the relationship between the insured's debtor and the insurer should be governed by the law applicable to the relationship between the insured and his debtor.[146]

27. THE RELATIONSHIP BETWEEN ARTICLES 13 (SUBROGATION) AND 6 (INDIVIDUAL EMPLOYMENT CONTRACTS)

A word needs to be said about the relationship between Article 13 and Article 6 of the Rome Convention. It has been debated in the legal literature whether the judge must apply Article 13 or Article 6 to determine whether the insurer who has satisfied the insured-worker is entitled to exercise against the employer–debtor of the insured the rights which the insured–worker had against his debtor under the law governing their relationship and, if so, whether he may do so in full or only to a limited extent.[147]

Looking at the mere fact that Article 6 lays down a special regime for individual employment contracts, one might be tempted to conclude that this provision should apply since the issue is undoubtedly related to the employment contract. However, it appears that such an interpretation would conflict with

[144] See Davì, *La responsabilità extracontrattuale nel diritto internazionale privato* (Torino, Utet, 1997) 86 *et seq*; Malatesta, *La cessione del credito nel diritto internazionale privato* (Padova, CEDAM, 1996) 119 *et seq*; Dubuisson, *Le droit applicable au contrat d'assurance*, 511–20; Frigessi di Rattalma, *Il contratto internazionale di assicurazione*, n 101 above, 245 *et seq*; Mari (1975) *Rivista di diritto internationale privato e processuale* 486 *et seq*.

[145] Dubuisson, *Le droit applicable au contrat d'assurance dans un espace communautaire integré* (Doctoral thesis, Université Catholique de Louvain, 1994) n 144 above, 515.

[146] For the same conclusion see Frigessi di Rattalma, *Il contratto internazionale di assicurazione*, n 101 above, 246.

[147] For a discussion of this point see Forlati Picchio, *La legge applicabile ai contratti di assicurazione* in Treves (ed), *Verso una disciplina della legge*, n 56 above, 56–57.

the fact that Article 13 applies in any situation in which the insured has a contractual claim upon another person. Moreover, it cannot be supported by the purpose of Article 6 which is the protection of the *worker's rights against the employer*.[148] Therefore, it follows that the law which governs the insurer's duty to satisfy the insured (ie the law applicable to the insurance contract) should determine whether the insurer is entitled to exercise against the employer–debtor of the insured the rights which the insured–worker had against his debtor. Article 6 should apply, however, to the content of the subrogated rights and the exceptions of the insured-worker's debtor against the insurer.[149]

28. THE LAW APPLICABLE TO INSURANCE WARRANTIES

Contracts of insurance generally consist of not just the policy document itself, but also the completed proposal form where pertinent, and frequently, as well, other documents including in certain cases renewal notices. These contracts can comprise three sorts of appropriate terms, namely conditions and clauses descriptive of the risk and warranties. The warranty is the most essential term and thus deserves special attention.

Warranty is a term of the insurance contract upon breach of which the insurer is discharged from all liability as from the date of the breach.[150] This date will change depending on the type of warranty. Warranties should be strictly complied with, and it is quite irrelevant that the breach is unrelated to a loss that occurs. Warranties are basically promises made by the insured concerning things or facts which he undertakes to do or not to do, as the case may be. They will always affect the risk to which the insurer is subject. There are three kinds of warranties; warranties as to the present or past facts as at the date they are made; warranties as to the future; and warranties of opinion.

In examining the conflict of laws issues which may arise from insurance warranties the starting point should be the legal character of the warranties and their differences with the purely contractual conditions. These matters having been established, we can go on to consider the law applicable to the different facets of the clauses containing warranties. The question of characterisation arises at two levels. First, there is the characterisation of the warranty itself. This has to be determined in most of the Member States according to the law of the forum. Is this a purely contractual condition, a collateral agreement or a combination of the two? Secondly, where a warranty is breached, which is the applicable law to the liability of the insured?

[148] See Morse, *The EEC Convention on the Law Applicable to Contractual Obligations* in North (ed), *Contract Conflicts* (Amsterdam and Oxford, North Holland, 1983) 145–46.

[149] *Ibid*, 45, 46.

[150] On the effects arising from the breach of warranties see inter alia Clarke, *Policies and Perceptions of Insurance* (Oxford, Clarendon Press, 1997) 132 *et seq*.

Under English law the term warranty has been described as a 'word of uncertain meaning'.[151] Any attempt to explain the significance of the term is complicated by the often indiscriminate use of the word to denote clauses in policies with widely varying functions.[152] In the *Good Luck* case[153] the English Court of Appeal stated that a warranty in marine insurance is equivalent to a condition precedent in general contractual law. Following the *Good Luck* case Professor Clarke stated that

> The place of insurance warranty in the rank of contractual terms is now clearer than before. As regards contracts in general, it is distinguished from the general warranty, in that the latter, if broken, gives rise to damages but not to discharge, whether automatically or by election. The insurance warranty is distinguished from the general condition, in that the latter, if broken, gives rise to both damages and discharge, but the discharge occurs only on the election of the party not in breach.

Being the warranty analogous to a purely contractual clause, the applicable law to the insurance warranty must be ascertained according to the provisions of the Rome Convention on the law applicable to contractual obligations. But these rules do not apply when the warranty forms part of a contract of insurance that covers risks situated outside the territories of the Member States of the European Community. In these cases, the governing law of the insurance warranty must be determined according to the choice of law rules of the EC Insurance Directives. The law, as designated by the Rome Convention or the Insurance Directives, will, in particular, govern the interpretation of the warranty, the performance of the obligations, the various ways of extinguishing these obligations and the issues of prescription and limitation of actions. Moreover, the applicable law will also govern the consequences of any breach of the warranty, but this will be done within the limits of the powers conferred on the judge by its procedural law. The consequences of any breach will include the assessment of damages in so far as they are governed by legal rules.[154]

29. *RENVOI*

At this stage, it is appropriate to mention shortly the notion of *renvoi*, if only to dispose of it. The issue is whether the 'applicable law' is the law which would be applied in the country of the applicable law to a domestic contract in that country (no *renvoi*), or whether it is the law that would be applied in the country of the applicable law to that particular contract with all its foreign elements (*renvoi*).

[151] Clarke, *Policies and Perceptions of Insurance* (Oxford, OUP, 1997) 132.
[152] *Ibid*, 132
[153] [1992] 1 AC 233.
[154] Art 10 of the Rome Convention.

This can become easier if you look at Article 15 of the Rome Convention which is headed 'Exclusion of *renvoi*'. This states that

> the application of the law of any country specified by this Convention means the application of the rules of law in force in that country other than its rules of private international law.

30. INCAPACITY

The Rome Convention excludes contractual capacity from its scope of application.[155] However, Article 11 provides that

> in a contract concluded between persons who are in the same country, a natural person who would have capacity under the law of that country may invoke his incapacity resulting from another law only if the other party to the contract was aware of this incapacity at the time of the conclusion of the contract or was not aware thereof as a result of negligence.[156]

In the context of insurance, this provision applies to life-insurance contracts which are generally concluded between persons who are in the same country. Due to the fact that this provision only refers to natural persons, it is unlikely to apply to reinsurance contracts which are usually concluded between two legal persons. Moreover, reinsurance contracts are often concluded between persons who are in different countries. Nevertheless, this article will apply to any type of insurance and reinsurance contract when the contract is concluded under the circumstances indicated in it.

31. VOLUNTARY ASSIGNMENT OF CREDITS

The Rome Convention lays down a distinction between the law applicable to the relationship between assignor and assignee and that to the relation between assignee and debtor. Article 12(1) provides that the law governing the contract between assignor and assignee applies to the obligations of assignor and assignee arising from a voluntary assignment of a right against another person. According to Article 12(2), the relationship between the assignee and the debtor is governed by the law of the right to which the assignment relates.

Although a different conclusion might be derived from the text of Article 12, it is clear that this provision applies also to the voluntary assignment of the contract.[157] Article 12(2) treats as matters within its scope and provides for, issues

[155] See Art 1(2)(a) which provides that the rules of the Rome Convention 'shall not apply to: questions involving the status or legal capacity of natural persons, without prejudice to Article 11'.

[156] See the Giuliano and Lagarde Report, n 12 above, 34; Kaye, *The New Private International Law of Contracts*, n 72 above, 312–19; Cheshire and North, n 3 above, 594–95.

[157] Foyer (1991) *Journal de droit international* 624, note 13; Dubuisson, *Le droit applicable au contrat d'assurance*, n 144 above, 508.

both as to whether the debtor owes monies to and should pay the assignee and under what conditions.[158] There is no indication in Article 12(2) of any intention to distinguish between proprietary and contractual aspects of the assignment. This is not surprising if you consider how difficult can be the task of distinguishing between the proprietary and contractual effects of the assignment in relation to contracts in respect of intangibles such as insurance policies and choices in action. Therefore, Article 12 will apply to the transfer of an insurance or reinsurance contract and the transfer of an insurance portfolio (ie the set of insurance and reinsurance contracts belonging to the same insurer).[159] Moreover, it applies to the voluntary assignment of an insurance or reinsurance contract made in security for a credit. As has already been pointed out by others,[160] there are no reasons, in fact, to introduce a distinction in conflict of laws between the ordinary transfer of an insurance contract and the transfer of an insurance contract made as security for a credit.

32. EVALUATION

(a) Strengths of the Rome Convention in Relation to Insurance and Reinsurance Contracts

(i) The Use of Suitable Connecting Factors

This is one of the major strengths of the Rome Convention. The choice-of-law rules which apply in the absence of a valid stipulation by the parties largely ensure that only the law of a State with which there are strong connections is applied. The fact that Article 4(1) provides that the contract shall be governed by the law of the country which is 'most closely connected' prevents the application of the law of a fortuitous place. Nevertheless, the presumption of the characteristic performance applies very well to simple contracts but it will be difficult to determine a characteristic performance in a contract which involves mutual obligations of confidence and collaboration. The presumption is also not the most efficacious means to determine the closest connection. However, the court shall not apply the rule of connection by characteristic performance if a single characteristic performance cannot be determined or it appears from the circumstances as a whole that the contract of insurance or reinsurance is most closely connected with another country.

Moreover, the Rome Convention's rules on party autonomy, by providing the parties with ample freedom to select the law they wish to govern their agreement, ensure that the interests of the parties to insurance and reinsurance contracts are respected.

158 Case *Raiffeisen Zentral Bank Osterreich AG v Five Star General Trading LLC (The Mount I)* [2000] 1 All ER (Comm) 897.

159 Dubuisson, *Le droit applicable au contrat d'assurance*, n 144 above, 508.

160 *Ibid*, 508.

(ii) Providing Certainty and Predictability, Simplicity and Thus Ease of Application

The Rome Convention takes adequately into account the interests of the claimant, defendant, and defendant's insurers that private international law provisions should be certain and predictable. This is particularly so if you look at the application of the Rome Convention's rules on party autonomy to insurance and reinsurance contracts. This is undoubtedly one of the major strengths of the Rome Convention. Insurers, in fact, need to be able to plan their transactions and to decide whether to make their services and products available abroad. This is particularly important in the context of the European Community where the free movement of services within the European internal market should not be hindered by insurer's concerns over the possible legal consequences of marketing their services and products elsewhere in the Community. Insured and third party beneficiaries need to have a clear idea what their rights are, after taking legal advice, including advice as to which States' substantive law will apply. Any uncertainty as to the applicable law means that claims are more likely to be litigated than settled by insurers, and it is in neither party's interest that this should happen.

(iii) Harmonisation of Choice of Law Rules

Another important strength of the Rome Convention is that, with 15 ratifications from European Community States, it has already achieved a measure of harmonisation of insurance and reinsurance choice of law rules within Europe. Given that in a Joint Declaration[161] annexed to the Convention the Contracting States express the wish that any state which joins the European Community must accede to the Rome Convention, the Convention has the potential for harmonisation throughout nearly all of Western Europe.

(b) Weakness of the Rome Convention in Relation to Insurance and Reinsurance Contracts

(i) Fairness to the parties

The Convention is fair to the insurer in the sense that he is usually protected from the application of an unforeseeable law. What is more questionable is whether the Rome Convention is always fair to the insured. Whilst the protective measures of Article 5 (consumer contracts) may apply to an insurance contract, the insured-consumer has to bear in mind the fact that in the absence of a valid stipulation by the parties the law of his habitual residence will apply even

[161] OJ 1980 L266/14.

if it is not the more favourable to him. Unlike Article 6 (individual employment contracts), Article 5, paragraph 3 does not provide that the law applicable in the absence of a choice can be disregarded if it appears from the circumstances as a whole that the contract is most closely connected with the law of another country. Moreover, by providing that the protective rules of Article 5 apply only if the three conditions laid down in Article 5, paragraph 2 are satisfied the Convention restricts the application of Article 5 to a very small number of consumer-insurance contracts.

33. OPTIONS FOR REFORM

(a) The US Restatement (Second) Conflict of Laws

§ 192 Comment (e) of the *Restatement (Second) on the Conflict of Laws* contains special choice of law rules for life insurance contracts, which provide that:

> . . . Effect will not be given to a choice of law provision in a life insurance contract designating a state whose local law gives the insured *less protection* than he would receive under the otherwise applicable law, which, as stated in Comment *c*, will usually be the local law of the state where the insured was domiciled at the time the policy was applied for.[162]

A similar provision in respect of general insurance is proposed in § 193 Comment (e). The purpose of section 192 Comment (e) is to protect the insured when the life insurance contract is 'drafted unilaterally by the insurer, and the insured is then given the opportunity on a "take-it-or-leave-it" basis of adhering to their terms'. It applies to both commercial and non-commercial insurance.

Would the introduction of a provision such as Section 192 Comment (e) in the Rome Convention bring fairness to the assured? One might be tempted to give a positive answer to this question as this provision prescribes the application of the law of the place in which the assured is domiciled only when it is most favourable to the assured. However, Section 192 Comment (e) casts 'the net of protection far wider than is warranted' as it applies to any type of insurance.[163]

(b) A Special Rule for Consumer Contracts of Insurance Services?

The most direct way of dealing with the problem of the unsuitability of Article 5 for use in *consumer-insurance* cases is to introduce a special provision for such cases. An additional special rule for consumer-insurance contracts is justified because of the unsatisfactory way in which Article 5 deals with such cases. However, it appears that Article 5 is unsuitable not only for use in consumer-

[162] My emphasis.

[163] See Nygh, *Autonomy in International Contracts* (Oxford, Clarendon, 1999) 152.

insurance contracts but also in any type of consumer contract. As has been highlighted on other occasions in this chapter, the unsuitability of this provision derives from the rigidity of the criterion used in Article 5, paragraph 3 to indicate the law applicable in the absence of choice.

(c) **Re-wording Article 5**

(i) The Proposal of the European Group of Private International Law[164]

Under the solution proposed by the European Group of Private International Law (or GEDIP: *Group européen de droit international privé*) Article 5 of the Rome Convention should be re-worded so that

> the law applicable by virtue of Articles 3, 4 and 9 cannot deprive the consumer of the protection afforded to him by the mandatory rules of the law of the country in which he has his habitual residence at the time of the conclusion of the contract unless the supplier can establish that he was not aware of the country in which the consumer has his habitual residence, as a result of the conduct of the consumer.

Undoubtedly this would represent a significant improvement of the current version of Article 5.[165] However, it seems not to be always fair to the consumer due to the fact that in the absence of a valid stipulation by the parties the mandatory rules of the law of the habitual residence of the consumer at the time of the conclusion of the contract would apply even if they are not the most favourable to him. Article 5 (2) of the Draft Proposal in fact provides that the protective provisions should apply

> (a) when the consumer travels to the supplier's country and there concludes the contract, or (b) when property or services were or ought to have been supplied in the country in which the place of business through which such supply was or ought to have been effected was situated, unless, in either case, the consumer was induced by the supplier to travel to the aforementioned country to conclude the contract.

(ii) An Alternative Solution

Under this solution Article 5 would be re-worded so that, in the absence of a valid stipulation by the parties, the law of the country in which the consumer has his habitual residence would apply only if it is objectively the more favourable to him. This would have the advantage of introducing the element of appropriateness into the text of this article. Moreover, it attempts to tackle the deficiencies in Article 5 head on by concentrating on this provision. Furthermore, it would stop the present version of Article 5 being applied to any type of consumer contract.

[164] For the text of the draft proposal see the website of the GEDIP at www.drt.ucl.ac.be/gedip

[165] For the same opinion see Fallon (2000) *Revue belgique de droit international* 640–48.

9

The Choice of Law Rules in the Second and Third Non-Life Directives

1. INTRODUCTION

IN THIS chapter, the concern is with non-life insurance contracts covering risks situated in the territories of the Member States of the European Community. These contracts may involve insurance which is not compulsory under Member States' national laws, as well as insurance which is compulsory. I propose to deal separately with each of these types of contract, as they are partially regulated by different choice of law provisions. The aim of the present chapter is to discuss the private international law rules for contracts concerning insurance which are not compulsory under the Member States' national laws.

The main instruments in relation to these contracts are now the Second Non-Life Directive of 1988 and the Third Non-Life Directive of 1992. Their impact will be analysed in detail and their provisions will be the starting point of this analysis. It should be noted from the outset that, although the above-named directives have certain special rules for insurance contracts covering risks situated in the territories of the Member States of the European Community, they do not lay down a complete set of choice of law provisions for these contracts. Therefore, the courts must refer to the general rules of private international law of the forum concerning contractual obligations to fill out any lacuna in the system.[1]

But before starting the examination of the private international law provisions of the Second and Third Non-Life Directives, the scheme of the set of choice of law rules and the definitions of 'large risks' and 'mass risks' will be discussed.

2. SCHEME OF THE SET OF CHOICE OF LAW RULES IN THE SECOND AND THIRD NON-LIFE INSURANCE DIRECTIVES

It may be helpful at this point to indicate in outline the main provisions of the Second and Third Non-Life Directives relating to the law applicable to insurance contracts covering risks situated in the territories of the Member States of

[1] See below, para 15.1.

the European Community, and then to discuss them in greater detail. They will be discussed in the same order in which they appear in the Directives.

3. SCHEME OF THE CHOICE OF LAW RULES IN THE SECOND NON-LIFE INSURANCE DIRECTIVE

The basic provisions in the Second Non-Life Directive are as follows:

1. Where a policyholder has his habitual residence or central administration (if a legal person) in the Member State in which the risk is situated, the law applicable to the contract shall be the law of that Member State; if the law of that Member State so allows, the parties can choose the law of another country (Article 7(1)(a)).
2. Where the policyholder's habitual residence or central administration is not in the Member State where the risk is situated, the parties to the insurance contract may choose either the law of the country in which the policyholder has his or her habitual residence or central administration or the law of the Member State in which the risk is situated (Article 7(1)(b)).
3. Where the Member States referred to in Article 7, paragraph 1(b) and (c) grant the parties greater freedom to choose the applicable law the parties may take advantage of this freedom (Article 7(1)(d)).
4. Where the risks covered by the contract are limited to events occurring in one Member State other than the Member State where the risk is localised the parties shall always choose the law of the former State (Article 7(1)(e)).
5. For the 'large risks' referred to in Article 5(d)(i) of the first Directive, the parties can choose any law.
6. If the parties have not made an express or implied choice of law, or they have made a choice which is not permitted by the rules in Article 7(1)(a) to (e), then the judge will apply the law of the country with which the contract is most closely connected.

As it appears from this exposition, the structure of the set of choice of law rules in the Second Non-Life Directive is quite different from that of the Rome Convention. Although there are some similarities between the two instruments, the basic rule of the Rome Convention which provides that a contract is to be governed by the law chosen by the parties cannot be found in the system of the Second Non-Life Directive.

4. SCHEME OF THE CHOICE OF LAW RULES IN THE THIRD NON-LIFE INSURANCE DIRECTIVE

The Third Non-Life Directive lays down a few special rules. Article 27, by amending Article 7(1)(f), extends freedom of choice to direct contracts insuring any large risks. Article 28 extends freedom of choice to contracts insuring mass risks, by providing that

> the Member State in which a risk is situated shall not prevent a policyholder from concluding a contract with an insurance undertaking . . . as long as that does not conflict with legal provisions protecting the general good in the Member State in which the risk is situated.

Article 31, by introducing a requirement that before an insurance contract is concluded the insurer must give the insured information regarding the applicable law has an impact on the choice of law.

5. THE DEFINITION OF 'MASS RISKS' AND 'LARGE RISKS'

A word needs to be said about the distinction between 'mass risks' and 'large risks' in the EC choice of law rules for insurance contracts. Article 5(d) of the First Non-Life Directive of 1973 lists 16 classes of large risks. It is worth noting that the criteria for the insertion of the risks into the list were the economic relevance of the risk and the bargaining power of the policyholder.[2] The category of 'mass risk' is a residual one. Therefore any risk which is not included in one of the 16 classes of large risks has to be qualified as mass risk.[3] Although it appears that Article 5(d) encompasses most of the risks which are covered by non-consumer contracts of insurance, it is not a complete coincidence that insurance contracts cover mass risks and consumer contracts.[4] This question will be discussed in greater detail in the paragraph concerning the application of Article 5 of the Rome Convention to insurance contracts covering risks situated in the territories of a Member State of the European Community.[5]

[2] See Berr (1988) *Revue trimestrelle de droit européen* 662–63.

[3] See Claret, *Contrats d'assurance and conflits de lois en droit communautaire* (Doctoral thesis, University of Lille, 1994) 70.

[4] *Cf* Schnyder, *Observations* in Facilides and d'Oliveira (eds), *International Insurance Contract Law*, 188.

[5] See below para 18.

I
The Choice of Law Rules in the Second Non-Life Insurance Directive

6. THE SCOPE OF APPLICATION

(a) Is the Establishment of the Insurer in a Member State of the European Community Necessary for the Application of the Choice of Law Rules of the Second Non-Life Insurance Directive?

As already stated above, the choice of law rules of the Second Non-Life Insurance Directive apply to insurance contracts covering risks situated in the territory of a Member State of the European Community. However, it is not clear whether these rules apply to insurance contracts covering risks situated in the territory of a Member State of the European Community under *any* circumstances. It has been suggested by some writers that the choice of law rules of the 'Second Generation' Insurance Directives only apply when the risk is situated in the territory of a Member State of the European Community *and* the insurer is established in a Member State.[6] Two arguments are generally put forward to maintain this thesis: the first argument is that such limitation derives from the Treaty of Rome provisions concerning the freedom to provide services within the Single Insurance Market; the second argument is that the choice of law rules of the 'Second Generation' Insurance Directives are strictly connected with the rules of the 'First Generation' Insurance Directives, which expressly apply to cases involving insurers established in the territory of a Member State of the European Community.

It is the present author's opinion that none of these arguments can be used to uphold this view. It is true that the Treaty of Rome grants the freedom to provide services in the Single Insurance Market only to insurers who are established in the territory of a Member State of the European Community. This conclusion is derived from the text of Article 49 (ex Article 59) of the Treaty of Rome which refers to '*nationals of Member States who are established in a State of the Community*'. Moreover, this is suggested by the objective of the Treaty of Rome to protect the competition between insurance companies which operate in the Single Insurance Market and by the objective of the Treaty to protect insurers and insureds habitually resident in the Member States of the European Community. However, is it possible to maintain that the competition in the Single Insurance Market and the interests of European insurers and insureds would be protected by a restriction on the scope of application of the choice of

[6] See Fallon, (1989) 1 *RGAT*, 249; Dubuisson, *Le droit applicable au contract d'assurance dans un espace communautaire integré* (Doctoral thesis, Université Catholique de Louvain, 1994) 88.

law rules of the Second Non-Life Insurance Directive to only the cases in which the insurer is established in a Member State of the European Community? The answer to this question must be negative. If, as it appears, a goal of the choice of law provisions contained in the Second Non-Life Insurance Directive was the protection of European policyholders (ie, the policyholders habitually resident in a Member State) then it would be unreasonable to deny this protection to some policyholders only because the establishment of their contractual counterpart is situated outside the territory of a Member State of the European Community. Moreover, this could create an obstacle to the freedom to *receive* insurance products and services granted by the Treaty of Rome provisions.[7] Moving on to the second argument that has been used to support a narrow interpretation of the scope of application of the choice of law rules contained in the Second Non-Life Insurance Directive, it can be observed that the insertion of the choice of law rules in the Title I of the Second Non-Life Directive, which contains provisions supplementary to the First Non-Life Insurance Directive, is not sufficient per se to demonstrate the intention of the drafters of the Second Non-Life Insurance Directive to submit the choice of law provisions for non-life insurance contracts covering risks situated in the Member State of the European Community to the same restrictions arising from the scope of application of the rules contained in the First Non-Life Insurance Directive. The wording of Article 7 of the Second Non-Life Directive which refers to 'the law applicable to contracts of insurance *referred to by this Directive* [the Second Non-Life Insurance Directive] covering risks situated within the Member States' makes it clear that the scope of application of these choice of law rules cannot be determined by reference to the scope of the rules contained in the First Non-Life Insurance Directive.[8] On the contrary, two arguments can be put forward to maintain the application of the choice of law rules of the Second Non-Life Insurance Directive to *any* contracts of insurance covering risks situated in the territory of a Member State of the European Community. First, the text of Article 7, paragraph 1 of the Second Non-Life Directive does not contain any reference to the *establishment of the insurer*. Secondly, the criterion of the risk which has been used in the private international law rules of the Second Non-Life Directive is the same criterion which has been used in Article 1, paragraph 3 of the Rome Convention. It can be concluded from this last point that the intention of the drafters of the Second Non-Life Insurance Directive was to complete the harmonisation of the private international law framework for insurance contracts and, therefore, the application of the choice of law rules of the Second Non-Life Insurance Directive should apply to *any* insurance contract beyond the scope of the 1980 Rome Convention.[9]

[7] For an illustration of the freedom to receive insurance products see above, ch 1, para 3(b).

[8] Emphasis added.

[9] The implementing legislation in the UK does not, as far are private international law provisions are concerned, limit itself to an insurer with an establishment in a Member State of the European Community. For a clear illustration of this point see Dicey and Morris, *The Conflict of Laws* by L Collins *et al*, 13th edn (London, Sweet & Maxwell, 1999) 34, 1353.

(b) Are the Choice of Law Provisions of the Second Non-Life Insurance Directive Applicable to Insurance Contracts *Beyond* the Scope of Application of the Non-Life Insurance Directives?

It appears that the choice of law rules contained in the Second Non-Life Insurance Directive do not apply to insurance contracts concluded by insurers who are *excluded* from the scope of application of the Non-Life Insurance Directives and to insurance contracts covering activities *beyond* the scope of application of these Directives.[10] This conclusion can be derived from the wording of Article 7 of the Second Non-Life Insurance Directive which refers to 'the law applicable to contracts of insurance *referred to by this Directive* and covering risks situated within the Member States . . .'.

7. THE PROBLEM OF CHARACTERISATION IN THE INSURANCE DIRECTIVES

Like the Second Life Directive the Second Non-Life Directive does not define the expression 'contract of insurance'. The absence of a definition in these Directives can be justified by the ambiguities of the term 'insurance' and also by the unsuccessful results of the European Community institutions in the harmonisation of insurance contract law in Europe.[11] Because of the absence of a definition of insurance contract a problem of characterisation may arise in the Directives. If you look at the legal writings it appears that characterisation must be made according to the law of the forum.[12] As the Insurance Directives do not depart from this rule, it is clear that questions of characterisation which might arise from the text of these Directives have to be decided according to the *lex fori*.

[10] For an indication of the insurers excluded from the scope of application of the Non-Life Insurance Directives see Arts 3 and 4 of Directive 73/239/EEC of 24 July 1973, OJEC, No L228 of 16 August 1973, amended by Art 3 of the Third Non-Life Insurance Directive. See also Art 3 of Directive 79/267/EEC of 5 March 1979, OJEC, No L 63 of 13 March 1979, p 1. But the choice of law rules of the Second Non-Life Directive are applied, with modifications, to contracts of insurance made by Friendly Societies, the effect of which constitutes general business and which cover risks situated in the UK or in another Member State of the European Community. See Dicey and Morris, n 9 above, 1362.

[11] For an illuminating illustration of the problems raised by the term 'insurance' see Kimball, (1995) 4 *International Journal of Insurance Law*, 226 *et seq*.

[12] See in the English literature especially Robertson, *Characterisation in the Conflict of Laws* (Cambridge, Mass., Harvard University Press, 1940); Dine, (1983) *Juridical Review*, 73; Cheshire and North, *Private International Law* (London, Edinburgh, Dublin, Butterworths, 1999) 35–45; Dicey and Morris, n 9 above, 34–48.

8. THE LAW APPLICABLE TO INSURANCE CONTRACTS COVERING A RISK SITUATED IN THE MEMBER STATE WHERE THE POLICYHOLDER HAS HIS HABITUAL RESIDENCE OR ITS CENTRAL ADMINISTRATION

The Second Non-Life Directive provides in Article 7(1)(a) that where the policyholder has his habitual residence or central administration in the territory of the Member State in which the risk is situated, the law applicable to the contract shall be the law of that Member State. Article 7(1)(a) also provides that the parties may choose the law of another country, if the law of the Member State where the policyholder has his habitual residence so allows.[13]

At first glance, this provision prohibits the choice of law by the parties, by imposing the law of the policyholder's residence when the policyholder is habitually resident in a Member State and the risk covered by the contract is situated in the same State. However, this prohibition on choosing the law applicable to the contract is mitigated by the second part of the provision which introduces an option for the Member States to grant the parties greater freedom, and by the imprecise formulation of the text of Article 7(1)(a).

It goes without saying that the option for the Member States to grant the parties greater freedom to choose the applicable law is the result of a political compromise between the delegates from the more liberal States, which were favourable to the freedom of the parties in the field of insurance contracts, and the delegates from the more protectionist States, which were favourable to restrictions of the freedom of the parties to choose the governing law of the contract. This conclusion is confirmed by the examination of the different solutions adopted by the Member States in their implementation statutes of the Second Non-Life Directive. Under the Insurance Companies Act 1982 the parties can choose the law of another country. However, under the Belgian Loi relative au controle des entreprise d'assurances du 9.7.95 as well as under the Spanish Ley 30/1995 de 8 noviembre de Ordenacion y Supervision de los Seguros Privados the parties cannot choose another law when the circumstances indicated in Article 7(1)(a) have occurred.[14] The option for the Member States to grant the parties greater freedom to choose the governing law of the contract raises the question of the number of laws the implementation statutes can indicate as applicable. Are the Member States allowed to indicate any law? If you look at the words 'the law of another country' in the text of Article 7(1)(a), it appears that this provision allows the Member States to grant the freedom of an additional law to those indicated in Article 7(1)(a).[15]

[13] See Dicey and Morris, n 9 above, 1357; Frigessi di Rattalma, *Il contratto internazionale di assicuratione* (Padova, 1990) 167–73; Dubuisson, *Le droit applicable au contrat d'assurance dans un espace communitaire integré* (Doctoral thesis, Université Catholique de Louvain, 1994) 212.

[14] See Merkin and Rodger, *EC Insurance Law* (London and New York, Longman, 1997) 149 ff.

[15] For the same conclusion see Claret, *Contrats d'assurance*, n 3 above, 75.

Despite the clear intention of the drafters to prohibit any choice of law in the situation considered in the first limb of Article 7(1)(a), the formulation of this provision suggests that there is room for a choice of the law applicable to the contract. This conclusion can be derived from two circumstances. First, the Second Non-Life Directive does not define the term 'habitual residence', therefore leaving room for different interpretations of this concept. Secondly, neither Article 7(1)(a) nor the other provisions of the Directive clarify whether the habitual residence is to be ascertained with reference to the conclusion of the contract. One might argue eventually that the habitual residence of the policyholder as a de facto connecting factor cannot be qualified, and the Rome Convention which refers to this concept in Articles 4 and 5 does not define it too. Nevertheless, some questions can arise when one or both parties have more than one habitual residence as is possible when someone shares his time equally between two different places. Article 7(1)(a) does not indicate the habitual residence the judge must take into account in such a case. Unlike the Second Non-Life Directive, the Rome Convention addresses the questions that arise when one or other of the parties has more than one habitual residences. Article 4(2) of the Rome Convention which concerns the characteristic performance of the contract makes clear that habitual residence must be ascertained at the time of conclusion of the contract. It appears that, in the absence of an indication in Article 7(1)(a) of the Second Non-Life Insurance Directive, this rule will apply to determine the habitual residence of the policyholder for the purpose of the application of Article 7(1)(a). This conclusion is suggested by Article 7(3) which provides the application of the rules in the Rome Convention to the questions that are not covered by the choice of law rules of the Second Non-Life Insurance Directive.

9. THE LAW APPLICABLE TO INSURANCE CONTRACTS COVERING A RISK SITUATED IN A MEMBER STATE WHERE THE POLICYHOLDER IS NOT HABITUALLY RESIDENT

Article 7(1)(b) provides that the parties to an insurance contract covering a risk situated in a Member State where the policyholder is not habitually resident can choose between the law of the Member State where the risk is situated and the law of the State where the policyholder is habitually resident or has its central administration. Additional choices for the parties are also available due to Article 7(1)(d) which provides that, where 'the Member State referred to' in Article 7(1)(b) and (c) grant greater freedom of choice, the parties can take advantage of this freedom.[16]

[16] See Dicey and Morris, n 9 above, 1358; Frigessi di Rattalma, *Il contratto internazionale di assicurazione*, n 3 above, 167 *et seq*; Dubuisson, *Le droit applicable au contrat d'assurance*, n 13 above, 211 *et seq*.

At first glance, one might argue that this provision is likely to be applied in most of the situations involving cross-border transactions of insurance services within the Single Market. However, this would be a false conclusion, as Article 2(d) of the Second Non-Life Directive, which defines the risks, makes clear that risks are generally considered to be situated in the Member State where the policyholder has his habitual residence (if an individual) or his 'establishment, to which the contract relates' (if a legal person). Nevertheless, Article 7(1)(b) applies in a number of situations where risks are not supposed to be localised in the policyholder's habitual residence or central administration. Article 7(1)(b) is, therefore, of relevance when the insured risk comprises buildings, travel and holiday risks, motor vehicles.[17] Furthermore, it appears that Article 7(1)(b) applies when the policyholder's habitual residence or central administration is not situated in a Member State. This conclusion is suggested by Article 7(1)(b) which does not require the policyholder's residence to be situated in a Member State. Thus, in the situation where the policyholder is habitually resident in Australia and an insurance contract covers risks for a house in France, the parties are free to choose either Australian or French law to govern the contract.

10. THE LAW APPLICABLE TO INSURANCE CONTRACTS COVERING RISKS SITUATED IN DIFFERENT MEMBER STATES

The Second Non-Life Directive provides in Article 7(1)(c) that where the policyholder pursues a commercial or industrial activity or a liberal profession and the contract covers two or more risks which relate to these activities and which are situated in different Member States, the freedom to choose the law applicable to the contract shall extend to the laws of those Member States and of the State in which the policyholder has his habitual residence or central administration.[18] Therefore, if a commercial company with its central administration in England insures its branches in France and Spain the parties can choose English, French or Spanish law. As already stated above, additional choices of law are also available as a result of Article 7(1)(d).

It is worth noting that Article 7(1)(c) does not grant the parties this choice when an insurance contract covers two or more risks situated in different Member States and is concluded by a non professional policyholder. The reason for this exclusion was the protection of the weaker party, ie the non-professional policyholder, from unilateral choices made by the insurance company which is considered to be in a stronger bargaining position.[19] On the contrary,

[17] See Merkin and Rodger, n 14 above, 150.

[18] See Dicey and Morris, n 9 above, 1359; Frigessi di Rattalma, *Il contratto internazionale di assicurazione*, n 13 above, 167 *et seq*; Dubuisson, *Le droit applicable au contrat d'assurance*, n 13 above, 211 *et seq*.

[19] See Berr, n 2 above, 670.

Article 7(1)(c) applies when an insurance contract covers two or more risks related to a commercial or industrial activity or a profession.

11. WHERE THE MEMBER STATES INDICATED IN ARTICLE 7(1)(B) AND (C) GRANT THE PARTIES GREATER FREEDOM TO CHOOSE THE GOVERNING LAW OF THE CONTRACT

Article 7(1)(d) states that:

> Notwithstanding subparagraphs (b) and (c), where the Member States referred to in those subparagraphs grant greater freedom to choose the applicable law to the contract, the parties may take advantage of this freedom.[20]

This provision has raised two questions in the legal literature which are discussed below.[21] The first question is whether the only States referred to are the Member States in which insured risks are situated. One might argue from the text of Article 7(1)(d) that this provision does not refer to the state in which the policyholder has its habitual residence or its central administration. Article 7(1)(b) and (c) use the word 'country' in relation to the state in which the policyholder has its habitual residence or its central administration. However, such an interpretation would conflict with the fact that risks are generally considered to be situated in the Member State where the policyholder has its habitual residence (if an individual) or its central administration (if a legal person). Therefore, it is unlikely that Article 7(1)(d) does not refer to the Member State in which the policyholder has its habitual residence.

The second question which should be discussed is whether all of the Member States' laws referred to in Article 7(1)(b) and (c) must allow the parties such freedom. It might be argued from the expression 'Member States' in Article 7(1)(d) that the judge must ascertain whether all of these Member States' laws grant the parties greater freedom to choose the governing law of the contract. However, such a liberal interpretation would conflict with the purpose of the choice of laws rules in the Second Non-Life Directive which is to restrict the choice of the applicable law to insurance contracts covering mass risks. Moreover, this interpretation does not take into account the fact that the Member States are free to grant greater freedom of choice. Thus, in the case of an English company insuring branches in Italy and France, if the parties chose Chinese law to govern their agreement and such a choice was permitted under Italian law but not under French law, the choice would not be valid.

[20] See Dicey and Morris, n 9 above, 1360; Frigessi di Rattalma, *Il contratto internazionale*, n 13 above, 167 *et seq*; Dubuisson, *Le droit applicable au contrat d'assurance*, n 13 above, 211 *et seq*.

[21] See Frigessi di Rattalma (1989) *Rivista di diritto internazionale privato e processuale* 578; Dubuisson, *ibid*., 212 *et seq*.

12. THE LAW APPLICABLE TO INSURANCE CONTRACTS COVERING RISKS WHICH ARE LIMITED TO EVENTS OCCURRING IN ONE MEMBER STATE OTHER THAN THE ONE IN WHICH THE RISK IS SITUATED

The Second Non-Life Directive contains a provision relating to insurance contracts covering risks which are limited to events occurring in one Member State other than the one in which the risk is situated. This is in the following terms (Article 7(1)(e)):

> Notwithstanding subparagraphs (a), (b) and (c), when the risks covered by the contract are limited to events occurring in one Member State other than the Member State where the risk is situated, as defined in Article 2(d), the parties may always choose the law of the former State.

This provision grants the parties to liability-insurance contracts an additional choice to those examined above. Article 7(1)(e) is a most unfortunate provision. Legal security is not advanced by it and, far from contributing to certainty in the law, it is likely to create uncertainty. Some uncertainties arise from the word 'events' in the text of this rule. Article 7(1)(e) does not clarify the meaning of this term. However it provides that the Member State in which the events occur has to be other than the Member State where the risk is situated. It appears from the fact that Article 7(1)(e) applies only if the events constituting the tort or delict occur in one Member State that the rule is not very important in practice. It is unlikely, in fact, to apply to an insurance contract covering risks which are limited to events occurring in one Member State. It is quite common especially in the sector of liability insurance for the policy to cover any risk, regardless of the fact that a risk is not limited to events occurring in one state. However, travel insurance policies often cover only risks which are limited to events occurring in the Member State of the trip or vacation.

13. THE LAW APPLICABLE TO INSURANCE CONTRACTS COVERING 'LARGE RISKS'

Article 7(1)(f) adopts the almost universal rule for contract choice of law that the parties are free to choose the law governing their contract. It reads as follows:

> For the risks referred to in Article 5(d)(i) of the First Directive, the parties to the contract may choose any law.[22]

As appears from the text, this rule contains no exception to this principle to the effect that the choice of the governing law must be 'genuine' or 'bona fide'.

[22] See Dicey and Morris, n 9 above, 1354; Frigessi di Rattalma, *Il contratto internazionale di assicurazione*, n 13 above 157 *et seq*; Dubuisson, *Le droit applicable au contrat d'assurance*, n 13 above, 269 *et seq*.

It is true that the first paragraph of Article 8 of the Rome Convention which is recalled by Article 7(3) of the Second Non-Life Directive provides that:

> the existence and validity of a contract, or of any term of a contract shall be determined by the law which would govern it under this Convention if the contract or term were valid.

However that provision relates only to defects in the consent of the parties as to the designation of the applicable law and probably does not deal with the question of genuineness.

Article 7(1)(h) makes clear that the choice referred to, *inter alia*, in Article 7(1)(f) must be 'expressed or demonstrated with reasonable certainty by the terms of the contract or the circumstances of the case'. Given that this rule is identical to Article 3(1) of the Rome Convention, it raises the same questions already discussed above.[23]

Does Article 7(1)(f) grant the parties the right to change the law applicable to the contract? Sir Peter North argues[24] that the right to change the applicable law is an essential aspect of the autonomy of the parties. That right is generally acknowledged, subject to the protection of vested rights and the interests of third parties. The law of the forum indicates whether a change of choice is allowed. Therefore, it appears that Article 7(1)(f) of the Second Non-Life Insurance Directive acknowledges the right to change the law applicable to the contract, subject to the protection of vested rights and the interests of third party beneficiaries.

14. THE LAW APPLICABLE IN THE ABSENCE OF A CHOICE OR A VALID CHOICE

Article 7(1)(h) applies in the absence of an implied or express choice of law. The basic provision is that the contract shall be governed by the law of the *country* with which it is most closely connected. In this respect the Second Non-Life Directive adopts the same approach as Article 4(1) of the Rome Convention. However, English cases prior to the introduction of the Rome Convention spoke of 'the system of law' with which the transaction has its closest and most genuine connection, rather than the country, although there are conflicting dicta on this. Article 7(1)(h) also provides that the law must be chosen from those laws which the parties could validly have chosen under the above provisions.[25]

There is a rebuttable presumption that the law of the country with which the contract is to be treated as being most closely connected is the Member State in which the risk is situated. This will usually be the Member State in which the

[23] See above ch 8, para 5, 146.

[24] See North, *Essays in private international law* (Oxford, Clarendon, 1993) 58–61 at note 123.

[25] See Dicey and Morris, n 9 above, 1361; Frigessi di Rattalma, *Il contratto internazionale di assicurazione*, n 13 above, 170 *et seq*; Dubuisson, *Le droit applicable au contrat d'assurance*, n 13 above, 283 *et seq*.

policyholder is habitually resident, except where the risk covered by the contract comprises motor vehicles, buildings, travel or holiday risks.[26]

Article 7(1)(h) provides no indication of the circumstances in which the rebuttable presumption can be overruled. In the English case of *Crédit Lyonnais v New Hampshire Insurance Company*[27] the Deputy High Court Judge Barbara Dohmann QC stated that two policies under a worldwide insurance programme of a multinational policyholder whose central administration was in France, were governed by English law (ie the law of the country in which the risk was situated), due to the fact that the policies were issued in England by an English underwriting agency to a British branch expressly and exclusively with respect to that UK business. However, some uncertainties remain if the insured's habitual residence or central administration is not in the Member State in which the risk is situated. Dubuisson suggests[28] that the presumption shall be overruled and the law of the country of residence or business establishment of the insurer has to be applied when the insured is not in a weaker bargaining position. This conclusion is supported by the argument that the application of the law of the country in which the insured is habitually resident can be unfair to the insurer as it favours the insured in the sense of being concerned predominantly with the interests of the insured. However this interpretation is not supported by the text of Article 7(1)(h). This provides that the applicable law shall be chosen only between those which the parties could validly have chosen under the preceding paragraphs of Article 7. There is no room therefore for the application of the law of the country in which the insurer is resident if no choice of law has been made.

15. *DÉPEÇAGE*

Unlike the Rome Convention, which grants the parties the right to submit different parts of the same contract to different laws, the Second Non-Life Directive is silent on the point. Article 7(1)(h) of the Second Non-Life Insurance Directive grants the judge, in the absence of a choice or a valid choice, the power to split issues away from the proper law of the contract and subject them to different laws. The difference between the Rome Convention and the Second Non-Life Directive is explained by the fact that the right of the parties to submit parts of the same contract to different laws is a logical consequence of the principle of autonomy.[29] As already stated above, the basic rule of the Rome Convention which provides that a contract has to be governed by the law chosen by the parties cannot be found in the system of the Second Non-Life Directive. Article 7(1)(f) grants the parties to insurance contracts covering certain large risks the

[26] See Art 2(d) of the First Non-Life Insurance Directive.
[27] [1997] 2 Lloyd's Rep 1, CA.
[28] See Dubuisson, *Le droit applicable au contract d'assurance*, n 15 above, 805–6.
[29] See Giuliano and Lagarde Report (1980) OJ C281 of 31 October 1980, 17.

freedom to choose any law. However, Article 7(1)(a), (b), (c), (e) restricts the choice to the laws indicated in the relevant subparagraphs.

Because the right of the parties to *dépeçage* is a logical result of the principle of autonomy it must be acknowledged in all cases that the parties are free to choose the governing law of the contract. Therefore, if an insurance contract covers one of the 'large risks' referred to in Article 7(1)(f) the parties have the right to split issues away from the governing law and subject them to different laws. In contrast, if the insurance contract does not cover one of the risks indicated in Article 7(1)(f), only the judge has the right to *dépeçage*. This is true, despite the fact that the Second Non-Life Insurance Directive does not provide the right of the parties to submit different parts of the same contract to different laws.[30]

Like Article 4 of the Rome Convention, Article 7(1)(h) of the Second Non-Life Directive provides that the *dépeçage* must be coherent, ie the parties cannot subject a part of the contract which is not 'severable' to a different law. Moreover, the part of the contract to be severed must have a closer connection with another country (which must be one of the countries indicated in Article 7(1)). Severance is allowed only 'by way of exception'.

16. THE LAW APPLICABLE TO INSURANCE CONTRACTS COVERING RISKS SITUATED WITHIN AND OUTSIDE THE TERRITORIES OF THE MEMBER STATES OF THE EUROPEAN COMMUNITY

A word needs to be said about the law applicable to insurance contracts covering risks situated both within *and* outside the territories of the European Community. One could be tempted to argue that the law applicable to these contracts shall be determined according both to the choice of law rules of the Rome Convention and the choice of law rules of the Insurance Directives.[31] This conclusion is suggested by Articles 3, paragraphs 1 and 4, paragraph 1 of the Rome Convention and Article 7(1)(h) of the Second Non-Life Insurance Directive, which allow the possibility of different laws applying to the same contract. However, the severance of the contract in such a situation, so that the applicable law would be ascertained according to the choice of law rules of the Second Non-Life Directive in so far as the risk is located within a Member State of the European Community but according to the choice of law provisions of the Rome Convention to the extent that the risk is located outside a Member State, can lead to inconsistent results as between the different laws that can be found to govern the contract under the different régimes.[32] Thus the most reasonable

[30] See Frigessi di Rattalma, *Il contratto internazionale di assicurazione*, n 13 above, 169 *et seq*; Celle, *I contratti di assicurazione grandi rischi nel diritto internazionale privato* (Padova, CEDAM, 2000) 182 *et seq*.

[31] See Dubuisson, *Le droit applicable au contrat d'assurance*, n 13 above 96.

[32] For these criticisms see Dicey and Morris, n 9 above, 1343.

solution is that if the risk covered is 'indivisible' (eg, in the case of a policy on the life of a person habitually resident in a Member State of the European Community and a non-Member State) then only the régime in the Second Non-Life Directive will apply. On the contrary, if the risk is 'divisible' (eg, a policy covering buildings, located in a Member State and a non-Member State of the European Community), then the contract can be split so that the governing law of the parts of the contract insuring each risk will be ascertained separately according to the régime which is pertinent to each of them.[33]

17. THE 'GENERAL PROVISIONS OF PRIVATE INTERNATIONAL LAW': ARTICLE 7(3)

Article 7(3) provides that:

> Subject to the preceding paragraphs, the Member States shall apply to the insurance contracts referred to by this Directive their general rules of private international law concerning contractual obligations.

Though this provision refers to the general rules of private international law of the Member States, it is clear that the reference is to the Rome Convention on the law applicable to contractual obligations.[34] This conclusion can be derived from the majority of the statutes implementing the Second Non-Life Insurance Directive which refer to the Rome Convention. Moreover, it is suggested by the fact that the choice of law rules of the Rome Convention apply in any situation involving a choice between the laws of different countries.

As has already been seen, the Second Non-Life Directive does not provide a complete set of choice of law rules for insurance contracts covering risks situated in a Member State of the European Community. Therefore Article 7(3) applies to issues which are not covered by the choice of law rules of the Second Non-Life Directive, such as the form of the contract, the capacity of the parties, and the existence and validity of the contract.

It goes without saying that the application of the general rules of private international law, ie the provisions in the Rome Convention, cannot be justified by the mere absence of an explicit regulation in the choice of law provisions of the Second Non-Life Directive. It is suggested by the language and meaning of Article 7(3) that this provision applies to issues which are not *explicitly* or *implicitly* governed by the choice of law rules of the Second Non-Life Directive. Thus the judge must ascertain from the circumstances in front of him whether

[33] For the same solution see Dicey and Morris, n 9 above, 1343. But see *American Motorists Insurance Co (AMICO) v Cellstar Corporation and Cellstar (UK) Limited* [2002] EWHC 421 (Comm); discussed, *supra*, ch 8, para 3.1, 138; where Steel D claimed that only the law of the State in which the risks are predominately located applies to a contract of insurance covering risks situated within and outside the territories of the Member States of the European Community.

[34] Dicey and Morris, n 9 above, 1365–66.

an issue is covered by the private international rules of the Second Non-Life Directive.[35]

18. DOES ARTICLE 5 OF THE ROME CONVENTION APPLY TO THE INSURANCE CONTRACTS REFERRED TO BY THE SECOND NON-LIFE DIRECTIVE?

As has already been seen, Article 5 of the Rome Convention applies to contracts of insurance covering risks situated outside the territories of the Member States of the European Community where insurance is provided to the insured for a purpose that can be regarded as being outside his trade or profession. Some uncertainties arise, however, as to whether the protective consumer rules of the Rome Convention apply to insurance contracts referred to by the Second Non-Life Directive. With regards to this, various arguments have been proposed in scholarly writings in favour and against the application of Article 5 of the Rome Convention to these contracts.

The arguments in favour of the application of the protective rules are as follows.

First, this solution can be supported on the basis that as a matter of consumer protection, there is no reason why policyholders with a residence in the European Community require protection by choice of law rules on a different basis from policyholders with a residence outside a Member State of the European Community. Roth argues[36] that the application of Article 5(2) and (3) of the Rome Convention was considered to be unacceptable for the reason that these rules could enable policyholders to buy an out-of-state insurance policy at terms that intra-state-insurers (being bound by the local regulations) might not offer, thereby putting the national insurance companies at a competitive disadvantage. Secondly, the application of the protective provisions of the Rome Convention is suggested by Article 7(3) of the Second Non-Life Directive. As has already been stated in the preceding paragraph, this provision applies to any issue not covered by the choice of law rules of that Directive.

Arguments against the application of Article 5 of the Rome Convention to the insurance contracts referred to by the Second Non-Life Directive are as follows.

One could argue that the only distinction in the text of the Second Non-Life Directive is between insurance contracts covering 'mass risks' and insurance contracts covering 'large risks'. Unlike the Rome and Brussels Conventions, the Second Non-Life Directive does not refer to consumer contracts. Nevertheless, the Directive grants protection to the policyholder of an insurance contract covering 'mass risks' who are supposed to be in a weaker bargaining position. However, unlike the Rome Convention and Brussels Regulation, the Second

[35] See also Dubuisson, *Le droit applicable au contract d'assurance*, n 13 above, 140.

[36] *Cf* Roth, *Article 59 EEC Treaty* in Facilides and d'Oliveira (eds), *International Insurance Law in the EC* (Deventer, Kluwer Law and Taxation, 1993) 75 note 45.

Non-Life Directive grants protection to the 'active consumer', ie the consumer who has not been solicited into a contract by the insurer.

On an arithmetical count the solution toward the application of the protective rules of the Rome Convention has nearly as many arguments in favour as against. However, if you take into account the relative weight to be attached to the different considerations, the picture changes. The distinction between 'mass risks' and 'large risks' shows clearly the intention of the drafters of the Second Non-Life Directive to avoid any other division between the insurance contracts referred to by the Directive. When it comes to the arguments against this solution, it cannot be said that they are sufficient to support the solution in favour of the application of the protective rules of the Rome Convention. The overall conclusion is that the arguments against the application of Article 5 of the Rome Convention to the insurance contracts referred to by the Second Non-Life Directive outweigh those in favour of the application of the protective rules.

19. MANDATORY RULES: ARTICLE 7(1)(G)

Article 7(1)(g) states that

> The fact that, in the case referred to in subparagraph (a) or (f), the parties have chosen a law shall not, where all the other elements relevant to the situation at the time of the choice are connected with one Member State only, prejudice the application of the mandatory rules of the law of that Member State, which means the rules from which the law of that Member State allows no derogation by means of a contract.

This provision deals with the narrow case in which all the relevant factors point to one country, but in which a foreign law has been chosen. In this case, the mandatory provisions of that one country will apply and these are defined as the rules one may not contract out of in a purely domestic situation, or in other words 'rules from which the law of that Member State allows no derogation by means of a contract'. This is a reference to the imperative law and a substantive matter is involved. It is clear that this matter must be dealt with under the criteria of the substantive law, not those of conflict of laws.[37] This provision parallels Article 3(3) of the Rome Convention. However, there are two differences between these provisions. First, it seems that a choice of jurisdiction is an element which shall be taken into consideration for the purpose of Article 7(1)(g) in contrast to the position under Article 3(3) of the Rome Convention.[38] Unlike Article 3(3), Article 7(1)(g) does not distinguish between the choice of a foreign tribunal and the other elements relevant to the situation at the time of the choice. Secondly, unlike Article 3(3), Article 7(1)(g) only applies when the risk covered is situated in a Member State. This conclusion is suggested by the

[37] See de Boer, 54 (1990) *RabelsZ* 24, 56.
[38] See Merkin and Rodger, *EC Insurance Law*, n 14 above, 154 note 119 .

words 'in the cases referred to in subparagraphs (a) or (f)' in the text of Article 7(1)(g).

In connection with the first two cases considered by Article 7(1), the situation in which the risk is located in the same country as the policyholder,[39] it has been questioned why this rule should hinder at all the laws of the Member States.[40] If it pertains to the laws of the Member States to ascertain whether the parties have a choice of law,[41] it could be expected that it would also be left to the laws of the Member States themselves to establish whether the choice of law can impair the application of mandatory rules, This reasoning does not adequately take into consideration one fundamental issue: once a Member State has conferred freedom to determine the applicable law, it becomes a matter of EU law to determine whether in fact 'all the other elements relevant . . . are connected with' that Member State only, in such a way as to warrant disregard of the choice made by the parties to an insurance contract.[42]

An example may illustrate this point. Claims-made policies have been maintained to be contrary to the public policy exception by the French Cour de Cassation, on the grounds that a part of the premium would be paid for a risk not borne by the insurer.[43] Imagine that a French insurer were to cover a French risk with a French resident by a claim-made policy in which English law is selected; or that the same choice is made by the French branch or agency of an insurer which has an English 'passport'; or, finally, that the same is done in the form of cross-border provision of services by London-based insurers. Should it be an issue of French or rather European Union law to establish whether such a choice of law can be overlooked in connection with the essential issue of the validity of the claims-made feature?

In the same vein, it is for the European Union law and not for the domestic laws of the Member States to establish whether 'all the other elements relevant to the situation . . . are connected with' a single Member State with respect to insurance of large risks.[44] Here, the principle of party autonomy finally rules, thanks to the progressive advance of European Union law. It would have been unwise to leave it to the unique discretion of the Member State to determine when such choice might be overridden by their own mandatory rules.[45]

39 Art 7(1)(a).

40 See Smulder and Glazener, *Harmonisation in the Field of Insurance Law through the Introduction of Community Rules of Conflict* (1992) *Common Market Law Review* 784 at note 3.

41 As it is pursuant to the second part of Art 7(1)(a).

42 In fact, the wording of Art 7(1)(g) and the structure of Art 7(1) as a whole show that a Member State cannot invoke Art 7(1)(g) if one of the connecting factors considered in Art 7(1)(b), (c) and (e) points to a different Member State.

43 Hankey (1994) *International Insurance Law Review* 267.

44 Art 7(1)(f).

45 For the same conclusion see Ricolfi (2000) *International Journal of Insurance Law* 147–48.

20. MANDATORY RULES: ARTICLE 7(2)(1)

Article 7(2)(1) provides that

> Nothing in this Article shall restrict the application of the rules of the law of the forum in a situation where they are mandatory, irrespective of the law otherwise applicable to the contract.

These rules to which Article 7(2)(1) refers have been qualified in the French and Belgian literature as *règles d'application immédiate*.[46] This means that they are priority rules in the sense that if a certain situation arises, this leads to the application of the mandatory provisions before recourse can be had to any normal choice of law rule. It has to be pointed out that the mandatory rules in Article 7(2)(1) of the Second Non-Life Directive refer to overriding the choice of law.[47] It may be added that it has to be 'a situation' where provisions are mandatory. Provisions are mandatory in certain situations. As it appears from a comparison between Article 7(2)(1) of the Second Non-Life Directive and Article 7(2) of the Rome Convention, the former closely parallels the latter.

21. MANDATORY RULES: ARTICLE 7(2)(2)

Article 7(2)(2) gives the courts of the forum a discretionary power to take into consideration the mandatory rules of the Member State in which the risk is situated or of the Member State imposing the obligation to take out insurance.

This latter provision is highly controversial. The United Kingdom has exercised its rights under Article 22(1)(a) of the Rome Convention to make a reservation allowing it not to apply Article 7(1) of the Rome Convention. But it is unclear whether English judges will also decline to apply the parallel rule set out in Article 7(2)(2) of the Directive. They are surely not obliged to do so by the reservation, which is restricted to an international agreement, the Rome Convention, that explicitly excludes contracts of insurance covering risks situated in the territories of the Member States of the European Community from its scope of application.[48]

Apart from that, unlike Article 7(2)(1) which closely parallels the corresponding provision of the Rome Convention, Article 7(2)(2) greatly differs from the corresponding Article 7(1) of the Rome Convention. The most relevant difference between these provisions is that Article 7(2)(2) does not give the court a discretionary power to take into account mandatory rules of a foreign country with which the situation has a close connection, but allows it to take into consideration only the imperative provisions of the Member State in which the risk

[46] See, eg Lagarde (1991) *Revue critique de droit international privé* 287.

[47] See Frigessi di Rattalma, *Il contratto internazionale di assicurazione*, n 13 above, 178 *et seq*.

[48] For same conclusion see Ricolfi, n 45 above.

covered is situated or of the Member State imposing the obligation to take out insurance. By drawing this distinction the drafters of Article 7(2)(2) no doubt intended to restrict the number of the laws applicable to the insurance contracts referred to by the Second Non-Life Insurance Directive. Another difference is the absence in Article 7(2)(2) of a reference to the 'nature' and 'purpose' of the mandatory rules. This solution was probably adopted to bypass the questions that can arise from these guiding principles. Nevertheless, it appears that the judge may refer to the 'nature' and 'scope' of a mandatory rule as well as to 'the consequences of their application or non application' to determine whether a rule is internationally mandatory for the purpose of Article 7(2)(2). However, other elements can be taken into consideration, such as the interests of the forum and the fact that a rule is necessary to safeguard the political, social and economic structures of a country.

Though the relevant rules in the Second Non-Life Insurance Directive only refer to mandatory provisions taking effect where a choice of law is made, the general objective of mandatory rules, which is to restrict the freedom of contract of the contracting parties, suggests that such rules should apply to attempts to evade such mandatory rules through contract terms as well as by a choice of foreign law.[49] This issue is relevant for insurers in the United Kingdom mainly as regards the transactions of insurance in other Member States whether on an establishment or service basis.[50] Due to the absence of mandatory provisions from the law of insurance contracts in the United Kingdom the issue is much less relevant for insurance products and services sold in the United Kingdom. This means that there will be no control over the incorporation of substantive rules of foreign law into policies sold in the United Kingdom, irrespective of whether the insurer is authorised in the United Kingdom or elsewhere (including countries outside the European Union).

22. THE RELATIONSHIP BETWEEN PUBLIC LAW PROVISIONS AND CHOICE OF LAW RULES IN THE SECOND NON-LIFE INSURANCE DIRECTIVE

A choice of law has no effect on the establishment of which national supervisory authority is responsible for the activities of insurers who sell insurance products and services on a cross-border basis because this issue is regulated by the system of the unique licence and home country control contained in the EC Insurance Directives.[51] Nevertheless, it is possible for public law provisions relating to the prudential supervision of insurers to have an impact on contractual conditions

[49] For the same conclusion see MacNeil, *UK Report on the implementation of the EC choice of laws rules for insurance* in Frigessi di Rattalma and Seatzu (eds), *The Implementation Provisions of the EC Choice of Law Rules for Insurance Contracts in Belgium, France, Germany, Italy, The Netherlands, Spain and the United Kingdom: A Commentary* (The Hague, Kluwer Law International, 2003) forthcoming.

[50] *Ibid.*

[51] *Ibid.*

and terms. For example, it is possible for the law on supervision of insurers to check the sum payable to a life policyholder where the policy is waived prior to the maturity date specified by the policy. The banning contained in the EC Insurance Directives on prior approval by national insurance supervisors of policy rates and forms has critically diminished the scope for public law rules to determine insurance contract terms but the issue is still of importance.[52]

The relationship between public law and conflict of laws is increasingly discussed in the legal writings.[53] It appears that this topic deserves particular attention in the present context due to the existence of a large number of public law rules especially in the non-life insurance sector.

Legal literature is very divided as to the relation between public law and choice of law rules. As regards this, one can identify three main views, which must be examined separately.

The first view tends to demonstrate the existence of a relationship between choice of law and public law provisions, albeit in a disguised manner. According to Baade,[54] the public law character of a provision of foreign law no longer creates an obstacle to its incidental application as part of the applicable law (*lex causae*) by the forum state. This author derives his conclusion mainly from the 1975 resolution adopted on this topic by the Institut de droit international in Wiesbaden.[55]

In contrast to the above view, a part of the legal literature tends to demonstrate that there is no relationship between choice of law and public law; such authors hold firmly to traditional positions on the nature of private international law rules, and maintain that the choice of law provisions are in essence indifferent to public law rules.[56]

Lastly, a third approach attempts to reconcile the above two views by sustaining the existence of a limited interaction between public law and conflict of laws. According to the supporters of this thesis, only the operation of the public law rules which govern the relationship between private parties can be achieved through the choice of law provisions.[57] In the sector of non-life insur-

[52] *The Implementation Provisions of the EC Choice of Law Rules for Insurance Contracts in Belgium, France, Germany, Italy, The Netherlands, Spain and the United Kingdom: A Commentary* (The Hague, Kluwer Law International, 2003) forthcoming.

[53] See the reports in the *Basle Symposium on the Rôle of Foreign Public Law in Private International Law* (Bâle et Francfort-sur-le-Main, 1986).

[54] See Baade, *Operation of Foreign Public Law*, in *International Encyclopedia of Comparative Law*, vol III, *Private International Law* (JCB Mohr, Tubingen, Boston, Lancaster, 1990) 40.

[55] See the text of the resolution in *Annuaire de l'Institut de droit International*, vol 56, 1975, 50 *et seq*.

[56] See Battifol and Lagarde, *Droit international privé*, vol I, (1981) 291.

[57] See *inter alia* Kreuzer, *Lausanner Kolloquium über den deutschen und den schweizerischen Gesetzenentwurf zur Neuregelung des Internationalen Privatrechts* (1984), 3, 4, 9; Picone, *L'applicazione extraterritoriale delle regole sulla concorrenza e il diritto internazionale*, in Capotorti, Di Sabato, Patroni Griffi, Picone, Ubertazzi, *Il fenomeno delle concentrazioni di imprese nel diritto interno e internazionale* (Milano, Giuffré, 1989) 174ff; Lugato, *Assicurazioni sociali e diritto internazionale privato* (Milano, Giuffré, 1994), especially 68, 143.

ance this means that the rules which fix the terms of the contract could be applied through the choice of law rules of the directive.

The Second Non-Life Directive does not clarify the relationship between its choice of law rules and the public law provisions of the Member States. It follows that due to the absence of indications in the text of the directive and the legal writings there is room for different approaches by the national courts of the Member States.

23. SOME REMARKS ON THE CONFLICT OF LAWS ISSUES ARISING FROM BAD FAITH INSURANCE

It is known that the law of insurance contracts in many countries provides that if the policyholder is shown to have misrepresented material facts about his risks in his application the insurer can cancel the contract ex post facto and refuse to pay any claims.[58] Moreover, a duty of good faith and fair dealing can be, and normally is, imposed upon the insurer towards his insured. This duty of good faith and fair dealing towards the insured is widespread, but implemented with unequal strictness under common law or civil law.[59]

The concern is here with the private international law issues arising from insurance policies that contain a duty of good faith and fair dealing upon the insurer towards his insured. In examining these issues the starting point should be the legal nature of the good faith principle. This matter having been established, we can go on to consider the law applicable to the different facets of the insurance policies containing an explicit or implicit obligation applicable to the insurer of 'good faith and fair dealing'. The question of characterisation arises at two levels. First, there is the characterisation of the good faith principle itself. Is this a purely contractual issue, a tort issue or a mixture of the two? This has to be determined according to the law of the forum. Secondly, where the duty of good faith is breached by the insurer, which is the applicable law to the liability of the insurer?

The identification of the substantive law is complicated by the fact that many bad faith cases include relevant events which occurred in different States. Consider this hypothetical case: an Italian insured drives to France. There he collides with a pedestrian who sues in that country. His carrier, from the home office in England, decides not to defend the suit. The insured is defaulted and sues his carrier, in Italy, for bad faith. Which State supplies the substantive law? Italy, the forum State and place where the policy was delivered? France, where the insured was defaulted? England, where the 'bad faith' decision was taken? Neither the Second Non-Life Insurance Directive nor the Second Life Insurance

58 See Houser (1994) *Tort and Insurance Law Journal* 37–45.

59 For further references see Zimmermann and Whittaker (eds), *Good faith in European contract law* (Cambridge, Cambridge University Press, 2000).

Directive clarify whether the obligation upon the insurer of 'good faith and fair dealing' towards his insured is governed by the law applicable to the insurance contract. This is probably due to the uncertainties surrounding this obligation under the laws of most Member States of the European Community. Thus you have to look at the real aim of the insurance bad faith actions against the insurer and the relationship between these actions and thc insurance policy. As these actions focus on the performance of the policy, the judge has to apply the law of the country in which performance takes place. This is true either for an insurance bad faith action, which is brought against an insurer for breach of his duty of 'good faith and fair dealing' in an insurance contract covering a risk situated in the territory of the Member States of the European Community, and for an insurance bad faith action which is brought against an insurer for breach of his duty of 'good faith and fair dealing' in an insurance contract covering a risk situated outside the territories of the Member States of the European Community.[60] The law of the place of performance (*lex loci solutionis*) will, in particular, apply to the consequences of the breach of the good faith principle, including the assessment of damages in so far as it is governed by rules of law and the issues of prescription and limitation of actions.

24. EVALUATION

(a) An Excessively Restricted Choice of Law

Some restrictions on the parties' right to choose the law applicable are inevitable in insurance cases, given the existence of situations in which the insured is in a weaker bargaining position. But to deny the parties the right to choose the law of the country in which the insurer is established (home country law) produces an excessively restricted choice. This is unfair to the insurance company.[61]

(b) Limiting the Freedom of Services Within the Single Insurance Market

By allowing the enforcement of mandatory provisions, Article 7(2) of the Second Non-Life Directive produces the effect that the enjoyment of the freedom of insurance services in different Member States cannot be identical. For the purposes of insurance services, and especially with regards to issues of application of the governing law of the contract, this might be a case for mandatory provisions of the forum or host State which set provisions aimed (a) at prescribing specific requirements for insurance undertakings in order to protect the purchases from them, (b) at protecting the insured, (c) at maintaining the

[60] Art 10(2) of the Rome Convention.

[61] For the same consideration see Lando in Facilides and Jessurum d'Oliveira (eds), *International Insurance Contract Law*, n 4 above, 111–12.

integrity of national insurance markets. It is clear that the application of such rules can modify the chances of the insurance company supplying its services in the same manner as in its home state. The application of the host State rules, in particular, can make the insurance company's activities more difficult.

In the *Alpine Investments* judgment[62] the European Court of Justice states that a regime which 'deprives the operators concerned of a rapid and direct technique for marketing and contacting potential clients' constitutes a restriction of the freedom of services. It is clear that, in order to market an insurance product easily and efficiently, operators needs to ascertain the law applicable to the contract rapidly. However, Article 7(1)(a), (b), (c), (e) of the Directive lays down a very complex set of rules on the law applicable to the insurance contracts referred to by the Second Non-Life Directive and therefore hinders the exercise of the freedom of insurance services within the Single Market.

(c) Lack of Co-ordination Between the Jurisdiction Rules of the Brussels Regulation and the Choice of Law Rules of the Second Non-Life Directive

It is well known that the relationship between jurisdiction and choice of law has become close during the eighties with its emphasis on the appropriate forum. Jurisdiction provisions have been affected by a consideration of choice of law policies so that, often, jurisdiction is being taken on the basis that a certain law is applicable and declined if it does not apply. Moreover, the development of choice of law is no longer independent of jurisdiction.[63]

Nonetheless, the choice of law provisions of the Second Non-Life Directive do not seem to fit in with the Brussels Regulation on jurisdiction. There is a difference in the way the scope of application is determined. Whilst choice of law matters are connected to the location of risks, jurisdiction is based on the domicile (usually of the policy-holder). Moreover, it appears that the choice of law rules of the Second Non-Life Directive do not provide any antidote to the excessively wide choice of fora in insurance cases. On the contrary, the Second Non-Life Directive encourages forum shopping. This is true for Article 2(d) which provides definitions of the risks for the purpose of the application of the choice of law rules in the directive. As already stated above, this provision gives the Member States a wide freedom of implementation and, therefore, encourages the parties to forum shop for substantive law reasons.

(d) Lack of Choice of Law Rules on the Agency Relationship

Another criticism which may be advanced against the choice of law rules in the Second Non-Life Directive is that they do not encompass the agency relationship.

[62] Case 384/93 [1995] ECR I-4795.
[63] See Fawcett (1991) *Current Legal Problems* 39 *et seq.*

This might discourage agents and brokers from entering into cross-border insurance transactions as they are unlikely to have a precise comprehension of their duties and rights. There is, in fact, little harmonisation of the substantive law in Europe on insurance agents and intermediaries.[64]

Due to the absence of a specific choice of law rule on the agency relationship, one might be tempted to conclude that the rules in the Rome Convention apply to this issue. Article 7(3) of the Second Non-Life Directive provides that the choice of law rules of the Rome Convention apply to the issues which are not covered by the Directive. However, such a conclusion would conflict with Article 1(2)(f) of the Rome Convention which excludes from the scope of the Convention 'the question whether an agent is able to bind a principal or an organ to bind a company or body corporate or unincorporate, to a third party'. Therefore, it appears that no uniform rules apply to the issue and traditional choice of law provisions will continue to govern the relationship between principal and third party. This raises some problems in the United Kingdom as it is not always easy to determine for whom an agent is acting. It has been maintained that a Lloyd's broker always acts for the insured but the case-law on other instances of agency is less clear.[65]

(e) Lack of Co-ordination Between Public Law and Choice of Law Rules

As has already been stated above, the Second Non-Life Insurance Directive totally fails to address the issue of whether the public law rules of a Member State can be applied through the choice of law provisions laid down in Articles 7 and 8. This is a failure of harmonisation which might seriously affect the operation of the Directive's choice of law provisions because of the existence of a large number of public law rules in the non-life insurance sector.

(f) An Excessive Freedom of Implementation of the Choice of Law Rules

One might be tempted to justify the wide freedom of implementation of the choice of law rules granted by the Second Non-Life Insurance Directive by looking at the nature of the Directives which are binding only 'as to the result to be achieved' and leave to the Member States of the European Community 'the choice of form and methods' for the implementation. However, an excessive freedom of implementation of the choice of law provisions merely reduces the level of conflicts law harmonisation between the Member States.

[64] See above ch 1, para 16.

[65] For further references on this point see MacNeil, *UK Report on the Implementation of the EC Choice of Laws Rules for Insurance* in Frigessi di Rattalma and Seatzu (eds), *The Implementation Provisions of the EC Choice of Law Rules for Insurance Contracts in Belgium, France, Germany, Italy, The Netherlands, Spain and the United Kingdom* (forthcoming).

II
The Choice of Law Rules in the Third Non-Life Insurance Directive

25. THE LAW APPLICABLE TO INSURANCE CONTRACTS COVERING 'LARGE RISKS': ARTICLE 27

Article 27 of the Third Non-Life Directive, by amending Article 7(1)(f) of the Second Non-Life Directive, enlarges the freedom of choice to insurance contracts insuring any large risk. The additional classes of risks covered are:

(a) classes 3 (land vehicles) and 10 (motor vehicle liability);
(b) classes 14 (credit) and 15 (suretyship) where the policyholder is engaged professionally in an industrial or commercial activity or in a profession and the risks relate to such activity;
(c) classes 8 (fire and natural forces), 9 (other damage to property), 13 (general liability) and 16 (miscellaneous financial loss) where the policyholder exceeds certain criteria as to size and financial status.[66]

By extending the freedom of choice to insurance contracts covering any large risk, Article 27 eliminates the questions raised by Article 7(1)(f) of the Second Non-Life Insurance Directive on the scope of the classes of risks and the types of non-life insurance contracts encompassed by them. Moreover, it eliminates discriminatory treatment as regards the law applicable to insurance contracts covering the same type of risks (large risks) and concluded by policyholders in the same bargaining position.

It is clear that Article 27 grants the parties the freedom to choose either the law of a Member or a non-Member State.[67] Unlike Article 7(1)(c) of the Second Non-Life Directive, Article 27 does not restrict the choice to the laws of the Member States. However, some restrictions of the freedom to choose the applicable law may arise from the public policy exception of Article 16 of the Rome Convention and the mandatory rules (the so-called *lois de police* or 'rules of immediate application') of Articles 7(1)(g) and 7(2)(1), (2) of the Second Non-Life Insurance Directive.

[66] As reported by Merkin and Rodger, *EC Insurance Law*, n 14 above 148.

[67] See Morse (CGJ), *Party Autonomy in International Insurance Contract Law* in Facilides and Jessurum d'Oliveira (eds), *International Insurance Contract Law, n 4 above*, 37 note 6; Fallon (1989) *Revue Giuridique de l'Assurance Terrestre* 252 note 6; Dubuisson, *Le droit applicable au contract d'assurance*, n 13 above, 272.

26. THE LAW APPLICABLE TO INSURANCE CONTRACTS COVERING 'MASS RISKS': ARTICLE 28

It is submitted that Article 28 of the Third Non-Life Insurance Directive contains a choice of law rule, albeit in a disguised manner.[68] By stating that 'the Member State in which a risk is situated shall not prevent a policyholder from concluding a contract with an insurance undertaking authorised under the conditions of Article 6 of Directive 73/239/EEC', this provision grants the parties the freedom to choose the applicable law. A words needs to be said in this section about the scope of application of this choice of law provision.

Article 28 applies to insurance contracts covering 'mass risks' (ie risks that are not major commercial risks). This conclusion is derived from the history of this provision and the wording of the corresponding Article 25 of the Draft Non-Life Insurance Directive which provided that:

> the Member State in which the risk is situated shall not prevent the policyholder from concluding a contract conforming with the *rules of the home Member State*, as long as it does not conflict with legal provisions protecting the general good in the Member State in which the risk is situated.

As appears from the text, Article 25 provided the application of the law of the country in which the policyholder is established. Due to the fact that Article 7(1)(f) of the Second Non-Life Directive as modified by Article 27 of the Third Non-Life Directive grants the parties to an insurance contract covering large risks the right to choose the law of the country in which the policyholder is established, it is clear that Article 28 (ex Article 25) does not apply to insurance contracts covering 'large risks'. It would be unreasonable, in fact, to maintain the existence in the system of private international law laid down by the EC Insurance Directives of two identical rules for insurance contracts covering 'large risks'. One might argue eventually, as regards this, that Article 28 of the Third Non-Life Directive is different from Article 25 of the Draft Non-Life Directive. However, like Article 25 of the Draft Directive, Article 28 of the Third Non-Life Directive provides for the application of the law of the country in which the policyholder is established (home country law). Article 28 applies therefore to insurance contracts which do not cover major commercial risks such as the contracts that cover all accident and sickness insurance, all insurance against loss or damage caused to or by land vehicles and all risks which fail to satisfy the conditions necessary for classification as major risks.

[68] See the observations about Art 25 of the draft third non-life directive of Reichert Facilides in Reichert Facilides and Jessurun d'Oliveira (eds), *International Insurance Contract Law*, n 4 above, 194–95. But see Dubuisson, *Le droit applicable au contract d'assurance*, n 13 above, 765 *et seq*.

27. THE RELATIONSHIP BETWEEN MANDATORY RULES AND 'GENERAL GOOD'

As already stated above, the notion of 'general good' has been developed by the European Court of Justice to widen the scope of the Treaty provisions on freedom of movement from mere non-discrimination principles to general prohibitions on all measures that constitute restrictions to the freedom of movement across borders.[69] A word needs to be said about the relationship between mandatory rules and general good exception in the non-life insurance sector.

It must be pointed out that the notion of 'general good' does not identify itself with that of *lois de police*. This conclusion is derived, inter alia, from the Third Non-Life Directive which does not refer to the general good exception in the same provisions as those concerning international mandatory rules. Moreover, it is suggested by the fact that mandatory rules and the general good exception do not pursue the same goals. Whilst the main purpose of the mandatory rules is to take account of national interests in evasion cases, the goal of the general good exception is to avoid the evasion of the Treaty of Rome provisions on the freedom to provide services. It appears that the reference to the general good exception in Article 28 is explained by the fact that trade barriers to the freedom to provide services usually arise from protective measures adopted in the field of insurance contracts covering mass risks (ie risks that are not major commercial risks). As already stated above, Article 28 of the Third Non-Life Directive applies to contracts of insurance which cover mass risks.

28. THE RELATIONSHIP BETWEEN ARTICLES 28 AND 7(1)(A), (B), (C), (D), (E) OF THE SECOND NON-LIFE DIRECTIVE

Has Article 7(1)(a), (b), (c), (d), (e) of the Second Non-Life Directive been repealed by Article 28 of the Third Non-Life Directive? This question arises from the fact that Article 28 applies to insurance contracts covering 'mass risks' and grants the parties a wider choice. However, it appears that Article 28 did not repeal Article 7(1)(a), (b), (c), (d), (e), which applies in the absence of a choice or a valid choice. As already stated above, Article 7(1)(h) provides that 'if no choice has been made, the contract shall be governed by the law of the country, from amongst those considered in the relevant subparagraphs above'. By allowing the parties a wider choice of law, Article 28 did not modify Article 7(1)(h) which does not deal with the freedom to choose the applicable law. Article 7(1)(h) refers to the laws indicated in Article 7(1)(a), (b), (c), (d), (e). Therefore, it is clear that these provisions have not been repealed by Article 28 of the Third Non-Life Directive but still operate if a choice or a valid choice has not been made.

[69] See above ch 1, para 12.3.

29. FROM THE FREE CHOICE OF LAW RULE TO THE 'AWARE CHOICE OF LAW' PRINCIPLE: ARTICLE 31(1), (2), (3)

It is undoubtedly true that one of the most interesting aspects of the Third Non-Life Directive is the duty imposed on the insurer to inform the policy-holder on the law applicable to the contract. Article 31 of the Directive reads as follows:

1. Before an insurance contract is concluded the insurance undertaking shall inform the policyholder of:
   —the law applicable to the contract where the parties do not have a free choice, or the fact that the parties are free to choose the law applicable and, in the latter case, the law the insurer proposes to choose,
   —the arrangements for handling policyholders' complaints concerning contracts including, where appropriate, the existence of a complaints body, without prejudice to the policyholders' right to take legal proceedings.
2. The obligation referred to in paragraph 1 shall apply only where the policyholder is a natural person.
3. The rules for implementing this Article shall be determined in accordance with the law of the Member State in which the risk is situated.[70]

This is a very long and complex provision which deserves attention due to its impact on the freedom of the parties to choose the law applicable to the contract. As appears from the text, this provision does not deal solely with private international law issues but also with co-operation matters. The present section is concerned with the choice of law issues.

Although a similar provision is laid down in the Second Non-Life Directive, Article 31 expands the scope of the duty of information imposed on the insurer in order to protect the policy-holder/natural person who is assumed to be in a weaker bargaining position. This constitutes a change since Article 21(1) of the Second Non-Life Directive applies to insurance contracts covering 'mass risks', regardless of whether the policy-holder is a natural or legal person. It is worth noting that this original technique is consistent with the single authorisation system which grants competence to the insurer's home State. Though the authorisation system does not deal with choice of law issues, it is clear that a rule imposing the application of a certain law to an insurance contract concluded by a policy-holder/natural person would affect the competence of the law of the insurer's home State. Nevertheless, the protective rules of Article 5 of the Rome Convention apply to

> a contract the object of which is the supply of goods or services to a person ('the consumer') for a purpose which can be regarded as being outside his trade or profession.

Although the 'consumer' is usually a natural person, it is clear that this provision applies also to the policy-holder/legal person when the contract is

[70] See Dubuisson, *Le droit applicable au contrat d'assurance*, n 13 above, 311–13.

concluded for a purpose which can be considered 'as being outside his trade or profession'. Similarly, Article 15 of the Brussels Regulation applies to 'a contract concluded by a person for a purpose which can be regarded as being outside his trade or profession'. Unlike Article 5 of the Rome Convention and Article 13 of the Brussels Regulation, Article 31 of the Third Non-Life Directive not only takes care to protect the 'passive' consumer, ie the consumer who has been solicited into a contract in his/her country of residence, but also the 'active consumer', ie the consumer who concludes a contract in another Member State. Apart from the fact that the consumer has to be a natural person, there are no other conditions in Article 31 for the application of the duty of information.

30. EVALUATION

(a) Strengths of the Choice of Law Rules of the Third Non-Life Directive

(i) Expanding an Excessively Restricted Choice

By allowing the parties of an insurance contract covering a mass risk to choose, *inter alia*, the law of the country in which the insurer is established, Art. 28 of the Third Non-Life Directive gives the insurer a wider choice than happens under Art. 7(1)(a), (b), (c) and (e) of the Second Non-Life Directive, with its excessively restricted choice to the parties.

(ii) Providing Protection for Insureds Within the European Community

This is one of the major strengths of the Third Non-Life Insurance Directive. The duty of information imposed on the insurer as regards the law applicable to the contract undeniably operates in a pro-insured way. However, if you look at Article 31 as a whole it is not as aggressively pro-insured as might appear at first sight. It only attempts to balance out the interests of the parties by making both responsible for the choice of law. The insurer can have no real cause for complaint as regards this obligation, because it does not affect his right to choose the applicable law.

(b) Weaknesses of the Choice of Law Rules of the Third Non-Life Directive

(i) Limiting the Freedom of Services Within the Single Insurance Market

Although the Third Non-Life Directive provides 'the operators concerned with *insurance transactions* of a rapid and direct technique for marketing and contacting potential clients', there are still restrictions on the freedom of insurance services within the Single Market arising from the conflict of law rules laid down in the Second and Third Non-Life Directives. As has been stated above, by permitting the enforcement of international mandatory rules Article 7(2) of the Second Non-Life Directive produces the effect that the enjoyment of the freedom of insurance services in different States cannot be identical.

(ii) Lack of Co-ordination Between the Jurisdiction Rules of the Brussels Convention and the Choice of Law Provisions of the Third Non-Life Insurance Directive

There is a lack of co-ordination between the jurisdiction rules of the Brussels Convention and the choice of law provisions of the Third Non-Life Insurance Directive. The choice of law rules of the Directive do not appear to fit in with the rules on jurisdiction in the Brussels Convention. There is a difference in the way the scope of application is determined. Whilst choice of law issues are connected to the location of the risk, jurisdiction is based on the domicile (usually of the policy-holder). Moreover, the choice of law provisions of the Third Non-Life Insurance Directive do not provide any antidote to the excessively wide choice of fora in insurance cases.

(iii) Lack of Choice of Law Provisions on the Agency Relationship

Like the choice of law rules of the Second Non-Life Directive, the choice of law rules of the Third Non-Life Directive do not encompass the agency relationship. It is worth noting that a different approach is taken in the American Restatement (Second) Conflict of Laws. Section 318 of the Restatement Second contains a special rule for insurance policies delivered by agents.[71] Moreover, section 319 lays down an *ad hoc* provision for insurance policies mailed to brokers.[72]

(iv) Lack of Co-ordination Between Public Law and Choice of Law Rules

Another criticism which can be made against the choice of law rules of the Third Non-Life Directive is that they do not address the issue of whether the public law provisions of the Member States can be applied through the EC choice of law rules.

(v) Uncertainty of the Notion of 'General Good'

The brevity of the reference to the 'general good' in Article 28 of the Third Non-Life Insurance Directive, which gives it its simplicity, has a downside in that it

[71] S 318 provides that: 'When an insurance policy becomes effective upon delivery and is sent by the company to its agent and by him delivered to the assured, the place of contracting is where it is this delivered to the assured'.

[72] S 319 reads as follows: 'When an offer for an insurance contract is received by the company through a broker who acts for a client, and the policy is effective on delivery, the place of contracting is where the policy is posted or otherwise delivered to the broker'.

leads to considerable uncertainty, both in relation to its meaning and its control by the national courts and insurance authorities. The drafters of the Third Non-Life Directive fail to clarify the meaning of general good beyond the terse statement that a definition of the general good is not possible due to its evolutionary nature. Tison argues[73] that the 'general good' can be described only as:

> an open-ended concept by nature, embracing the possibilities for Member States to maintain, in the absence of Community legislation, their regulation for the protection of special social values which are not incompatible with the objectives of the Treaty.

But how can the 'general good' be ascertained? What is the relationship between the 'general good' and the Treaty of Rome provisions on free movement of services? What is the difference between the 'general good' and the public order exception to the Treaty freedom? What kind of control can the national insurance authorities exercise on the application of the 'general good'? What is the balance between the fundamental Treaty freedoms and the Member States' interests in the regulation of their values? It is clear that these uncertainties may discourage insurers from selling insurance products and services by way of freedom of services within the Single Insurance Market.

(vi) Conclusion

On an arithmetical count the weaknesses of the choice of law rules laid down in the Third Non-Life Insurance Directive greatly exceed the strengths. This picture does not change if you take into consideration the relative weight to be attached to the different characteristics. The Third Non-Life Directive does not score very well in terms of providing harmonising choice of law provisions, which is one of the most important considerations in Europe. Moreover, it produces an unacceptable degree of complexity and incompatibility with the objective of the Single Market of abolishing obstacles to the free movement of insurance services in Europe.

31. OPTIONS FOR REFORM

(a) Providing an Answer to the Questions Arising from the Notion of 'General Good'

The most direct way of dealing with the lack of certainty as regards the 'general good' is to introduce a definition in the text of Article 28. However, it appears that this is a difficult task to achieve as is demonstrated by the attempts that have been made by legal scholars and recently by the EU Commission. Similar considerations apply to most of the questions arising from the notion of 'general

[73] See Tison, (1997) *Legal Issues of European Integration* 11.

good' and especially to the relationship between the fundamental Treaty freedoms and the Member States' interests. Moreover, this solution would not stop the other basic failings of the choice of law rules of the Third Non-Life Directive.

(b) Re-wording Article 1(3) of the Rome Convention

Under this solution Article 1(3) of the Rome Convention would be re-worded so that it would encompass contracts of insurance which cover risks situated in the territories of the Member States of the European Community. This would have the advantage of introducing a single set of choice of law rules for insurance contracts, regardless of whether the risk is situated in or outside the territories of a Member State. As already stated above, the choice of law rules of the Rome Convention adopt suitable connecting factors for insurance contracts and thus ensure that the interests of the parties are respected.[74] Moreover, due to the fact that the Third Non-Life Directive grants the parties a wide choice of law in relation to contracts of insurance which cover mass risks there is no reason for a parallel set of choice of rules to the provisions in the Rome Convention.[75] Furthermore, this solution would eliminate or reduce differences between the laws applicable to the contracts of original insurance and reinsurance and, therefore, inconsistency between the two contracts.[76] It goes without saying that the choice of law rules of the Rome Convention shall be modified to encompass the agency relationship and to co-ordinate them with public law rules of the Member States. However, this does not appear to be a serious problem as the Rome Convention will be re-negotiable from the year 2001.[77] It is worth noting that the 1994 Inter-American Convention on the law applicable to contractual obligations, which reproduces most of the choice of law rules of the 1980 Rome Convention, does not contain a provision equivalent of Article 1, paragraph 3 of the Rome Convention. Therefore, in Venezuela and Mexico which have implemented this Convention the same choice of law rules apply to insurance contracts regardless of the fact that the risk is situated in or outside the territories of a Member State.[78]

[74] See above ch 5, para 26(1).

[75] But see Delaume (1981) *Virginia Journal of International Law* 104, who advocates the adoption of special choice of law rules for the different types of contracts; see also Cavers (1975) *South California Law Review* 603; Nadelmann (1976) *American Journal of Comparative Law* 1 *et seq*; Nadelmann (1974) *Harvard International Law Journal* 213 *et seq*.

[76] See Law Commission and the Scottish Law Commission, *Private International Law Report on the choice of law rules in the Draft Non-Life Insurance Service Directive* (London, HMSO, 1979) note 47.

[77] Article 26

[78] For a commentary of this Convention see Juenger (1994) *American Journal of Comparative Law* 381–93; Fernandez Arroyo (1995) *Revue critique de droit international privé* 178 *et seq*; Fernandez Arroyo, *La codificación del Derecho internacional privado en América Latina* (Madrid, Eurolex, 1994).

10

The Applicable Law Under the Second and Third Life Assurance Directives

1. INTRODUCTION

IN THIS chapter, the concern is with life assurance contracts covering risks situated in the territories of a Member State of the European Economic Community. These contracts take various forms, such as, for example, fixed sum life insurance and fixed annuities, on the one hand, and more complex forms, such as variable annuities and group assurance, that involve more than a simple transfer of the mortality risk, on the other hand. I do not propose however to deal separately with each of these types of contract, as they all have in common the fact that they involve a transfer and distribution of risk which is not within the control of either party. Any such distribution and transfer can, irrespective of the type of contract, be subject to restriction of time and scope, so it is submitted that the distribution and transfer are the essential points. When the discussion is based on the example of a traditional life insurance it is, therefore, submitted that the same discussion and analysis would equally apply to variable annuities and other formats.

The main instruments in relation to life assurance contracts choice of law are now the Second and Third Life Directive. I will analyse their impact on this topic in detail. Their provisions will be the starting point of the analysis.

But before starting the examination of the choice of law provisions of the Second and Third Life Directives, the scheme of the set of choice of law rules will be discussed.

2. SCHEME OF THE SET OF CHOICE OF LAW PROVISIONS IN THE SECOND AND THIRD LIFE ASSURANCE DIRECTIVES.

The rules on the applicable law are contained in Article 4 of the Second Life Assurance Directive of 1990 and Article 28 of the Third Life Assurance Directive of 1992 and are 'brief and clear-cut'.[1]

[1] Fallon, *The Law Applicable to Compulsory Insurance and Life Insurance: Special Problems* in Reichert-Facilides and Jessurun d'Oliveira (eds), *International Insurance Contract Law* (Deventer, Kluwer Law and Taxation, 1993) 123; Dicey and Morris, *The Conflict of Laws* by L Collins *et al* (London, Sweet & Maxwell, 1999) 34, 1368–75; Frigessi di Rattalma, *Il contratto internazionale di assicurazione* (Padova, 1990) 213–23; Fuentes Camacho, *Los contratos de seguro y el Derecho Internacional Privado* (Civitas, 1999) 119–23.

(a) The Choice of Law Provisions in the Second Life Assurance Directive

Two connecting factors are used in Article 4: the place of the commitment; the nationality of the policyholder. According to Article 1(e) of the Second Life Assurance Directive, the 'Member State of the commitment' means the Member State where the policyholder has his habitual residence or, if the policyholder is a legal person, the Member State where the latter's establishment, to which the contract relates is situated. In most cases, the applicable law is determined by using these connecting factors in various combinations, and according to a hierarchy of combinations. However, in some cases the claimant is allowed to elect whether he wishes to base his claim on one connecting factor rather than another. This is true regardless of whether the law of the Member State of the commitment gives the parties greater freedom to choose the applicable law. Moreover, due to Article 28 the parties have a choice of law if the contract is concluded between a policyholder who takes the initiative to take out an assurance and an insurer in the State of origin (case of *libre prestation de services passive* or *LPSP*). Finally, a principle of foreseeability is used in certain circumstances, to deny the application of what would otherwise be the applicable law.

Like Article 7 of the Non-Life Directive, Article 4 only provides the designation of the applicable law, without prejudice to other contract choice of law provisions in force in the State.

(b) The Choice of Law Rules in the Third Life Assurance Directive

The Third Life Assurance Directive lays down few choice of law provisions. Article 28, by providing that:

> the Member State of the commitment shall not prevent a policyholder from concluding a contract with an assurance undertaking authorised under the conditions of Article 6 of Directive 79/267/EEC, as long as that does not conflict with legal provisions protecting the general good in the Member State of the commitment,

extends the freedom of choice of law to the situations in which the policyholder takes the initiative to take out an assurance and enters into contact with the insurer in the State in which the insurer is established. Article 31 and point 16 of Annex II, by introducing a requirement that before an assurance contract is concluded the insurer must give the insured information regarding the applicable law, have an impact on the choice of law process.

3. THE RELEVANT CONNECTING FACTORS

(a) The law of the Member State of the Habitual Residence of the Policyholder

The law of the Member State of the habitual residence of the policyholder or, in the case of a legal person, of the Member State where the latter's establishment to which the contract relates is situated is the first connecting factor that is mentioned in Article 4 of the Second Life Assurance Directive. The Directive does not deal with the issue of when habitual residence is determined. Should the habitual residence of the policyholder be ascertained with reference to the conclusion of the contract? And eventually is the contract governed by another law when the policyholder gives up habitual residence in a Member State? All these issues are left to the national courts and the law that they apply, although they may wish to be guided by the Rome Convention which seems to prefer that habitual residence is determined at the time when the contract was concluded.[2] This interpretation is to be supported as it creates legal certainty for both of the parties. They can determine, at the time of the conclusion of the contract, the scope of their rights and duties, and that certainty cannot be undermined by later changes in the habitual residence of the policyholder of which the insurers are not necessarily aware of and of which they cannot reasonably be expected to keep track.

Though Article 4, paragraph 1 undeniably provides a hard rule which can be rebutted in two situations. These are described in Articles 4, paragraph 1, second part and 4, paragraph 2.[3]

Due to its rigidity, the designation of the law of the habitual residence of the policyholder as the governing law of the contract presents the advantages that uniformity between the courts of the different Member States will be easier to achieve, but it has also been subjected to a lot of criticism. The rule applies very well to simple contracts, such as a life insurance contract concluded by a policyholder for his own benefit, but it will be difficult to justify when applied to a life insurance contract of a slightly more complicated nature, especially if it involves obligations in favour of a third party beneficiary. Though a number of considerations have to be taken into account by the judge in ascertaining the meaning of this rule, it is clear that the intention of the drafters of the Second Life Assurance Directive was to propose a connecting factor able to establish the

[2] See *inter alia* Cheshire and North, *Private International Law*, PM North and JJ Fawcett, 13th edn (London, Edinburgh, Dublin, Butterworths, 1999) 571.

[3] See below paras 3(b) and 4.

relationship between life assurance and family law issues.[4] The habitual residence of the natural person could be a pertinent factor in the field of family conflict of laws. However, it appears that the law of the habitual residence of the policyholder does not necessarily protect the third party beneficiary of the life assurance contract more than any other law, eg the law chosen by the contracting parties or the law of the country in which the insurer is established.[5]

The same point has to be made with regards to the application of the law of the habitual residence of the policyholder to group assurances taken out by the employer for his work force. Moreover, the rule may not be the most effective way to localise the labour relations at stake. Are the labour relations always closely connected with the place of residence of the employer/policyholder? One might argue eventually in this regard that the labour relations are not closely linked with the place of residence of the employer if the work force operates in another country. Therefore, a so-called labour connection would be improperly extended to group assurances taken out by the employer for his workers.

(b) Nationality

Article 4, paragraph 2 of the Second Life Assurance Directive adds another narrow connecting factor, which can apply when the criteria of this provision are met. Article 4, paragraph 2 provides that, when the policyholder does not reside in the State of his nationality, the parties may choose the law of this State. This law must be the law of a Member State of the European Community. Moreover, Article 4, paragraph 2 provides that this rule applies only when the policyholder is a natural person. Thus a group assurance contract taken out by the employer/legal person for his work force will be governed by the law of the Member State of the commitment. Some questions might arise whether Article 4, paragraph 2 applies when one of the policyholders is a natural person but the other policyholder(s) is a legal person. Though one could find some reasons to grant the parties the freedom to choose the law of the State of the nationality of the policyholder/natural person, the text of Article 4, paragraph 2 clearly excludes such a possibility.

One might argue that the designation of the law of the nationality of the policyholder as the governing law of the contract was made because the State of the nationality of the policyholder corresponds to the State where the risk is situated.[6] However, it appears that the intention of the drafters of Article 4,

[4] Explanatory report of the European Commission, cited by K Lenaerts, (1990) *Annales de droit de Louvain*, 145–68, especially at 155. But see Dubuisson, *Le droit applicable au contrat d'assurance dans un espace communitaire integré* (Doctoral thesis, Université Catholique de Louvain, 1994) especially at 202.

[5] Fallon, *The Law Applicable to Compulsory Insurance and Life Insurance: Special Problems* in Reichert-Facilides and Jessurun d'Oliveira (eds), *International Insurance Contract Law in the EC* (Deventer, Kluwer Law and Taxation, 1993) n 1 above, 125.

[6] Fallon, *ibid*, 123.

paragraph 2 was to introduce a connecting factor able to establish the relationship between life assurance and family law issues. This is suggested by the fact that the policyholder is a pertinent factor in the field of family conflict of laws.[7] It is well known, in fact, that, at least under the law of most civil law countries, family legal issues are regulated by the law of the nationality of the persons concerned.[8] However, this is not true for some common law countries such as the United Kingdom and Ireland.

Unlike Article 4, paragraph 1, Article 4, paragraph 2 makes clear that the nationality of the policyholder must be ascertained with reference to the conclusion of the contract. Nevertheless, some questions might arise in the United Kingdom which does not have a national law of contract. As has already been pointed out by others,[9] this difficulty cannot be overcome by referring to Article 4, paragraph 3 which provides that:

> where a State includes several territorial units each of which has its own rules of law concerning contractual obligations, each unit shall be considered a country for the purposes of identifying the law applicable under this Directive.

This rule means that the law of Scotland or the law of England can be considered as the law of a country but it does not provide any guidance for the identification of the national law of a British subject since it does not clarify what link must exist between the natural person and one of the territorial units for these purposes. Though the question has been discussed in scholarly writings,[10] it has not been addressed in the implementing legislation. Therefore, one has to refer to the various solutions which have been suggested in legal literature. The first of these solutions proposes the application of the law of that unit with which the British subject is most closely connected.[11] This solution can be supported on the basis that the intention of the drafters of Article 4, paragraph 2 was to ensure that only the laws of States with which there are strong connections are applied. Nonetheless, this test is quite hard to apply since the policyholder might be habitually resident elsewhere.[12] Another solution is to identify the national law as the law of the unit in which the policyholder is domiciled.[13] An argument in

[7] For a clear exposition of the principle of nationality in comparative conflict of laws see Castangia, *Il criterio di collegamento della cittadinanza nel diritto internazionale privato* (Naples, Jovene, 1984)

[8] See Morse, *Party Autonomy in International Insurance Contract Law* in Reichert-Facilides and Jessurun d'Oliveira (eds), *International Insurance Contract Law* (Deventer, Kluwer Law and Taxation, 1993) 49.

[9] *Ibid*, 49.

[10] See Morse, n 8 above, at note 8; Dubuisson, *Le droit applicable au contrat d'assurance*, n 4 above, 233.

[11] See Wills Act 1963, s 6(2)(b) as quoted by Morse, n 8 above.

[12] For the same remark see Morse, *Party Autonomy in International Insurance Contract Law* in Reichert-Facilides and Jessurun d'Oliveira (eds), *International Insurance Contract Law in the EC*, n 8 above, 49.

[13] See *Re O'Keefe* [1940] Ch 124 as cited by Morse, *Party Autonomy in International Insurance Contract Law* in Reichert-Facilides and Jessurun d'Oliveira (eds), *International Insurance Contract Law in the EC*, n 8 above, 49.

favour of this solution is that the domicile of the person is a pertinent factor in the field of family conflict of laws. However, one could argue that a person could be a British subject without being domiciled in any part of the United Kingdom.[14] Moreover, the criterion of domicile has never played a relevant role in contractual relations in the British legal system.[15] In conclusion, there are arguments either in favour or against both the proposals and therefore there is room for different approaches by the courts in the identification of the national law of a British subject.

(i) Conflict mobile

Article 4, paragraph 2 does not clarify whether a change of the nationality of the policyholder/natural person allows the parties to choose the law of the new place of nationality. It goes without saying that this question arises only if the new state of nationality is a Member State of the European Community. The facility of the parties to choose the law of the new state of nationality can be derived from the fact that the Rome Convention grants this choice. Nevertheless, one might argue eventually that the freedom of choice of law is a basic principle in the Rome Convention but not in the Second Life Assurance Directive. Moreover, the meaning of Article 4, paragraph 2 suggests that the intention of the drafters was to introduce a connecting factor which localises objectively the contractual relationship. It appears therefore that the parties of a life insurance contract encompassed by the choice of law rules of the Second Life Assurance Directive can not change the governing law of the contract as a result of the change of the nationality of the policyholder.[16]

4. WHERE THE MEMBER STATE OF THE COMMITMENT GRANTS THE PARTIES GREATER FREEDOM TO CHOOSE THE GOVERNING LAW OF THE CONTRACT

Article 4, paragraph 1, states that the parties may freely choose any law, provided that such choice is valid under the law of the Member State of the commitment. This law might be a law of a third State, ie not a EC/EFTA Member State. As regards this, Article 4, paragraph 1 adopts the same approach towards party autonomy as Article 7(1)(a) of the Non-Life Insurance Directive. Thus it deserves the same considerations already made with regard to Article 7(1)(a). From the perspective of policyholders habitually resident in the United Kingdom, this provision has the effect of granting the parties the freedom to choose the law applicable to the contract.

[14] See Morse, n 8 above, at n 12, 49.

[15] *Ibid*, 49.

[16] For the same conclusion see Lenaerts (1990) *Annales de Droit de Louvain* 157 n 22; Dubuisson, *Le droit applicable au contrat d'assurance*, n 4 above, 235.

5. 'THE GENERAL PROVISIONS OF PRIVATE INTERNATIONAL LAW': ARTICLE 4, PARAGRAPH 5

Article 4, paragraph 5 provides that:

> Subject to the preceding paragraphs, the Member States shall apply to the assurance contracts referred to in this Directive their general rules of private international law concerning contractual obligations.

This rule is identical to Article 7, paragraph 3 of the Second Non-Life Insurance Directive. It grants the possibility of the Member States of the European Community adopting diverging provisions in their implementation rules of the Directive. As already stated above, the Second Life Assurance Directive does not lay down a complete set of choice of law provisions for life assurance contracts covering risks situated in a Member State of the European Community. Thus the rules of the Rome Convention apply to issues which are not covered by the choice of law rules of the Second Life Assurance Directive. These concern the consent and the capacity of the parties, the existence and validity of the contract. Like Article 7, paragraph 3 of the Second Non-Life Directive, the application of the rules in the Convention cannot be justified by the mere absence of an explicit regulation in the choice of law provisions of the Second Life Assurance Directive. The language and reason underlying Article 4, paragraph 5 suggest that this rule applies to issues which are not *explicitly* or *implicitly* governed by the choice of law rules of the Second Life Assurance Directive. Therefore the judge must ascertain in the circumstances of the case whether an issue is governed by the choice of law rules of the Second Life Assurance Directive.

6. *DÉPEÇAGE*

Like the Second Non-Life Insurance Directive, the Second Life Assurance Directive does not provide a right to *dépeçage*, ie, the right to submit different parts of the same contract to different laws. However, the Rome Convention grants the parties the right to submit different issues of the same contract to different laws. Thus only the assurance contracts covering a risk situated outside the territories of a Member State of the European Community can be governed by different laws. Perhaps one could argue that the right to split issues away from the governing law of a life-insurance contract covered by the directive and subject them to different laws may be inferred from Article 4, paragraph 5 of the Second Life Assurance Directive. This provides the application of the choice of law provisions of the Rome Convention to the issues not covered by the choice of law rules of the Directive. But the application of the rules of the Rome Convention cannot be justified by the mere absence of an explicit indication in the choice of law rules of the Second Life Assurance Directive.[17] On the contrary, it appears that the Second Life Assurance Directive does not grant the parties the right to split issues away from the governing law of the contract as this right is a logical consequence of the principle of autonomy in the field of contract conflict of laws.[18]

7. DOES ARTICLE 5 OF THE ROME CONVENTION APPLY TO THE ASSURANCE CONTRACTS REFERRED TO BY THE SECOND LIFE ASSURANCE DIRECTIVE?

Another question which deserves attention is the application of Article 5 of the Rome Convention to life insurance contracts covering risks situated in the territories of a Member State of the European Community where assurance is provided to the assured for a purpose that can be regarded as being outside his trade or profession. As already stated above, the protective consumer rules of Article 5 of the Rome Convention apply to assurance contracts covering risks situated outside the territories of the Member States of the European Communities.[19] Nevertheless, there are a number of arguments in favour of the application of Article 5 of the Rome Convention to the life insurance contracts referred to by the Second Life Assurance Directive. First, the application of the protective consumer rules of the Rome Convention to these contracts can be supported on the basis that as a matter of consumer protection, there is no reason why policyholders habitually resident in a Member State of the European Community require protection by private international law rules on another basis than the policyholders who are not habitually resident in a Member State of the European Community. Secondly, the application of Article 5 is suggested by Article 4, paragraph 5 of the Second Life Directive. As already stated above, this rule applies to the issues not covered by the choice of law rules of that Directive. Finally, unlike the Second Non-Life Directive the Second Life Directive does not lay down a distinction between contracts such as that between insurance contracts covering 'mass risks' and insurance contracts covering 'large risks'. As already seen above, such a distinction shows clearly the intention of the drafters of the Second Non-Life Insurance Directive to avoid any other division between the contracts referred to by the Directive and thus militates against the application of the protective rules of Article 5 of the Rome Convention to these contracts.

8. PUBLIC POLICY

A word needs to be said about the exception of public policy or *ordre public* in life insurance cases. It is questionable whether Article 16 of the Rome

[17] See above para 5 5.
[18] See above ch 8, para 7.
[19] See above ch 8, para 9.

Convention, which allows the judge to refuse the application of any rule of the governing law of the contract if this would be 'manifestly incompatible' with the public policy of the forum, applies when the governing law is designated by a choice of law rule of the Second Life Assurance Directive. Some uncertainties in this regard might arise from the fact that Article 14, paragraph 5 of the Second Life Assurance Directive has been repealed by the Third Life Assurance Directive. This rule provided that a Member State cannot prevent a policyholder from taking out an assurance contract valid under the law of the Member State of the insurer's establishment, unless it is contrary to the *public policy provisions* of the Member State of the commitment (ie, the Member State where the policyholder has his habitual residence). One might derive from the repeal of this provision that the intention of the drafters of the Third Life Assurance Directive was to impede recourse to the public policy exception when the law applicable to the contract is designated by a private international law rule of the Second Life Assurance Directive. However, it appears that the expression 'public policy provisions' in Article 14, paragraph 5 of the Second Life Assurance Directive did not cover the public policy exception in the sense in which this concept is used in conflict of laws but only rules of an administrative character.[20] Thus, the fact that Article 14, 5 of the Second Life Directive has been repealed by the Third Life Assurance Directive does not prevent the judge from refusing the application of any rule of the governing law designated by a choice of law provision of the Second Life Directive if this would be 'manifestly incompatible' with the public policy of the forum.

9. MANDATORY RULES: ARTICLE 4(4)

Article 4, paragraph 4 of the Second Life Assurance Directive is a double limbed choice of law rule. The first limb deals with mandatory rules of the forum. The second limb is concerned with the application of the mandatory rules of the Member State of the commitment (ie, the Member State where the policyholder has his habitual residence). Like Article 7 of the Rome Convention, Article 4 of the Second Life Assurance Directive deals with mandatory rules which are mandatory in an international sense. These rules also want to be applied in an international context.[21]

We are concerned here with substantive law rules which are intended to apply, regardless of the law applicable to the contract. In English private international law before the Rome Convention, these were known as overriding statutes. It is on these provisions that our analysis will focus.

[20] See Fallon, *The Law Applicable to Compulsory Insurance and Life Insurance: Special Problems* in Reichert-Facilides and Jessurun d'Oliveira (eds), *International Insurance Contract Law*, n 00 above 128.

[21] Frigessi di Rattalma, *Il contratto internazionale di assicurazione*, n 1 above, 221 *et seq.*

(a) Article 4(4)(1)

Article 4(4)(1) states that:

> Nothing in this Article shall restrict the application of the rules of the law of the forum in a situation where they are mandatory, irrespective of the law otherwise applicable to the contract.

These rules to which Article 4(4)(1) refers can be described as *règles d'application immédiate*.[22] This means that they override the conflicts process. They are priority rules in the sense that if a certain situation arises, this leads to the application of the mandatory rule before recourse can be had to any normal choice of law provision.

These rules have an imperative character. They want to be applied in a certain situation irrespective of the choice of law provisions. For example, state regulations concerning life assurance contracts often want to be applied whatever the law applicable to the contract. State regulations concerning life assurance contracts are, indeed, the traditional example of mandatory rules in the field of life assurance. Often this specific category is described as provisions which are close to public law, but this description is of little practical use in England as the category of public law is not used in England in the way that it is in many civil law countries.

It can be added that the mandatory rules in Article 4(4)(1) refer to overriding the choice of law. They even appear to override the mandatory provisions determined by Article 5 of the Rome Convention. Another relevant point is that it has to be a 'situation' where provisions are mandatory. As has already been said above, the provisions are only mandatory in certain situations.

(b) Article 4(4)(2)

Article 4(4)(2) gives the judge a discretionary power to take into account mandatory provisions of the law of the Member State of the commitment, ie the Member State of the habitual residence of the policyholder or, in the case of a legal person, the Member State where the latter's establishment to which the contract relates is situated. Due to the fact that the governing law of the contract is generally that of the Member State of the commitment, the provision has a modest relevance in practice. The law of the Member State of the commitment, in fact, generally applies to the contract entirely. But Article 4(4)(2) might apply when the parties choose the law of another country if such choice is permitted by the law of the Member State of the commitment or when the parties choose the law of the Member State of which the policyholder is a national. Some Member States of the European Community used their right to make a reserva-

[22] See Lagarde (1991) *Revue critique de droit international privé* 287.

tion which means that Article 4(4)(2) does not apply in these countries and because the United Kingdom is amongst these Member States I will not discuss Article 4(4)(2) in further detail.

10. THE SCOPE OF APPLICATION OF THE GOVERNING LAW OF THE CONTRACT

The law of the contract, as designated by the Second Life Assurance Directive, will, in particular, govern the interpretation of the contract, the performance of the contractual obligations, the various ways of extinguishing these obligations and the issues of the prescription and limitation of actions. The applicable law will also govern the consequences of any breach of a contractual obligation, but this will be done within the limits of the powers conferred on the judge by its procedural law. The consequences of any breach will include the assessment of damages in so far as it is governed by legal provisions.[23]

11. THE LAW APPLICABLE TO GROUP LIFE, HEALTH AND DISABILITY INSURANCE CONTRACTS

It is known that health, disability and especially group life insurance contracts, unlike individual insurance contracts cover multiple lives and generally involve different jurisdictions.[24] Therefore, it is not remarkable that more problems may arise when construing a health, disability or a group insurance contract than other types of individual insurance contract. Faced with this complication, how do courts establish whether coverage in question is a group policy? And given such a conclusion, which State's substantive law applies when health, disability or group insurance issues are litigated?

The standard group policy is made accessible through an employer as an employment benefit. Normally, it consists of either life insurance solely or life insurance in combination with disability and health benefits, accident or a retirement/pension scheme. The policyholder, normally an employer or group of employers, applies for and receives the policy covering the employees. Therefore, the contract exists between the policyholder and the insurer for the benefit of the insureds and their beneficiaries. Group insurance can be defined as the coverage of several individual persons by one all-embracing policy.[25] The insured can vary from time to time as the constitution of the group is remodelled, but the basic features of the group entity never changes. The employer provides an intermediary between the insurer and the employees. The employer

[23] Art 10 of the Rome Convention 1980.

[24] For some references to these types of insurance see *inter alia* Birds, *Modern Insurance Law* (London, Sweet & Maxwell, 2001) 338–39. See also Hansel, *Introduction to Insurance law* (London, New York, Hong Kong, LLP, 1996) 66–67.

[25] See Birds, *Modern Insurance Law*, n 24 above.

contracts terms for the group, so as to minimise arbitrary provisions in the master policy; provides information regarding coverage to its employees, and resolve any disputes with the insurer. Furthermore, the employer is responsible for communicating with the insurer about which persons are covered at any given time, and also ascertains the payment of premiums, whether upon a contributory or non-contributory basis.[26] The employees normally apply for coverage by enrolment cards or single applications. The participants in the group, who are normally employees, receive certificates of insurance. A fundamental distinction has to be made between the 'master policy' and the group policy itself and the certificate of insurance issued to each group member under the policy.[27] These certificates cannot be considered as policies as they are usually evidence of coverage under a group policy held by the employer. The certificates issued to the insured are not meant to be part of the insurance contract. They normally function as an outline of the master policy.

In discussing the choice of laws issues that may arise from health, disability and group life insurance contracts the starting point must be the law applicable to the relationship between the insurer and the master policyholder. This matter having been established, we can then go on to consider the law applicable to the certificate of insurance issued to each group member under the policy.

There is little doubt about the fact that the law applicable to the relationship between the master policyholder and the insurer is the law of the State applicable to the master policy.[28] The initial contract is indicated by the master policy issued to the employer. Much more difficult is to determine the law applicable to the relationship between the insurer and the individual insureds. The issue was examined in detail by the US Supreme Court in the leading case *Boseman v Connecticut General Life Insurance Co.*[29] In this case the US Supreme Court established the principle that the law of the State where the group policy was issued controls not only the rights between the employer and the insurer but also the rights between the insurer and the individual insureds. The US Supreme Court derives its conclusion from the fact, *inter alia* that the certificate issued to the individual insureds do not form part of the insurance contract but only evidence of Boseman's insurance under the group policy, that would exist unchanged even without delivery of the certificate to him. Therefore, the delivery of the certificate cannot have impact on the issue of which law must apply to the relationship between the insurer and individual insureds.[30]

It appears that the same arguments can be used to maintain the competence of the governing law of the master policy with regard to the relationship

[26] See Hansel, n 24 above.

[27] For the relevance of this distinction in conflict of laws see Schuman, *Conflict of law analysis in group life, health and disability insurance contract cases* at the website www.thefederation.org/public/Quarterly/Fall99/Schumann.htm

[28] *Ibid.*

[29] 301 US 196 (1937) as quoted by Schuman, n 27 above.

[30] Accordingly see Schuman, n 27 above.

between the insurer and individual insureds under the European system of private international law for insurance contracts. Thus, when an employer arranges for group life assurance for its employees, the right of a particular employee against the insurer will usually be determined, in the absence of a valid choice of law, not by the law of the place where the employee was habitually resident but rather by the law governing the master policy with respect to that issue. This will usually be the State where the employer has his principal place of business.

The determination of the law applicable to the insurance certificate becomes relevant when there is a discrepancy between the certificate and the group policy. This might occur when the certificate omits any reference to some provisions of the insurance policy or differs in certain respects from the master policy. It could also occur when the more specific clauses of the insurance contract are material. In these circumstances, one has to distinguish between the certificate which merely provides evidence of the existence of the terms and provisions of the master policy and the certificate that creates liabilities and rights. It is clear that the certificate which is part of the contract of insurance, ie that only provides information concerning the existence and terms of the contract formed by the master policy, should be construed according to the law applicable to the insurance contract.[31] But the certificate which creates rights and liabilities, as it is not part of the insurance contract, must be construed according to its own set of rules.[32]

12. THE LAW APPLICABLE TO THE RIGHTS OF THE THIRD PARTY BENEFICIARY OF A LIFE ASSURANCE CONTRACT

The rights of the third party beneficiary

As already stated above, most contracts in relation to life assurance contain two elements. First, there is the determination of the rights and duties of the parties and, secondly, there are the rights of the third party beneficiary. Both elements warrant separate attention in relation to choice of law. It must be emphasised, however, that the second aspect can be absent from certain life assurance contracts in which the policyholder is also the beneficiary of the contract.

Let us consider the life assurance contracts which contain both elements. Here, the non-contractual issues have to be separated from the contractual ones. The laws applicable to most non-contractual issues are the laws of the marriage/divorce or the proper law of the labour relation.[33] It is worth listing

[31] For the same conclusion see Schuman, n 27 above.

[32] *Ibid.*

[33] See Fallon, *The Law Applicable to Compulsory Insurance and Life Insurance: Special Problems* in Reichert-Facilides and Jessurun d'Oliveira (eds), *International Insurance Contract Law*, n 5 above, 132.

briefly the items that fall within this category. First of all, the issue of whether a matrimonial relationship still exists between the policyholder and the third party beneficiary is covered. A second issue that is covered is whether or not, in the case of group assurances taken out by employers, the labour relationship between the employer/policyholder and his employee/third beneficiary is valid. Finally, the issue of whether an action for fraud on a creditor (*actio pauliana*) is covered. The law of the State of the habitual residence of the creditor or debtor will determine whether such an action exists and whether and in which circumstances the action can be taken.[34]

What is left is the determination of the rights and obligations of the policyholder and third party beneficiary inside the framework and borderlines that are provided by the non-contractual provisions of the law of the marriage/divorce or the proper law of the labour relation. These contractual aspects are governed by the choice of law rules of the Second Life Assurance Directive and the Rome Convention. The starting point is again Article 4(1) of the Second Life Assurance Directive. The law applicable to the rights and obligations of the policyholder and third party beneficiary is usually the law of the Member State of the commitment, ie the law of the habitual residence of the policyholder.

13. SOME REMARKS ON THE CONFLICT OF LAWS ISSUES ARISING FROM THE SPECIAL CLAUSES INDICATING THE THIRD PARTY BENEFICIARY IN A LIFE ASSURANCE CONTRACT

A word needs to be said about the choice of law issues raised by the interpretation of special terms indicating the third party beneficiary in a life assurance contract.

It is known that life assurance contracts in which provisions for modification of the third party beneficiary either were not enacted by the insured or were not included present complex construction problems in the law of insurance contracts when the expression indicating the beneficiary is either 'to my wife, if she survives, and otherwise to my children' or to 'my wife and children'.[35] Although with regard to the insured, these policies may be considered as constituting interests in the third beneficiaries, a question yet persists as to which persons are included.

When the special term is 'to my wife and children' the rule is that the interests vest in equal parts in the wife and children living at the time of the execution of the contract if it does not incorporate a power of modification. There is, however, a difference of opinions in the legal literature as to whether after-born children can be admitted to partake in the final allocation.[36] Questions can also

[34] See Dubuisson, *Le droit applicable au contrat d'assurance*, n 4 above, 524.

[35] See Carnahan, *Conflict of Laws and Life Insurance Contracts* (Buffalo and New York, Dennis and Co Inc, 1958) 361–73.

[36] For an excellent and still valid exposition of the different opinions on this subject see Carnahan, n 35 above, 363.

arise from the death, before insured, of one of the children. In that event distribution of his share could possibly be transferred to his children, to his personal representative, or by survivorship to the other children.[37]

The term of the second type mentioned above, that 'to my wife, if she survives, and otherwise to my children', can also be considered as creating, as against the insured, vested rights. Yet, as between the beneficiaries, the interests of the children are subject to the defeat of the mother to survive the insured. Is there also a chance of the child or children remaining alive after the wife? In other words, does the interest of children vest in those children living at the time the policy is realised? If so, and a child dies before the wife of the insured, does the interest of the child pass to its children or its representative? Or does the part of the deceased pass by survivorship to those children who outlive the insured and his wife?[38]

As Professor Carnahan pointed out correctly a long time ago, in order to answer these questions fully you have to make a choice between two different approaches: one of which considers the third beneficiary's right as derived from contract and the other of which considers the beneficiary's rights as being similar to interests originating by testamentary disposition.[39] If the beneficiary's interest be likened to a testamentary provision, it is maintained that if the wife predeceases the insured, the right of the child who has passed away before its mother will pass by descent. On the contrary, if the right of the third beneficiary is regarded as contractual, the child is considered as having merely an incidental interest which is hindered by its death prior to the mother and hence is not transferable.[40]

Neither the Second Life Assurance Directive nor the Third Life Assurance Directive clarify whether the interest of the third party beneficiary should be analogised to a testamentary provision or considered as purely contractual. Thus, one should look at the traditional rules of private international law which usually request judges to characterise issues for conflict of laws purposes according to the law of the forum.

14. THE LAW APPLICABLE TO LOANS CONTAINED IN LIFE INSURANCE POLICIES

Life insurance policies, issued in some Member States, such as Italy, may contain a promise by the insurer to make loans on the security of the policy to the insured upon his request. The introduction of such a loan does not form a separate and distinct agreement since the insurer was already under an absolute duty to make the loan. Instead, it must be considered as a consummation of the original contract. The law ascertained by application of the choice of law rules

[37] *Ibid*, 363.
[38] *Ibid*, 363.
[39] *Ibid*.
[40] *Ibid*.

of the Second Life Assurance Directive determines the validity of the loan and the rights created thereby. If, however, the insurer has to make the insured a loan on terms different from those indicated in the original contract, the loan would be a separate agreement governed by its own proper law, specifically by the law of the state which, with respect to the particular issue, has the closest connection with the loan.[41]

15. THE RELATIONSHIP BETWEEN BUSINESS RULES AND CHOICE OF LAW PROVISIONS IN THE SECOND LIFE ASSURANCE DIRECTIVE

A word needs to be said about the relationship between business rules for investment business and choice of laws provisions in the Second Life Assurance Directive. Life Assurance (including pensions and related business) falls within the definition of 'investment business' for the purposes of the Financial Services Act 1986 and 'regulated business' for the purposes of the successor of that Act, the Financial Services and Market Act 2000. The result has been that life assurance has been included within the financial services in respect of which the Financial Services Authority has made conduct of business rules. These rules are not meant to control contract terms but cover matters such as pre-contractual information and advertising given to the policyholder. Nevertheless, as the provisions are superimposed on the traditional duties of insurers and agents, they can be considered as relevant to insurance contract law. The separate character of these provisions is emphasised by the remedies available to the policyholder when the insurer is in breach of a provision of a Self-Regulating Organisation ('SRO') or Recognised Professional Body ('RPB').[42]

The choice of law rules of the Second Life Assurance Directive do not refer to conduct of business. Both the Department of Trade and Industry and the European Commission maintain that a choice of law provision does not encompass such rules.[43] This conclusion is supported by the fact that not all Member States have conduct of business rules.[44]

However, one might argue eventually that the choice of law provisions of the Second Life Assurance Directive are relevant to the conduct of business rules at least for the following two reasons. First, the application of the conduct of business rules to life assurance contracts reduces the sphere of the applicable law which is designated by a private international law provision since the rules are superimposed on the common law duties of the insurer and agent. Secondly, the

[41] See Art 4(1) of the Rome Convention.

[42] For a clear exposition of these rules see MacNeil (1995) *International and Comparative Law Quarterly* 33.

[43] See House of Lords Select Committee on the European Communities, 12th Report (1990–91), *A Single Insurance Market* (DTI evidence: answer to question 19). See also the DTI Consultative Document on the implementation of the Framework Directives (Dec. 1993) as cited by MacNeil, n 42 above, note 88.

[44] MacNeil, n 42 above.

application of the conduct of business rules to *all* investment business concluded with policyholders habitually resident irrespective of whether the fact that the assurance product is sold on a 'service basis' conflicts with the notion of 'general good' as it has been developed by the European Court of Justice. As already seen above, this allows the application of the mandatory rules only if the conditions attached to the general good are fulfilled.[45] Thus it appears that, despite the suggestions which have been made by the Department of Trade and Industry and the European Commission in order to deny the existence of an impact of choice of law provisions on the conduct of business rules, these are are not completely neutral vis-à-vis the functioning of the private international law rules of the Life Assurance Directives.

16. EVALUATION

(a) Strengths of the Choice of Law Rules of the Second Assurance Directive

(i) Discouraging Forum Shopping

The harmonisation of choice of law rules in Europe for life assurance contracts covering risks situated in a Member State of the European Community means that forum shopping for substantive law advantages is not a problem in Europe. The harmonised choice of law rules for assurance contracts produce the same effect in the international sphere as would complete harmonisation of the substantive law of assurance contracts. Every Member State has the same or at least very similar choice of law rules for life assurance contracts. Accordingly, every Member State of the European Community should apply the same substantive law as the applicable law, even though their own national law of life insurance contracts may be different from that of another Member State. But harmonisation of choice of law rules for life assurance contracts can only stop forum shopping for substantive law advantages and does nothing to stop forum shopping for procedural law advantages. This can only be achieved by harmonisation of procedural provisions.

(ii) Certainty

The brevity of Article 4 of the Second Assurance Directive, which gives it its simplicity, leads to certainty in relation to its scope and its rules on the applicable law. The governing law of the contract is usually designated by a choice of law provision, whose purpose can be said to localise *objectively* the contractual relationship. The applicable law being the law of the Member State with which the contract has the closest connection. Indeed, the set of rules in relation to the

[45] See ch 1, para 12.3.

applicable law in the Second Life Assurance Directive provides a degree of certainty which is missing from other special insurance choice of law schemes. It is also missing in States where there are no special insurance choice of law schemes and resort has to be made to the general contract choice of law rules, with little or no authority as to how these apply in insurance cases.

It is in the interests of the insurer, policyholder and third party beneficiary that any choice of law rule should be certain and predictable. Insurance companies need to be able to plan their transactions and to decide whether to make their services available abroad. It is particularly important in the context of the European Community that the free movement of services within the European internal market should not be hindered by insurers' concerns over the possible legal consequences of marketing their services elsewhere in the Community. Insureds and third party beneficiaries need to have a clear idea of what their rights are, including information as to which States' substantive law will apply. Any uncertainty as to the applicable law means that the claims are more likely to be litigated than settled by insurers,[46] and it is in neither party's interest that this should have occurred.

Moreover, the 'policyholder's habitual residence or the policyholder's establishment are generally easy to define.'[47] However, the place of nationality might raise problems in some common law countries such as the United Kingdom which does not have a national law of contract.

(iii) Co-ordinating Jurisdiction and Choice of Law Rules

The choice of law rules of the Second Life Assurance Directive seem to fit in with the Brussels Convention. Article 8(1), (2) of the Brussels Convention allows a policyholder who takes the initiative to take out an assurance contract and enters into contact with an insurer in a state other than that in which he is habitually resident to bring his action in the courts of the state where he is domiciled. As the place of domicile generally coincides with that of the habitual residence, there is co-ordination between the jurisdiction rules of the Brussels Convention and the choice of law provisions of the Second Life Assurance Directive. This is convenient since the courts of a Contracting State can apply their own law better than the courts of any other state.

[46] Park (1978) 12 *International Lawyer* 845–54.

[47] But it has been questioned in the legal writings whether reference to a personal connecting factor such as a habitual residence is pertinent to commercial contracts. See Collins (1976) *International and Comparative Law Quarterly* 45–46.

(b) Weaknesses of the Choice of Law Rules of the Second Life Assurance Directive

(i) An Excessively Restricted Choice of the Governing Law

Some restrictions on the freedom of the parties to choose the applicable law are inevitable in life assurance cases, due to the existence of situations in which the policyholder is in a weaker bargaining position. But to deny the parties the right to choose the law of the Member State in which the insurer is established produces an excessively restricted choice. This is unfair to the insurance company. Moreover, such a restriction seems to be unjustified in the case of a group insurance contract taken out by an employer for the benefit of his employees. In this case, the restriction on the choice of law cannot be motivated by the fact that the policyholder is in a weaker bargaining position. On the contrary, it is likely that the policyholder has more bargaining power than his contractual counterpart.

(ii) Limiting the Freedom of Services Within the Single Insurance Market

Following on from the last point, the restriction of the freedom of the parties to choose the law of the Member State in which the insurer is established would mean that the free movement of insurance products and services would remain a problem in Europe. Insurance companies will be reluctant to offer their assurance services to consumers in other EU countries, because of the duty imposed by the Directive to subject the policies to the laws of the countries in which the policyholders are habitually resident. Moreover, by denying the choice of the governing law to the parties of an assurance contract referred to by the Directive, Article 4 of the Second Life Assurance Directive unduly limits the right of the recipient of insurance services to travel across state borders and make a choice among the services offered by insurance companies established in different Member States. Since the European Court's judgment in *Luisi & Carbone*,[48] it is commonly recognised that not only the provider, but also the recipient of services derives certain rights from the Treaty of Rome provisions on the free movement of services.[49]

(iii) The Use of Unsuitable Connecting Factors

This is one of the major weaknesses of the set of choice of law rules in the Second Life Assurance Directive. The use of the habitual residence of the policyholder as the main connecting factor in Article 4 cannot be considered to be beneficial to the protection of the policyholder in all cases. Within a single insurance market, where people can move freely, the state of the habitual

[48] Case 286/82 and 26/83 *Luisi & Carbone v Ministero del Tesoro* [1984] ECR 377.
[49] See Smulders and Glazener (1992) *Common Market Law Review* 796.

residence of the policyholder (which determines the degree of consumer protection) does not logically correspond to the legal system which the policyholder knows best.[50] Moreover, by denying the policyholders the right to sign insurance contracts which are subject to foreign law the Directive steps back from the conditions for free movement of insurance companies. However, it is true that insurance companies are usually very reluctant to offer their policies to subjects in other countries, because of the complexity of the legal regulations involved.[51]

Finally, the Second Life Assurance Directive does not lay down a provision for 'mobile' consumers of insurance products; therefore it will not be possible for a consumer acting on his own initiative (active consumer) to sign an insurance contract subject to foreign law.[52] The possibility for active consumers of assurance products in the Second Life Directive to take out foreign assurance, but only when their national consumer provisions do not apply, has been deleted from the draft proposal.[53]

(iv) Preventing Distortions of Competition

Reference to the law of the Member State of the habitual residence of the policyholder or, in case of a legal person, of the State of the establishment which the contract concerned prevents distortions of competition. Thus an assurance product sold in France which has been produced by a Luxembourg company is not generally subject to a different governing law from an assurance product sold in France produced by a French company or an English company. This was probably one of the reasons why the connecting criterion of the habitual residence was adopted in Article 4 of the Second Life Assurance Directive and is one of its major strengths.

In so far as the parties opt to apply the law of the country where the premium is paid, this might lead to distortions of competition. Therefore an assurance product sold in Italy which has been produced by a French company may be subject to a different governing law from a product sold in Italy produced by an Italian company or an English company. But obviously in some cases the law of the country where the premium is paid will be more favourable than the law of the habitual residence of the policyholder and parties will opt for this instead. The problem of distortions of competition will accordingly remain.

(v) An Excessive Protection for Assureds Within the European Community

It would be possible to justify very pro-assured choice of law rules if the substantive law was itself equally pro-assureds. However, it has been seen that,

[50] See European Consumer Law Group Opinion on the Third Generation of Directives in the Life and Non-Life Insurance Sector (1992) *Journal of Consumer Policy* 207–14.

[51] *Ibid*, 212.

[52] *Ibid*, 213.

[53] *Ibid*, 213, n 1.

overall, the Second Life Assurance Directive is not noticeably pro-assured. Although the Directive contains a number of provisions which are pro-assured,[54] this does not mean that an assured should be allowed excessive protection of his interests by the conflict of laws. To allow this would be unfair to the insurer.

(vi) Lack of Choice of Law Rules on the Agency Relationship

Another criticism which can be made against the choice of law provisions of the Second Life Directive is that they do not encompass the agency relationship. This might discourage agents and brokers from entering into cross-border assurance transactions since they are unlikely to have a clear comprehension of their obligations and rights. There is in fact a little harmonisation of the substantive rules in Europe on assurance intermediaries and agents.[55]

(vii) Lack of Co-ordination Between Public Law and Choice of Law Rules

Like the Second Non-Life Insurance Directive, the Second Life Assurance Directive fails to address the issue of whether the public law provisions of the Member States may be applied through the choice of law rules laid down in Article 4. This is a failure of harmonisation which could seriously affect the operation of the EC choice of law rules due to the number of public law provisions in the life assurance sector. Nevertheless, the importance of this question must not be exaggerated as some of those rules, which are more common in civil law countries than in common law countries, are mandatory in an international sense and thus should be applied in an international context.

(viii) Lack of Co-ordination Between Family Law, Labour Law Issues and the Choice of Law Rules of the Second Life Assurance Directive

There is a lack of co-ordination between the choice of law rules in the Second Life Assurance Directive and the family and labour law issues. As already stated above, the governing law of the contract, as designated by the choice of law rules of the Second Life Assurance Directive, does not apply to these issues.[56] Although that lack of co-ordination between the choice of law provisions and family and labour law issues is not really detrimental to the operation of the choice of law rules, it does not deserve a positive consideration due to the fact that the interpretation thereof would have been facilitated by such a co-ordination.[57]

[54] *Cf* ch 1 above, para 13.

[55] See Merkin and Rodger, *EC Insurance Law* (London and New York, Longman, 1997) 88 *et seq*; ch 8 above, para 17(c).

[56] *Cf* para 8.

[57] See Fallon, *The Law Applicable to Compulsory Insurance and Life Insurance: Special Problems* in Reichert-Facilides and Jessurun d'Oliveira (eds), *International Insurance Contract Law*, n 5 above, 133.

(ix) Conclusion

The reader will not be surprised by my final statement that the weaknesses of the set of choice of law rules laid down in the Second Life Assurance Directive greatly outweigh its strengths.

II
The Choice of Law Rules in the Third Life Assurance Directive

17. WHERE THE POLICYHOLDER TAKES THE INITIATIVE TO TAKE OUT AN ASSURANCE AND ENTERS INTO CONTACT WITH THE INSURER IN THE STATE OF ORIGIN: ARTICLE 28

Like Article 28 of the Third Non-Life Insurance Directive, Article 28 of the Third Life Assurance Directive contains a choice of law rule, albeit in a disguised manner. It provides that:

> the Member State of the commitment shall not prevent a policyholder from concluding a contract with an assurance undertaking authorised under the conditions of Article 6 of the Directive 79/267/EEC, as long as that does not conflict with legal provisions protecting the general good in the Member State of the commitment.

This provision grants the parties the freedom to choose the governing law of the contract. Some observations must be made about the scope of application of this choice of law provision.

It appears that the provision applies when the policyholder takes the initiative to take out an assurance and enters into contact with the insurer in the State of origin (ie, the Member State in which the insurer is established). Though there is no explicit reference to these cases in the text of Article 28, the application of this provision in these circumstances is suggested both by the history of this rule and the scope of application of the corresponding Article 14, paragraph 5 of the Second Life Assurance Directive. Article 14, paragraph 5 is applied in cases where the policyholder takes the initiative to take out an assurance and he enters into contact with the insurer in the State of origin. The fundamental consideration was that the policyholder should not require any special protection as to the law to be applied in these cases.[58]

It is clear that the same reason underlies the text of Article 28 of the Third Life Assurance Directive. It would be unreasonable to maintain the need for a special protection under the law to be applied in the cases where the policyholder takes the initiative to take out an assurance and he enters into contact with the insurer in the State of origin. On the contrary, it appears that Article 28 does not apply to life assurance contracts concluded by the policyholder in the State of his residence when he received an offer or was the recipient of advertising in this State (case of *libre prestation de service active*). These contracts are covered by Article 4 of the Second Life Directive which prescribes the application of the law of the Member State of the commitment.

[58] Fallon, *The Law Applicable to Compulsory Insurance and Life Insurance : Special Problems* in Facilides and Jessurun d'Oliveira, *International Insurance Contract Law in the EC*, n 5 above, 127.

18. THE RELATIONSHIP BETWEEN ARTICLES 28 OF THE THIRD LIFE ASSURANCE DIRECTIVE AND 4 OF THE SECOND LIFE ASSURANCE DIRECTIVE

One might question whether Article 4 of the Second Life Assurance Directive has been repealed by Article 28 of the Third Life Assurance Directive. Some uncertainties in this respect could arise from the fact that Art. 28 applies in cases where the policyholder takes the initiative to take out an assurance and he enters into contact with the insurer in the State of origin and grants the parties a wider choice than Article 4 of the Second Life Assurance Directive. Nevertheless, it appears that Article 28 did not repeal Article 4, paragraph 1(i) of the Second Life Assurance Directive which applies in the absence of a choice or a valid choice. Article 4, paragraph 1(i) provides that 'the law applicable to contracts relating to the activities referred to in the First Directive shall be the law of the Member State of the commitment'. By allowing the parties a wider choice of law, Article 28 did not modify Article 4, paragraph 1(i) which does not deal with the freedom to choose the applicable law. It goes without saying that Article 4, paragraph 1(ii) and Article 4, paragraph 2 has been superseded by Article 28 which provides a wider choice of law. However, these provisions apply to life assurance contracts concluded by the policyholder in the State of his residence when he received an offer or was the recipient of advertising in this State.

19. FROM THE FREE CHOICE OF LAW RULE TO THE 'AWARE CHOICE OF LAW' PRINCIPLE: ARTICLE 31

It is clear that one of the most interesting features of the Third Life Assurance Directive is the obligation imposed on the insurer to inform the policyholder on the law applicable to the contract. Article 31 and point (a)16 of Annex II read as follows:

> Before the assurance contract is concluded, at least the information listed in point A of Annex II shall be communicated to the policyholder.
>
> (a)16. Law applicable to the contract where the parties do not have a free choice or, where the parties are free to choose the law applicable, the law the assurer proposes to choose.

Though a similar rule is laid down in the Third Non-Life Insurance Directive, Article 31 and point 16 of Annex II expand the scope of the obligation of information imposed on the insurer in order to protect the policyholder who is assumed to be in a weaker bargaining position. This constitutes a change since Article 31 of the Third Non-Life Directive only applies when the policyholder is a natural person. Like its counterpart for the non-life insurance sector, Article 31 and point (a)16 not only take care to protect the 'passive' consumer of insurance services, ie the consumer who had been solicited into a contract in his/her country of residence, but also the 'active consumer', ie the consumer who concludes a contract in another Member State of the European Community.

20. EVALUATION

(a) Strengths of the Choice of Law Rules of the Third Life Assurance Directive

(i) Expanding an Excessively Restricted Choice

By granting the parties to a life assurance contract, in the cases where the policyholder takes the initiative to take out an assurance and he enters into contact with the insurer in the State of origin, the right to choose, inter alia, the law of the country in which the insurance company is established, Article 28 of the Third Life Assurance Directive gives the insurer a wider choice of law than happens under Article 4 of the Second Life Assurance Directive, with its excessively restricted choice for the parties.

(ii) Providing Protection for Assureds Within the European Community

This is one of the major strengths of the Third Life Assurance Directive. The obligation imposed on the insurance company to provide information to the insurer about the governing law of the contract undeniably operates in a pro-assured way. Nevertheless, if one looks at Article 31 as a whole it is not as aggressively pro-assured as could appear at first glance. Like Article 31 of the Third Non-Life Directive, which is the counterpart of Article 31 of the Third Life Assurance Directive in the non-life insurance sector, this provision just tries to balance out the interests of the parties by making both responsible for the applicable law. The insurance company can have no cause for complaint because of the duty, since this does not affect his right to choose the applicable law.

(b) Weaknesses of the Choice of Law Rules of the Third Life Assurance Directive

(i) Limiting the Freedom of Services Within the Single Insurance Market

Though the Third Life Assurance Directive takes a step further to the realisation of the freedom to provide assurance products and services within the Single Market, there are still some restrictions on this freedom deriving from the sets of choice of law rules laid down in the Second and Third Life Assurance Directives. By imposing the application of the law of the place of the habitual residence of the policyholder when the policyholder takes the initiative to take out an assurance and he enters into contact with the insurer in the State of origin, Article 4 of the Second Life Assurance Directive produces the effect that the enjoyment of assurance services in different States of the European Community cannot be the same.

(ii) Lack of Choice of Law Rules on the Agency Relationship

Like the choice of law rules of the Second Life Assurance Directive, the choice of law provisions of the Third Life Assurance Directive do not encompass the agency relationship. As already stated above, this might discourage agents and brokers from entering into cross-border assurance transactions since they are unlikely to have a clear comprehension of their obligations and rights.[59]

(iii) Lack of Co-ordination Between Public Law and Choice of Law Rules

Another criticism which can be made against the Third Life Assurance Directive is that it does not address the issue whether the public law rules of the Member States of the European Community can be applied through the choice of law rules.

(iv) Lack of Co-ordination Between Family Law, Labour Law Issues and the Choice of Law Rules of the Second Life Assurance Directive

Like the Second Life Assurance Directive, the Third Life Assurance Directive does not raise the question of co-ordination between family law, labour law issues and the EC choice of law rules for life assurance contracts.

(v) Conclusion

On an arithmetical count the weaknesses of the choice law rules laid down in the Third Life Assurance Directive greatly exceeded the strengths. This situation does not change if you take into account the relative weight to be attached to the different issues. The Third Life Assurance Directive does not score well in terms of providing harmonising choice of law rules. Moreover, it is submitted that the private international law provisions in the Third Life Assurance Directive create an obstacle to the free movement of life assurance services in Europe.

[59] *Cf* above para 16(b)(vi).

21. OPTIONS FOR REFORM

(a) Providing an Answer to the Questions Arising From the Notion of 'General Good'

As already stated above, the notion of 'general good' in Article 28 leads to considerable uncertainty, both in relation to its meaning and its control by the national insurance authorities in charge of the surveillance of the insurance markets.[60] The most direct way of dealing with the lack of clarity as regards the 'general good' is to introduce a definition in the text of Article 28. Nevertheless, it appears that this is quite a difficult task to achieve as is demonstrated by the attempts that have been made in legal writings and recently by the European Commission.[61] Moreover, this solution would not stop the other basic failings of the choice of law provisions of the Third Life Assurance Directive.

(b) Re-wording Article 1(3) of the Rome Convention

Under this solution Article 1(3) of the Rome Convention would be re-worded so that the Convention would encompass contracts of assurance which cover risks situated in the territories of the Member States of the European Community. This would have the advantage of introducing a single set of choice of law rules for assurance contracts, regardless of whether the risk is situated in or outside the territories of a Member State. As already stated above, the choice of law rules of the Rome Convention adopt suitable connecting factors for assurance contracts and thus ensure that the interests of the parties are respected.[62] Furthermore, due to the fact that the Third Life Assurance Directive grants the parties a wide choice of law in cases where the policyholder takes the initiative to take out an assurance and he enters into contact with the insurer in the State in which the insurer is established (case of *libre prestation de services passives or LPSP*), there is no reason for a parallel set of choice of law provisions to the conventional rules.

It is clear that the choice of law rules of the Rome Convention should be modified to encompass the agency relationship and to co-ordinate them with public law rules of the Member States. But this does not appear to be a problem as the Rome Convention will be renegotiable after the year 2001.[63]

[60] See above ch 1, para 12.3.
[61] See especially Tison (1998) *Legal Issues of European Integration* 1 *et seq*.
[62] See above ch 8, para 26.1.
[63] Art 26.

11

The Implementation of the EC Choice of Law Provisions for Insurance Contracts in the United Kingdom

1. INTRODUCTORY REMARKS

THE AIM of this brief chapter is merely to provide an overview of the implementation of the EC choice of law rules for insurance contracts in the United Kingdom, though certain issues which are considered to be of special relevance will be highlighted in greater depth. This approach is intended to complement and consolidate the preceding analysis of the core concepts on which the Rome Convention and the EC Insurance Directives are based.

2. THE IMPLEMENTING ACTS OF THE ROME CONVENTION AND INSURANCE DIRECTIVES

The United Kingdom has implemented the Rome Convention by the Contracts (Applicable Law) Act 1990 with effect from 1 April 1991.[1] It has also ratified the two Brussels Protocols of 1988 providing for references to be made by national courts to the European Court of Justice for interpretation of the Conventions, but these are not yet in force due to the absence of the minimum number of ratifications by other Contracting States. The United Kingdom has implemented the Second Directive of Non-Life Insurance by the Insurance Companies (Amendment) Regulation 1990, inserting new provisions into the Insurance Company Act 1982 which entered into force on July 1990.[2] The introduction of new provisions in the Insurance Company Act 1982 as a result of the Second Directive on Life Assurance is done by the Insurance Company (Amendment) Regulation 1993.[3] These provisions entered into force on 20 May 1992. The Third Directives on Non-Life and Life Insurance were implemented by the Insurance Companies (Third Insurance Directive) Regulations 1994, in force from 1 July 1994.[4]

1 The Contracts (Applicable Law) Act (Commencement) (No 1) Order 1991 (SI 1991/707).
2 The Insurance Companies (Amendment) Regulations 1990 (SI 1990/133).
3 The Insurance Companies (Amendment) Regulations 1993 (SI 1993/174).
4 The Insurance Companies (Third Insurance Directives) Regulations 1994 (SI 1994/1696).

The implementation of the choice of law provisions contained in the EC Insurance Directives has significantly enhanced the intricacy of the provisions that apply to the determination of the applicable law governing insurance contracts in the United Kingdom. Nevertheless, the traditional common law approach of allowing a free choice of law has been left to a great degree intact by both the Rome Convention and the Insurance Directives. The UK implementation legislation is quite obscure, mainly literally reproducing sections of the relevant directives.[5] It does not clarify the content of the rules concerning choice of applicable law in the United Kingdom. In order to consider these rules, the provisions that are contained in the implementing statutes of the Insurance Directives, the Rome Convention and the common law provisions on choice of law need to be gathered together. Whilst, as already stated above, the Rome Convention is not relevant to the determination of the governing law for insurance contracts covering risks situated within the European Community, the implementing legislation does not represent a thorough framework for choice of law in insurance and the implementing legislation thus demands courts and tribunals in the United Kingdom to act in accordance with the rules of the Contracts Applicable Law Act 1990 in circumstances not encompassed by the special insurance provisions.[6] It also demands courts and tribunals in the United Kingdom to look at the Contracts Applicable Law Act 1990 to establish whether a choice of law is granted to the contracting parties in circumstances in which the insurance directives demand Member States to determine if the contracting parties are allowed any choice or a more substantial choice than that granted by the Directives.[7]

3. THE FORMAT OF THE PROVISIONS

Looking at the way in which most rules of the implementing legislation of the EC Insurance Directives are worded, it is evident that the legislator was not primarily concerned with those cases in which English law can apply on objective bases. On the contrary, it also examined those situations where English law is not applicable to the contract. This becomes visible particularly due to the fact that most of the choice of laws rules are not worded in a unilateral way (that would have unduly privileged the application of the law of the forum) but in a bilateral/multilateral fashion.

[5] See MacNeil, *UK Report on the Implementation of the EC Choice of Law Rules for Insurance* in Frigessi di Rattalma and Seatzu (eds), *The Implementation Provisions of the EC Choice of Law Rules for Insurance Contracts in Belgium, France, Germany, Italy, The Netherlands, Spain and the United Kingdom: A Commentary* (The Hague, Kluwer Law International, 2003) forthcoming.

[6] *Ibid*.

[7] Section 94B and Sch 3 A part 1, para 5 and part 2, para 10 of the Insurance Company Act 1982 as quoted by MacNeil above at note 12.

4. THE CHOICES MADE

(a) The Extent of Party Autonomy

A relevant aspect of the implementing statutes of the EC Insurance Directives in the UK is that whenever the directives grant some discretion to the Member States to enforce party autonomy a positive approach has been taken.[8] This is so as regards the English private international law rules themselves (that one might call 'primary' party autonomy). However, as regards the rules of an elected foreign law, ie in the case of a possible '*renvoi*' ('secondary' party autonomy) a more negative approach has been adopted.

(b) Party Autonomy According to English Law

It is worth noting that none of the possible restrictive choices granted by the Second Non-Life and Life Insurance Directives have been taken by the implementing statutes in the United Kingdom, with the result that the implementation of the directives can be considered to have had no real impact on the UK law relating to circumstances in which the parties have made (expressly or by implication) a choice of applicable law.[9] Here you can see a reflection of the very relevant role of 'party autonomy' in insurance contracts which was stated earlier.

(c) Party Autonomy by Way of Renvoi

Under Article 7(1)(b) of the Second Non-Life Insurance Directive, where the risk and the policyholder's residence or seat are located in different States, the parties can choose any one of both laws. Again, under Article 7(1)(c) of the Second Non-Life Insurance Directive, where the policyholder is acting in a commercial capacity and the risk is spread out in more than one State, the parties can choose the law of any of them. In both instances the directive granted a wider degree of choice, if permitted by the law of the States involved, which may be considered as a type of renvoi. Nevertheless, despite the choice given by the Directive, the implementing legislation does not permit any such extensions. The rational behind is that the issue of expanded choice is not significative for the UK implementing legislation as the United Kingdom does not attempt to reduce choice in the first instance. Thus the question of enlarging choice is not a real consideration.[10]

[8] For the same remark see MacNeil n 5 above at note 12.
[9] *Ibid.*
[10] For the same conclusion see MacNeil n 5 above at note 12.

(d) Where There is No Choice of Law by the Parties

Where no choice is made by the contracting parties, the contract is governed by the law of the three countries with which the contract is most closely connected. Those countries are: the Member State in which the risk is located; the Member State of the policyholder's habitual residence or central administration; and the Member State where the events occur when the risks covered by the contract are restricted to events occurring in a Member State other than the Member State where the risk is situated. The presumption may be rebutted but the English courts will apply a stricter standard to any attempt to rebut this presumption than to any attempt to displace the presumption in Article 4(2) of the Rome Convention that relates a contract with the country of the party who is to effect 'characteristic performance'. This is because the provision of Article 4(5) of the Rome Convention permitting the presumption to be set aside if all circumstances of the case show that the contract is most closely related to another country does not appear in the UK implementation statutes of the EC Insurance Directives.

(e) Choice of Law Within the United Kingdom

The implementing legislation in the United Kingdom complies with the principle founded in the EC Insurance Directives that where a Member State encompasses different territorial units, each of which has its own rules of law concerning contractual obligations, each unit must be considered as a country for the purposes of ascertaining the applicable law.[11] The effect of this is that England and Wales, Scotland and Northern Ireland will be regarded as separate countries for the purposes of ascertaining the applicable law although the provisions concerning the applicable law are the same in each country.

The implementing legislation also applies the provisions derived from the Insurance Directives to conflicts between the laws of the different parts of the United Kingdom, although this is not imposed by the Directives.

[11] Para 4(1), Part 1 and para 9(1), Part II of Sch 3A, Insurance Companies Act 1982.

PART IV

The European Private International Law of Compulsory Insurance

In this Part the concern is with compulsory insurance contracts covering risks situated either in or outside the territories of a Member State of the European Community. Chapter 12 deals with the fundamental issues raised by the EC choice of law rules in the compulsory insurance sector. Chapter 13 is concerned with the special questions and issues raised by the European private international law rules in the field of motor vehicle insurance contracts.

12

The EC Choice of Law Rules for Compulsory Insurance Contracts: The General Rules

1. INTRODUCTION

As is well known, national legislators commonly impose a duty to take out insurance in relation to certain types of dangerous activities. The aim is usually to protect the victim, being the insured party or a third party.[1] The popularity of compulsory insurance policies is apidly growing. Until recently, the compulsory insurance scheme in the large majority of Member States of the European Community was almost entirely confined to the narrow field of motor vehicle insurance but now an increasing number of laws of the Member States of the European Community impose a direct or indirect obligation to take out compulsory insurance in a wider range of circumstances. In the UK, for example, there are provisions which impose a direct or indirect obligation to take out compulsory insurance in relation to estate agents who are subject to compulsory insurance requirements by statute, and to insurance brokers, osteopaths and chiropractors who may be subject to such requirements if their professional associations exercise their statutory entitlement to make provision requiring compulsory insurance.[2] The popularity of the compulsory scheme has contributed to the development of a discussion about the utility of this device and its relationship to liability regimes in general.

The vast majority of compulsory insurance contracts do not cover mass risks, ie, insurances of a consumer nature. Moreover, in a considerable number of contracts the purchaser of the insurance policy acts in the course of business and is thus in a position different from that of a genuine consumer in terms of consumer protection. Nevertheless, in the field of motor vehicle insurance the purchaser of the policy is usually a natural person acting for private purposes.

Compulsory insurance may well involve a foreign element and is then of interest to the private international lawyer. A hunting insurance policy, which is compulsory in Italy, might be taken out in Italy by a French resident. This is,

[1] See Fallon, *The Law Applicable to Compulsory Insurance and Life Insurance: Special Problems* in Reichert-Facilides and Jessurun d'Oliveira (eds), *International Insurance Contact Law* (Deventer, Kluwer Law and Taxation, 1993) 113.

[2] See Purves (1998) *International Journal of Insurance Law* 4.

on its facts, a simple case. However, a much more complex case might arise when the policy is taken out in Italy to cover Italian territory by an Italian resident and it also gives extended coverage, for example, to hunting in France. Complex cases in the field of compulsory insurance can arise also where the insurance policy provides cover in several Member States of which at least one imposes an obligation to take out insurance. Furthermore, complex cases might arise where there are large numbers of joint policyholders who are resident in different States.

The purpose of this chapter is to examine the choice of law problems that arise in Europe in relation to compulsory insurance, and the possible solutions to these problems. Due to the fact that motor vehicle insurance has been the subject of a significant harmonisation programme within the European Community, it is proposed not to deal with this type of insurance in the present chapter. This will be the subject of the next chapter. The examination of the conflict of law problems in transnational compulsory insurance will be carried out against the substantive law background in Europe. Part I will therefore look at the substantive law background and its significance for the private international lawyer. Part II will look at problems regarding the applicable law and the solutions which are suggested by the 1980 Rome Convention and the Second Non-Life Insurance Directive. Finally, Part III will lay down some recommendations to improve some choice of law provisions of the Second Non-Life Insurance Directive.

2. THE SUBSTANTIVE LAW BACKGROUND IN EUROPE

The substantive law of compulsory insurance in Europe is undeniably complex, involving as it does, two very different types of insurance schemes.

First and foremost, there are compulsory insurance schemes which concern non-contractual liability. These are very popular especially in the field of transport and of motor vehicle insurance. Alongside the compulsory insurance schemes which concern non contractual liability there are compulsory insurance schemes concerning contractual liability which are designed to ensure the compensation of injuries to the contractual counterpart of the policyholder.

Secondly, there are a number of compulsory insurance coverage schemes which belong to the field of social security. This is the case for occupational accident insurance. The application of the pertinent substantive provisions depend in these cases on the criteria governing this field. Like motor vehicle insurance, social security has been the subject of a comprehensive harmonisation programme within the European Community.[3]

The rest of this chapter will deal with the private international law aspects of compulsory insurance.

[3] For an illuminating exposition of this programme see Lugato, *Assicurazioni sociali e diritto internazionale privato* (Milan, 1994).

3. CHOICE OF LAW PROBLEMS IN TRANSNATIONAL COMPULSORY INSURANCE

Because of the increasing number of cross-border transactions in the field of compulsory insurance and because of the increasing variety of usages of the compulsory insurance scheme for different purposes, there is a growing need for clear and universally applicable solutions for the possible problems of conflict of laws with regard to compulsory insurance. The need stems from the diversity of cases where national legislation imposes a direct or indirect obligation to take out compulsory insurance and the uncertainty which would arise for the parties whenever two or more national laws competing for application to the particular instance of compulsory insurance represent such diversity. The insurance company and the insured, as well as the third party, want to know precisely what the applicable law is and what the relationship is between the law imposing the obligation to take out compulsory insurance and the law applicable to the contract.

A few examples will illustrate the point. As already stated above, hunting insurance might be taken out in Belgium to cover Belgian territory by a Belgian resident but also to give extended coverage, for example, for hunting in France. Some questions may arise with regards to the law applicable to this policy. Would it be governed by French law before a French court if an accident occurred in France for the sole reason that French law imposes a duty to take out compulsory insurance? To what extent should a court apply the specific provisions relating to that insurance as laid down by the French State? To take another example, an insured in Italy obtains cover in respect of a large risk from an English insurer; the risk is of a kind which Italian law requires to be insured; the contract contains an express choice of English law. Suppose that Italian law imposes the application of the law of the Member State (Italy) imposing the obligation to take out insurance. There may be a question as to whether English or Italian law applies to that contract.

This chapter addresses some of the questions which the formulation of unified choice of law rules on compulsory insurance raises and deals with some of the problems encountered in such a process of unification of choice of law rules.

(a) Different Types of Compulsory Insurance

Much of writers' attention has been focused on the one situation where the Member State which imposes an obligation to take out insurance is not the same as the Member State in which the risk is situated.[4] Transnational compulsory insurance, however, may be encountered in other situations as well. Even the

[4] See inter alia Fallon, *The Law Applicable to Compulsory Insurance and Life Insurance: Special Problems in Facilides and d'Oliveira (eds), International Insurance Contract*, n 1 above, 113 *et seq*; Dubuisson (Doctoral thesis, Université Catholique de Louvain, 1994) 633 *et seq*.

one situation mentioned above is susceptible to various different manifestations, the distinctions between which are not without interest.

Four distinct types of compulsory insurance can be identified:

1. The Member State which imposes an obligation to take out insurance does not correspond with the Member State in which the risk is situated but the law of the Member State imposing the obligation to take out insurance and that of the Member State in which the risk is situated do not contradict each other.
2. The Member State which imposes an obligation to take out insurance does not correspond with the Member State in which the risk is situated and the law of the Member State imposing the obligation to take out insurance and that of the Member State in which the risk is situated contradict each other.
3. The Member State which imposes an obligation to take out insurance corresponds only with one of the Member States in which the risk is situated but the law of the Member State imposing an obligation to take out insurance and those of the Member States in which the risk is situated do not contradict each other.
4. The Member State which imposes an obligation to take out insurance corresponds only with one of the Member States in which the risk is situated and the law of the Member State imposing an obligation to take out insurance and those of the Member States in which the risk is situated contradict each other.

In all four of these types of compulsory insurance the contract could contain a foreign element and therefore more than one municipal law would contend for governing the insurance contract. The need for a solution to any potential conflict of laws is present in all four situations.

(b) The Need for Specific Choice of Law Rules on Compulsory Insurance

The tardiness with which the search for specific private international law rules on compulsory insurance was undertaken is no cause for surprise. Private international law rules are usually devised to fit well-established categories in municipal laws such as contracts, the capacity of the parties and inheritance. The category called 'compulsory insurance' is a relative newcomer. No wonder, then, that it is relatively recently that efforts have been directed towards devising specific conflict solutions in the field of compulsory insurance.

The application of the law applicable to the contract to compulsory insurance contracts may not raise complex problems but can be questionable. When a State imposes an obligation to take out insurance the contract must be in accordance with the specific provisions relating to that insurance laid down by that State. For self evidently, this does not raise questions when the State which imposes the obligation is the State whose law governs the contract. In these cases, in fact, there is no overlap between the law applicable to the contract and the law which imposes the obligation to take out insurance. But the State which imposes the obligation to take out insurance does not always correspond to the State whose law applies to the contract. In these cases some questions may arise about the relationship between the law applicable to the contract and the special provisions relating to compulsory insurance.[5] These questions suggest that the standard choice of law rules for insurance contracts are not readily adaptable to the particular circumstances of compulsory insurance contracts. Thus there is a need for more specific choice of law rules on compulsory insurance which would take the proper characteristics of that insurance policy into account.

The rest of this section will look in detail at the law applicable to compulsory insurance under the 1980 Rome Convention and the Second Non-Life Insurance Directive.

4. CHOICE OF LAW RULES

European States face the complication of having two different sets of choice of law rules for insurance contracts: the rules contained in the Rome Convention and the choice of law provisions in the Insurance Directives.

(a) The 1980 Rome Convention and the Law Applicable to Compulsory Insurance Contracts Covering Risks Situated Outside the Territories of the Member States of the European Community

The Rome Convention says nothing about its application in cases involving compulsory insurance. Neither does the English statute implementing the Convention. There is nothing unusual about this. Private international law statutes seldom make provision for compulsory insurance contracts. Moreover, the Rome Convention and the English statute of implementation do not lay down specific provisions for any type of insurance contract. The point has either been overlooked altogether or it has been decided that, rather than add an extra layer of complexity to what may already be a complex statute, the problem of the applicable law to compulsory insurance should be left to the courts to apply the general rules of private international law for contracts. In cases involving compulsory insurance contracts covering risks situated outside the territories of a Member State of the European Community this would involve turning to the choice of law rules set out in chapter four.

[5] See below para 5.4.

(b) The Applicable Law

Article 3 of the Rome Convention (freedom of choice) does not raise any particular problems in relation to compulsory insurance contracts. Accordingly, our analysis will focus on compulsory insurance contracts which do not contain a choice of law. It would be wrong to conclude that this analysis is concerned with a problem that can only arise in a very marginal number of international compulsory insurance contracts, because quite a number of these do not contain a choice of law clause, nor do they imply a choice of law by the insurer and the insured. The main reason for this fact is probably that the parties were unable to agree on a choice of law. Neither the insurer nor the insured want to accept the law of the country of the other party for reasons of prestige or because they do not trust the law proposed by the other party, suspecting that it will contain unpleasant surprises.

Typically, a compulsory insurance contract creates a transfer from the idea of civil liability, contractual or non-contractual, to a system of compensation. The coverage is usually linked to a mechanism of indemnity to the victims. Such a link may be manifested directly, where the legislator lays down in the same statute a specific regime of liability and a duty to cover this liability by way of an insurance contract or, alternatively, of an equivalent financial guarantee. Compliance with such a duty might be a pre requisite for having access to a professional or non-professional activity.[6] In these cases the policyholder has to present to the public authorities a certificate stating that valid insurance has been taken out. In order to assure the reality of the protection offered to the victim, the legislator tends to give a direct right of action to the victim against the insurer (*action directe*).

On this basis, at least three countries could claim to have the closest connection with the compulsory insurance scheme. First, the country which imposes the obligation to take out insurance could rely on the fact that such an obligation could be seen as the most important element. Secondly, the country whose law governs the liability could rely on the fact that the *lex loci delicti* is usually the protecting law for the victim. Finally, the country whose law applies to the direct action of the victim if different to that which imposes the obligation to take out insurance could rely on the fact that, without this action, the victim would not receive compensation in a large number of circumstances.

Like Article 3 of the Rome Convention, Article 4(2), which deals with the presumption of characteristic performance, does not raise any special problems in relation to compulsory insurance. It is clear that the obligation to take out insurance does not affect the performance of the contractual parties. Therefore the question of the identification of the party whose performance is characteristic of the contract has to be solved according to the principles set out in chapter four.

[6] See Fallon, *The Law Applicable to Compulsory Insurance and Life Insurance: Special Problems* in Reichert-Facilides (eds), *International Insurance Contract Law*, n 1 above, 114.

(c) Article 5 of the Rome Convention and the Law Applicable to Contracts of Compulsory Insurance

Article 5 deals with consumer contracts that arise in three defined sets of circumstances. In these cases, the mandatory provisions of the country of habitual residence of the consumer cannot be contracted out of, and apply in the absence of a choice of law by the parties. This Article can be relevant to certain contracts of compulsory insurance, for example in the case of motor vehicle insurance if the policyholder does not plan to use the car for professional purposes. Mandatory consumer protection rules such as Article 5 may also take on significance in relation to yachting or hunting.[7] But Article 5 does not appear to be directly or indirectly relevant to most compulsory coverage which concerns large risks, because the policyholder is a professional.

5. THE SECOND NON-LIFE INSURANCE DIRECTIVE AND THE LAW APPLICABLE TO THE CONTRACTS OF COMPULSORY INSURANCE COVERING RISKS SITUATED IN THE TERRITORIES OF A MEMBER STATE OF THE EUROPEAN COMMUNITY: AN OVERVIEW OF THE SET OF CHOICE OF LAW RULES

Unlike the Rome Convention, the Second Non-Life Directive lays down specific provisions of conflict of laws for compulsory insurance. However, the Second Life Insurance Directive does not provide special rules of private international law for compulsory coverage. The reason for this fact is probably that much compulsory coverage belongs to the areas of motor vehicle insurance and transport. Nevertheless, the use of a compulsory scheme is also possible in the field of life insurance. For example, a Member State might impose an obligation on an employer to take out life insurance for the benefit of his employees. In such cases the problem of the law applicable to the compulsory coverage should be left to the courts to apply the general rules of private international law for contracts.

It can be useful at this point to indicate in outline the main provisions of choice of law in the Second Non-Life Directive concerning compulsory coverage, and then to discuss them in greater detail. They will be discussed in the same order in which they appear in the Directive.

[7] See Fallon, *The Law Applicable to Compulsory Insurance and Life Insurance: Special Problems* in Reichert-Facilides and Jessurun d'Oliveira (eds), *International Insurance Contact Law*, n 1 above, 116.

(a) Scheme of the Set of Choice of Law Rules for Compulsory Insurance in the Second Non-Life Directive

The basic provisions concerning compulsory insurance in the Second Non-Life Directive are as follows:

1. Under the conditions set out in Article 8, insurance undertakings can offer and conclude contracts of compulsory insurance in accordance with the provisions of this Directive and of the first Directive (Article 8(1)).
2. When a Member State imposes a duty to take out insurance, the contract shall not satisfy that duty 'unless it is in accordance with the specific provisions relating to that insurance laid down by that Member State' (Article 8(2)).
3. When in the case of compulsory coverage, the law of the Member State in which the risk is located and the law of the Member State imposing the duty to take out insurance 'contradict each other, the latter shall prevail' (Article 8(3)).
4. Subject to subparagraphs (b) and (c) of paragraph four, the third subparagraph of Article 7(2) shall apply where the contract of insurance provides cover in several Member States of which at least one imposes a duty to take out insurance (Article 8(4)).
5. A Member State can, by way of derogation from Article 7, provide that the governing law of a contract of compulsory insurance is the law of the country which imposes the duty to take out insurance (Article 8(4)(c)).
6. Where a Member State imposes a duty to take out compulsory coverage and the insurance company shall notify the competent authorities of any cessation of cover, 'such cessation may be invoked against injured third parties only in the circumstances laid down in the legislation of that State' (Article 8(40(d)).

As it appears from this exposition, the structure of the set of choice of law rules for compulsory insurance in the Second Non-Life Directive is not very different from the structure of the set of choice of law provisions for the other types of insurance in the same directive. Although there are some differences between the two instruments, the similarities greatly outweigh the differences. This conclusion emerges clearly if you take into consideration the basic rule of Article 8(1) which provides that, subject to Article 8(2), (3), (4) of the Second Non-Life Directive, the compulsory insurance contract is governed by the other rules of the Second Non-Life Directive.

(b) Article 8(1)

The Second Non-Life Directive provides in Article 8(1) that insurance undertakings may conclude under the conditions laid down in Article 8 contracts of compulsory insurance in accordance with the provisions of that Directive and of the First Non-Life Directive.

At first glance, this provision calls for little comment. It appears to state the obvious principle that compulsory insurance contracts shall be concluded in accordance with the rules of the insurance directives. However, if you look at the provision from the perspective of the private international lawyer the picture changes.

Some uncertainties might arise from the text of Article 8(1) about the relationship between the set of choice of laws rules for compulsory insurance contracts in the Second Non-Life Directive and the Rome Convention. Article 8(1) says nothing about the application of the rules of the Rome Convention to contracts of compulsory insurance. The question is not purely academic as the special choice of law rules for contracts of non-life insurance in the Second Non-Life Directive do not cover all the issues related to the contract of insurance. A possible explanation for the omission is that the Second Non-Life Directive provides in Article 7(3) for the application of the rules in the Rome Convention to the questions not covered by the specific rules of private international law for insurance contracts. Thus the rules of the Rome Convention would apply to the issues of compulsory insurance contracts which are not covered by the specific provisions laid down in Articles 7 and 8 of the Second Non-Life Directive. Nevertheless, there are some arguments against the application of the rules of the Rome Convention to compulsory insurance contracts. Unlike the Rome Convention, Article 8 of the Second Non-Life Directive does not adopt the rule that the parties are free to choose the law governing their contract. On the contrary, Article 7(1)(f) of the Second Non-Life Directive adopts this rule for insurance contracts covering 'large risks'. One might derive from this different approach of Article 8 of the Second Non-Life Directive to the applicable law an incompatibility between the choice of law provisions for compulsory insurance and the conventional rules under the Rome Convention. Moreover, in the vast majority of cases in which the compulsory insurance concerns civil liability the prominent interest of the protection of the victim suggests the application of the *lex loci delicti* rather than the governing law of the contract to the issues which are not covered by the specific rules of choice of laws for compulsory insurance. It is likely that the law of the country in which the damage occurred is more in keeping with the needs of the victim than the governing law of the contract, which is usually chosen by the contractual parties taking into account their own convenience. However, it is quite improbable that the intention of the drafters of Article 8(1) was to exclude the application of Article 7(3) and thus the rules of the Rome Convention to compulsory insurance contracts. On the contrary, the application of Article 7(3) to compulsory insurance contracts is suggested by the fact that the set of choice of laws rules for compulsory insurance is not complete but very much dependent on the special set of choice of law rules for contracts of non-life insurance.

(c) The Law Applicable to Compulsory Insurance Contracts Covering Risks Situated in Different Member States: Article 8(4)(a)

The Second Non-Life Directive provides in Article 8(4)(a) that where the insurance contract gives cover in several Member States of which at least one imposes a duty to take out insurance, Article 7(2)(3) of the Second Non-Life Directive shall apply, ie the contract is to be considered as constituting several contracts relating to only one Member State.

It is worth noting that Article 8(4)(a) is similar but not identical to Article 7(2)(3). However, if you look at the text of Article 8(4)(a) this does not go further than the mere reference to Article 7(2)(3). Nevertheless, the latter article does not apply to compulsory insurance contracts under the same conditions set out in it for non-life insurance contracts. Article 7(2)(3) provides that 'where the contract covers risks situated in more than one Member State, the contract is considered for the *purposes of applying this paragraph* as constituting several contracts . . .'.[8] Paragraph two of Article 7 deals with the application of the mandatory rules of the law of the forum and the Member State in which the risk is situated. Where the insurance contract provides cover in several Member States of which at least one imposes a duty to take out insurance, the contract is considered as constituting several contracts not only for the purpose of applying the mandatory rules of the law of the forum and the Member State in which the risk is situated but also for the purpose of applying the specific provisions relating to insurance laid down by the Member State which imposes the duty to take out insurance. This conclusion is suggested by the fact that the latter provisions have very often a mandatory character, ie apply irrespective of the law otherwise applicable to the contract. Moreover, it is supported by the scope of Article 7(2)(3). This provision aims to restrict the application of mandatory rules to only the parts of the contract which are strictly connected with the law of the forum or the law of the country to which the mandatory provisions belong. Thus no distinction has to be made for the purpose of applying Article 8(4)(a) between the mandatory provisions of the law of the forum/of the Member State in which the risk is situated and the specific rules laid down by the Member State which impose the duty to take out insurance, provided, of course, these rules are mandatory.

(d) The Law of the Member State Imposing the Obligation to Take Out Insurance and the Law Applicable to Compulsory Insurance Contracts: Article 8(4)(c)

Article 8(4)(c) provides that a Member State can lay down that the governing law of a compulsory insurance contract is the law of the State which imposes the duty to take out insurance.

[8] Emphasis added.

It goes without saying that the option for the Member States to provide that the law applicable to compulsory insurance is the law of the Member State which imposes the obligation to take out insurance is the result of a political compromise between the delegates from the more protectionist States, which were favourable to restrictions to the freedom of the parties, and the delegates from the more liberal States, which were favourable to the freedom of the parties in the field of compulsory insurance contracts. This conclusion is confirmed by the different solutions adopted by the Member States in their statutes implementing the Second Non-Life Directive. Article 8(4)(c) has not been implemented in the UK, Ireland and Italy. However, the provision has been implemented in most of the Member States, such as Belgium, France, Germany, Luxembourg, The Netherlands and Spain.

This option for the Member States to prohibit any choice of law in relation to compulsory insurance contracts deserves 'a welcome' since it avoids the *dépeçage* of the contract. It is clear that the right to split issues away from the governing law of the insurance contract may conflict with the interest of the parties in predicting the law applicable to their policy. However, the application of the law of the State which imposes the duty to take out insurance is not always the most convenient one for the contractual parties. Moreover, the law of the State which imposes the duty to take out insurance is not usually the one most closely connected to the contract. It is not unusual that a Member State imposes an obligation to take out insurance coverage but does not lay down specific provisions for the insurance contract. In such cases, the application of the mandatory rules and the specific provisions relating to that insurance laid down by the Member State which imposes the duty to take out insurance is sufficient to avoid the evasion of that duty.

(e) The Specific Provisions Relating to Compulsory Insurance Laid Down by the Member State Imposing an Obligation to Take Out Insurance and the Law Applicable to Compulsory Insurance Contracts: Article 8(2)

Article 8, paragraph 2 states that:

> When a Member State imposes an obligation to take out insurance, the contract shall not satisfy that obligation unless it is in accordance with the specific provisions relating to that insurance laid down by that Member State.

At first glance, one might argue that this provision deals with mandatory rules. However, this would be a false conclusion, as the words 'in accordance with' in the text of Article 8(2) make it clear that the 'specific provisions' relating to compulsory insurance shall not apply irrespective of the law otherwise applicable to the contract. Nevertheless, it is true that a large number of specific provisions relating to insurance laid down by the Member State which imposes the obligation to take out insurance have a mandatory character. Technically,

Article 8, paragraph 2 looks like some choice of laws provisions in torts such as Article 142(2) of the Swiss statute of private international law which provides that whatever the applicable law, in determining liability *account shall be taken* of rules of conduct and safety which were in force at the place and time of the occurrence of the harmful event. Although the words 'in accordance with' in Article 8(2) do not exactly have the same meaning as the expression 'account shall be taken' in the text of Article 142(2) of the 1987 Swiss statute, the idea expressed by these provisions is almost identical. According to these articles, the court, in order to decide whether or not to apply the 'specific rules' relating to compulsory insurance laid down by the Member State which imposes the duty to take out insurance (or in tort cases the rules of safety and conduct which were in force at the place and time of the occurrence of the harmful event), must compare the interests protected by these rules with those protected by the law governing the insurance contract. Only if the governing law of the contract does not take into consideration the interests protected by the specific provisions relating to compulsory insurance laid down by the Member State which imposes the obligation to take out insurance (or in tort cases the interests protected by the rules of safety and conduct which were in force at the place and time of the occurrence of the harmful event) will the court apply these provisions. In all the other cases, the court can depart from the competence of the governing law of the contract when the conditions set out in Article 8(3) and (4)(d) for the application of mandatory rules have occurred.

(f) Mandatory Rules: Article 8(3)

Article 8(3) deals with mandatory rules. However, unlike Articles 7 of the Rome Convention and 7(2) of the Second Non-Life Directive, this provision does not set out conditions for the application of mandatory provisions to compulsory insurance contracts. Article 8(3) reads as follows:

> When, in the case of compulsory insurance, the law of the Member State in which the risk is situated and the law of the Member State imposing the obligation to take out insurance contradict each other, the latter shall prevail.

This provision must be read together with Article 7, paragraph 2, last sentence, of the Second Non-Life Directive. According to the latter provision, if the law of a Member State so provides, the mandatory rules of

> the law of the Member State in which the risk is situated or of *the Member State imposing the obligation to take out insurance* may be applied in so far as, under the law of those States, those rules must be applied whatever the law applicable to the contract.[9]

Some questions might arise in the field of compulsory insurance when both the conditions for the application of the mandatory rules of the law of the Member

[9] Emphasis added.

State imposing the obligation to take out insurance and those for the application of the mandatory provisions of the law of the Member State in which the risk is situated are satisfied. In these cases a conflict might arise between the law of the Member State in which the risk is situated and the law of the Member State imposing the obligation to take out insurance. Article 8(3) states that the latter law should prevail. This solution is consistent with the role given in the set of choice of laws rules for compulsory insurance to the law of the Member State imposing the obligation to take out insurance. Article 8(3) does not deal, however, with the conflicts which might arise between the laws of two Member States both imposing obligations to take out insurance.[10] In these cases the rule laid down in Article 8(3) cannot be used. These conflicts do not raise any particular problem when the insurance contract covers risks situated in more than one Member State. Article 7(2) of the Second Non-Life Directive provides that the contract is considered as constituting *several contracts* each relating to only one Member State. Nevertheless, some difficulties might arise when two Member States impose conflicting obligations to take out insurance and the contract covers risks localised only in one Member State. In the absence of any indication in the text of Article 8(3) the judge perhaps should refer to the law of the forum to decide which law must prevail in these circumstances.

(g) Mandatory Rules: Article 8(4)(d)

The Second Non-Life Directive provides in Article 8(4)(d) that:

> Where a Member State imposes compulsory insurance and the insurer must notify the competent authorities of any cessation of cover, such cessation may be invoked against injured third parties *only in the circumstances laid down in the legislation of that State.*[11]

As suggested in the introduction to this chapter, the obligation to take out insurance is, in a proper way, connected with the governing law of the contract. A close link between the duty to take out insurance and the law applicable to the contract exists where the Member State which imposes the obligation to take out an insurance coverage does not establish a comprehensive regime for the insurance contract. In these cases some questions might arise with regards to the issues which are governed by the law applicable to the contract and the issues to which the law of the Member State which imposes the obligation to take out insurance apply. While the law of the State which imposes the duty to take out insurance coverage does not establish a comprehensive regime for the contract in any circumstance, it often lays down some provisions concerning the contract.

[10] For a clear illustration of this point see Dubuisson, *Le droit applicable au contrat d'assurance*, n 4 above, 652.

[11] Emphasis added.

The Second Directive raises the question of the relationship between the law applicable to the contract and the obligation to take out insurance in Article 8(4)(d). This provision is concerned with the particular case in which a Member State imposes compulsory insurance and the insurer must notify the competent authorities of any cessation of cover. That any cessation of cover can be invoked against an injured third party only in the circumstances laid down in the legislation of the Member State which imposes the duty to take out insurance is suggested by the protection of the injured third parties. Moreover, this is consistent with the obligation to notify the competent authorities of any cessation of cover.

6. THE DUTY OF THE MEMBER STATES TO COMMUNICATE TO THE COMMISSION THE RISKS AGAINST WHICH INSURANCE IS COMPULSORY: ARTICLE 8(5)(A) AND (B)

Article 8(5) of the Second Non-Life Directive does not lay down a choice of law provision, but deals exclusively with matters of co-operation amongst the Member States. According to Article 8(5)(a), each Member State must

> communicate to the Commission the risks against which insurance is compulsory under its legislation, stating: the specific legal provisions relating to that insurance, the particulars which must be given in the certificate which an insurer must issue to an insured person where that State requires proof that the obligation to take out insurance has been complied with. A Member State may require that those particulars include a declaration by the insurer to the effect that the contract complies with the specific provisions relating to that insurance.

Though paragraph five of Article 8 does not lay down a private international law rule, neither is it completely indifferent to the choice of law process. The imposition on the Member States of a duty to communicate to the Commission the risks against which insurance is compulsory under their legislation avoids complex problems of qualification which might arise because of the different approaches taken in the Member States with regards to compulsory insurance. This point is clearly illustrated by the example of occupational accidents. These accidents are considered in France as belonging to the field of social security and thus the applicability of pertinent substantive provisions depends on the criteria governing this field. However, in other Member States such as Belgium and the United Kingdom occupational accidents belong to the field of private insurance. The impact of the duty to communicate the risks against which insurance is compulsory on the issue of qualification proves the very close link that exists between matters of co-operation amongst Member States and choice of law issues in the field of compulsory insurance.

7. EVALUATION

A number of criticisms can be made of the choice of law rules in Article 8 of the Second Non-Life Directive.

(a) Complexity

One of the Belgian and French writers' major criticisms of the set of choice of law rules for compulsory insurance contracts was its complexity,[12] and the same criticism has been made by lawyers from Italy and Denmark.[13] It is undeniable that this set of provisions is complex. Any set of choice of laws rules which uses combinations of connections, an elective solution and a foreseeability rule cannot be regarded as being a simple one.

However, the degree of complexity under Article 8 of the Second Non-Life Directive should not be exaggerated.

First, the basic idea under Article 8(4)(c) of granting the Member States the option to state in their implementation statutes the application of the law of the State which imposes the obligation to take out insurance is a remarkably simple one. Moreover, paragraph three of Article 8 provides for every conflict between the law of the Member State in which the risk is situated and the law of the Member State imposing the obligation to take out insurance that can arise. To that extent the choice of law provisions for compulsory insurance contracts are easy to apply. The real complexity only arises in relation to Article 8(4)(2), but this provision will only apply in relatively rare cases.

Second, the absence of special rules for particular issues and particular types of compulsory insurance contracts is a feature of Article 8 that involves simplicity of approach.

Third, it must be doubtful whether a short simple rule can satisfy the complex range of policy considerations that should underlie choice of law provisions for compulsory insurance.

(b) An Excessive Freedom of Implementation of the Choice of Law Rules

By granting the Member States the option to provide, by way of derogation from Article 7, that the law applicable to a compulsory insurance contract is the

[12] See inter alia Dubuisson, *Le droit applicable au contrat d'assurance*, n 4 above, 635 *et seq*; Berr (1988) *Revue trimestrelle de droit européen*, 672.

[13] See Frigessi di Rattalma, *Il contratto internazionale di assicurazione* (Padova, 1990) 206 *et seq*; Lando, *Mandatory Rules Governing Insurance Contracts and Private International Law* in Reichert-Facilides and d'Oliveira (eds), *International Insurance Contract in the EC* (Deventer, Kluwer Law and Taxation, 1993) 109.

law of the State which imposes the duty to take out insurance, Article 8 gives them a wide freedom of implementation of the choice of law rules for compulsory insurance. The exercise of that option, in fact, can result in very different regimes of private international law for compulsory insurance contracts in Europe, as is demonstrated by the examination of the national rules of implementation of Article 8.

One might perhaps explain this wide freedom of implementation with the character of the European directives which are binding only 'as to the result to be achieved' and give the Member States 'the choice of form and methods' for the implementation. Transposition of a European Directive into domestic law does not require in any case that 'its provisions be incorporated formally and verbatim in express, specific legislation'; it is possible that:

> a general legal context may, depending on the content of the directive, be adequate for the purpose provided that it does indeed guarantee the full application of the directive in a sufficiently clear and precise manner. . .[14]

In order to ensure the complete application of Directives, Member States should make sure only that there is a clear legal framework for the area in question.[15] Moreover, Article 7 of the Second Non-Life Directive grants the Member States a wide freedom of implementation of the choice of law provisions concerning the other types of non-life insurance contracts. Nevertheless, an excessive freedom of implementation of the choice of law provisions merely reduces the programmed level of conflicts of law harmonisation between the Member States.

(c) Objections to This

There are a number of objections which can be made to giving the Member States a wide freedom of implementation.

(d) Forum Shopping

The lack of harmonisation of choice of law rules for compulsory insurance in the European Union resulting from such a wide freedom of implementation merely encourages forum shopping for substantive law advantages, as the following example shows. A French national is injured in England by a vehicle covered by an insurance policy issued by a French insurer and wishes to sue the French insurance company. Let us assume that French substantive law is more

[14] See Lenaerts and van Nuffel, *Constitutional Law of the European Union* (London, Sweet & Maxwell, 1999) 573 *et seq*.

[15] *Ibid*, 572.

favourable to the claimant than English law. If the claimant sues in France, which is the natural forum for trial, the French courts would apply the law of the State which imposes the obligation to take out insurance, and that would probably be French law. The claimant would do better to come to England, where there would be jurisdiction under Article 9 of the Brussels Convention. The English courts, on the face of it, would apply English law as the law of the place in which the risk is situated.

(e) The Objective of the Second Non-Life Directive

The Second Non-Life Directive is concerned to introduce freedom of insurance services within the European Community, by allowing an insurance company authorised and established in any Member State to sell insurance products in any other Member State without the need for further authorisation or establishment.[16] To achieve this it is necessary, *inter alia*, to reach a reasonable level of choice of law harmonisation in the field of insurance (including that of compulsory insurance). Accordingly, the Second Directive lays down a set of choice of law provisions for insurance contracts. However, the low level of harmonisation in the field of compulsory insurance resulting from the excessive freedom of implementation for the Member States clearly undermines this objective.

(f) Uncertainty

A wide freedom of implementation cannot also be supported on the grounds of certainty and simplicity. This, of course, is not an absolute factor but one which is relative. The law of the Member State imposing the obligation to take out insurance as indicated in Article 8(4)(c) is no more certain or easy to apply than the law of the country in which the risk is situated. Indeed, it is clearly less certain than the law of the country in which the risk is situated in cases where the law of the state imposing the duty to take out insurance does not establish a comprehensive regime for the contract and therefore it shall apply to the contract together with the *lex contractus*. But if you contrast the law of the Member State which imposes the obligation to take out insurance with the proper law or American interest analysis approaches then it is infinitely more certain and easy to apply. Nevertheless, the alternative in the Second Directive was between the law of the state which imposes the obligation to take out insurance and the law of the place of the risk.

[16] See above ch 1, para 9(a).

(g) Lack of Co-ordination Between the Jurisdiction Rules of the Brussels Regulation and the Choice of Law Rules for Compulsory Insurance

There is a lack of co-ordination between the jurisdiction rules of the Brussels Regulation and the choice of law provisions of the Second Non-Life Directive for compulsory insurance contracts. The choice of law rules in Article 8 of the Second Directive do not appear to fit in with the jurisdiction provisions of the Brussels Regulation. Indeed, the law of the Member State which imposes the obligation to take out insurance does not fit in well with the competence of the courts for the place where the harmful event occurred under Article 10 of the Brussels Regulation. This article applies in respect of liability insurance or insurance of immovable property. It allows an insurer to be sued in a State other than that in which he is domiciled. The country where the harmful event occurred may be the same one which imposes an obligation to take out insurance. However, the State which imposes a duty to take out insurance may not coincide with the country where the harmful event occurred. Take the example of a State which provides for an obligation to cover yachting, such as Italy. The accident, ie the harmful event raising the duty of the insurer to repair the damage, may occur in another country, for example in France. In such a case the State (Italy) which imposes the obligation to take out insurance does not coincide with the State (France) where the harmful event occurred. If the injured party sues the insurer of the wrongdoer in France, according to Article 10, the French courts would apply Italian law as the law of the state which imposes the obligation to take out insurance. However, that would probably not be a very satisfactory outcome for the injured party. It is clear that the injured party would benefit more from the application of French law which is the law of the place where the harmful event occurred. This is suggested especially by reasons of litigational convenience, such as the close proximity to the evidence and witnesses. Nevertheless, this lack of co-ordination between the jurisdiction rules of the Brussels Regulation and the choice of law provisions for compulsory insurance in the Second Non-Life Directive should not be exaggerated. Choice of law is concerned, in fact, not only with connections and matters such as litigational convenience but also with such matters as mandatory provisions and public policy.

8. OPTIONS FOR REFORM

(a) Repealing the Implementation Provisions of Article 8(4)(c)

The most direct way of dealing with the problem of the unsuitability of Article 8(4)(c) of the Second Non-Life Directive is to repeal the corresponding implementation rules in those statutes, such as the Belgian, Dutch, French, German,

Spanish statutes of implementation of the Second Non-Life Directive, which provide that the law applicable to a compulsory insurance contract is the law of the Member State which imposes the obligation to take out insurance.

However, this solution would not tackle the other deficiencies in the choice of law rules for compulsory insurance contracts. Indeed, it would not stop the common criticism in legal writings that the set of choice of law rules for compulsory insurance contracts is too complex.

(b) Re-wording Article 1(3) of the Rome Convention

Under this solution Article 1(3) of the Rome Convention would be re-worded so that the Convention would apply to compulsory insurance contracts which cover risks situated in the territories of the Member States of the European Community. This would have the advantage of introducing a single set of choice of law rules for compulsory insurance contracts regardless of whether the risk is situated in or outside the territories of a Member State. As has already been seen, the choice of law provisions of the Rome Convention adopt suitable connecting factors for insurance contracts (including compulsory insurance contracts) and thus ensure that the interests of the parties are respected. Indeed, Article 7(1) of the Rome Convention which deals with the application of the mandatory rules of the law of a country with which the situation has a close connection, can be used by the courts to ensure that the mandatory provisions relating to compulsory insurance laid down by the Member State which imposes the obligation to take out insurance are respected. Moreover, the application of the rules of the Rome Convention to compulsory insurance contracts covering risks situated in the territories of Member States of the European Community would avoid the forum shopping for substantive law advantages caused by the present low level of harmonisation of choice of law rules for compulsory insurance contracts in Europe.

13

The EC Choice of Law Rules for Motor Vehicle Insurance Contracts

1. INTRODUCTION

THE CHOICE of laws problems which may arise when the insurance policy in relation to motor vehicle accidents has an international character (ie, covers liability for damages incurred in an accident abroad) have received little sustained judicial or academic treatment in European countries.[1] In this respect, the European position provides a striking contrast to its American counterpart. It appears that the relative dearth of specialist consideration of the field can be attributed to four principal factors. Firstly, the absence of specific choice of law rules for compulsory insurance contracts in most of the European countries. Secondly, the acceptance by nearly all Western-European countries of the 'green card' system (international motor insurance card) which is an alternative tool to private international law for resolving the problems of road victims' damages. Thirdly, the general tendency of national courts in Europe to apply the law of the country which imposes the obligation to take out insurance to any aspect of the insurance contract for motor vehicles.[2] Fourthly, at least in some common law countries, the flexibility of the proper law of the contract.

These observations, however, apply more to the past than to the present. At the present, most of the European systems of private international law provide specific choice of law rules for compulsory insurance contracts as a result of the implementation of the Non-Life Insurance Directive. As already explained below, these rules apply to motor vehicle insurance.[3] Moreover, there are also ad hoc provisions of private international law for insurance contracts covering motor vehicle risks. Furthermore, the law of the country which imposes the obligation to take out insurance is not exclusively competent to govern the insurance policy against motor vehicle accidents. Accordingly, consideration of the choice of laws problems which may arise when the insurance policy in relation to motor vehicle accidents has an international character is now seen as a necessity.

[1] But see L Garau Juaneda, *El seguro de responsabilidad civil pour el uso de automóviles en derecho internacional privado* (Madrid, Civitas, 1977); Dubuisson, *Le droit applicable au contrat d'assurance* (Doctoral thesis, Université Catholique de Louvain, 1994) 665–735.

[2] See above ch 12, para 5.4.

[3] See above ch 12, para 5.1.

Indeed, motor vehicle insurance contracts present many challenging questions for the private international lawyer, which are heightened by the international mobility of motor vehicles resulting from the principle of free movement within the European Economic Community. Some of these questions are aspects of general problems current in private international law; for example, the relationship between administrative and private law rules, the interaction between tort and contract in an international context, the plethora of issues surrounding the effect of statutes in the conflict of laws. Other questions are more specifically germane to motor vehicle insurance, for example ascertainment of the law governing insurance contracts covering motor vehicle risks. Is this law to be discovered by reference to the choice of laws provisions for insurance contracts or do the particular issues raised by international contracts of motor vehicle insurance require a more particularised rule for the choice of law applicable to them? The Motor Vehicle Insurance Directives suggest that international contracts of motor vehicle insurance merit special consideration in this regard.

As already stated above, principles of choice of law in the field of contracts as embodied in the Rome Convention attempt to give a response to the needs of international commerce. The basic characteristic of this response was its flexibility as indicated by the wide freedom of the parties to choose the law applicable to the contract and the rule that the presumptions in paragraphs 2, 3 and 4 of Article 4 relating to the applicable law in the absence of choice shall be disregarded if it appears from the circumstances as a whole that the contract is most closely connected with another country. However, the policies and interests at work in international commerce are quite different from those at work in international compulsory insurance concerning motor vehicles. Almost all countries seek to regulate insurance contracts covering motor vehicle risks through protective legislation designed to provide adequate compensation for the victims of traffic accidents. And where the compulsory insurance relationship is of an international character, choice of law principles have to accommodate the existence of these policies and interests. Clearly this is the rationale behind the special choice of law rules for motor vehicle insurance contracts, insofar as it carves out exceptions to the choice of law provisions contained in the Non-Life Insurance Directive.

The rest of this chapter will consider the choice of laws rules for motor vehicle insurance contracts in Europe and their impact on the European mechanism of indemnification of the victims of traffic accidents.

2. APPLICABLE LAW

(a) The 1980 Rome Convention and the Law Applicable to Motor Vehicle Insurance Contracts Covering Risks Situated Outside the Territories of the Member States of the European Community

Under the 1980 Rome Convention, there are no special rules of private international law dealing with the law applicable to motor vehicle insurance contracts. This means that the private international law rules of general application have to be applied to the specific contracts. Two very different sets of rules come into play. The first are contract choice of law rules. The second are the mandatory rules of the forum. In cases involving motor vehicle insurance contracts covering risks situated outside the territories of a Member State of the European Community this would involve turning to the conflict of laws rules set out in chapter four.

(b) The Second Non-Life Insurance Directive and the Law Applicable to Motor Vehicle Insurance Contracts Covering Risks Situated in the Territories of a Member State of the European Community

Like the Rome Convention, the Second Non-Life Directive does not lay down special rules of private international law for motor vehicle insurance contracts. However, this Directive provides choice of law rules for compulsory insurance contracts. It appears that these provisions as well as the choice of law rules of general application in Article 7 of the Second Non-Life Directive apply to motor vehicle insurance contracts. This conclusion is suggested by the fact that motor vehicle insurance policies are not excluded from the scope of application of the title I of the Second Non-Life Directive which contains choice of law rules for non-life insurance and compulsory insurance contracts.[4] On the other hand, motor vehicle insurance policies are excluded from the scope of application of the rules in title II of the Second Non-Life Insurance Directive. Therefore in cases involving motor vehicle insurance contracts covering risks situated in the territories of a Member State of the European Community the judge must turn to the private international law provisions discussed in chapters five and seven.

[4] For the same opinion see Dubuisson, *Le droit applicable au contrat d'assurance* (Doctoral thesis, Université Catholique de Louvain, 1993) 672.

(c) Article 7(1)(a) of the Second Non-Life Directive and the Law Applicable to Motor Vehicle Insurance Contracts

A word needs to be said about the application of Article 7(1)(a) in the field of motor vehicle insurance. This provision together with Article 2(d) of the Second Non-Life Directive provides that where a policy holder has his habitual residence within the territory of the Member State in which the vehicle is registered the law applicable to the insurance contract shall be the law of that Member State.

In the field of motor vehicle insurance Article 7(1)(a) raises some questions in relation to non-registered vehicles. Which is the law applicable to an insurance policy covering motor vehicles that have no registration? Article 2(d) of the Second Non-Life Insurance Directive suggests that in the absence of specific rules the risk shall be considered as situated in the country where the policy holder is habitually resident. Therefore the law of the place of the habitual residence of the policyholder should apply to an insurance contract covering a non-registered vehicle. However, another solution can be derived from Article 6 of 1971 Hague Convention on the law applicable to traffic accidents. This provides that in the cases of vehicles which have no registration (or which are registered in several States) the internal law of the State in which they are usually stationed shall replace the law of the state of registration. Article 6 lays down a clearly cut and reasonable rule which deals both with the cases of motor vehicles that have no registration and the cases of motor vehicles which are registered in several states. The application of this rule to insurance contracts covering motor vehicles which are registered in several Member States would avoid the *dépeçage* of the contract, ie the severance of the different parts of the contract from the governing law of the contract and their subjection to different laws. Moreover, it would be favourable to the victim being the place in which the vehicle is usually stationed, which is generally coincident with the place of the accident. One perhaps might argue that the 1971 Hague Convention on the law applicable to traffic accidents does not apply to insurance and therefore Article 6 of the Hague Convention can not provide an alternative solution to Article 2(d) of the Second Non-Life Directive. However, this would be a false conclusion as Article 3 of the Hague Convention excludes from the scope of application of the convention only '. . . the recourse actions and . . . subrogation in so far as insurance companies are concerned'.[5] Therefore, Article 6 of the 1971 Hague Convention applies to insurance contracts covering motor vehicles which are registered in several Member States of the European Community. But Article 6 of the Hague Convention can not provide an alternative solution to Article 2(d) of the Second Non-Life Directive in the United Kingdom, Italy, Spain, the Netherlands which have not ratified the 1971 Hague Convention.

[5] Emphasis added.

(d) Article 8(4)(c) of the Second Non-Life Insurance Directive and the Law Applicable to Motor Vehicle Insurance Contracts

Another provision which deserves attention is Article 8(4)(c) of the Second Non-Life Insurance Directive. This deals with compulsory insurance contracts. It provides that a Member State can decide that the governing law of a compulsory insurance contract is the law of the country which imposes the duty to take out insurance. Article 8(4)(c) may raise some problems in the motor vehicle insurance sector since it creates an obstacle to the conclusion of insurance policies covering the territories of two or more Member States. It is clear, in fact, that the conclusion of an insurance policy covering risks situated in the territories of two or Member States is possible only if the Member States involved recognise the validity of the policy made according to a foreign law. The conclusion of a policy covering risks situated in the territories of two or more Member States is not possible if one or all the Member States involved provide that the governing law of the policy is the law of the country which imposes the duty to take out insurance. It is submitted that Article 8(4)(c) conflicts with the objective of the Motor Vehicle Insurance Directives to allow the conclusion of insurance policies covering the entire territory of the Community.[6] Notably, this provision is incompatible with Article 2(1) of the Third Motor Vehicle Insurance Directive which provides that:

> Member States shall take the necessary steps to ensure that all compulsory insurance policies against civil liability arising out of the use of vehicles: cover, on the basis of a single premium, *the entire territory of the Community* . . .

The contradiction between Article 8(4)(c) of the Second Non-Life Directive and Article 2(1) of the Third Motor Insurance Directive is relevant to those Member States which have implemented Article 8(4)(c). In the absence of specific indications in the implementation statutes Article 2(1) of the Third Motor Insurance Directive must prevail over Article 8(4)(c). This conclusion is suggested by the fundamental principle of European law according to which the following rule prevails on the former rule (*lex posterior derogat priori*).[7]

Moreover, it is supported by the fact either private international law and substantive law rules must be interpreted in conformity with European Community law.

[6] See Fallon, *The Law Applicable to Compulsory Insurance and Life Insurance: Special Problems* in Reichert-Facilides and Jessurun d'Oliveira (eds), *International Insurance Contract Law* (Deventer, Kluwer Law and Taxation, 1993) 119.

[7] For a clear illustration of this principle see J Shaw, *Law of the European Union* (Houndmills, Basingstoke, Hampshire, New York, Palgrave, 2000) 184.

(e) Private International Law Aspects of the Third Motor Vehicle Insurance Directive

On reading the Third Motor Vehicle Insurance Directive for the first time one might have the impression that it does not lay down any private international law rules. However, this would be a false idea, as Article 2(2) of the Directive provides that Member States are requested to:

> take the necessary steps to ensure that all compulsory insurance policies against civil liability arising out of the use of vehicles: guarantee, on the basis of the same single premium, in each Member State, the cover required by its law or the cover required by the law of the Member State where the vehicle is normally based when that cover is higher.

Undoubtedly, the formulation which has been adopted for this rule is rather unusual for a choice of law provision and may also be confusing. Nevertheless, it is clear that the objective of Article 2(2) of the Third Motor Vehicle Insurance Directive is to guarantee the application of the most favourable law to the victim of traffic accidents. In this respect the provision resembles Article 5 of the Rome Convention which grants special protection to the weaker party to a consumer contract.

Being concerned with the interests of the victim, Article 2(2) deals exclusively with torts, as is proved by the absence of a reference to the governing law of the contract in the text of the provision. Dubuisson argues that this rule is questionable as it may subject the tort issues to different laws.[8] It is clear that the splitting of issues away from the governing law of the tort, such as the reparation of the damage, the criteria for the evaluation of the behaviour of the wrongdoer, the exceptions that the victim can invoke against the wrongdoers and the insurer, may be unfair both to the damaging party and insurance company. The *dépeçage* of the governing law of the tort may affect the (legitimate) expectations of the insurer and wrongdoer for the application of the *lex delicti*. However, the meaning of Article 2(2) of the Third Motor Vehicle Insurance Directive suggests that the judge should ascertain the most favourable law to the victim by taking into consideration the overall norms, ie the provisions on the reparations of the damage, the criteria for the evaluation of the behaviour of the wrongdoer, etc. Moreover, this conclusion can be derived from the words of the provision which refer to the 'cover' required by the law but not to the single rights of the victim.

(f) The Relationship Between Contract and Tort in the Field of Motor Vehicle Insurance

Numerous problems arise out of the interaction between contract and tort in conflict of laws, and some of the problems are highlighted in the context of

[8] See Dubuisson, *Le droit applicable au contrat d'assurance*, n 4 above, 674–76.

motor vehicle insurance contracts. These issues are discussed extensively in the legal literature:[9] it is only intended here to give a brief sketch of the problem.

The problem arises particularly in relation to the direct action of the victim against the insurer of the person liable, especially in the French and Italian systems of law which regard this action as sounding both in contract and in tort.[10] The direct action against the insurer of the person liable is of crucial importance for the victims of traffic accidents who often need rapid and substantial reparation of the damages suffered. However, the Motor Vehicle Insurance Directives do not provide a rule dealing with the law applicable to the direct action of the victim of traffic accidents. That cannot be justified by the fact that the 1971 Hague Convention on the law applicable to traffic accidents lays down an ad hoc provision on the law applicable to the direct action of the victim. Article 2 of the 1971 Hague Convention excludes actions in so far as insurance companies are concerned. Moreover, the Convention on the law applicable to traffic accidents has only been ratified by a limited number of Member States.[11] The Rome Convention gives no help in answering the question of the law applicable to the 'direct action' of the victim against the insurer. However, the draft proposal of the 'European Group of Private International Law' for a European Convention on the law applicable to non contractual obligations (Rome II) contains a rule on the direct action of the victim.[12] Nevertheless, like Article 9 of the 1971 Hague Convention on the law applicable to traffic accidents the proposed rule only deals with tort issues.

(g) The Law Applicable to Punitive Damages

A word needs to be said about the choice of laws problems which may arise when the insurance policy in relation to motor vehicle accidents does not contain a specific exclusion for punitive (exemplary) damages, ie damages that are separate and in excess of the compensatory damages awarded to a claimant in a

[9] See Kahn-Freund, (1968) II Hague Recueil 149–57; Ferrari Bravo, (1975) III Hague Recueil 387–90; North, (1977) *International and Comparative Law Quarterly* 914–31; Morse, *Torts in Private International Law* (Amsterdam, New York, North-Holland Pub Co, 1978) 187–94.

[10] See above ch 8, para 25.

[11] The 1971 Hague Convention on the law applicable to traffic accidents has been ratified by only 7 Member States (Austria, Belgium, France, Luxembourg, Netherlands, Portugal, Spain).

[12] Art 6 of the draft proposal of the 'European Group of Private International Law' for a European Convention on the law applicable to non contractual obligations provides that: ' 1. A person who has suffered injury or damage shall have a right of direct action against the insurer of the person liable if he has such a right under the law applicable to the non-contractual obligation. 2. If the law applicable to the non-contractual obligation does not provide for such a right, it shall nevertheless exist if it is available to the person who suffered damage or injury under the law applicable to the contract of insurance'. For the text of the proposal see the website of the European Group of Private International Law www. drt.ucl.ac.be/gedip For a commentary of the draft proposal see Fallon (2000) *Revue belgique de droit international* 322 to 325; Seatzu (2001) *Jus-Rivista di Scienze Giuridiche* 37 to 67.

legal suit which arises from the malicious or wanton misconduct of the defendant.[13]

It is known that many insurance policies in relation to motor vehicle accidents (but also other insurance policies such as policies in relation to aviation vehicle accidents)[14] do not specifically address coverage for punitive damages, though in certain distinct circumstances exclusions for intentional conduct or known risks can work to preclude coverage. As has been pointed out correctly, some insurers are quite reluctant to insert a specific exclusion for punitive damages due to the competitive marketplace for insurance services and apprehensions that such exclusion will lead prospective insureds to look elsewhere for coverage.[15] Therefore, noting that the laws of numerous States prohibit the insurability of exemplary damages, a number of insurers have sought to safeguard themselves against punitive damage awards via policy clauses which state that the insured will not be compensated for an award of punitive damages where to do so would violate the law.

Where the insurance policy at issue does not unequivocally exclude coverage for exemplary damage awards, the public policy of the place whose law applies to the interpretation of insurance contract should be referred in order to ascertain whether coverage can be allowed for such damages.[16] In the default of pending declaratory judgments, this issue cannot be settled on as the ascertainment of the applicable law depends on the private international law provisions of the forum in which coverage litigation is brought. Thus, the most feasible forum for coverage litigation (usually the place where the insured is habitually resident or where the primary action is pending) should be determined prior to embarking on any choice of law examination.[17]

In principle, once the jurisdiction whose law will apply to the insurance contract has been determined, the public policy of that State will establish whether an insurer should compensate a policyholder for a punitive damage award. Where punitive damages are awarded pursuant to the law of the State that also applies to the insurance policy, there is rarely any query that the issue of coverage for exemplary damages will be established by that State's public policy on insurability.[18] Therefore, if Italian law (which prohibits the insurability of punitive damages) is the applicable law to the insurance policy and exemplary damages are awarded against the policyholder by an Italian court, the answer is easy. There will be no coverage for the exemplary damage award. But if punitive damages are awarded against an insured in a State other than Italy it is not clear that Italian law will continue to apply to the interpretation of the insurance contract.

[13] See inter alia Saravalle (1993) *Rivista di diritto internazionale privato e processuale* 867–92.
[14] See Margo (1994) *Air & Space Law* 4–5.
[15] See Posner (1993) *International Insurance Law Review* 402.
[16] For the same conclusion see Posner (1993) *International Insurance Law Review* 403.
[17] *Ibid.*
[18] *Ibid.*

(h) Examples of Mandatory Rules in the Field of Motor Vehicle Insurance

The following sub-paragraphs will highlight some examples of international mandatory rules in the field of motor vehicle insurance. As already stated above, Articles 7 and 8 of the Second Non-Life Insurance Directive lay down some provisions dealing with the application of internationally mandatory rules (ie, rules which apply despite the parties choice on the law applicable to the contract). Like the other choice of law rules contained in Articles 7 and 8 of the Second Non-Life Insurance Directive these rules apply to motor insurance contracts.

(i) Mandatory Rules in the Motor Vehicle Insurance Directives

Article 2(1) of Directive 85/2 provides that any term in a compulsory policy is void in so far as it seeks to exclude liability for traffic accidents caused by any of the following persons: (a) a person who does not have express or implied authorisation to drive; (b) a person not licensed to drive the vehicle; (c) a person driving the vehicle in breach of safety requirements laid down by domestic law. It is likely that this provision has to be considered as internationally mandatory as it aims to safeguard the social and economic structures of the Member countries (the forum for the purposes of Article 7(2) of the Rome Convention). The social goal of this provision emerges clearly from the fact that it provides that these extensions may be removed where a Member state's social security provisions make compensation available in place of insurance.[19]

(ii) Section 149 of the British Road Traffic Act 1988

Section 149 deals with possible defences that a driver might have to a civil claim by a passenger. It provides that any agreement between the driver and the passenger restricting the driver's liability is of no effect. It states also that a driver can not plead the defence of *volenti non fit injuria* against a passenger, eg, where the passenger has voluntarily accepted a lift with a drunken driver or where the driver has warned the passenger that the driver accepts no liability for injuries caused.[20] The interests of the forum and the social purpose of these rules suggest the conclusion that these provisions are international mandatory rules.[21]

[19] For a clear illustration of the social goal of the legislation as a test to determine whether a rule is internationally mandatory see Barmat de Winter, *De sociale functies der rechtsnormen als grondslag voor de oplossing van internationaal privatrechteliijke wetsconflicten* (Berlin, Themis, 1947), reprinted in Kisch, Dubbink, van Hoogstraaten, Kotting and Jessurun d'Oliveira (eds), *Naar een sociaal IPR: Een keus uit het werk van LI de Winter* (The Hague, Kluwer Law International, 1979), at 3–52; de Winter in Kisch, Dubbink, [1940] *WPNR* 245–49 (No 3675) and 257–61 (No 3676), reprinted in Kisch, Dubbink, van Hoogstraaten, Kotting and Jessurun d'Oliveira (eds), *Naar een sociaal IPR: Een keus uit het werk van LI de Winter* (The Hague, Kluwer Law International, 1979), at 164–81.

[20] For a clear exposition of these rules see Merkin and Rodger, *EC Insurance Law* (London and New York, Longman, 1997) 66.

[21] See Barmat de Winter, n 19 above.

This is true despite the absence of an express provision or an indication about their territorial scope. Therefore a choice of a law other than English or Scots will not prevent the application of these provisions.

(iii) Rules Ensuring Payment to the Victim of a Traffic Accident

As already seen, there are Member States, such as Italy and the United Kingdom, which confer upon the victim of a traffic accident a direct claim against the insurer of the person liable. Section 151 of the British Road Traffic Act of 1988 and Article 18 of the Italian statute of 1969 n 990 grant the victim a direct claim against the insurer. Whichever law is applicable to the insurance contract, if the action is brought in the United Kingdom, then Section 151 of the Road Traffic Act of 1988 imposes its own applicability, as does Article 18 of the statute of 1969 n 990 if the action is brought in Italy. This conclusion is suggested by the social purpose of these rules, which is to ensure rapid and complete compensation for the victim. As Francescakis pointed out correctly, the fact that a rule is essential to safeguard the social structures of a country is a clear indication of its mandatory character.[22] Undoubtedly, the rules concerning the direct action of the victim are not neutral but play an essential role in the protection of the weaker party in the context of road traffic accidents.

(i) The Law Applicable to Claims for Damages Under the Motor Insurers Bureau System

It is arguable that it is impossible to resolve satisfactorily the problems of road victims' claims for damages by traditional choice of law techniques. While Article 2(2) of the Third Motor Vehicle Insurance Directive has much to commend it, it nevertheless is not entirely apt to guarantee prompt reimbursement to the victims of traffic accidents.[23]

Indeed, one suspects that concern with the suitability of dealing with claims for damages through relatively simple techniques seems to have been present within the European institutions. For in 1972, the European Council adopted the Directive 72/166 on the approximation of the laws of the Member States relating to insurance against civil liability in respect of the use of motor vehicles, and to the enforcement of the obligation to insure against such liability. The

[22] See Francescakis, (1966–1969) *Travaux du Comité français de Droit international privé*, at 149 *et seq*.

[23] The new proposal for a European Parliament and Council directive on the approximation of the laws of the Member States relating to insurance against civil liability in respect of the use of motor vehicles and amending Directives 73/239/EEC and 92/49/EEC (Fourth Motor Insurance Directive) aims to provide specific provisions applicable to victims of accidents '(a) occurring in a Member State other than the State of residence of the victim and (b) caused by a vehicle insured by an undertaking established in a Member State other than the State of residence of the victim, and registered in a Member State other than the State of residence of the victim' (Art 1).

directive is important since it became the starting point for the EC's ultimate objective of freedom of cross-border transfer movement. Following Directive 72/166 numerous agreements between national Motor Insurers Bureaux of the Member States of the European Community and between those Bureaux and those of other European states were concluded. Under those agreements, the Bureau of the country in which any accident occurs becomes responsible for settling the victim's loss, and that Bureau (the 'handling bureau') is then entitled to be indemnified by the Bureau of the place in which the vehicle is usually based (the 'paying bureau'). In March 1999 the various agreements were consolidated into one single agreement, called the Multilateral Guarantee Agreement between National Insurers Bureaux.[24]

To all intents and purposes the main differences between the protection of the victim of a traffic accident under the choice of law rules of the Insurance Directives and the protection of the victim under the provisions concerning the reparation of the victim's loss in the Multilateral Agreement between National Insurers Bureaux are differences of degree rather than of kind. The rules on reimbursement in the Multilateral Agreement of 1991 are more detailed and specific, and accordingly more inflexible than the relatively flexible choice of law provisions of the Motor Vehicle Insurance Directive. In that regard the rules concerning the victim's claims for damage under the Multilateral Agreement between National Insurers Bureaux are more in keeping with the need of the road victim to get prompt reparation of damages than the choice of laws provisions of the Insurance Directives.

At first glance, one might argue that the Multilateral Agreement between National Insurers Bureaux is an alternative strategy to the private international law approach to the settlement of the road victim's loss. However, this would be a false conclusion. Article 1(e) of the Multilateral Agreement makes clear that every National Insurers Bureaux settles the victim's loss according to its *own national law* and the *governing law of the insurance policy*.[25] Thus the victim of a road accident who claims compensation of the damages to a National Insurance Bureau according to the rules laid down in the 1991 Multilateral Agreement will receive the same treatment of a victim who sues the insurer of the person liable in the competent court.

(j) Final Remarks

The purpose of this chapter has been to highlight the most relevant questions arising from the European private international law rules in the field of motor vehicle insurance. From the above analysis, it is fairly clear that the choice of

[24] For a clear exposition of these points see Merkin and Rodger, *EC Insurance Law*, n 20 above, 53–54.

[25] *Cf* CE Claeys, (1979) *Revue critique de droit international privé* 723, at note 21; for the same conclusion see Dubuisson, *Le droit applicable au contrat d'assurance*, n 4 above, 723.

law rules in Articles 7 and 8 of the Second Non-Life Insurance Directive are unsuitable connecting factors for motor vehicle insurance contracts. At present the outcome of actions requiring determination of the law applicable to motor vehicle insurance contracts covering risks situated in the EC is far from being straightforward, certain and predictable. This view is based on two considerations. First, there are very different regimes of private international law for motor vehicle insurance contracts in Europe as a result of the excessive freedom of implementation granted to the Member States by Article 8 of the Second Non-Life Directive. Second, there is a lack of co-ordination between tort law issues and the EC choice of law rules which apply to motor vehicle insurance contracts. On the contrary, the choice of law provisions of the Rome Convention use suitable connecting factors for motor vehicle insurance contracts. Nevertheless, like the Second Non-Life Directive, the Rome Convention gives little help to answer the numerous questions arising out of the interaction between contract and tort. Thus it is very much to be hoped that the law applicable to motor vehicle insurance contracts will be a matter which will engage the attention of the Member States when they renegotiate the Rome Convention. It is submitted that Article 1(3) of the Rome Convention should be re-worded so that it might encompass motor vehicle insurance contracts covering risks situated in the territories of the Member States of the European Community.

PART V

The European Private International Law Rules of Insurance and Reinsurance Contracts by Electronic Means

INTRODUCTION

European countries are increasingly becoming familiar with electronic commerce. By 2001 on-line revenues in commercial trade, consumer sales and content in the Member States of the European Union are expected to step over 70 billion Euro, with 53 million people connected to the world-wide collection of interconnecting networks known as the Internet.[1] This revolutionary development of the Internet is leading to profound structural changes. Online commerce is radically transforming the relationship between provider of services and consumer. A one-to-one relationship between the supplier and consumer is replacing traditional mass-marketing and mass-distribution techniques.[2] Moreover, consumers are already benefiting from increased choice by being able to choose from an impressive range of offers. Lower prices are possible in the online environment as general costs reduce and efficiency increases.

However electronic commerce is not limited to the Internet. It includes a large number of applications in the narrowband (videotext), broadcast (teleshopping), and off-line environment (catalogue sales on CD-ROM). Nevertheless, the Internet is federating different types of online commerce. Corporate networks are rapidly becoming Intranets.[3]

The institutions of the European Union are already supporting the promotion of electronic commerce for a more competitive Europe in the global marketplace by producing a body of substantive law which can be called *European* electronic commerce law, as opposed to merely, for example, English or French or Dutch law on electronic commerce. Two Directives were adopted in 1988 containing procedures for the provision of information in the sector of technical standards on provisions on information society services. These Directives lay down an obligation on Member States of the European Union to ensure that the standards drawn up by their national bodies are communicated to the Commission and do not create obstacles to the functioning of the internal market. Legislation has been proposed on the 'private law infrastructure of the Community electronic marketplace'.[4]

[1] S Micossi, *Electronic Commerce in Europe: Editorial* at <http://www.electronicmarkets.org>.

[2] See COM (97) 157 'A European Initiative in Electronic Commerce' *Communication to the European Parliament, the Council, the Economic and Social Committee and the Committee of the Regions* <http://www.ispo.cec.be/Ecommerce>.

[3] *Ibid.*

[4] The expression 'private law infrastructure of the Community electronic marketplace' is used by Dickie, *Internet and Electronic Commerce Law in the European Union* (Oxford, Hart Publishing, 1999) 3.

However, electronic commerce is not just a matter of interest to the substantive lawyer. It also raises important questions for the private international lawyer. These range from establishing which court has jurisdiction and which is the applicable law to securing recognition and enforcement of foreign judgments. By its nature, online commerce is transnational and encourages cross-border ordering and delivery of goods and services. As users connected to the Internet, we are continually being exposed to the offers of foreign products and services. At present large economic sectors, such as the distance selling industry in Europe, are actively integrating the Internet into their marketing strategies. In the field of insurance commerce the Internet is rapidly becoming an acceptable marketing tool from the standpoint of legal compliance. This is true in the sectors of life insurance and travel insurance.[5] The Single Insurance Market in Europe offers online commerce the prospect of a critical mass of business and customers across national borders.

Business contacts and contracts conducted via the Internet can engender disputes in the same way as traditional business and trade activity. These relations will have connections with more than one legal system if only because the parties are domiciled in two different Member States.[6] To the private international lawyer these raise the fundamental question of jurisdiction and choice of law. There is now an internal market with nearly 400 million consumers in the European Community. As trade grows within the Community and consumers and lawyers become increasingly aware of rights under the substantive law these private international law problems are likely to arise with increasing frequency.

Whilst the substantive law of electronic commerce has be taken into account by the institutions of the European Union, the private international law aspects of electronic commerce have been almost ignored. There are European rules on jurisdiction contained in the Brussels Convention and in the parallel Lugano Convention. However, these Conventions contain no provision to deal specifically with electronic business. When it comes to choice of law, the EEC Convention on the law applicable to contractual obligations of 1980 and the EC Insurance Directives do not provide rules dealing with contracts concluded by electronic means. It follows that the judge must apply the general rules on jurisdiction and applicable law to online contracts.

The time is ripe for the examination of the jurisdiction and choice of law problems that arise in Europe in relation to insurance and reinsurance contracts concluded by electronic means, and the possible solutions to these problems. But this has to be carried out against the most recent directives and proposals for directives on the substantive law of electronic commerce in Europe. Chapter 14 will therefore look at the substantive law background and its significance for

[5] See Barger and McKennon (1998) *International Journal of Insurance Law* 96.

[6] For a clear illustration of this point see K Boele-Woelki and C Kessedijan (eds), *Internet: Which Court Decides? Which Law Applies? Quel tribunal décide? Quel droit s'applique?* (The Hague, Kluwer Law International, 1998).

the private international lawyer. Chapters 15 and 16 will look respectively at jurisdictional and choice of law problems and possible solutions.

As the present thesis deals with the European rules of private international law for insurance and reinsurance contracts, the perspective will be unashamedly European. At the same time, when thinking of solutions to these problems, much can be learnt from an examination of developments in non-European States, in particular the United States of America.

Finally, a word is needed on terminology. 'Electronic commerce' is often used to describe:

> all forms of commercial transactions involving both organisations and individuals, that are based upon the electronic processing and transmission of data, including text, sound and visual images. It also refers to the effect that the electronic exchange of commercial information may have on the institutions and processes that support and govern commercial activities.[7]

Much of the following chapters will be concerned with 'electronic commerce' in this sense.

[7] OECD, *Electronic Commerce: Opportunities and challenges for government* ('The Sachter Report') (Paris, OECD, 1997) at 11 as quoted by Dickie, n 4 above.

14

Electronic Commerce Law in Europe

1. INTRODUCTION

THE INITIATIVES currently undertaken by the institutions of the European Union to create a body of substantive law for electronic commerce in Europe are undeniably complex, resulting, as they do, from different types of directives and proposals for directives.

First, there are proposals for directives which attempt to complete and adapt the legal framework for off-line commerce with regard to electronic commerce. Examples of this category are the draft directives on electronic signatures and on the distance marketing of financial services, which contain specific rules for business contacts and contracts conducted online.

Second, there is the directive on electronic commerce, which is designed to enable the internal market to work for electronic commerce. Alongside this directive there are a number of directives which abolish technical obstacles to the smooth functioning of the single market.

Third, there are a number of directives not directly or exclusively concerned with online commerce but which may have an impact on the electronic commerce. An example is the Directive of the European Parliament and of the Council of 6 October 1997 amending Directive 84/450/EEC concerning misleading advertising so as to include comparative advertising. This Directive applies to commercial communications, advertisements and promotion of goods and services even when they are made in cyberspace.

After a brief illustration of the freedom to provide insurance products and services by electronic means in the Single Market, the rest of this chapter will consider the directive on electronic commerce and the draft directive on the distance marketing of financial services.

2. THE FREEDOM TO PROVIDE INSURANCE PRODUCTS AND SERVICES BY ELECTRONIC MEANS IN EUROPE

It appears that the vigorous growth of electronic commerce in Europe will modify the form in which international insurance and reinsurance contracts are written in the near future. In the United States of America insurance sales online are already a reality.[8] According to a recent article published in the *New York*

[8] See Barger and McKennon, n 5 above, 97.

Times, Internet sales of life insurance are becoming in the USA alternative tools to the use of an agent.[9] It is interesting to point out that a White Paper by the National Association of Insurance Commissioners ('the NAIC') entitled the 'Marketing of Insurance over the Internet' was recently adopted at the winter meeting of the NAIC in Seattle, Washington.[10]

The White Paper lays down a series of recommendations which included, inter alia, that the NAIC (a) consider providing technical support to insurance regulators in the development of their web sites to improve consumer education; and (b) adopt a specific programme of education to help state insurance regulators in monitoring possible fraudulent activities in the sale of insurance products. In the United Kingdom the London International Insurance and Reinsurance Market Association (LIRMA) has already opened the facilities of its subsidiary, the London Processing Centre (LPC), to underwriters established in European countries and their worldwide branches. Through the LPC, a large number of countries are trading in London market business electronically. In the European context, a series of initiatives has been taken recently by the European Commission to encourage business transactions (including insurance commerce) across state frontiers which utilise electronic commerce.[11]

As already stated above, the Single Insurance Market offers online commerce the prospect of a critical mass of customers across national borders. Accordingly, the 2000 Directive on Electronic Commerce grants the freedom to provide insurance products by electronic means in the European Market. Article 3(2) of the Electronic Directive provides that 'Member States may not, for reasons falling within this Directive's co-ordinated field, restrict the freedom to provide Information Society services from another Member State'. The aim of this provision, which is to facilitate the free movement of Information Society services between the Member States of the European Union, leaves no doubt about the introduction of the freedom to provide insurance products and services by electronic means in the Single Market. The Directive establishes ad hoc harmonised rules only where necessary to ensure that business and consumers can supply and receive Information Society services throughout the European Union, irrespective of national borders.

3. THE 2000 DIRECTIVE ON ELECTRONIC COMMERCE[12]

(a) The Aim of the Directive

The recent directive on certain legal aspects of electronic commerce in the single market aims to unify the different strands of law such as commercial com-

[9] *New York Times*, 6 September 1996 as quoted by Barger and McKennon, n 5 above, 135.

[10] For a concise analysis of this document see Barger and McKennon, n 5 above, 135.

[11] For a clear illustration of these points see recently Rossi and Leonard (1998) 1 *International Insurance Law Review* 8.

[12] See Dickie, n 4 above, 23 *et seq*.

munications, contracts, liability, licensing and enforcement drawn together by the online commerce. The 2000 Directive on Electronic Commerce followed from the Commission's 1997 Communication on electronic commerce, which has as its purpose the introduction of a coherent Community legal framework by the year 2000.[13]

(b) The Scope of Application

The Directive applies only to service providers established within the European Union and not those established outside. Nevertheless, the Directive on Electronic Commerce attempts to avoid incompatibility and inconsistency with legal developments in other regions of the world in order to eliminate obstacles to global online commerce.

(c) Commercial Communications/Advertising and Promotions

The Directive on electronic commerce shows that there is a need for harmonisation in the area of commercial communications, advertising and promotions. These areas seem to be differently regulated within the European Community: some Member States prohibit advertising by some professions, others do not impose any restriction but allow commercial communications, advertising and promotions by any professions. The prohibitions imposed by some Member States do not concern, however, insurers, brokers and agents.

The Directive states that commercial communications must be clearly identifiable as commercial communications. Perhaps of more importance in the field of insurance sales, the new Directive on electronic commerce also provides that the natural or legal person on whose behalf the commercial communication is made must be clearly identifiable. The identification of the person (the insurer) on whose behalf the commercial communication is made is important especially when the communication concerns life insurance and insurance contracts covering 'large risks', as the sums that the insurer might be requested to pay as compensation for damage under the insurance policy can be very significant. It is worth noting that promotional offers, such as discount and premiums are allowed by the directive if they can be clearly identifiable as such, and the conditions which are to be met to qualify for them are easily accessible and presented accurately and unequivocally.

Commercial communications, advertisements and promotions emanating from a service provider (in the field of insurance sales: the insurer, broker or agent) established in the European Community are subject to the control of the country of origin.

[13] See COM (97) 157, n 2 above.

(d) Contracts Concluded by Electronic Means

It is not clear whether the national laws of a number of Member States allow for the validity of contracts concluded by electronic means, both generally and in specific situations. Article 9 of the Directive provides for the generalised validity of these contracts. It states that:

> Member States shall ensure that their legislation allows contracts to be concluded electronically. Member States shall in particular ensure that the legal requirements applicable to the contractual process neither prevent the effective use of electronic contracts nor result in such contracts being deprived of legal validity because of the fact that they have been concluded electronically.

As it appears from the text, this provision aims to introduce 'equal treatment' for users of paper and electronic media. The types of provisions identified are those concerning all stages of the contractual process, including invitation to treat, offer, acceptance, registration, cancellation etc. In the field of insurance sales, this will affect requirements for there to be 'writing', 'an original copy', and for contracts to be 'printed' or 'published'. The Directive allows Member States of the European Community to derogate from Article 9 in respect of a number of contracts. However, Article 9 cannot be derogated from in respect of insurance and reinsurance contracts.

4. DRAFT DIRECTIVE ON THE DISTANCE MARKETING OF FINANCIAL SERVICES[14]

(a) The Aim of the Draft Directive

The aim of the proposal by the European Commission for a European Parliament and Council directive on distance marketing of financial services is to ensure a high standard of protection for consumers of retail financial services (insurance, banking and investment services) provided by mail, by telephone, by fax or by electronic means such as the Internet. The proposal concerns the contracts for financial services which are excluded from the scope of the 1997 Directive on distance contracts.

(b) Distance Contracts

Article 2 of the draft directive provides that 'distance contract' means:

> any contract concerning financial services concluded between a supplier and a consumer under an organised distance sales or service-provision scheme run by the

[14] See Dickie, *Internet and Electronic Commerce Law in the European Union*, n 4 above, 9–20.

supplier, who, for the purpose of that contract, makes exclusive use of means of distance communication up to and including the time at which the contract is concluded.

(c) Other Definitions

Article 2 of the proposal also clarifies the meaning of other concepts for the purpose of the directive.

Article 2(b) provides that 'financial services' means 'any banking, insurance, investment or payment services'.

Article 2(c) and (d) lays down definitions for 'supplier' and 'consumer'. The 'supplier' is any legal or natural person:

> who, acting in his commercial or professional capacity, is the actual provider of services subject to contracts covered by this directive or acts as intermediary in the supply of those services or in the conclusion of a distance contract between those parties.

The 'consumer' is defined as 'any natural person who, in contracts covered by this Directive, is acting for purposes which are outside his trade, business or profession'.

Article 2(e) makes clear that 'means of distance communication' refers to 'any means which, without the simultaneous physical presence of the supplier and the consumer, may be used for the distance marketing of service between those parties'.

(d) Information to the Consumer Before Conclusion of the Contract

Article 3 of the draft Directive requires the supplier of online products to inform the consumer of, inter alia, the identity of the supplier, the main characteristics and inclusive prices of the services, and the consumer's right of withdrawal. The information is required to be provided 'in good time prior to the conclusion of the contract'. The meaning of 'in good time' is rather unclear, but appears to mean that the consumer must have time to examine the information before the conclusion of any contract.[15] In particular, the supplier must not send the information in such a way that it does not reach the consumer until after the contract is concluded (eg sending the information by mail when the contract is concluded online). The information is required to be provided 'with regard . . . to the principles of good faith in commercial transactions' (Article 3(2)). The introduction of the principles of good faith would enable the directive to respond to changing circumstances and take into consideration the individual characteristics of the relationship between a supplier and a consumer.

[15] For similar remarks see Dickie, *Internet and Electronic Commerce Law*, n 4 above, 91 who refers to the identical text of the Directive on distance contracts.

5. ARE THE EC DIRECTIVES AND PROPOSALS RELATED TO ONLINE COMMERCE PRO-CONSUMERS?

Although the preamble of the 2000 Directive on certain aspects of electronic commerce and the preamble of the proposal for a directive on distance marketing make it clear that they are concerned with the protection of the consumer, it would be a mistake to assume that overall these are pro-consumer measures in the sense of being concerned predominantly with the interests of the consumer. Certain provisions in the new Directive on electronic commerce and the proposal for a directive on financial marketing are pro-consumer, whilst others are pro-supplier. Moreover, some provisions are neutral, favouring neither party, whereas others are seen as being in the interests of both parties.

It is clear that the main *aim* of the rules on commercial communications, advertisements and promotions in the new Directive on Electronic Commerce is to protect the consumer of online products. This is certainly true for the provision which states that the natural or legal person on whose behalf the commercial communication is made must be clearly identifiable. The rule stating that promotional offers, such as discounts, premiums and gifts must be clearly identifiable as such and the conditions which must be met to receive them must be easily accessible and be presented accurately and unequivocally is also pro-consumer. The rules on the information to be given to the consumer before conclusion of the contract in the draft directive on distance marketing are in favour of the consumer. On the other hand, the rules which limit the liability (other than for injunctive relief) of 'mere conduits' of information services for the content of those services are noticeably pro-supplier.

The rules which indicate the types of derogation from the generality of the Directive on electronic commerce are neutral provisions in that it has been left to the Member States to decide whether to take a pro-consumer or a pro-provider stance in relation to certain matters such as contractual obligations concerning consumer contracts and unsolicited commercial communications by electronic mail, or by an equivalent individual communication. Moreover, the provisions on enforcement and implementation in the Directive on electronic commerce are neutral, as they favour neither the consumer nor the supplier.

The rules concerning the contracts concluded by electronic means are intended to be in the interests of both parties.

The conclusion has to be that, overall, the 2000 Directive on certain aspects of electronic commerce and the recent proposal for a directive on distance marketing produce a balanced package, taking into account the interests of both consumer and provider of online products.

15

Insurance and Reinsurance Contracts Concluded by Electronic Means: Jurisdictional Problems and Possible Solutions

1. INTRODUCTION

IN THIS chapter, the concern is with insurance and reinsurance contracts concluded by electronic means. These contracts may concern insurance which is not compulsory under Member States' national laws, as well as insurance which is compulsory. However, the following analysis does not propose to deal separately with each type of contract, as they are regulated by the same jurisdictional provisions. The aim of the present chapter is to discuss the jurisdictional rules for insurance and reinsurance contracts which are concluded online.

The main instruments in relation to these contracts are the Brussels Regulation and Lugano Convention which are concerned to determine the 'international jurisdiction' of courts in the European Community and the EFTA. I propose to analyse their impact in detail. Their provisions will be the starting point of the analysis.

But before starting the examination of the jurisdictional rules in Europe for insurance and reinsurance contracts concluded by electronic means, the jurisdictional problems which might arise in transnational insurance transactions conducted online will be discussed.

2. JURISDICTIONAL PROBLEMS IN RELATION TO TRANSNATIONAL INSURANCE AND REINSURANCE CONTRACTS CONCLUDED BY ELECTRONIC MEANS

Because of the increasing number of cross-border transactions in the fields of life insurance and travel insurance on the web, there is a growing need for clear and universally applicable solutions for the possible problems of jurisdiction with regard to contracts concluded online. The need stems from the special situation in which firms doing business at a distance using electronic means conduct transnational transactions. E-commerce is different from traditional commerce due to its virtual nature. From the virtual nature of electronic commerce and the different positions of consumer and supplier in the transactions conducted on the web one might derive the conclusion that the jurisdictional rules in the Brussels Regulation and Lugano Convention cannot apply when the contract is signed with a firm doing business on the web. It has been maintained that some grounds of jurisdiction in the Brussels Regulation are inadequate to achieve jurisdictional fairness in e-commerce, as they fail 'to bridge the gap between the virtuality of cyberspace and the territoriality of jurisdiction'.[1] The operators involved in e-commerce must know precisely the competent courts for cases arising eventually from contracts concluded on the web. A few examples will illustrate the point. It is well known that a possible ground for jurisdiction in the Brussels Regulation and Lugano Convention is, in matters related to contract, the place of performance of the obligation in question.[2] The determination of the place of performance can prove difficult with respect to some contracts concluded on the web.[3] This is true when the contract is not only concluded but also performed on the web because of the absence of physical contacts with a given jurisdiction.[4] Again, another possible ground for jurisdiction is the domicile of the defendant. At first glance, this forum does not raise any problem in the field of electronic commerce, as it is always available. But what if the domicile of the defendant is so far away from the claimant's place of residence that, the latter because of the distance is deprived of any judicial remedy? In matters relating to insurance, Article 9(1) provides that an insurance company based in a Contracting State can be sued (a) in the courts of the state where he is based; or (b) in another Member State, in the courts for the place where the claimant is domiciled. Indeed the authorisation for the claimant bringing his action before his home courts can become unfair to the defendant who has to litigate in such a distant forum that his defence becomes very difficult because of the costs involved.

This chapter addresses some of the questions which the jurisdictional provisions on insurance matters in the Brussels Regulation and Lugano Convention raise in the field of electronic commerce and deal with some of the problems encountered in the process of adaptation of these rules to the needs of online commerce.

[1] See Kaufmann-Kohler, *Internet: mondialisation de la communication-mondialisation de la résolution des litiges* in K Boele-Woelki and C Kessedijan (eds), *Internet: Which court decides? Which law applies?* (The Hague, Boston, Kluwer Law International, 1988) 89 *et seq.*

[2] Art 5(1).

[3] For a clear illustration of the difficulties of localising financial products and services provided online see Dassese (2000) *International Journal of Insurance Law* 315 *et seq.*

[4] See Preliminary Document No 12 of August 2000 ('*Electronic Commerce and International Jurisdiction*') for the attention of the Nineteenth Session of June 2001. Summary of the discussion (Ottawa, 28 February–1 March 2000), prepared by Catherine Kessedijan with the co-operation of the private international law team of the Ministry of Justice of Canada at the website address <www. hcch.net/e/workprog/e-comm.html>; See also the Geneva Round Table on the Questions of Private International Law raised by Electronic Commerce and the Internet, Commission I-Contracts at <www. hcch.net/e/workprog/genve31e.html>.

3. JURISDICTION UNDER THE BRUSSELS REGULATION AND LUGANO CONVENTION

(a) The Absence of Special Rules for Contracts Concluded by Electronic Means

Though the Brussels Regulation and Lugano Convention have special jurisdictional rules for matters relating to insurance, consumer contracts and individual contracts of employment, they have no special rules for contracts concluded by electronic means. Instead, the normal rules on jurisdiction set out in the Conventions will have to be used. In the field of insurance, the insurer is expected, under Article 12, to sue the policyholder in the European State in which the policyholder is domiciled. However, the policyholder has the option, under the special rules contained in Article 9, of suing the insurer in a European State other than the one in which the insurer is domiciled.

(b) Jurisdiction in Matters Relating to Insurance

In cases where an action concerns insurance matters and the Brussels Regulation or Lugano Convention applies, jurisdiction normally will be founded on special jurisdiction under Articles 8 to 14 of the Regulation. The operation of these provisions in cases concerning insurance contracts concluded by electronic means will now be considered, as well as the operation of the other jurisdictional rules which apply in matters relating to insurance.

(i) Action Against Insurer: Article 9

Article 9(1)(1) and (2) provides that an insurer may be sued in his home courts or in the courts of the place where the claimant (policyholder/insured/beneficiary) is domiciled. Article 9(1)(3) states that a co-insurer may also be sued 'in the courts of a Member State in which proceedings are brought against the leading insurer'.

In cases related to contracts concluded by electronic means the option for the policyholder to bring action against the insurer before the courts of the state where the insurer is domiciled poses an acute problem because the policyholder may ignore the State where the insurer is domiciled. As is well known, one of the major risks associated with electronic transactions is the ease with which a supplier may offer services for sales through a website which he can set up without revealing his identity. For example, there is nothing to prevent an insurance seller based in France from setting up a website in English using an Internet domain name ending in the standard letters '.co.uk' (purchased from the UK domain name registry).[5] These uncertainties about the place where the insurer

[5] See on this point King (2000) *Communications Law* 14.

is domiciled can also prejudice the application of Article 9(1)(3), as it refers to the courts of the state in which proceedings are brought against the main insurer.

Everything said about Article 9(1) is equally applicable to Article 9(2). This provides that:

> an insurer who is not domiciled in a Member State but has a branch, agency or other establishment in one of the Member State shall, in disputes arising out of the operations of the branch, agency or establishment, be deemed to be domiciled in that State.

(ii) Actions Against Insurer in Matters Relating to Liability Insurance or Insurance of Immovable Property: Articles 10 and 11

As already said above, Articles 10 and 11 of the Brussels Regulation and Lugano Convention deal with actions in matters relating to liability insurance or insurance of immovable property.[6]

Unlike Article 9, these provisions do not pose special problems in cases concerning contracts concluded online. It is clear that the determination of the 'place where the harmful event occurred', which is a basis of jurisdiction in Article 10, does not prove difficult when the contract of liability insurance is concluded on the web. However, if the harm is, for example, causing economic loss by negligently advising the policyholder, it may be unclear where the harmful event occurs. That is equally applicable to the determination of the criteria for court jurisdiction in Article 11.

(iii) Actions by Insurers: Article 12

This provides that an insurer may bring proceedings against the policyholder, insured or beneficiary only in the courts of the Member States in which they are domiciled.

At first glance, one might argue that Article 12 does not pose special problems in the context of electronic commerce. However, this would be false, as everything said about the option of the policyholder of bringing an action against the insurer before the courts of the State where the insurer is domiciled is equally applicable to the forum of the domicile of the policyholder in Article 12. The determination of the domicile of the policyholder, in fact, can prove difficult when the transaction is concluded over the Internet, as the e-mail message containing the order of purchase of the insurance policy may not provide an indication of the geographical location of the web site. Moreover, the location of the web site does not coincide with the physical location of the consumer when the consumer sends the e-mail containing the order of purchase from his home country through his old email account connected to a web server localised abroad.[7]

[6] See above ch 5, paras 2(e) and (f).

[7] For a clear illustration of this point see Schu (1997) 5(2) *International Journal of Law and Information Technology* 192 *et seq*.

On the contrary, the determination of the domicile of the third party beneficiary or the insured, in case the insured is different to the policyholder, does not prove difficult because the transaction is conducted in the online environment. The conclusion of the contract online, in fact, changes the position of the parties but not the contents of the contract (eg, contractual clauses, indications in the text of the contract of the third beneficiary and the insured, indications of the places where the third beneficiary and the insured are domiciled, etc). Therefore the third party's domicile or the insured's domicile will be determined, as usual, according to the indications in the text of the contract.

(iv) Jurisdiction Agreements: Article 13

In disputes arising from an insurance contract concluded online, the parties may have concluded an agreement conferring jurisdiction on the court or courts of a European State, which is then given exclusive jurisdiction under Article 13. It is worth noting that such an agreement conferring jurisdiction will doubtless come in a standard form contract containing conditions on the back of the contract; there may then be difficulties in satisfying the formalities required under Article 13. There can also be difficulties in satisfying the requirements in Article 23 which apply to the jurisdiction agreements in matters relating to insurance. How can the parties of an online transaction make a jurisdiction agreement 'in a form which accords with practices which the parties have established between themselves'? Which are the usages of which 'the parties are or ought to have been aware and which in *electronic commerce are* widely known to, and regularly observed by, parties to contracts involved in the *electronic commerce*'?[8] But the writing requirements in Article 23(1)(a) are no longer a serious obstacle to the enforceability of a choice of court agreement contained in an online contract, as paragraph 2 of the same article provides that 'any communication by electronic means which provides a durable record of the agreement shall be equivalent to "writing"'. Nevertheless, these difficulties in satisfying the formalities required under Article 23 should not be overestimated. There is, in fact, a clear tendency at the international level to recognise an electronic record as the equivalent of a written record.[9]

The situation where the parties are most likely to have entered into an agreement conferring jurisdiction is that where the transaction involves two

[8] Emphasis added.

[9] See the Proposed Uniform Electronic Transactions Act (18 September 1998 Draft, National Conference of Commissioners on Uniform State Law <http://www.law.upenn.edu/library/ulc/ulc.htm>, which states in Section 201(b) that, if a rule of law requires a record to be in writing, or provides consequences if it is not, an electronic record satisfies this writing requirement. Similarly, the Draft International Convention on Electronic Transactions, proposed by the USA to the UNCITRAL Working Group on Electronic Commerce (A/CN.9/WG.IV/WP.77 of 25 May 1998). As quoted by Kaufmann-Kohler, *Internet: mondialisation de la résolution des litiges?* in K Boele-Woelki and Kessedijan (eds), *Internet—which Court Decides? Which Law Applies?* n 1 above, 125 ff.

commercial actors such as two insurance companies (business to business transactions). An example would be where you have an action for a contractual indemnity brought by an insurer against his reinsurer. Two such business parties may well have an agreement on jurisdiction which confers jurisdiction on the courts of a European State. However, a choice of court clause can also be found in an online contract between an insurance company and a consumer (business to consumer transactions). Nevertheless, the requirements of jurisdictional agreements in Article 13 make a choice of court clause difficult when the online contract of insurance does not cover a large risk. The rapidity of the transactions between suppliers and consumers in the online environment, in fact, cannot easily cope with some requirements of jurisdiction agreements contained in Article 13, such as the requirement that a jurisdictional clause is allowed if it 'is entered into after the dispute has arisen'. Therefore, it seems unlikely that the jurisdictional rules of Section 3 (jurisdiction in matters relating to insurance) will usually be departed from a choice of court clause contained in contracts concluded on the web.

(v) Consumers: Article 15

As already stated above, in actions related to insurance contracts there is a possibility of Section 4 (jurisdiction over consumer contracts) of the Brussels Regulation applying. However, the narrow definition of consumer contract contained in Article 15 means that many contractual insurance cases would fall outside the scope of Section 4. Although a contract for the supply of insurance services comes with Article 15 this will only be a 'consumer contract' if it can be proven that (a) the other party (a business) pursues commercial or professional activities in the Member State of the consumer's domicile, or (b) such party directs such activities to that Member State or several Member States including that one.

The determination of these requirements may, however, prove difficult with respect to contracts concluded on the Internet. How to ascertain the State where the consumer of online services is domiciled? How to establish that the commercial and professional activities of the other party are directed to the Member State where the consumer is domiciled or several States including that one?[10] The recitals to Article 15 are of little assistance. In a joint statement on this matter at the Justice, Home Affairs and Civil Protection Council meeting of 30 November and 1 December 2000 the Council and Commission held that:

> the mere fact that an Internet site is accessible is not sufficient for Article 15 to be applicable, although a factor will be that this Internet site solicits the conclusion of distance contracts and that a contract has actually been concluded at distance, by whatever means. In this respect, the language or currency which a website uses does not constitute a relevant factor.[11]

[10] For similar criticisms see Harris (2001) *Civil Justice Quarterly* 220.
[11] For the text of the joint statement see the website www.europa.eu.int

But this is clearly not sufficient to solve all the problems arising from the ambiguous expression of 'directed activities' contained in Article 15 of the new Regulation. Thus, in the absence of official guidance, we will have to expect precedents on the matter of what can be regarded as 'directing' activities at a Member State. These precedents may well be slow to emerge because of the rather modest level of cross-border disputes. But, enhancing consumer confidence in Internet commerce may result in the growth in the number of such cases and perhaps, in the long term, greater benefits for businesses and consumers alike.

4. EVALUATION

(a) Article 13: An Unsuitable Provision for Jurisdictional Agreements Concluded in the Online Environment

It is arguable from the exposition above that Article 13 is an unsuitable provision for jurisdictional agreements concluded in the online environment. The requirements in Article 13 are adequate to deal with complex questions of form, such as the questions of form arising from the choice of court clauses contained in insurance contracts concluded offline. However, the questions of form arising from jurisdictional agreements contained in online contracts are often far simpler than the questions of form arising from jurisdictional agreements contained in contracts concluded in the world outside the Internet.

There appear to be three reasons for simple requirements in jurisdictional agreements concluded over the Internet. First, online transactions are much more rapid than offline transactions. The personalised, one to one relationships between the supplier and consumer in the Internet environment encourages the agreement of the parties more than the traditional mass-marketing and mass-distribution techniques. Secondly, unlike most of the traditional transactions in the field of insurance between the supplier of the online services and the consumer there is usually no middleman eg, an agent, broker. That clearly helps to make agreements on the web easy as there are few parties involved. Thirdly, because of the different approaches to the question of jurisdiction in Internet e-commerce transactions by the national courts in Europe and the United States of America, it is very much in the interests of both the supplier and consumer to reach a prompt and simple agreement on the competent forum for contractual disputes. It is clear that uncertainties over the competent forum favour neither the supplier nor the consumer of an online service.

The use of Article 13 in jurisdictional agreements concluded online, because of its requirements, results in uncertainty and unfairness to the supplier of online services.

(i) Uncertainty

The fulfilment of the requirements in Article 13 prove difficult with respect to insurance contracts concluded on the Internet. The case law of the European Court of Justice and the national courts does little to resolve this difficulty since there are very few cases dealing directly or indirectly with online contracts.

(ii) Unfairness to the Supplier of Online Services

The difficulty for the operators involved in the online environment in departing from the bases of jurisdiction contained in Section 3 (jurisdiction in matters relating to insurance) is that it results in unfairness to the supplier of online services. Though the purpose of the jurisdictional rules in Section 3 was not the protection of the policyholder, insured or beneficiary, there are rules in Articles 8 to 14 which favour the policyholder, insured or beneficiary. Indeed, Article 12(1) which provides that 'an insurer may bring proceedings only in the courts of the Member State in which the defendant is domiciled' favours the policyholder, insured and beneficiary.

It would be possible to justify very pro-consumer/insured jurisdiction provisions in cases relating to online contracts if the substantive law on electronic commerce was itself equally pro-consumer/insured. However, it has been seen that, overall, the EC Directives and Proposals related to online commerce are not noticeably pro-consumer.

5. OPTIONS FOR REFORM

The problem is in relation to Article 13. This needs to be reformed to ensure that there is certainty in the law and the law is not unfair to the supplier of online services. When it comes to achieving these objectives two possible options for reforms should be considered. The first is the option of deleting the requirements contained in paragraphs 1 and 2 of Article 12 as they are inadequate to deal with the questions of form arising from jurisdictional agreements contained in insurance contracts formed over the Internet. The second is to introduce a special rule into Article 13 to deal with jurisdictional agreements concluded over the Internet.

(a) **Re-wording Article 13**

Under this solution Article 13 would be re-worded so that it would have to be shown that the provisions of Section 3 may be departed from with a jurisdictional agreement which relates to an insurance contract concluded by electronic means. This would have the advantage of equalising jurisdictional agreements relating to insurance contracts concluded by traditional means with jurisdictional agreements relating to insurance contracts concluded by electronic means. Instead, it attempts to tackle the deficiencies in Article 13 head on by concentrating on this provision.

However, it would affect the jurisdictional agreements contained in insurance contracts concluded by traditional means and not just those contained in contracts concluded online.

(b) A Special Rule for Jurisdictional Agreements Contained in Contracts Concluded by Electronic Means[12]

The most direct way of dealing with the problems of the unsuitability of Article 13 for use in jurisdictional agreements contained in insurance contracts formed over the Internet is to introduce a special provision under Article 23 (prorogation of jurisdiction) for jurisdictional agreements contained in online contracts. The Brussels Regulation and Lugano Convention already contain special rules for jurisdictional agreements contained in consumer contracts and insurance contracts. An additional special rule for jurisdictional agreements contained in contracts formed over the Internet is justified because of the unsatisfactory way in which Articles 13 and 23 deal with such jurisdictional agreements.

(i) A Proposal for a New Rule

This rule would grant the operators involved in the online environment a wide freedom to conclude jurisdictional agreements. Because of the rapidity of electronic transactions and because of the stronger bargaining position of the consumer in the online environment than in the offline environment the rule should not provide complex requirements for such jurisdictional agreements. Following the Draft Directive on a common framework for electronic signatures it could affirm the legal validity of electronic signatures which are based on a qualified certificate issued by a certification service provider that fulfils certain specified requirements as well as the equivalence of the electronic signature and hand written signature.[13]

[12] See also the recommendations of a new rule of jurisdiction for contracts concluded and performed online in the Preliminary Document 12 of August 2000, n 3 above. But the new Council Regulation on jurisdiction and enforcement of judgments in civil and commercial matters does not provide a special rule for jurisdictional agreements contained in contracts concluded online. Art 23(2) tersely states that 'Any communication by electronic means which provides a durable record of the agreement should be equated to writing'.

[13] For the text of the amended proposal for a European Parliament and Council Directive on a common framework for electronic signatures see the website www.europa.eu.int

(ii) The Virtues of the Proposed Rule

(1) Certainty

This rule would provide certainty in the law, since a choice of court clause in an online contract would avoid definitional problems that could arise from the use of the traditional bases of jurisdiction in cases relating to Internet contracts.

(2) Limiting an Excessively Pro-insured Approach

By introducing this rule for jurisdictional agreements formed over the Internet, parties who are in the same bargaining position would be able to depart from the provisions of Section 3 such as Articles 9(2) and 12(1) which favour the policyholder.

16

Choice of Law in Relation to Insurance and Reinsurance Contracts Concluded by Electronic Means

1. INTRODUCTION

MUCH CRITICISM has been directed at the use of the choice of law rules contained in the Rome Convention on the law applicable to contractual obligations in cases relating to contracts concluded by electronic means. Concerns have focused largely on the appropriateness of the connecting factors used in Article 5 of the Rome Convention for the determination of the law applicable to consumer contracts concluded online. It has been questioned whether these connecting factors will be able to provide certainty and predictability to consumer transactions concluded on the Internet as these are indeed not easy to define.[1]

Anxiety has also been expressed about the application of the choice of law rules which refer to 'real' places, such as the domicile or the habitual residence of a natural person or the principal place of business of a company to contracts concluded over the Internet. The question arises whether these rules are suitable for online contracts. The Internet is indeed characterised by the fact that the national borders no longer exist. Moreover, a web-site may be accessed from every country and is not located in the place where the party who sets it up is established.

Yet some problems could arise from the use of the choice of law rules contained in the European Insurance Directives in cases relating to insurance contracts concluded over the Internet. Article 28 of the Third Life Insurance Directive states that the law applicable to the contract should not conflict with legal provisions protecting the general good in the Member State of the commitment. The use of this rule is far from being easy in cases relating to contracts concluded by electronic means as the determination of the place of the commitment may prove difficult with respect to life insurance contracts concluded over the Internet. Moreover, some problems might arise from Articles 7 and 8 of the Second Insurance Directives. These provide complex choice of law rules which do not apply well to simple contracts, such as online contracts in

[1] See inter alia Schu (1997) 5 2 *International Journal of Law and Information Technology* 192 *et seq*; Stone (1998) *Information and Communication Technology Law* 23 *et seq*; Carrascosa González in Caravaça et alios (ed), *Contratos internacionales* (Madrid, Tecnos, 1997) 1707–36.

which the parties are usually in the same bargaining position. However these problems have not attracted significant attention from the legal writers and the participants to the recent public hearings on the jurisdiction and applicable law to electronic commerce.

The following analysis will examine the main questions arising from the use of the choice of law rules to be found in the European Insurance Directives in cases relating to insurance contracts concluded by electronic means. As these rules only apply to insurance contracts which cover risks situated in the territories of the Member States of the European Community, the following analysis will also examine the questions arising from the use of the choice of law rules contained in the Rome Convention in cases relating to online contracts of reinsurance and insurance covering risks situated outside the territories of the Member States of the European Community.

2. THE 1980 ROME CONVENTION AND THE LAW APPLICABLE TO INSURANCE CONTRACTS CONCLUDED BY ELECTRONIC MEANS

The Rome Convention says nothing about its application in cases involving online contracts. Neither does the English statute implementing the Convention. There is nothing unusual about this. Until recently no more than business-to-business transactions on closed proprietary networks were conducted in the online environment. Moreover, the Rome Convention and the English statute of implementation lay down specific provisions for few types of contracts. The point has either been overlooked altogether or it has been decided that, rather than add an extra layer of complexity to what may already be a complex statute, the problem of the applicable law to online contracts should be left to the courts to apply the general choice of law rules in contract. In cases involving online contracts of reinsurance or insurance covering risks situated outside the territories of a Member State of the European Community this would involve turning to the choice of law rules set out in chapter four.

(a) The Applicable Law

Article 3 of the Rome Convention (freedom of choice) does not raise any particular problems in relation to insurance contracts concluded by electronic means. Accordingly, our analysis will focus on insurance contracts concluded by electronic means which do not contain express or implied choice of law clauses.

Some questions might arise from the use of the presumption of characteristic performance to ascertain the law of the country with which the online contract is most closely connected. The determination of this presumption may prove difficult with respect to contracts concluded on the Internet as Article 4(2) of the Rome Convention refers to:

> the country where the party who is to effect the performance which is characteristic of the contract has, at the time of conclusion of the contract, his habitual residence or, in the case of a body corporate or unincorporate, its central administration.

In most of the Member States of the European Union there is as yet neither any specific rule nor any specific judicial guidance on the actual time of formation of a cyber-contract.[2] In some civil law countries such as Germany the question of the precise time of contract formation on the net has been solved by reference to the general rule on the contract formation inter absentes which states that the contract is concluded when the proposal of the sender reaches the receiver.[3] However, in other countries such as the United Kingdom there are arguments in favour of the application of the postal rule to emailing.[4] For self evidently these different approaches to the questions of the precise time of formation of a cyber-contract might alter the correct operation of the characteristic performance test. Due to the principle of uniform interpretation of the conventional rules set out in Article 18 of the Rome Convention national courts must interpret and apply the uniform rules taking into account their international character. Whenever it is possible courts must give independent community meanings to the terms used in the Convention. Nevertheless these difficulties applying the rule of connection by characteristic performance to online contracts must not be overestimated. As already said above, it appears that this rule shall apply as a last resort, if consideration of all circumstances of the case fails to identify the applicable law to the contract.[5]

3. ARTICLE 5 OF THE ROME CONVENTION AND THE LAW APPLICABLE TO INSURANCE CONTRACTS CONCLUDED BY ELECTRONIC MEANS

Article 5 deals with consumer contracts that arise in three defined sets of circumstances. The first and second sets of circumstances were also found in Article 13 (jurisdiction over consumer contracts) of the Brussels Convention. However the third set of circumstances is only in Article 5 of the Rome Convention. The present analysis will focus on the problems which arise from these sets of circumstances (previous advertising, steps taken in the country of residence, order received in the country of consumer's habitual residence) in the field of insurance contracts concluded by electronic means.

[2] See Niemann (2000) 5 *Communications Law* 48 *et seq*.
[3] *Ibid*, 48.
[4] *Ibid*, 48.
[5] *Cf* ch 8, para 9.

(a) Specific Invitation

In a virtual environment such as the Internet a specific invitation is usually sent to the consumer by email. This poses acute problems because Article 5(2) requires that the specific invitation precede the conclusion of the contract in the country of the consumer's domicile. Though not expressed in the text of Article 5(2) this means that the invitation must be received by the consumer in his home country.[6] Email is usually received and stored by the server where the email account of the consumer is located and is later accessed by the consumer. Usually the server is physically close to the consumer's location. However the email server can be located in a different country. Also a consumer might have moved to a different country but might still use his previous email account. In these situations it is fundamental to establish whether the invitation is received by the consumer when the email is stored on the email server or when the user actually accesses it.[7]

(b) Previous Advertising

The question of previous advertising in an online environment arises when the supplier appears on the World Wide Web (WWW). The World Wide Web is a non-coordinated worldwide database to which anybody may add information on any computer connected to the net.

Are the websites new forms of 'advertising'? To answer this question properly a distinction has to be made between the different types of activity on the World Wide Web. It appears that the mere presence of a business site on the Web cannot be seen as advertising in the sense of Article 5. In a very hypothetical scenario, a supplier might set up a website but not make any effort to link that site with another site. As the whole structure of the World Wide Web consists of links the user follows, nobody would reach the supplier's site.[8] It is clear that such a site could not be seen as advertising. On the other hand, the presence of a website in some Internet directories, comparable with an advertisement in specialised magazines, can be considered a form of advertising. That is true despite the fact that once the site is listed in a Internet directory the information about the website spreads further in the net even without the supplier's intervention.

[6] See Stone (1998) *Information and Communications Technology Law* 156 *et seq.*

[7] For a clear illustration of these and further questions see Schu (1997) 5(2) *International Journal of Law and Information Technology* 192.

[8] See Schu, n 7 above, 194.

c) Steps Necessary for the Conclusion of the Contract

What are the 'steps' necessary for the conclusion of an Internet contract? In an online environment the consumer can place his order either by email or by filling in and posting the order onto the supplier's web server.[9] It is clear that the former is equivalent to posting the order by ordinary mail, which is considered to be all the steps necessary to be taken by the consumer. Though the posting of a form directly onto the supplier's web server involves factual changes on that server, no distinction has to be made with posting an email, as the location of the server is fortuitous and the means of communication should not be decisive.[10] However, some difficulties may still occur in cases where the consumer has posted his order electronically from another country, eg while travelling. The wording of Article 5 suggests that this provision cannot apply where the steps necessary for the conclusion of the contract are not taken in the country of the consumer's domicile. Moreover, the same conclusion can be derived from the Giuliano and Lagarde Report. In commenting on the wording in Article 5 the Giuliano and Lagarde Report makes clear that the factual and not the legal steps must be taken by the consumer in his country of domicile.

(d) Order Received in the Country of Consumer's Habitual Residence

Article 5(2) provides that:

> Notwithstanding the provisions of Article 3, a choice of law made by the parties shall not have the result of depriving the consumer of the protection afforded to him by the mandatory rules of the law of the country in which he has his habitual residence: . . . if the other party or his agent received the consumer's order in that country.

The determination of the place where the consumer's order was received by the supplier or his agent may prove difficult with respect to contracts concluded over the Internet. An order placed by email or posted onto a website can be saved there or on an email server respectively but can be accessed later from a different location. The requirement of the order received by the supplier or his agent in the country of consumer's habitual residence was meant to apply mainly in situations where the consumer has addressed himself to a foreign firm at a fair or exhibition or at its branch in the consumer's country.[11] However in the online environment the consumer will often ignore the physical location of the site where the email containing his order or WWW-form is posted to.

[9] *Ibid*, 194.
[10] *Ibid.*
[11] See the Giuliano and Lagarde Report (1980) OJ C281 of 31 October 1980, 24.

Article 5(4) makes clear that the protective rules do not apply to:

> a contract for the supply of services where the services are to be supplied to the consumer exclusively in a country other than that in which he has his habitual residence.

This provision may raise some questions in cases relating to contracts for the supply of electronic services (provision of information, provision of software or other material stored in computer files etc) as the location of these services is difficult to ascertain.[12] However insurance services cannot be compared with electronic services which are provided online. For self evidently an insurance service can only be supplied offline regardless of whether the contract of insurance is concluded by traditional means.

4. THE LAW APPLICABLE TO THE FORM OF INSURANCE AND REINSURANCE CONTRACTS CONCLUDED BY ELECTRONIC MEANS

As already seen above, Article 9(2) of the Rome Convention lays down a system of alternative laws governing formal validity of contracts concluded between persons who are in different countries (contracts *inter absentes*). This provides that a contract concluded between persons who are in different countries is formally valid if it satisfies the formal requirements of the law which governs it under the Convention (*lex causae*) or the requirements of the law of the country where it is concluded. In the context of electronic commerce this provision raises the same questions of the precise time of contract formation already examined above.[13]

5. THE 2000 DIRECTIVE ON ELECTRONIC COMMERCE AND THE LAW APPLICABLE TO INSURANCE AND REINSURANCE CONTRACTS CONCLUDED BY ELECTRONIC MEANS

As already stated above, the Directive on certain aspects of electronic commerce in the internal market lays down principles of access to the market, liability of professional persons and some issues concerning the contract (information to the consumer prior to the conclusion, moment of the conclusion, admissibility). It clarifies that it 'does not establish additional rules of private international law'.[14] Moreover, each Member State has the obligation to guarantee that the 'information society services provided by a service provider established on its territory comply with the national provisions applicable in the Member State'.[15] This duty encompasses the rules concerning access to the market, torts as well

[12] See Schu (1997) *International Journal of Law and Information Technology* 192.
[13] See ch 15, para 2.
[14] Art 1(4).
[15] Art 3(1).

as contractual obligations. Nevertheless, the provision enacting this obligation (Article 3) does not apply to 'contractual obligations concerning consumer contracts'.[16]

It has been pointed out correctly that the part of Article 3 which refers to the national provisions applicable in the State of establishment adopts a single rigid factor pertaining to the territory of the implementing State.[17] This provision being an applicable law rule it contains a conflict of laws rule, notwithstanding the wording of Article 1(4) of the Directive.[18]

By excluding consumer contracts from the scope of Article 3(1), it means that, in this subject matter, establishing the territorial scope of application of the imperative provisions at stake is left completely to the private international law rules of the forum. In other terms, Article 5 of the Rome Convention can still be adopted and can determine the law of a third State, even if the insurer is established in the territory of a Member State of the European Community.[19]

6. THE SECOND NON-LIFE DIRECTIVE AND THE LAW APPLICABLE TO INSURANCE CONTRACTS CONCLUDED ON THE INTERNET COVERING RISKS SITUATED IN THE TERRITORIES OF A MEMBER STATE OF THE EUROPEAN COMMUNITY

Like the Rome Convention, the Second Non-Life Directive does not lay down specific choice of law provisions for online contracts. This means that the private international law rules of general application have to be applied to the specific contracts. Two very different sets of rules come into play. The first are choice of law in contract rules. The second are the mandatory rules of the forum. In cases relating to insurance contracts concluded online covering risks situated in the territories of a Member State of the European Community this would involve turning to the choice of law rules set out in chapter five.

7. ARTICLE 7(1)(A), (B), (C) OF THE SECOND NON-LIFE DIRECTIVE AND THE LAW APPLICABLE TO INSURANCE CONTRACTS CONCLUDED BY ELECTRONIC MEANS

A word needs to be said about the application of Article 7(1)(a),(b),(c) of the Second Non-Life Directive in the field of insurance contracts concluded by electronic means. This provision may raise some problems in relation to online contracts as it uses 'real' connecting factors such as the habitual residence or central

[16] Annex to the Directive.

[17] Fallon and Franq, *Internationally mandatory rules for consumer contracts?* in Basedow, Meier, Schnyder, Einhorn, Girsberg (eds), *Private Law in the International Arena* (The Hague, TMC Asser Press, 2000) 162–64.

[18] *Ibid.*

[19] *Ibid.*

administration of the policyholder. The determination of the habitual residence and central administration of the policyholder may, in fact, prove difficult with respect to insurance contracts concluded on the Internet. It has been pointed out correctly in legal writings that one of the major risks associated with electronic transactions is the ease with which anyone can buy services through the Internet without revealing their location or identity.[20] However, these risks must not be overestimated. It is a current practice amongst suppliers of online services to set up their electronic ordering facilities so that the order form insists on customers stating their address. Self-evidently that is not sufficient to avoid the risk of misleading statements by the customer. Nevertheless 'a customer would not be permitted to rely on the application of the law of his home country where he has misled the supplier as to his habitual residence or central administration, and the supplier has therefore reasonably concluded that this law does not apply'.[21]

8. THE SECOND LIFE DIRECTIVE AND THE LAW APPLICABLE TO INSURANCE CONTRACTS CONCLUDED BY ELECTRONIC MEANS

As already seen, two connecting factors are used in Article 4 of the Second Life Directive to determine the law applicable to contracts of direct insurance covering life risks: the place of the commitment (the place where the policyholder has his habitual residence) and the nationality of the policyholder.[22]

Article 4 bears analogies with Article 7 of the Second Non-Life Directive which deals with the law applicable to non-life insurance contracts. It adds a further connecting factor (the nationality of the policyholder), which can apply when the criteria of Article 4, paragraph 2 are met.

Whether the rule's concentration on the policyholder's nationality pays adequate attention to the purposes of life insurance contracts concluded by electronic means must be open to doubt. However, the application of the national law of the policyholder does not in turn become unfair to the insurer as Article 4(2) makes clear that 'the parties . . . choose the law of the Member State of which the policyholder is a national.'[23] In the absence of a choice, the law of the Member State of the commitment applies to the contract.

9. FINAL REMARKS

In a sense, what one can draw from the above analysis is straightforward. Both the choice of law in contract rules to be found in Articles 4, paragraph 2 (characteristic performance), 5 (consumer contracts), 9, paragraph 2 (formal validity)

[20] See inter alia King (2000) 5 1 *Communications Law* 14.
[21] Stone (1999) *Information and Communication Technology* 23 *et seq*.
[22] See above ch 10, para 3.1.
[23] Emphasis added.

of the Rome Convention and Article 7 of the Second Non-Life Insurance Directive, as well as the choice of law rules in Article 4 of the Second Life Insurance Directive, do not apply well to contracts concluded by electronic means. The writer would submit that this is not surprising in view of the state of flux in the substantive law applicable to electronic transactions in Europe and the United States. In such circumstances the approach of the new Directive on certain legal aspects of electronic commerce offers the best prospects of international standardisation given that the country of origin's applicable law serves the interests of the parties involved in online transactions, by harnessing the advantages that electronic commerce has to offer and encouraging its growth throughout the European Union.

The law applicable to contracts concluded by electronic means is a matter which must engage the attention of the European legislator when it revises the Rome Convention and the Insurance Directives. It is very much to be hoped that the revised text of the Rome Convention will provide that, in the absence of a choice or a valid choice, the contact shall be governed by the law of the country of origin of the service, regardless of whether the electronic transaction resulted from advertising or not. Such a rule would apply both to insurance contracts covering risks situated within and outside the European Community.

17

General Conclusions

THE AIM of this book has been to isolate and describe from a European perspective the legal regulation of jurisdiction and choice of law problems in relation to transnational insurance and reinsurance. What emerges from the analysis is that European countries have adopted a complex and, at times, inefficient response to the private international law problems posed by insurance contracts. This is due largely to the unsatisfactory nature of the special rules of jurisdiction for insurance contracts contained in Articles 8, 9, 13 and 14 of the Brussels Regulation and Lugano Convention and the special choice of law rules for insurance contracts contained in the European Insurance Directives.

1. THE NEED FOR A REVIEW OF THE RULES ON JURISDICTION IN INSURANCE MATTERS

By stating that 'in matters relating to insurance, jurisdiction shall be determined by the rules of Section 3, without prejudice to the provisions of Articles 4 and 5(5)' Article 8 fails to indicate all the bases of jurisdiction which apply to insurance contracts. Moreover, the Brussels Regulation and Lugano Convention have displayed a remarkable rigidity in adapting the general requirements for jurisdiction agreements to accommodate expectations of the party in a weaker bargaining position, ie usually the insured. Although this rigidity responds to the need of protection of the insured, this response is unfair to the insurer and cannot be squared with the substantive insurance law, which is not itself equally pro-insured. Furthermore, the interaction between the special rules of jurisdiction agreements in insurance matters and general rules of jurisdiction agreements in civil and commercial matters has resulted in a complex system of regulation. One consequence, illustrated in chapter 5, is that the parties often ignore whether a choice of court clause which departs from the special rules of jurisdiction for insurance contracts is enforceable. Moreover, the special regime for jurisdiction agreements in insurance matters is not suited to dealing with agreements on the forum contained in insurance and reinsurance contracts formed over the Internet.

(a) The Solution

As was urged at the conclusion of chapter 5 above, Article 8 should be re-worded so that it should appear that not only Articles 4 and 5(5) but also Articles 6(2), 14, 23, 24, 25, 26, 27, 28, 29 and 31 are not affected by the rules contained in Section 3 of Chapter II of the Brussels Regulation. This would eliminate the uncertainties arising from the present version of Article 8. Again, it is very much to be hoped that the European Commission will take active steps to ensure that Article 9 of the Brussels Regulation is re-worded so that it is shown that an insurer domiciled in a Member State can be sued only in the courts of the Member State in which proceedings are brought against the leading insurer.

Moreover, it was suggested in the concluding section of chapter 14, and is again submitted here, that the regime of jurisdiction agreements contained in Article 13 needs to be reformed to ensure that the protective rules of jurisdiction for insurance contracts can be departed from when there is a jurisdiction agreement which relates to a contract of insurance concluded by electronic means. As was urged at the conclusion of chapter 14, the most direct way of dealing with the problems of the unsuitability of Article 13 for use in jurisdictional agreements contained in insurance contracts concluded in the online environment is to introduce a special provision under Article 23 (prorogation of jurisdiction) for jurisdictional agreements contained in online contracts. By granting the operators involved in the online environment a wide freedom to conclude jurisdictional agreements this rule would provide certainty in the law and allow the parties who are in the same bargaining position to depart from jurisdiction rules such as Article 9(2) and 12(1) of the Brussels Regulation and Lugano Convention which favour the policyholder.

2. THE UNSATISFACTORY STATE OF THE LAW APPLICABLE TO INSURANCE CONTRACTS

The present law in Europe in relation to choice of law for insurance contracts covering risks situated in the EC is in a very unsatisfactory condition.

First and most noticeably, the law is not completely harmonised. The Second Non-Life Insurance Directive grants the Member States an excessive freedom of implementation of the choice of law rules for insurance contracts. In conflict of law there are, in Europe, harmonised rules on jurisdiction, enforcement of judgments and contract choice of law. In light of this, the failure to harmonise choice of law rules for insurance contracts covering risks situated in the EC has become highly anomalous. The result is that claimants are encouraged to forum shop in Europe for substantive law advantages. For the different choice of law rules may produce a different outcome depending on which set of provisions is applied.[1] Furthermore, the jurisdiction provisions in matters relating to insurance allow such forum shopping.

Second, there is uncertainty in the law applicable to insurance contracts under the Third Insurance Directives because of the concept of 'general good'. It is uncertain, because of a lack of authority, how the limit of the 'general good' operates in relation to the freedom of the parties to choose the applicable law. This, combined with the lack of complete harmonisation of choice of law rules in Europe, makes it difficult for the legal adviser to advise his client on the choice of law aspects in cases relating to insurance contracts covering risks situated within the EC.

Third, the application of Directive choice of law rules fails to acknowledge the argument that the European private international law should not hinder the exercise of the freedom of services provided by the Treaty of Rome.

Fourth, in so far as the choice of law rules contained in the Second Life Insurance Directive are applied this involves rules which are unsuitable for the protection of the policyholder in all cases.

(a) The Solution

The Rome Convention stands out as the best solution for solving choice of law problems in respect of insurance contracts in Europe regardless of whether the risk covered by the contract of insurance is situated within or outside the EC. It best achieves the policy considerations that choice of law rules for insurance contracts should achieve, such as predictability, certainty and fairness to the parties. Whilst no solution is perfect, application of the Rome Convention to any type of insurance contract would be a considerable improvement over the present position.

The Convention has already achieved a measure of harmonisation in Europe. Application of Directive choice of law rules to insurance contracts covering risks situated within the EC is not the answer since these rules differ markedly from one European Union State to another.[2]

Neither is reform of the choice of law rules in the Insurance Directives and adaptation to the contract choice of law rules of the Rome Convention the answer since adoption of this approach would maintain two sets of rules, one for insurance contracts covering risks situated outside the EC (which would be completely harmonised), the other for insurance contracts covering risks situated within the EC (which would not be completely harmonised).

[1] For a clear discussion of this point see Fawcett, *General Report*, in Fawcett (ed), *Declining Jurisdiction in Private International Law* (Oxford, Clarendon, 1998) 1 *et seq*.

[2] See Frigessi di Rattalma and Seatzu (eds), *The Implementation Provisions of the EC Choice of Law Rules for Insurance Contracts in Belgium, France, Germany, Italy, The Netherlands, Spain and the United Kingdom: A Commentary* (The Hague, Kluwer Law International, 2003) forthcoming.

The Rome Convention contains a detailed code, which ensures that in the absence of a valid stipulation by the parties only the law of a State with which there are strong connections is applied. Moreover, the Rome Convention's provisions on party autonomy by providing the parties with ample freedom to select the law they wish to govern their agreement ensures that the interests of the parties to insurance and reinsurance contracts are respected.

Furthermore, the Convention provides contract choice of law rules which acknowledge the argument that European private international law must not hinder the exercise of the freedom of services within the Single Market.

Finally, the Convention adopts a sophisticated approach towards connecting factors which acknowledges the complexity of international insurance and reinsurance cases.

The European Commission should be encouraged to make a proposal to reword Article 1(3) of the Rome Convention so that the choice of law rules contained in the Convention would apply to any type of insurance contracts.[3] It was suggested in the concluding section of chapter 8 above, and is again submitted here, that Article 5 (consumer contracts) of the Rome Convention should be re-worded so that in the absence of a valid stipulation by the parties the law of the country in which the consumer has his habitual residence would apply *only* if it is objectively more favourable to him. As was urged at the conclusion of chapter 16, a special rule for contracts formed over the Internet must be adopted in the revised text of the Rome Convention. This rule should provide that, in the absence of a choice or a valid choice, the contract shall be governed by the law of the country of origin of the service, regardless of whether the electronic transaction resulted from advertising or not.

[3] See Claret, *Contrats d'Assurance et Conflits de lois en droit communitaire* (Thesis, University of Lille, 1994) especially 325 ff; North in North (ed) *Contract Conflicts* (Amsterdam and Oxford, North Holland, 1982) 11; The Law Com and Scottish Law Com Report on the Choice of Law Rules in the Draft Non-Life Insurance Services Directive, 11 April 1979, especially 66. But see Smulders and Glazener, (1992) *Common Market Law Review* 796. See also Delaume, (1981) *Virginia Journal of International Law*, 120–21 who criticises the idea of a general Convention on the law applicable to contractual obligations and advocates the adoption of special choice of law rules for the different types of contracts. For the same criticism see also Nadelmann, (1976) *American Journal of Comparative Law* 19; Cavers, (1975) 48 *South California Law Review* 603.

APPENDICES

Appendix 1

Convention on the Law Applicable to Contractual Obligations

Opened for Signature in Rome on 19 June 1980 (80/934/EEC)

PREAMBLE

THE HIGH CONTRACTING PARTIES to the Treaty establishing the European Economic Community,

ANXIOUS to continue in the field of private international law the work of unification of law which has already been done within the Community, in particular in the field of jurisdiction and enforcement of judgments,

WISHING to establish uniform rules concerning the law applicable to contractual obligations,

HAVE AGREED AS FOLLOWS:

TITLE I

SCOPE OF THE CONVENTION

Article 1
Scope of the Convention

1. The rules of this Convention shall apply to contractual obligations in any situation involving a choice between the laws of different countries.
2. They shall not apply to:
   (a) questions involving the status or legal capacity of natural persons, without prejudice to Article 11;
   (b) contractual obligations relating to:
   wills and succession,
   rights in property arising out of a matrimonial relationship,
   rights and duties arising out of a family relationship, parentage,
   marriage or affinity, including maintenance obligations in respect of children who are not legitimate;
   (c) obligations arising under bills of exchange, cheques and promissory notes and other negotiable instruments to the extent that the obligations

under such negotiable instruments arise out of their negotiable character;

(d) arbitration agreements and agreements on the choice of a court;

(e) questions governed by the law of companies and other bodies corporate or unincorporated such as the creation by registration or otherwise, legal capacity, internal organisation or winding up of companies and other bodies corporate or unincorporated and the personal liability of officers and members as such for the obligations of the company or body;

(f) the question whether an agent is able to bind a principal, or an organ to bind a company or body corporate or unincorporated, to a third party;

(g) the constitution of trusts and the relationship between settlors, trustees and beneficiaries;

(h) evidence and procedure, without prejudice to Article 14.

3. The rules of this Convention do not apply to contracts of insurance which cover risks situated in the territories of the Member States of the European Economic Community. In order to determine whether a risk is situated in these territories the court shall apply its internal law.
4. The preceding paragraph does not apply to contracts of re-insurance.

Article 2
Application of non-Contracting States

Any law specified by this Convention shall be applied whether or not it is the law of a Contracting State.

TITLE II
UNIFORM RULES

Article 3
Freedom of Choice

1. A contract shall be governed by the law chosen by the parties. The choice must be express or demonstrated with reasonable certainty by the terms of the contract or the circumstances of the case. By their choice the parties can select the law applicable to the whole or a part only of the contract.
2. The parties may at any time agree to subject the contract to a law other than that which previously governed it, whether as a result of an earlier choice under this Article or of other provisions of this Convention. Any variation by the parties of the law to be applied made after the conclusion of the contract shall not prejudice its formal validity under Article 9 or adversely affect the rights of third parties.

3. The fact that the parties have chosen a foreign law, whether or not accompanied by the choice of a foreign tribunal, shall not, where all the other elements relevant to the situation at the time of the choice are connected with one country only, prejudice the application of rules of the law of that country which cannot be derogated from by contract, hereinafter called 'mandatory rules'.
4. The existence and validity of the consent of the parties as to the choice of the applicable law shall be determined in accordance with the provisions of Articles 8, 9 and 11.

Article 4
Applicable Law in the Absence of Choice

1. To the extent that the law applicable to the contract has not been chosen in accordance with Article 3, the contract shall be governed by the law of the country with which it is most closely connected. Nevertheless, a severable part of the contract which has a closer connection with another country may by way of exception be governed by the law of that other country.
2. Subject to the provisions of para 5 of this Article, it shall be presumed that the contract is most closely connected with the country where the party who is to affect the performance which is characteristic of the contract has, at the time of conclusion of the contract, his habitual residence, or, in the case of a body corporate or incorporate, its central administration. However, if the contract is entered into in the course of that party's trade or profession, that country shall be the country in which the principal place of business is situated or, where under the terms of the contract the performance is to be effected through a place of business other than the principal place of business, the country in which that other place is situated.
3. Notwithstanding the provisions of para 2 of this Article, to the extent that the subject matter of the contract is a right in immovable property or a right to use immovable property it shall be presumed that the contract is most closely connected with the country where the immovable property is situated.
4. A contract for the carriage of goods shall not be subject to the presumption in para 2. In such a contract if the country in which, at the time the contract is concluded, the carrier has his principal place of business is also the country in which the place of loading or the place of discharge or the principal place of business of the consignor is situated, it shall be presumed that the contract is most closely connected with that country. In applying this paragraph single voyage charter-parties and other contracts the main purpose of which is the carriage of goods shall be treated as contracts for the carriage of goods.
5. Paragraph 2 shall not apply if the characteristic performance cannot be determined, and the presumptions in paras 2, 3 and 4 shall be disregarded if it

appears from the circumstances as a whole that the contract is more closely connected with another country.

Article 5
Certain Consumer Contracts

1. This Article applies to a contract the object of which is the supply of goods or services to a person ('the consumer') for a purpose which can be regarded as being outside his trade or profession, or a contract for the provision of credit for that object.
2. Notwithstanding the provisions of Article 3, a choice of law made by the parties shall not have the result of depriving the consumer of the protection afforded to him by the mandatory rules of the law of the country in which he has his habitual residence:
   —if in that country the conclusion of the contract was preceded by a specific invitation addressed to him or by advertising, and he had taken in that country all the steps necessary on his part for the conclusion of the contract; or
   —if the other party or his agent received the consumer's order in that country; or
   —if the contract is for the sale of goods and the consumer travelled from that country to another country and there gave his order, provided that the consumer's journey was arranged by the seller for the purpose of inducing the consumer to buy.
3. Notwithstanding the provisions of Article 4, a contract to which this Article applies will, in the absence of choice in accordance with Article 3, be governed by the law of the country in which the consumer has his habitual residence if it is entered into in the circumstances described in para 2 of this Article.
4. This Article shall not apply to:
   (a) a contract of carriage;
   (b) a contract for the supply of services where the services are to be supplied to the consumer exclusively in a country other than that in which he has his habitual residence.
5. Notwithstanding the provisions of para 4, this Article shall apply to a contract which, for an inclusive price, provides for a combination of travel and accommodation.

Article 6
Individual Employment Contracts

1. Notwithstanding the provisions of Article 3, in a contract of employment a choice of law made by the parties shall not have the result of depriving the

employee of the protection afforded to him by the mandatory rules of the law which would be applicable under para 2 in the absence of choice.

2. Notwithstanding the provisions of Article 4, a contract of employment shall, in the absence of choice in accordance with Article 3, be governed:
   (a) by the law of the country in which the employee habitually carries out his work in performance of the contract, even if he is temporarily employed in another country; or
   (b) if the employee does not habitually carry out his work in any one country, by the law of the country in which the place of business through which he was engaged is situated;

   unless it appears from the circumstances as a whole that the contract is more closely connected with another country, in which case the contract shall be governed by the law of that country.

Article 7
Mandatory Rules

1. When applying under this Convention the law of a country, effect may be given to the mandatory rules of the law of another country with which the situation has a close connection, if and in so far as, under the law of the latter country, those rules must be applied whatever the law applicable to the contract. In considering whether to give effect to these mandatory rules, regard shall be had to their nature and purpose and to the consequences of their application or non-application.
2. Nothing in this Convention shall restrict the application of the rules of the law of the forum in a situation where they are mandatory irrespective of the law otherwise applicable to the contract.

Article 8
Material Validity

1. The existence and validity of a contract, or any term of a contract, shall be determined by the law which would govern it under this Convention if the contract or term were valid.
2. Nevertheless a party may rely upon the law of the country in which he has his habitual residence to establish that he did not consent if it appears from the circumstances that it would not be reasonable to determine the effect of his conduct in accordance with the law specified in the preceding paragraph.

Article 9
Formal Validity

1. A contract concluded between persons who are in the same country is formally valid if it satisfies the formal requirements of the law which governs it under this Convention or of the law of the country where it is concluded.
2. A contract concluded between persons who are in different countries is formally valid if it satisfies the formal requirements of the law which governs it under this Convention or of the law of one of those countries.
3. Where a contract is concluded by an agent, the country in which the agent acts is the relevant country for the purposes of paras 1 and 2.
4. An act intended to have legal effect relating to an existing or contemplated contract is formally valid if it satisfies the formal requirements of the law which under this Convention governs or would govern the contract or of the law of the country where the act was done.
5. The provisions of the preceding paragraphs shall not apply to a contract to which Article 5 applies, concluded in the circumstances described in para 2 of Article 5. The formal validity of such a contract is governed by the law of the country in which the consumer has his habitual residence.
6. Notwithstanding paras 1 to 4 of this Article, a contract the subject matter of which is a right in immovable property or a right to use immovable property shall be subject to the mandatory requirements of form of the law of the country where the property is situated if by that law those requirements are imposed irrespective of the country where the contract is concluded and irrespective of the law governing the contract.

Article 10
Scope of the Applicable Law

1. The law applicable to a contract by virtue of Articles 3 to 6 and 12 of this Convention shall govern in particular:
   (a) interpretation;
   (b) performance;
   (c) within the limits of the powers conferred on the court by its procedural law, the consequences of breach, including the assessment of damages in so far as it is governed by rules of law;
   (d) the vicarious ways of extinguishing obligations and prescription and limitation of actions;
   (e) the consequences of nullity of the contract.
2. In relation to the manner of performance and the steps to be taken in the event of defective performance regard shall be had to the law of the country in which performance takes place.

Article 11
Incapacity

In a contract concluded between persons who are in the same country, a natural person who would have capacity under the law of that country may invoke his incapacity resulting from another law only if the other party to the contract was aware of this incapacity at the time of the conclusion of the contract or was not aware thereof as a result of negligence.

Article 12
Voluntary Assignment

1. The mutual obligations of assignor and assignee under a voluntary assignment of a right against another person ('the debtor') shall be governed by the law which under this Convention applies to the contract between the assignor and assignee.
2. The law governing the right to which the assignment relates shall determine its assignability, the relationship between the assignee and the debtor, the conditions under which the assignment can be invoked against the debtor and any question whether the debtor's obligations have been discharged.

Article 13
Subrogation

1. When a person ('the creditor') has a contractual claim upon another ('the debtor'), and a third person has a duty to satisfy the creditor, or has in fact satisfied the creditor in discharge of that duty, the law which governs the third person's duty to satisfy the creditor shall determine whether the third person is entitled to exercise against the debtor the rights which the creditor had against the debtor under the law governing their relationship and, if so, whether he may do so in full or only to a limited extent.
2. The same rule applies where several persons are subject to the same contractual claim and one of them has satisfied the creditor.

Article 14
Burden of Proof

1. The law governing the contract under this Convention applies to the extent that it contains, in the law of contract, rules which raise presumptions of law or determine the burden of proof.

2. A contract or an act intended to have legal effect may be proved by any mode of proof recognised by the law of the forum or by any of the laws referred to in Article 9 under which that contract or act is formally valid, provided that such mode of proof can be administered by the forum.

Article 15
Exclusion of Renvoi

The application of the law of any country specified by this Convention means the application of the rules of law in force in that country other than its rules of private international law.

Article 16
Ordre Public

The application of a rule of law of any country specified by this Convention may be refused only if such application is manifestly incompatible with the public policy ('ordre public') of the forum.

Article 17
Non-retrospective Effect

The Convention shall apply in a Contracting State to contracts made after the date on which this Convention has entered into force with respect to that State.

Article 18
Uniform Interpretation

In the interpretation and application of the preceding uniform rules, regard shall be had to their international character and to the desirability of achieving uniformity in their interpretation and application.

Article 19
States with More Than One Legal System

1. Where a State comprises several territorial units each of which has its own rules of law in respect of contractual obligations, each territorial unit shall be considered as a country for the purposes of identifying the law applicable under this Convention.

2. A State within which different territorial units have their own rules of law in respect of contractual obligations shall not be bound to apply this Convention to conflicts solely between the laws of such units.

Article 20
Precedence of Community Law

This Convention shall not affect the application of provisions which, in relation to particular matters, lay down choice of law rules relating to contractual obligations and which are or will be contained in acts of the institutions of the European Communities or in national laws harmonised in implementation of such acts.

Article 21
Relationship With Other Conventions

This Convention shall not prejudice the application of international conventions to which a Contracting State is, or becomes, a party.

Appendix 2

Second Non-Life Directive (80/934/EEC)

(Official Journal of the European Communities 1988, No L 172/1)

THE COUNCIL OF THE EUROPEAN COMMUNITIES

Having regard to the Treaty establishing the European Economic Community, and in particular Articles 57(2) and 66 thereof,
Having regard to the proposal from the Commission,
in cooperation with the European Parliament,
Having regard to the opinion of the Economic and Social Committee,

3. Whereas, for practical reasons, it is desirable to define the provision of services taking into account both the insurer's establishment and the place where the risk is situated; whereas therefore a definition of the situation of the risk should also be adopted; whereas, moreover, it is desirable to distinguish between the activity pursued by way of establishment and the activity pursued by way of freedom to provide services;

...

4. Whereas policyholders who, by virtue of their status, their size or the nature of the risk to be insured, do not require special protection in the State in which the risk is situated should be granted complete freedom to avail themselves of the widest possible insurance market; whereas, moreover, it is desirable to guarantee other policyholders adequate protection;

...

7. Whereas the provisions in force in the Member States regarding insurance contract law continue to differ; whereas the freedom to choose, as the law applicable so the contract, a law other than that of the State in which the risk is situated may be granted in certain cases, in accordance with rules taking into account specific circumstances;
8. Whereas the scope of this Directive should include compulsory insurance but should require the contract covering such insurance to be in conformity with the specific provisions relating to such insurance, as provided by the Member State imposing the insurance obligation;

...

12. Whereas the taking-up and pursuit of freedom to provide services should be subject to procedures guaranteeing the insurance undertaking's compliance

with the provisions regarding both financial guarantees and conditions of insurance; whereas these procedures may be relaxed in cases where the activity by way of provision of services covers policyholders who, by virtue of their status, their size or the nature of the risk to be insured, do not require special protection in the State in which the risk is situated;

TITLE I
GENERAL PROVISIONS

Article 2

For the purpose of this Directive:

(a) 'first Directive' means: Directive 73/239/EEC;

(b) 'undertaking'
for the purposes of applying Titles I and II, means:
any undertaking which has received official authorisation under Article 6 or 23 of the first Directive,
for the purposes of applying Title III and Title V, means:
any undertaking which has received official authorisation
under Article 6 of the first Directive;

(c) 'establishment':
means the head office, agency or branch of an undertaking account being taken of Article 3;

(d) 'Member State where the risk is situated' means:
the Member State in which the property is situated, where the insurance relates either to buildings or to buildings and their contents, in so far as the contents are covered by the same insurance policy,
the Member State of registration, where the insurance relates to vehicles of any type,
the Member State where the policyholder took out the policy in the case of policies of a duration of four months or less covering travel or holiday risks, whatever the class concerned,
the Member State where the policyholder has his habitual residence or, if the policyholder is a legal person, the Member State where the latter's establishment, to which the contract relates, is situated, in all cases not explicitly covered by the foregoing indents;

(e) 'Member State of establishment' means:
the Member State in which the establishment covering the risk is situated;

(f) 'Member State of provision of services' means:
the Member State in which the risk is situated when it is covered by an establishment situated in another Member State.

TITLE II

PROVISIONS SUPPLEMENTARY TO THE FIRST DIRECTIVE

Article 5

The following is added to Article 5 of the first Directive:

(a) 'large risks' means:

(i) risks classified under classes 4, 5, 6, 7, 11 and 12 of point A of the Annex;

(ii) risks classified under classes 14 and 15 of point A of the Annex, where the policyholder is engaged professionally in an industrial or commercial activity or in one of the liberal professions, and the risks relate to such activity;

(iii) risks classified under classes 8, 9, 13 and 16 of point A of the Annex in so far as the policyholder exceeds the limits of at least two of the following three criteria;

first stage: until 31 December 1992:
balance sheet total: 12, 4 million ECU,
net turnover: 12, 8 million ECU,
average number of employees during the financial year; 250.

If the policyholder belongs to a group of undertakings for which consolidated accounts within the meaning of Directive 83/239/EEC are drawn up, the criteria mentioned above shall be applied on the basis of the consolidated accounts.

Each Member State may add to the category mentioned under (iii) risks insured by professional associations, joint ventures or temporary groupings.

. . .

Article 7

1. The law applicable to contracts of insurance referred to by this Directive and covering risks situated within the Member States is determined in accordance with the following provisions:

(a) Where a policyholder has his habitual residence or central administration within the territory of the Member State in which the risk is situated, the law applicable to the insurance contract shall be the law of that Member State. However, where the law of that Member State so allows, the parties may choose the law of another country.

(b) Where a policyholder does not have his habitual residence or central administration in the Member State in which the risk is situated, the parties to the contract of insurance may choose to apply either the law of the

Member State in which the risk is situated or the law of the country in which the policyholder has his habitual residence or central administration.

(c) Where a policyholder pursues a commercial or industrial activity or a liberal profession and where the contract covers two or more risks relating to these activities and situated in different Member States, the freedom of choice of the law applicable to the contract shall extend to the laws of those Member States and of the country in which the policyholder has his habitual residence or central administration.

(d) Notwithstanding subparagraphs (b) and (c), where the Member States referred to in those subparagraphs grant greater freedom of choice of the law applicable to the contract, the parties may take advantage of this freedom.

(e) Notwithstanding subparagraphs (a), (b) and (c), when the risks covered by the contract are limited to events occurring in one Member State other than the Member State where the risk is situated, as defined in Article 2(d), the parties may always choose the law of the former State.

(f) For the risks referred to in Article 5(d)(i) of the first Directive, the parties to the contract may choose any law.

(g) The fact that, in the cases referred to in subparagraph (a) or (f), the parties have chosen a law shall not, where all the other elements relevant to the situation at the time of the choice are connected with one Member State only, prejudice the application of the mandatory rules of the law of that Member State, which means the rules from which the law of that Member State allows no derogation by means of a contract.

(h) The choice referred to in the preceding subparagraphs must be expressed or demonstrated with reasonable certainty by the terms of the contract or the circumstances of the case. If this is not so, or if no choice has been made, the contract shall be governed by the law of the country, from amongst those considered in the relevant subparagraphs above, with which is most closely connected. Nevertheless, a severable part of the contract which has a closer connection with another country, from amongst those considered in the relevant subparagraphs, may by way of exception be governed by the law of that other country. The contract shall be rebuttably presumed to be most closely connected with the Member State in which the risk is situated.

(i) Where a State includes several territorial units, each of which has its own rules of law concerning contractual obligations, each unit shall be considered as a country for the purposes of identifying the law applicable under this Directive.

A Member State in which various territorial units have their own rules of law concerning contractual obligations shall not be bound to apply the provisions of this Directive to conflicts which arise between the laws of those units.

2. Nothing in this Article shall restrict the application of the rules of the law of the forum in a situation where they are mandatory, irrespective of the law otherwise applicable to the contract.

   If the law of a Member State so stipulates, the mandatory rules of the law of the Member State in which the risk is situated or of the Member State imposing the obligation to take out insurance may be applied if and in so far as, under the law of those States, those rules must be applied whatever the law applicable to the contract.

   Where the contract covers risks situated in more than one Member State, the contract is considered for the purposes of applying this paragraph as constituting several contracts each relating to only one Member State.
3. Subject to the preceding paragraphs, the Member States shall apply to the insurance contracts referred to by this Directive their general rules of private international law concerning contractual obligations.

Article 8

1. Under the conditions set out in this Article, insurance undertakings may offer and conclude compulsory insurance contracts in accordance with the rules of this Directive and of the First Directive.
2. When a Member State imposes an obligation to take out insurance, the contract shall not satisfy that obligation unless it is in accordance with the specific provisions relating to that insurance laid down by that Member State.
3. When, in the case of compulsory insurance, the law of the Member State in which the risk is situated and the law of the Member State imposing the obligation to take out insurance contradict each other, the latter shall prevail.
4. (a) Subject to subparagraphs (b) and (c) of this paragraph, the third subparagraph of Article 7(2) shall apply where the insurance contract provides cover in several Member States of which at least one imposes an obligation to take out insurance.

   (b) A Member State which, on the date of notification of this Directive, requires that any undertaking established within its territory must obtain approval for the general and special conditions of its compulsory insurance, may also, by way of derogation from Articles 9 and 18, require such conditions to be approved in the case of any insurance undertaking offering such cover, within its territory, under the conditions provided for in Article 12(1).

   (c) A Member State may, by way of derogation from Article 7, lay down that the law applicable to a compulsory insurance contract is the law of the State which imposes the obligation to take out insurance.

   (d) Where a Member State imposes compulsory insurance and the insurer must notify the competent authorities of any cessation of cover, such cessation may be invoked against injured third parties only in the circumstances laid down in the legislation of that State.

4. (a) Each Member State shall communicate to the Commission the risks against which insurance is compulsory under its legislation, stating:
   the specific legal provisions relating to that insurance,
   the particulars which must be given in the certificate which an insurer must issue to an insured person where that State requires proof that the obligation to take out insurance has been complied with. A Member State may require that those particulars include a declaration by the insurer to the effect that the contract complies with the specific provisions relating to that insurance.
   (b) The Commission shall publish the particulars referred to in subparagraphs (a) in the *Official Journal of the European Communities.*
   (c) A Member State shall accept, as proof that the insurance obligation has been fulfilled, a certificate, the content of which is in conformity with the second indent of subparagraph (a).

TITLE III

PROVISIONS PECULIAR TO THE FREEDOM TO PROVIDE SERVICES

Article 21

1. Where insurance is offered by way of provision of services, the policyholder shall, before any commitment is entered into, be informed of the Member State in which the head office, agency or branch with which the contract is to be concluded is established.
   Any document issued to the policyholder must contain the information referred to in the preceding subparagraph.
   The requirements in the first two subparagraphs shall not apply to the risks referred to in Article 5(d) of the First Directive.
2. The contract or any other document granting cover, together with the insurance proposal where it is binding upon the proposer, must specify the address of the insurance establishment which is granting the cover and also that of the head office.

Appendix 3

Third Non-Life Directive (92/49/EEC)

(Official Journal of the European Communities 1992, No L 228/11)

Article 27

Article 7(1)(f) of Directive 88/357/EEC shall be replaced by the following:
'(f) in the case of the risks referred to in Article 5(d) of Directive 73/239/EEC, the parties to the contract may choose any law'.

Article 28

The Member State in which a risk is situated shall not prevent a policyholder from concluding a contract with an insurance undertaking authorized under the conditions of Article 6 of Directive 73/239/EEC, as long as that does not conflict with legal provisions protecting the general good in the Member State in which the risk is situated.

Article 31

1. Before an insurance contract is concluded the insurance undertaking shall inform the policyholder of:
   —the law applicable to the contract where the parties do not have a free choice, or the fact that the parties are free to choose the law applicable and, in the latter case, the law the insurer proposes to choose,
   —the arrangements for handling policyholders' complaints concerning contracts including, where appropriate, the existence of a complaints body, without prejudice to the policyholder's right to take legal proceedings.
2. The obligation referred to in paragraph 1 shall apply only where the policyholder is a natural person.
3. The rules for implementing this Article shall be determined in accordance with the law of the Member State in which the risk is situated.

Appendix 4

Second Life Assurance Directive (99/619/EEC)

(Official Journal of the European Communities 1990, No L 330/50)

THE COUNCIL OF THE EUROPEAN COMMUNITIES,
Having regard to the Treaty establishing the European Economic Community, and in particular Articles 57(2) and 66 thereof,

Having regard to the opinion of the Economic and Social Committee,

. . .

4. Whereas, for practical reasons, it is desirable to define provisions of services taking into account both the assurer's establishment and the place where the commitment should also be defined; whereas, moreover, it is desirable to distinguish between activities pursued by way of establishment and activities pursued by way of freedom to provide services;

. . .

5. Whereas policyholders who, by virtue of the fact that they take the initiative in entering into a commitment in another State and thus place themselves under the protection of the legal system of that other State, do not require special protection in the State of the commitment, should be granted complete freedom to avail themselves of the widest possible market in life assurance and in the operations referred to in the First Directive; whereas other policyholders should also be afforded adequate protection;

. . .

7. Whereas the provisions in force in the Member States regarding contract law applicable to the activities referred to in the First Directive continue to differ; whereas the freedom to choose, as the law applicable to the contract, a law other than of the State of the commitment may be granted in certain cases, in accordance with rules which take into account specific circumstances;

. . .

11. whereas for life assurance contracts entered into by way of the free provision of services the policyholder should be given the opportunity of cancelling the contract within a period between 14 and 30 days;

HAS ADOPTED THIS DIRECTIVE:

TITLE I

GENERAL PROVISIONS

Article 2

For the purposes of this Directive:

(a) 'First Directive' means Directive 79/267/EEC;

(b) 'undertaking':

—for the purposes of Titles I and II, means any undertaking which has received official authorization under Article 6 or Article 27 of the First Directive;

—for the purposes of Titles III and IV, means any undertaking which has received official authorization under Article 6 of the First Directive;

(c) 'establishment:

—means the head office, an agency or a branch of an undertaking, having regard to Article 3;

(d) 'commitment':

—means a commitment represented by one of the kinds of insurance or operation referred to in Article 1 of the First Directive;

(e) 'Member State of the commitment':

—means the Member State where the policyholder has his habitual residence or, if the policyholder is a legal person, the Member State where the latter's establishment, to which the contract relates is situated;

(f) 'Member State of establishment':

—means the Member State in which the establishment covering the commitment is situated;

(g) 'Member State of provision of services':

—means the Member State of the commitment where the commitment is covered by an establishment situated in another Member State;

. . .

TITLE II

PROVISIONS SUPPLEMENTARY TO THE FIRST DIRECTIVE

Article 4

1. The law applicable to contracts relating to the activities referred to in the First Directive shall be the law of the Member State of the commitment. However, where the law of that State so allows, the parties may choose the law of another country.
2. Where the policyholder is a natural person and has his habitual residence in a Member State other than that of which he is a national, the parties may choose the law of the Member State of which he is a national.

3. Where a State includes several territorial units, each of which has its own rules of law concerning contractual obligations, each unit shall be considered a country for the purposes of identifying the law applicable under this Directive.
   A Member State in which various territorial units have their own rules of law concerning contractual obligations shall not be bound to apply the provisions of this Directive to conflicts which arise between the laws of those units.
4. Nothing in this Article shall restrict the application of the rules of the law of the forum in a situation where they are mandatory, irrespective of the law otherwise applicable to the contract.
   If the law of a Member State so stipulates, the mandatory rules of the law of the Member State of the commitment may be applied and in so far as, under the law of that Member State, those rules must be applied whatever the law applicable to the contract.
5. Subject to the preceding paragraphs, the Member States shall apply to the assurance contracts referred to in this Directive their general rules of private international law concerning contractual obligations.

TITLE II

PROVISIONS RELATING SPECIFICALLY TO THE FREEDOM TO PROVIDE SERVICES

Article 13

1. Commitments covered by way of freedom to provide services shall be subject to Article 14 where the policyholder takes the initiative in seeking a commitment from the undertaking.
   The policyholder shall be deemed to have taken the initiative:
   —where, on the one hand, the contract is entered into by both parties in the Member State in which the undertaking is established or by each of the parties in that party's own State of establishment or of habitual residence, and where, on the other hand, the policyholder has not been contracted in his State of habitual residence by the undertaking or through an insurance intermediary or any person authorized to act for it or by means of any solicitation of business addressed to him personally.
   —where the policyholder approaches an intermediary established in the Member State in which the policyholder has his habitual residence and carrying on the professional activities defined in Article 2(1)(a) of Directive 77/92/EEC, in order to obtain information on assurance contracts offered by undertakings established in Member States other than his State of habitual residence or with a view to entering into a commitment through the intermediary with such an undertaking. In that event the policyholder shall sign a statement, the text of which is set out, under item A in the Annex, expressly so requesting.

2. Before entering into a commitment in the cases referred to in the first and second indents of paragraph 1, the policyholder shall sign a statement, the text of which is set out under item B in the Annex, to the effect that he notes that the commitment is subject to the rules of supervision of the Member State of establishment which is to cover the commitment.

Article 14

1. Each Member State within whose territory an undertaking intends, by way of freedom to provide services, to cover commitments in accordance with Article 13 shall require that the undertaking abide by the following procedure:
   (a) production of a certificate issued by the competent authorities of the head office Member State certifying that it possesses for its activities as a whole the minimum solvency margin calculated in accordance with Article 19 of the First Directive and that, in accordance with Article 16(1) of the said Directive, the authorization enables the undertaking to operate outside the Member State of establishment;
   (b) production of a certificate issued by the competent authorities of the Member State of establishment indicating the classes in respect of which the undertaking is authorized to transact business and certifying that those authorities do not object to the undertaking's transacting business by way of freedom to provide services;
   (c) statement of the nature of the commitments which it proposes to cover in the Member State of provision of services.

   The above procedure shall not apply where an activity falling within this Directive is not subject, in the Member State of the commitments, to supervision by the administrative authorities responsible for supervising private insurance.
2. Each Member State shall make provision for the right to apply to the courts in respect of a refusal to issue the certificate referred to in paragraph 1(a) or (b).
3. The undertaking may commence activities as from the certified date on which the authorities of the Member State of provision of services are in possession of the documents referred to in paragraph 1.
4. This Article shall also apply where the Member State in whose territory an undertaking intends, by way of freedom to provide services, to cover commitments in accordance with arrangements other than those referred to in Article 13 of this Directive does not make the taking-up of such activity conditional on official authorization.
5. Member States may not prevent the policyholder from entering into any commitment which may be lawfully undertaken in the Member State of establishment unless it is contrary to public policy in the Member State of the commitment.

Appendix 5

Third Life Assurance Directive (92/96/EEC)

(Official Journal of the European Communities 1992, No L 360/27)

TITLE III

HARMONISATION OF THE CONDITIONS GOVERNING PURSUIT OF BUSINESS

Article 28

The Member State in which a risk is situated shall not prevent a policyholder from concluding a contract with an insurance undertaking authorised under the conditions of Article 6 of Directive 73/239/EEC, as long as that does not conflict with legal provisions protecting the general good in the Member State in which the risk is situated.

ARTICLE 31

1. Before the assurance contract is concluded, at least the information listed in point A of Annex II shall be communicated to the policyholder.
2. The policyholder shall be kept informed throughout the term of the contract of nay chance concerning the information listed in point B of Annex II.
3. The Member State of the commitment may require assurance undertakings to furnish information in addition to that listed in Annex II only if it is necessary for a proper understanding by the policyholder of the essential elements of the commitment.
4. The detailed rules for implementing this Article and Annex II shall be laid down by the Member State of the commitment.

Appendix 6

Council Regulation on Jurisdiction and the Recognition and Enforcement of Judgments in Civil and Commercial Matters (EC/No 44/2001)

(Official Journal of the European Communities 2001, No L 0/12)

CHAPTER I

SCOPE

Article 1

1. This Regulation shall apply in civil and commercial matters whatever the nature of the court or tribunal. It shall not extend, in particular, to revenue, customs or administrative matters
2. The Regulation shall not apply to:
   (a) the status or legal capacity of natural persons, rights in property arising out of a matrimonial relationship, wills and succession;
   (b) bankruptcy, proceedings relating to the winding-up of insolvent companies or other legal persons, judicial arrangements, compositions and analogous proceedings;
   (c) social security;
   (d) arbitration.
3. In this Regulation, the term 'Member State' shall mean Member States with the exception of Denmark.

CHAPTER II

JURISDICTION

Section 1
General Provisions

Article 2

1. Subject to this Regulation, persons domiciled in a Member State shall, whatever their nationality, be sued in the courts of that Member State.
2. Persons who are not nationals of the Member State in which they are domiciled shall be governed by the rules of jurisdiction applicable to nationals of that State.

. . .

Article 4

1. If the defendant is not domiciled in a Member State, the jurisdiction of the courts of each Member State shall, subject to Articles 22 and 23, be determined by the law of that Member State.
2. As against such a defendant, any person domiciled in a Member State may, whatever his nationality, avail himself in that State of the rules of jurisdiction there in force, and in particular those specified in Annex I, in the same way as the nationals of that State.

Section 2
Special Jurisdiction

Article 5

A person domiciled in a Member State may, in another Member State, be sued:

. . .

3. in matters relating to torts, *delict or quasi-delict*, in the courts for the place where the harmful event occurred or may occur;

. . .

4. as regards a dispute arising out of the operations of a branch, agency or other establishment, in the courts for the place in which the branch, agency or other establishment is situated;

. . .

Article 6

A person domiciled in a Member State may also be sued:

1. where he is one of a number of defendants, in the courts for the place where any one of them is domiciled, provided the claims are so closely connected that it is expedient to hear and determine them together to avoid the risk of irreconcilable judgments resulting from separate proceedings;
2. as a third party in an action on a warranty or guarantee or in any other third party proceedings, in the court seized of the original proceedings, unless these were instituted solely with the object of removing him from the jurisdiction of the court which would be competent in his case;
3. on a counter-claim arising from the same contract or facts on which the original claim is pending;
4. in matters relating to a contract, if the action may be combined with an action against the same defendant in matters relating to rights in *rem* in immovable property, in the court of the Member State in which the property is situated.

. . .

Section 3
Jurisdiction in Matters Relating to Insurance

Article 8

In matters relating to insurance, jurisdiction shall be determined by this Section, without prejudice to Article 4 and point 5 of Article 5.

Article 9

1. An insurer domiciled in a Member State may be sued:
   (a) in the courts of the Member State where he is domiciled,
   or
   (b) in another Member State, in the case of actions brought by the policyholder, the insured or a beneficiary, in the courts for the place where the plaintiff is domiciled,
   (c) if he is a co-insurer, in the courts of a Member State in which proceedings are brought against the leading insurer.
2. An insurer who is not domiciled in a Member State but has a branch, agency or other establishment in one of the Member States shall, in disputes arising out of the operations of the branch, agency or establishment, be deemed to be domiciled in that Member State.

Article 10

In respect of liability insurance or insurance of immovable property, the insurer may in addition be sued in the courts for the place where the harmful event occurred. The same applies if movable and immovable property are covered by the same insurance policy and both are adversely affected by the same contingency.

Article 11

1. In respect of liability insurance, the insurer may also, if the law of the court permits it, be joined in proceedings which the injured party has brought against the insured.
2. Articles 8, 9 and 10 shall apply to actions brought by the injured party directly against the insurer, where such direct actions are permitted.
3. If the law governing such direct actions provides that the policyholder or the insured may be joined as a party to the action, the same court shall have jurisdiction over them.

Article 12

1. Without prejudice to Article 11(3), an insurer may bring proceedings only in the courts of the Member State in which the defendant is domiciled, irrespective of whether he his the policyholder, the insured or a beneficiary.
2. The provisions of this Section shall not affect the right to bring a counter claim in the court in which, in accordance with this Section, the original claim is pending.

Article 13

The provisions of this Section may be departed from only by an agreement:
1. which is entered into after the dispute has arisen, or
2. which allows the policyholder, the insured or a beneficiary to bring proceeding in courts other than those indicated in this Section, or
3. which is concluded between a policyholder and an insurer, both of whom are at the time of conclusion of the contract domiciled or habitually resident in the same Member State, and which has the effect of conferring jurisdiction on the courts of that State even if the harmful event were to occur abroad, provided that such an agreement is not contrary to the law of that State, or
4. which is concluded with a policyholder who is not domiciled in a Member State, except in so far as the insurance is compulsory or relates to immovable property in a Member State, or

5. which relates to a contract of insurance in so far as it covers one or more of the risks set out in Article 14.

Article 14

The following are the risks referred to in Article 13(5):

1. any loss of or damage to:
   (a) seagoing ships, installations situated offshore or on the high seas, or aircraft, arising from perils which relate to their use for commercial purposes;
   (b) goods in transit other than passengers' baggage where the transit consists of or includes carriage by such ships or aircraft;
2. any liability, other than for bodily injury to passengers or loss of or damage to their baggage:
   (c) arising out of the use or operation of ships, installations or aircraft as referred to in point 1(a) in so far as, in respect of the latter, the law of the Member State in which such aircraft are registered does not prohibit agreements on jurisdiction regarding insurance of such risks;
   (d) for loss or damage caused by goods in transit as described in point 1(b);
3. any financial loss connected with the use or operation of ships, installations or aircraft as referred to in point 1(a), in particular loss of freight or charter-hire;
4. any risk or interest connected with any of those referred to in points 1 to 3;
5. notwithstanding points 1 to 4, all 'large risks' as defined in Council Directive 73/239/EEC,[1] as amended by Council Directives 88/357/EEC[2] and 90/618/EEC,[3] as they may be amended.

Section 4
Jurisdiction Over Consumer Contracts

Article 15

1. In matters relating to a contract concluded by a person, the consumer, for a purpose which can be regarded as being outside his trade or profession, jurisdiction shall be determined by this Section, without prejudice to Article 4 and point 5 of Article 5, if:
   (a) it is a contract for the sale of goods on instalment credit terms; or
   (b) it is a contract for a loan repayable by instalments, or for any other form of credit, made to finance the sale of goods; or

[1] OJ L228, 16.8.1973, 3. Directive as last amended by Directive 2000/26/EC of the European Parliament and of the Council OJ L 181, 20.7.2000, 65.

[2] OJ L 172, 4. 7. 1988, 1. Directive as last amended by Directive 2000/26/EC.

[3] OJ L330, 29.11.1990, 44.

(c) in all other cases, the contract has been concluded with a person who pursues commercial or professional activities in the Member State of the consumer's domicile or, by any means, directs such activities to that Member State or to several States including that Member State, and the contract falls within the scope of such activities.

2. Where a consumer enters into a contract with a party who is not domiciled in the Member State but has a branch, agency or other establishment in one of the Member States, that party shall, in dispute arising out of the operations of the branch, agency or establishment, be deemed to be domiciled in that State.
3. This Section shall not apply to a contract of transport other than a contract which, for an inclusive price, provides for a combination of travel and accommodation.

Article 16

1. A consumer may bring proceedings against the other party to a contract either in the courts of the Member State in which that party is domiciled or in the courts for the place where the consumer is domiciled.
2. Proceedings may be brought against a consumer by the other party to the contract only in the courts of the Member State in which the consumer is domiciled.
3. This Article shall not affect the right to bring a counter-claim in the court in which, in accordance with this Section, the original claim is pending.

Article 17

The provisions of this Section may be departed from only by an agreement:
1. which is entered into after the dispute has arisen; or
2. which allows the consumer to bring proceedings in courts other than those indicated in this Section; or
3. which is entered into by the consumer and the other party to the contract, both of whom are at the time of conclusion of the contract domiciled or habitually resident in the same Member State, and which confers jurisdiction on the courts of that Member State, provided that such an agreement is not contrary to the law of that Member State.

. . .

Section 7
Prorogation of Jurisdiction

Article 23

1. If the parties, one or more of whom is domiciled in a Member State, have agreed that a court or the courts of a Member State are to have jurisdiction to settle any disputes which have arisen or which may arise in connection with a particular legal relationship, that court or those courts shall have jurisdiction.
2. Such jurisdiction shall be exclusive unless the parties have agreed otherwise. Such an agreement conferring jurisdiction shall be either:
   (a) in writing or evidenced in writing: or
   (b) in a form which accords with practices which the parties have established between themselves; or
   (c) in international trade or commerce, in a form which accords with a usage of which the parties are or ought to have been aware and which in such trade or commerce is widely known to, and regularly observed by, parties to contracts of the type involved in the particular trade or commerce concerned;
3. Any communication by electronic means which provides a durable record of the agreement shall be equivalent to 'writing'.
4. Where such an agreement is concluded by parties, none of whom is domiciled in a Member State, the courts of other Member States shall have no jurisdiction over their disputes unless the court or courts chosen have declined jurisdiction.

. . .

Article 24

Apart from jurisdiction derived from other provisions of this Regulation, a court of a Member State before which a defendant enters an appearance shall have jurisdiction. This rule shall not apply where appearance was entered to contest the jurisdiction, or where another court has jurisdiction by virtue of Article 22.

. . .

Section 9
Lis Pendens—Related Actions

Article 27

1. Where proceedings involving the same cause of action and between the same parties are brought in the courts of different Member States, any court other than the court first seized shall of its own motion stay its proceedings until such time as the jurisdiction of the court first seized is established.
2. Where the jurisdiction of the court first seized is established, any court other than the court first seized shall decline jurisdiction in favour of that court.

Article 28

1. Where related actions are pending in the courts of different Member States, any court other than the court first seized may stay its proceedings,
2. Where these actions are pending at first instance, any court other than the court first seized may also, on the application of one of the parties, decline jurisdiction if the court first seized has jurisdiction over the actions in question and its law permits the consolidation thereof.
3. For the purposes of this Article, actions are deemed to be related where they are so closely connected that it is expedient to hear and determine them together to avoid the risk of irreconcilable judgments resulting from separate proceedings.

. . .

CHAPTER III
RECOGNITION AND ENFORCEMENT

Article 32

For the purposes of this Regulation, 'judgment' means any judgment given by a court or tribunal of a Member State, whatever the judgment may be called including a decree, order decision or writ of execution, as well as the determination of costs or expenses by an officer of the court.

Section 1
Recognition

Article 33

1. A judgment given in a Member State shall be recognised in the other Member States without any special procedure being required.

2. Any interested party who raises the recognition of a judgment as the principal issue in a dispute may, in accordance with the procedures provided for in Sections 2 and 3 of this Chapter, apply for a decision that the judgment be recognised.
3. If the outcome of proceedings in a court of a Member State depends on the determination of an incidental question of recognition that court shall have jurisdiction over that question.

Article 34

A judgment shall not be recognised:
1. if such recognition is manifestly contrary to public policy in the Member State in which recognition is sought;
2. where it was given in default of appearance, if the defendant was not served with the document which instituted the proceedings or with an equivalent document in sufficient time and in such a way as to enable him to arrange for his defence, unless the defendant failed to commence proceedings to challenge the judgment when it was possible for him to do so;
3. if it is irreconcilable with a judgment given in a dispute between the same parties in the Member State in which recognition is sought;
4. if it is irreconcilable with an earlier judgment given in another Member State or in a third State involving the same cause of action and between the same parties provided that the earlier judgment fulfils the conditions necessary for its recognition in the Member State addressed.

Article 35

1. Moreover, a judgment shall not be recognised if it conflicts with Sections 3, 4 or 6 of Chapter II, or in a case provided for in Article 72.
2. In its examination of the grounds of jurisdiction referred to in the foregoing paragraph, the court or authority applied to shall be bound by the findings of fact on which the court of the Member State of origin based its jurisdiction.
3. Subject to paragraph 1, the jurisdiction of the court of the Member State of origin may not be reviewed. The test of public policy referred to in point 1 of Article 34 may not be applied to the rules relating to jurisdiction.

Article 36

Under no circumstances may a foreign judgment be reviewed as to its substance.

. . .

Section 2
Enforcement

Article 38

1. A judgment given in a Member State and enforceable in that State shall be enforced in another Member State when, on the application of any interested party, it has been declared enforceable there.
2. However, in the United Kingdom, such a judgment shall be enforced in England and Wales, in Scotland and Northern Ireland when, on the application of any interested party, it has been registered for enforcement in that part of the United Kingdom.

. . .

Article 41

The judgment shall be declared enforceable immediately on completion of the formalities in Article 53 without any review under Articles 34 and 35. The party against whom enforcement is sought shall not at this stage of the proceedings be entitled to make any submission on the application.

CHAPTER IV
AUTHENTIC INSTRUMENTS AND COURT SETTLEMENTS

Article 57

1. A document which has been formally drawn up or registered as an authentic instrument and is enforceable in one Member State shall, in another Member State, be declared enforceable there, on application made in accordance with the procedures provided for in Articles 38, *et seq*. The court with which an appeal is lodged under Article 43 or Article 44 shall refuse or revoke a declaration of enforceability only if enforcement of the instrument is manifestly contrary to public policy in the Member State addressed.
2. Arrangements relating to maintenance obligations concluded with administrative authorities or authenticated by them shall also be regarded as authentic instruments within the meaning of paragraph 1.
3. The instrument produced must satisfy the conditions necessary to establish its authenticity in the Member State of origin.
4. Section 3 of Chapter II shall apply as appropriate. The competent authority of a Member State where an authentic instrument was drawn up or registered shall issue, at the request of any interested party, a certificate using the standard form in Annex VI to this Regulation.

Article 58

A settlement which has been approved by a court in the course of proceedings and is enforceable in the Member State in which it was concluded shall be enforceable in the State addressed under the same conditions as authentic instruments. The court or competent authority of a Member State where a court settlement was approved shall issue, at the request of any interested party, a certificate using the standard form in Annex V to this Regulation.

Bibliography

BOOKS, MONOGRAPHS AND THESES

Anton and Beaumont, *Civil Jurisdiction in Scotland*, 2nd edn (1995).

——*Private International Law: A treatise from the standpoint of Scots law*, 2nd edn (1990).

Auclair, *La loi applicable au contrat d'assurance communautaire d'assurance: etude de droit international privé* (Doctoral thesis, University of Paris 'La Sorbonne', 1999).

Audit, *Droit international privé* (1991).

Badiali, *Le droit international privé des Communautés europeenes*, in Hague Recueil, II, 1985.

Ballarino, *Diritto internazionale privato*, with the assistance of A Bonomi, 3rd edn (1999).

——*Internet nel mondo della legge* (1998).

——*Lineamenti di diritto comunitario e dell'Unione Europea*, 5th edn (1999).

——(ed), *La convenzione di Roma sulla legge applicabile alle obbligazioni contrattuali, II, Limiti di applicazione*, Lectio notariorum (1994).

Baratta, *Il criterio del collegamento più stretto nel diritto internazionale privato dei contratti* (1991).

Bariatti, *L'interpretazione delle convenzioni internazionali di diritto uniforme* (1986).

Basedow, *Le droit international privé des assurances. Collection d'etudes sur le droit des assurances*, T XX (1939).

Bennett, *Law of Marine Insurance* (1996).

Bianca and Giardina (eds), *Commentario alla Convenzione sulla legge applicabile alle obbligazioni contrattuali*, NLCC, 1995, pp 902–1127.

Birds' *Modern Insurance Law* (2000).

Blanco Morales Limones, *El seguro español en el Derecho internacional privado (Derecho comunitario)* (1989).

Boggiano, *International Standard Contracts. The price of fairness* (1991).

Bonolis, *Les assurances sur la vie en droit international privé*, Ouvrage traduit et annoté par J Valery et J Lefort (1902).

Bonomi, *Le norme imperative nel diritto internazionale privato* (1998).

Boschiero, *Appunti sulla riforma del sistema italiano di diritto internazionale privato* (1996).

Broggini (ed), *Il nuovo diritto internazional privato in Svizzera* (1987).

Bucher, 'L'ordre public et le but social du lois en droit international privé', Hague, 1993, I, pp 9–116.

——*Droit international privé suisse* (1988).

Briggs and Rees, *Civil Jurisdiction and Judgments*, 3nd edn (2001).

Brulhart, *La competence internationale en matiere d'assurance dans l'espace judiciaire européen* (1997).

Calvo Caravaca (ed), *Contratos internacionales* (1997).

Calvo Caravaca (ed), *Comentario al Convenio de Bruselas de 27 septiembre 1968 relativo a la competencia judicial y al reconocimento de resoluciones judiciales en materia civil y mercantil* (1995).
Campeis-De Pauli, *La procedura civile internazionale* (1991).
Capotorti, Di Sabato, Patroni Griffi, Picone, Ubertazzi, *Il fenomeno delle concentrazioni di imprese nel diritto interno e internazionale* (1989).
Carbone, *Lo spazio giudiziario europeo. Le Convenzioni di Bruxelles e di Lugano* (1995).
Carbone and Ivaldi, *Lezioni di diritto internazionale privato* (2000).
Carella, *Autonomia della volontà e scelta di legge nel diritto internazionale privato* (1999).
Carey Miller and Beaumont, *The option of litigating in Europe* (1993).
Carnaham, *Conflict of Laws and Life Insurance Contracts* (1958).
Carrascosa Gonzalez, *El contrato internacional (Fraccionamento versus unidad)* (1992).
Carrillo Salcedo, *Le renouveau du particularisme en droit international privé*, Hague Recueil, II, 1978.
Castangia, *Il criterio di collegamento della cittadinanza nel diritto internazionale privato* (1984).
Castel, *Canadian Conflicts of Law*, 2nd edn (1986).
Celle, *I contratti di assicurazione grandi rischi nel diritto internazionale privato* (2000).
Cheshire and North, *Private International Law*, by PM North and JJ Fawcett, 13th edn (1999).
Claret, *Contrats d'assurance et conflits de lois en droit communautaire* (Doctoral Thesis, University of Lille, 1994).
Clarke, *The Law of insurance contracts*, 3rd edn (1997).
——*Policies and perception of insurance: an introduction to insurance law* (1997).
Clifford Chance (ed), *Insurance Regulation in Europe* (1993).
Collins, *Essays in International Litigation and the Conflict of Laws* (1997).
Craig and de Burca, *EU Law: text, cases and materials*, 2nd edn (1998).
Crawford, *International Private Law* (1998).
Curti Gialdino, L'autonomie de la volonté de parties en droit international privé, Hague Recueil, III, 1972, pp 745–914.
Daintith (ed), *Implementing EC Law in the United Kingdom: Structures for indirect rule* (1997).
Daniele, *Il diritto materiale della Comunità Europea: introduzione allo studio delle libertà di circolazione e delle politiche comunitarie*, 2nd edn (1995).
Davi', *La responsabilita' extracontrattuale nel nuovo diritto internazionale privato italiano* (1997).
De Donatis, *L'autonomia delle parti e la scelta della legge applicabile al contratto internazionale* (1991).
Deidda, *Il sistema internazionale del certificato di assicurazione* (1986).
Di Blase, *Connessione e litispendenza nella Convenzione di Bruxelles* (1993).
Dicey and Morris, *The Conflicts of Laws*, by L Collins and others, 13th edn (2000).
Dolinger, 'Evolution and Principles for Resolving Conflicts in the Field of Contracts and Torts', Hague Recueil, 2000, I, pp 187–512.
Draetta e Parisi, *Elementi di diritto dell'Unione Europea: parte speciale—il diritto sostanziale*, 2nd edn (1999).
Droz, *Compétence judiciaire et effets de jugements dans le Marché Commun* (1972).
Dubler, *Le clauses d'exception en droit international privé* (1983).

Dubuisson, *Le droit applicable au contrat d'assurance dans un espace Communautaire integré*, (Doctoral thesis, Université Catholique de Louvain, 1994).
Ellis, *European Integration and Insurance* (1980).
Fallon, *Les accidents de la consommation et le droit* (1982).
——*Les conflits de lois et de jurisdictions dans un espace économique intégré. L'espérience de la Communauté Européenne*, in Hague Recueil, II, 1995.
Fallon and Rigaux, *Droit international privé 2, Droit positif belge*, 2nd edn (1993).
Fawcett, *Product Liability in Private International Law: A European perspective*, in Hague Recueil, I, 1993.
——(ed), *Declining Jurisdiction in Private International Law* (1995).
Fentiman, *Foreign law in English Courts* (1998).
——Nuyts, Tagaras and Watté, *L'espace judiciaire européen en matières civile et commerciale/ The European Judicial Area in Civil and Commercial Matters* (1999).
Fernández Arroyo, *La codificación del Derecho internacional privado en América Latina* (1994).
Fernandez Rozas y Sanchez Lorenzo, *Curso de Derecho internacional privado*, 3rd edn (1996).
Ferrari Bravo, Les rapports entre les contrats e les obligations délictuelles en droit international privé, Hague Recueil, III, 1975, pp 347 *et seq*.
Ferry (C), *La validité des contrats en droit international privé* (1989).
Fletcher, *Conflict of Laws and European Community Law* (1982).
Forget, *Les conflits de loi en matiere de la circulation routière* (1973).
Frignani, *Il contratto internazionale* (1990).
Frigessi di Rattalma, *Il contratto internazionale di assicurazione* (1990).
Frigessi di Rattalma and Seatzu (eds), *The Implementation Provisions of the EC Choice of Law Rules for Insurance Contracts in Belgium, Frace, Germany, Italy, The Netherlands, Spain and the United Kingdom* (Kluwer Law International, 2003 forthcoming).
Fuentes Camacho, *Los contratos de seguro y el Derecho Internacional Privado en la Unión Europea* (1999).
Garau Juaneda, *El seguro de responsabilidad civil pour el uso de automóviles en derecho internacional privado* (1977).
Gaudemet Tallon, *Les Conventions de Bruxelles et de Lugano: competence internationale, reconnaisance et execution des jugements en Europe* (1996).
Giardina and Villani, *Garanzie bancarie, commercio internazionale e diritto internazionale privato* (1984).
Gothot and Holleaux, *La Convention de Bruxelles du 27.9.1968* (1985).
Hartley, 'Mandatory Rules in International Contracts: The Common Law Aprroach', Hague Recueil, 1997, IV, pp 337–426.
Hay, 'Flexibility versus Predictability and Uniformity in Choice of Law, Reflections on Current European and United States Conflicts Law', II, Hague Recueil, 281–412.
Hertz, (K), *Jurisdiction in Contracts and Torts* (1998).
Hill, *The law relating to international commercial disputes*, 2nd edn (1998).
Imhoff-Scheier, *Protection du consommateur et contrats internationaux* (1981).
Jacquet, *Le contrat international* (1992).
——*Principe d'autonomie et contrats internationaux* (1989).
Jayme e Picchio Forlati (eds), *Giurisdizione e legge applicabile ai contratti nella CEE* (1990).

Kahn Freund, 'General Problems of Private International Law', Hague Recueil, 1974, II, pp 1–340.
Kassis, *Le noveau droit européen des contrats internationaux* (1993).
Kaye, *Civil Jurisdiction and Enforcement of Foreign Judgments* (1987).
——*The New Private International Law of Contracts of the European Community* (1993).
Kennett, *Enforcement of Judgments in Europe* (2000).
Kessedjian, *Internet: which court decides? which law applies? Quel tribunal decide? Quel droit s'applique?* (1998).
Kropholler, *Europäisches Zivilprozessrecht, Kommentar zum Eu*GVU, 4th edn (1993).
Lasok and Stone, *Conflict of Laws in the European Communities* (1987).
Leclerc, *La protection de la partie faible dans le contrats internationaux (Etude de conflits de lois)* (1995).
Lenaerts and Bray, *Constitutional Law of the European Union* (1999).
——*Procedural Law of the European Union* (1999).
Lenaerts and van Nuffel, *Constitutional Law of the European Union* (1999).
Levie (G), *Droit européen des assurances* (1992).
Lipstein (ed), *Harmonisation of Private International Law by the EEC* (1977).
Loussouarn and Bourel, *Précis de droit international privé*, 4th edn (1993).
Lowry and Rawlings, *Insurance law—Doctrines Principles* (1999).
Lugato, *Assicurazioni sociali e diritto internazionale privato* (1994).
Magagni, *La prestazione caratteristica caratteristica nella Convenzione di Roma sulla legge applicabile alle obbligazioni contrattuali* (1989).
Malatesta, *La cessione del credito nel diritto internazionale privato* (1996).
Mari, *Il diritto processuale civile della Convenzione di Bruxelles—Il sistema della competenza* (1999).
Marini, *Commercio Elettronico—Profili di diritto comunitario* (1998).
McClean, '*De Conflictu Legum*. Perspectives on Private International Law at the Turn of the Century. General Course on Private International Law' Hague Recueil, I, 2000, 41–228.
Mercier and Dutuoit, *L'Europe judiciarie: Le Conventions de Bruxelles et de Lugano* (1995).
Merkin and Rodger, *EC Insurance Law* (1997).
Mistelis, *Characterisierungen und Qualifikation im internationalen Privatrecht* (1999).
Monaco, 'Les assurances en droit international', Hague Reueil, II, 1960, pp 381 ff.
Morse (CGJ), *Torts in private international law* (1978).
Mosconi, *Diritto internazionale privato e processuale—Parte generale e contratti* (1999).
North (ed), *Contract Conflicts* (1982).
North, 'Reform, but not Revolution', Hague Recueil, I, 1990, pp 13–288.
Nygh, *Autonomy in International Contracts* (1999).
O'Malley and Layton, *European Civil Practice* (1989).
Orlando, *Il problema internazional privatistico nell'ordinamento comunitario europeo* (1981).
Paul Croly, *EC Insurance Law* (1991).
Philip, 'General Course on Private International Law', Hague Recueil, I, 1978, pp 9–73.
Picone, 'Les methods de coordination entre ordre juridiques en droit international privé', Hague Recueil, II, 1999, pp 1–296.
——, *La riforma italiana del diritto internazionale privato* (1998).

Plender, *The European Contracts Convention* (2001).
Pocar, *Il diritto dell'Unione e delle Comunità Europee*, 6th edn (2000).
——*Il nuovo diritto internazionale privato italiano*, with the assistance of C Honorati (1997).
——Treves, Carbone, Giardina, Luzzato, Mosconi, Clerici (eds), *Commentario del nuovo diritto internazionale privato italiano* (1996).
——*La Convenzione di Bruxelles sulla giurisdizione e l'esecuzione delle sentenze straniere*, 3rd edn, with the assistence of S Bariatti (1995).
——*La protection de la partie faible en droit international privé*, Hague Recueil, V, 1984.
Pommier, *Principe d'autonomie et loi du contrat en droit international privé conventionnel* (1992).
Pool, *The Creation of the Internal Market in Insurance* (1990).
Pryles, 'Tort and Related Obligations in Private International Law', Hague Recueil, II, 1991, pp 9–206.
Queirolo, *Gli accordi sulla competenza giurisdizionale. Tra diritto comunitario e diritto interno* (2000).
Quigley, *Droit communautiare des contrats: l'effet du droit communautaire sur les obligations contractuelles* (1998).
Radicati di Brozolo, *Operazioni bancarie internazionali e conflitti di leggi* (1984).
Rammeloo, *Corporations in Private International Law: A European Perspective* (2001).
——*Das neue EG-Vertaskollisionrecht* (1992).
Reicher-Facilides and Jessurum d'Oliveira (eds), *International insurance contract law in the EC: proceedings of a comparative law conference held at the European University Institute Florence, May 23–24 1991* (1993).
Rigaux (F), 'Les situations juridiques individuelles dans un système de relativité générale', Hague Recueil, I, 1989, pp 1–407.
Rigaux and Fallon, *Précis de droit international privé*, t. II, 2nd edn (1993).
Robertson, *Characterisation in the Conflict of Laws* (1940).
Rose (ed), *Lex Mercatoria: Essays on International Commercial Law in Honour of Francis Reynolds* (2000).
Rossolillo, *Mutuo riconoscimento e tecniche conflittuali* (2002).
Roth, *Internationales Versicherungsvertragsrecht* (1985).
Sacerdoti e Frigo (eds), *La Convenzione di Roma sul diritto applicabile ai contratti internazionali*, 2nd edn (1994).
Salerno (ed), *La Convenzione di Bruxelles del 1968 e la sua revisione* (2000).
Sarcevic (ed), *International Contracts and Conflicts of Laws* (1990).
Saulle, *Diritto comunitario e diritto internazionale privato* (1983).
Schlosser, 'Jurisdiction and International Judical and Administrative Co-operation', Hague Recueil, I, 2000, pp 9–428.
Schnyder, *Internationale Versicherungsaufsicht zwischen Kollisionrecht und Wirtschaftsrecht* (1989).
Scoles and Hay, *Conflict of Laws*, 2nd edn (1982).
Shaw, *Law of the European Union*, 3rd edn (2000).
Stein, *Le droit international des assurances*, in Hague Recueil, IV, 1927, pp 1–142.
Stone, *Civil Jurisdiction and Judgments in Europe* (1998).
Strenger, 'La notion de *lex mercatoria* en droit du commerce international', Hague Recueil', I, 1991, 207–356.

Strozzi, *Diritto istituzionale dell'Unione Europea: dal Trattato di Roma al Trattato di Amsterdam* (1998).

Struycken, 'Les consequences de l'integration européenne sur le développement du droit international privé', Hague Recueil, I, 1992, pp 257–384.

Tetley, *International conflict of laws: common, civil and maritime* (1994).

Treves, *Il controllo dei cambi nel diritto internazionale privato* (1967).

Treves (ed), *Verso una disciplina comunitaria della legge applicabile ai contratti* (1983).

Villani, *La Convenzione di Roma sulla legge applicabile ai contratti* (1997).

Vischer (F), '*The antagonism Between Legal Security and the Search for Justice in the Field of Contracts*', Hague Recueil, II, 1974, pp 1–70.

Weatherill, *EC Consumer Law* (1997).

——and Beaumont, *EU Law*, 3rd edn (1999).

Weintraub, *Commentary on the Conflict of Laws*, 3rd edn (1986).

Whittaker (ed), *Good faith in European contract law* (2000).

ARTICLES AND CHAPTERS IN BOOKS

Adrián Arnaiz, 'El coaseguro comunitario: problemas de tráfico externo y problemas de armonización en la consecución del mercado interior' *Revista española de seguros* 1987, pp 57–75.

Baratta, 'La Convenzione di Roma del 1980 sulla legge applicabile alle obbligazioni contrattuali' *Dir. UE*, 1997, pp 633–705.

——'Sull'adattamento del diritto interno alla Convenzione di Roma del 1980' *RDI*, 1993, pp 118–30.

Benedettelli, 'La giurisdizione internazionale in materia assicurativa secondo la Convenzione di Bruxelles' *DCI*, 1998, pp 593–632; 885–930.

Berr (CJ), 'Droit européen des assurances: la directive du 22 juin 1988 sur la libre prestation de services' *Revue trimestrielle de droit européen*, 1988, pp 655–88.

Berr and Groutel, 'Droit européen des assurances: accidents de la circulation causés dans un Etat de la CEE par un véhicule étranger', 1984, *Revue trimestrielle de droit européen*, pp 643–54.

Besson, 'La loi applicable aux contrats d'assurance dans le cadre de la liberté de prestation de services' *RGAT*, 1987, pp 236 ff.

Biancarelli, 'L'application du droit du contrat d'assurance dans le marché unique européen' 12ème Colloque juridique international du Comité Européen des Assurances, Avignon, 4–7 Octobre 1991, *RGAT*/LGDJ, 1992, pp 7–73.

Bigot and Parleani, 'La liberté de prestations de services en assurances de dommage au point de vue juridique' *RGAT*, 1989, pp 11–44.

Blanco Morales Limones, 'La determination del Derecho applicabile al contrato internacional de Seguro: elementos de Derecho comparado para la solución de una cuestión abierta en el ordenamiento español' *RES*, 1997, pp 15–58.

——'Capitulo III. Contrato internacional de seguro' in Calvo Caravaca y Fernández de la Gándara (eds), *Contratos internacionales* (Madrid: Tecnos, 1997).

Capotosti, 'La discipline juridique des contrats d'assurance "communitaire" selon le système des diretives CEE' in *L'Europe de l'Assurance. Les directives de la troisième generation* (Bruxelles, Maklu/Academia/Bruyland, 1992) pp 259–68.

Carter (PB), 'The role of public policy in English Private International Law', 1993, *International and Comparative Law Quarterly* pp 1–10.

——'Towards an internal market for insurance companies' *Cahiers de droit européen*, 1989, pp 552 ff.

Celle, 'L'assicurazione marittima merci nel nuovo regime di diritto internazionale privato' in *Diritto marittimo*, 1995, pp 630–708.

——'Le nuove norme di diritto internazionale privato applicabili ai contratti di assicurazione merci relativi a rischi localizzati nella CEE' *DCI*, 1995, pp 165–215.

Cerini, 'Note in tema di esercizio dell'attività assicurativa in regime di libertà di prestazione di servizi e in regime di stabilimento' *Dir. econ. ass.*, 1999, pp155–79.

Chapatte, 'Freedom to Provide Insurance Services in the European Community' *European Law Review*, 1984, pp 3–27.

Claassens, 'La libre prestation de services en assurance vie et en assurance RC automobile' *RGAT*, 1989, pp 269–78.

Clerici, 'Forum solutionis e Convenzione di Roma del 19 giugno 1980 al vaglio della giurisprudenza italiana', in *Studi Capotorti*, II, pp 611–35.

Collins, 'Interaction between Contracts and Torts' *International and Comparative Law Quarterly*, 1967, pp 103–28.

Conetti, 'La legge regolatrice del contratto di assicurazione in regime di libera prestazione di servizi' *Dir. e prat. ass.*, 1984, pp 148 ff.

Cousy, 'Le droit applicable au contrat d'assurance dans le marché unique européen' *Risques*, 1991, pp 101–20.

Crespo Hernández, 'Contrato de seguro' in Fernández Rozas (ed), *Derecho del comercio internacional* (Madrid, Eurolex, 1996), pp 369–80.

Dehousse, 'Le marché unique et la protection des consommateur' *JT*, 1993, pp 701–4.

Diamond, 'Conflict of Laws in the EEC', *Current Legal Problems*, 1979, pp 155–70.

Dubuisson, 'La loi applicable au contrat de réassurance' *Melanges RO Dalcq. Responsabilités et assurances* (Brussels, Larcier, 1994) pp 11–133.

——'Les véhicules en circulation internationale et le droit international privé' *RGAR*, 1991, N 11781.

Fallon, 'La loi applicable au contrat d'assurance selon la directivedu 22 juin 1988' *RGAT*, 1989, pp 243–69.

——'The Law Applicable to Compulsory Insurance and Life Insurance: Special Problems' in Facilides and Jessurun d'Oliveira (eds), *International Insurance Contract in the E.C.* (The Hague, Kluwer Law International) pp 113–35.

Fallon and Francq, 'Towards Internationally Mandatory Directives for Consumer Contracts?' in *Liber Amicorum Kurt Siehr*, pp 155–70.

——'Le conflits de lois en matière d'obligations contractuelles et non contractuelles: 1986–1997' *JT*, 1998, pp 683–700.

Fawcett, 'Multi-Party Litigation in Private International Law' *International and Comparative Law Quarterly*, 1995, pp 774–70.

——'The Interrelationship of Jurisdiction and Choice of Law in Private International Law' *Current Legal Problems*, 1991, pp 39–62.

——'Evasion of Law and mandatory Rules in Private International Law' *Cambridge Law Journal*, 1990, pp 44–66.

——'The Lugano Convention' *European Law Review*, 1989, pp 105–9.

——'Forum Shopping—Some Questions Answered' *Northern Ireland Legal Quarterly*, 1984, pp 141–52.

Floridi, 'Disciplina nazionale e disciplina comunitaria della legge applicabile ai contratti di assicurazione' *Assicur.*, 1988, pp 556 ff.

Fois, 'I conflitti tra le convenzioni di diritto internazionale privato e l'ordinamento comunitario' in *Studi Giuliano*, pp 435–70.

Forlati Picchio, 'La legge applicabile ai contratti di assicurazione e diritto comunitario' *Dir. comm. e scambi int.*, 1983, pp 35–80.

Foyer, 'Entrée en viguer de la Convention de Rome du 19 juin 1980 sur la loi applicable aux obligations contractuelles' *Journal de droit international*, 1991, pp 601–31.

Frigessi di Rattalma, 'La libertà di prestazione assicurative nel diritto comunitario derivato' *Dir. e prat. ass.*, 1989, pp 381–408.

——'Osservazioni sui profili internazionalprivatistici della seconda direttiva comunitaria sull'assicurazione contro i danni' *Rivista di diritto internationale privato e processuale*, 1994, pp 563–94.

Garofalo (L), 'Volonta' delle parti e norme imperative nella Convenzione di Roma sulla legge applicabile ai contratti e nel nuovo sistema di diritto internazionale privato italiano' *Rivista di diritto internationale privato e processuale*, 1996, pp 481 *et seq.*

Gaudemet Tallon, 'La Convention de Rome du 19 juin 1980 sur la loi applicable aux obligations contractuelles-Vingt ans après' in *Liber Amicorum Siehr*, pp 329–40.

——'Le nouveau droit international privé européen des contrats (Commentaire de la convention CEE n. 80/934 sur la loi applicable aux obligations contractuelles, ouvertes à la signature à Rome le 19 juin 1980)' *Revue trimestrielle de droit européen*, 1981, pp 215–70.

Gestri, 'Alcune questioni in materia di responsabilità contrattuale ed extracontrattuale' *Rivista di diritto internationale privato e processuale*, 1988, pp 53 *et seq.*

Giardina, 'La Convenzione comunitaria sulla legge applicabile alle obbligazioni contrattuali e il diritto internazionale privato italiano', *RDI*, 1981, pp 795 ff.

Gillies, 'A Review of the New Jurisdiction Rules for Electronic Consumer Contracts within the European Union' *Journal of Information Law and Technology*, 2001, at http://elj.warwick.ac.uk/jilt/01-1/gillies.html.

Harris, 'The Brussels Regulation', *Civil Justice Quarterly*, 2001, pp 218–24.

Hartley, 'Consumer protection provisions in the EEC Convention' in North (ed), *Contract Conflicts* (Amsterdam, New York, Oxford, 1982), p 111.

Hunter, 'Reinsurance Litigation and the Civil Jurisdiction and Judgements Act 1982' *Journal of Business Law*, 1987, pp 344–52.

Kahn Freund, 'Contractual Obligations and Conflict of Law: Contracts of Insurance' *Modern Law Review*, 1959, pp 195–98.

Kessler, 'Equilibre ou déséquilibre des marchés d'assurance en Europe?', *Risques*, 1991, pp 41–68.

Knöfel, 'EC legislation on conflict of laws: interactions and incompatibilities between conflicts rules', *International and Comparative Law Quarterly*, 1998, pp 439–53.

——'Mandatory rules and choice of law: a comparative approach to Article 7(2) of the Rome Convention, *Journal of Business Law*, 1999, pp 239–53.

Lagarde, 'The European Convention On The Law Applicable To Contractual Obligations: An Apologia', *Virginia Journal of International Law*, 1981, pp 91–101.

——'Le depeçage dans le droit international privé des contrats' *Rivista di diritto internationale privato e processuale*, 1975, pp 649–90.

——'Assurance–Assurance directe—Risque situé dans un Etat Membre.—Loi applicable. Deuxième directive du Conseil (88/357/CEE) du 22 juin 1988 portant coordination des dispositions législatives, réglementaires et administratives concernant l'assurance directe autre que l'assurance sur la vie, fixant les dispositions destinées à faciliter l'exercice effectif de la libre prestation des services et modifiant la directive 73/239/CEE' *Revue critique de droit international privé*, 1989, pp 144–49.

Lando, 'Party Autonomy in the EC Convention on the Law Applicable to Contractual Obligations' in *L'influence des Communautés Européennes sur le droit international privé des Etats members*, Luxemburg, 1981, pp 91–121.

Legrand, 'Carte verte et contrat d'assurance: le miroir à deux faces' *Gaz. Pal.* (1972) I, Doct., pp 241–43.

Lenaerts, 'La loi applicable et la libre prestation des services en matière d'assurance vie' *Ann. Dr. Louvain*, 1990, pp 145–68.

Mari, 'Ambito di applicazione della Convenzione di Bruxelles del 27 settembre 1968 e problemi di qualificazione della nozione di "materia civile e commerciale"' *Dir. com. e scambi internaz.*, 1977, pp 271 *et seq.*

——'Sulla legge regolatrice della c.d. surroga assucuratoria' *Rivista di diritto internationale privato e processuale*, pp 475–86.

Mayer 'Le lois de police' *Trav. Com. fr. d.i.p.*, 1988, pp 105–44.

McNeil, 'The legal framework in the United Kingdom for Insurance Policies Sold by European Insurers Under Freedom of Services' *International and Comparative Law Quarterly*, 1995, pp 19–37.

Miguel Asensio, 'La ley aplicable en defecto de elección a los contatos internacionales: el articulo 4 del Convenio de Roma' *La Ley. Com. Eur.*, 4 de abril de 1995, pp 1–6.

Monachos, 'Re-insurance in English Private International Law' *Journal of Business Law*, 1972, pp 206–20.

Morales Segura, 'La ley aplicable a los contratos de reaseguro' *Revista española de seguros*, 1993, pp 49–55.

Morse (CGJ), 'The EEC Convention on the Law Applicable to Contractual Obligations' *Yearbook of European Law*, 1982, pp 107–60.

——'Party Autonomy in International Insurance Contract Law' in Reichert-Facilides and Jessurun d'Oliveira (eds), *International Insurance Contract Law in the EC* (1993).

Partesotti, 'La localizzazione del rischio assicurato secondo il diritto italiano' in Treves (ed), *Verso una disciplina comunitaria della legge applicabile ai contratti* (1983) pp 201–14.

Pau, 'Le norme imperative nella Convenzione CEE sulla legge applicabile alle obbligazioni contrattuali' *RDI*, 1982, pp 868–72.

——'Il diritto internazionale privato *de jure condendo*' *RDI*, 1988, pp 285–302.

Pfennigstorf, 'Public Law of Insurance' in *International Encyclopedia of Comparative Law*, vol. IX (1988).

Philip, 'Mandatory Rules, Public Law (Political Rules) and Choice of Law in the EEC Convention on the Law Applicable to Contractual Obligations' in North (ed), *Contract Conflicts*, (1982), pp 81–108.

Picar, 'L'autonomie de la volonté en matière de contrats d'assurance' *Trav. Com. Fr. Dr. Int. Priv.*, 1937–38, pp 137–55.

Pierce, 'Post-formation choice of law in contract', *Modern Law Review*, 1987, pp 176–95.

Pocar, 'La comunitarizzazione del diritto internazionale privato: una European conflicts of law revolution?' *Rivista di diritto internationale privato e processuale*, 2000, pp 873–84.

Pocar,'L'entrata in vigore della convenzione di Roma del 1980 sulla legge applicabile alle obbligazioni contrattuali' *Rivista di diritto internationale privato e processuale*, 1991, pp 249–52.

——'Linee di tendenza della Convenzione di Bruxelles sulla giurisdizione e l'esecuzione delle sentenze dopo l'adesione di nuovi Stati' *Rivista di diritto internationale privato e processuale*, 1990, pp 5–16.

——'Alcune considerazioni sulla Convenzione di Roma del 1980' *Foro pad.*, 1987, 31–34.

——'Conflitti di leggi e di giurisdizioni in materia di assicurazioni nella Comunita' economica europea' *Rivista di diritto internationale privato e processuale*, 1987, pp 417–28.

Rigaux, 'New Problems of Private International Law in the Single Market' *King's College Law Journal*, 1993–94, 23–43.

Ripoll, 'Les conflits des lois en matière de droit des assurances' *Trav. Com. Fr. Dr. Int. Priv.*, 1993, pp 1989–90.

Roth, 'Article 59 EEC Treaty fifty-nine and its Implications for the Conflicts Law in the Field of Insurance Contracts' in Facilides and Jessurun d'Oliveira (eds), *International Insurance Contracts in the EC* (1993), pp 59–77.

Sacerdoti, 'Diritto di stabilimento e libera prestazione dei servizi assicurativi dopo la l. 10 giugno 1978, n. 295' *Dir. econ. ass.*, pp 81–96.

——'Contratti di assicurazione e libertà di stabilimento dopo la l. 295/1978 in attuazione della prima direttiva cee in materia di assicurazione' *Dir. com. e scambi int.*, 1979, pp 745–51.

Saravalle,'Clausole con scelta di legge variabile e Convenzione di Roma del 1980', *Rivista di diritto internationale privato e processuale*, 1991, pp 895–912.

Sauveplanne (JG), 'Consumer protection in private international law' *Netherlands International Law Review*, 1985, pp 100–22.

Schu, 'Consumer Protection and Private International Law in Internet Contracts' *International Journal of Law Information Technology*, 1997, pp 192 *et seq.*

Seatzu, 'Verso una disciplina comunitaria della legge applicabile alle obbligazioni contrattuali? Considerazioni in margine ad una recente proposta del 'Gruppo Europeo di Diritto Internazionale Privato', *Jus*, 2001, pp 37–67.

——'Diritto alla difesa, Ordine Pubblico dello Stato richiesto dell'exequatur e Convenzione di Bruxelles del 1968' *NGCC*, 2001, pp 587–97.

——'The scope of application of the Rome Convention on the law applicable to contractual obligations under the Italian statute of private international law' *Revista Mexicana de derecho internacional privado*, 2001, pp 59–68.

——'Jurisdiction Agreements under Article 17 (1) (c) of the Brussels Convention' *Northern Ireland Legal Quarterly*, 1998, pp 327–31.

——'La responsabilità civile nel nuovo diritto internazionale privato italiano' *Resp. civ prev.*, 1997, pp 816–23.

Smulders and Glazener, 'Harmonisation in the Field of Insurance Law through the Introduction of Community Rules of Conflict' *Common Market Law Review*, 1992, pp 775–97.

Steindorff, 'Insurance and Freedom to provide Services' *Common Market Law Review*, 1977, pp 133–53.

Thierry, 'Les assureurs vie et le grand marché européen' *Risques*, 1992, pp 65–66.

Tison, 'What is "General Good" in EU Financial Services Law?' *Legal issues of European integration*, 1997, pp 1–45.

Turci, 'La legge applicabile ai contratti internazionali di assicurazione marittima' *Diritto marittimo*, 1992, pp 850 ff.

Ubertazzi, 'Studi sul contratto internazionale di assicurazione nel diritto internazionale privato' *RDI*, 1962, pp 352 *et seq.*

Van Gerven and Ingberg, 'A la recherché de la prestation caractéristique' *Revue Université Libre de Bruxelles*, 1994, pp 55–70.

Villani 'L'azione comunitaria in materia di diritto internazionale privato', *Revue de droit européen*, 1981, pp 373–85.

Visher, 'The Concept of the Characteristic Performance Reviewed', in *Liber Droz*, pp 899 ff.

Volpe Putzolu, 'L'influenza della normativa comunitaria sul contratto di assicurazione' *Ass.*, 1991, pp 114–20.

Von Overbeck, 'L'irresistible extension de l'autonomie en droit international privé' in *Hommage Rigaux*, pp 619 ff.

——*La contribution de la Conference de la Haye au development du droit international privé* [1992] *Hague Recueil* 208.

Watté and Nuyts, 'Vers une interprétation uniforme et cohérente des Conventions de Rome et de Bruxelles' *Revue Université Libre de Bruxelles*, 1994, pp 21–34.

Weintraub, 'How to Choose Law for Contracts, and How Not to: The EEC Convention', *Texas International Law Journal*, 1982, pp 155–75.

Williams, 'The EEC Convention on the Law Applicable to Contractual Obligations' *International and Comparative Law Quarterly*, 1986, pp 1–31.

Zanelli, 'La convenzione di Roma del 19 giugno 1980 e l'attività assicurativa' in Treves, 'Norme imperative e di applicazione necessaria nella Convenzione di Roma del 19 giugno 1980' *Rivista di diritto internationale privato e processuale*, 1983, pp 25–41.